Athens of the New South

Athens
of the New South

College Life and the
Making of Modern Nashville

Mary Ellen Pethel

THE UNIVERSITY OF TENNESSEE PRESS
Knoxville

Copyright © 2017 by The University of Tennessee Press / Knoxville.
All Rights Reserved. Manufactured in the United States of America.
Cloth: 1st printing, 2017.
Paper: 1st printing, 2018.

LIBRARY OF CONGRESS CATALOGING-IN-PUBLICATION DATA
Names: Pethel, Mary Ellen, author.
Title: Athens of the New South: college life and the making of modern Nashville / Mary Ellen Pethel.
Description: First edition. | Knoxville: The University of Tennessee Press, 2017. | Includes bibliographical references and index. |
Identifiers: LCCN 2016053764 (print) | LCCN 2017022033 (ebook) |
ISBN 9781621903437 (pdf) | ISBN 9781621903420 (printed case) |
ISBN 9781621904571 (pbk.)
Subjects: LCSH: Education, Higher—Tennessee—Nashville—History. | Education, Higher—Social aspects—Tennessee—Nashville—History. | Universities and colleges—Tennessee—Nashville—History. | Women—Education (Higher)—Tennessee—Nashville—History. | African Americans—Education (Higher)—Tennessee—Nashville—History. | Nashville (Tenn.)—Social life and customs. | Nashville (Tenn.)—History.
Classification: LCC LA369.N2 (ebook) | LCC LA369.N2 P47 2017 (print) | DDC 378.768/55—dc23
LC record available at https://lccn.loc.gov/2016053764

FOR JACK

Contents

	Acknowledgments	xi
	Introduction: Athens of the (New) South	1
Chapter 1	Southern Style: Urbanization and Higher Education	33
Chapter 2	Modern Belle: Gender and Higher Education	65
Chapter 3	Beyond the Talented Tenth: Race and Higher Education	107
Chapter 4	Pursuit(s) of Happiness: College Youth Culture, Campus Life, and Leisure	151
Chapter 5	Students of Sport: Athletics and Higher Education	195
Chapter 6	Athens of the New, New South: A Conclusion	233
	Appendix: Nashville Maps	253
	Notes	261
	Bibliography	307
	Index	331

Illustrations

Fig. 0.1. Vanderbilt University Chancellor James H. Kirkland — 14
Fig. 0.2. University of Nashville, 1864 — 17
Fig. 0.3. George Peabody College for Teachers, 1920s — 19
Fig. 0.4. Nashville Bible School Faculty, 1914 — 21
Fig. 0.5. Dr. William E. Ward and Eliza Hudson Ward — 22
Fig. 0.6. Ida E. Hood and Susan L. Heron — 24
Fig. 0.7. Jubilee Hall, 1876, and Livingston Hall, 1881, at Fisk University — 25
Fig. 0.8. Roger Williams University Main Building — 27
Fig. 0.9. Central Tennessee College (later Walden University), 1894 — 29
Fig. 0.10. Tennessee A&I campus, 1930 — 31
Fig. 1.1. Nashville's "New South prophet" Arthur Colyar — 34
Fig. 1.2. Union Station, 1931 — 36
Fig. 1.3. Tennessee Centennial Exposition — 38
Fig. 1.4. 1897 Centennial Exposition Board of Directors — 39
Fig. 1.5. 1894 Belmont Mansion and Early Students — 42
Fig. 1.6. Neighborhood West of Vanderbilt University and Belmont College — 43
Fig. 1.7. 1897 Ward Seminary Students — 46
Fig. 1.8. Anne Dallas Dudley and Children — 56
Fig. 1.9. Downtown Nashville from Capitol Hill, 1864 — 62
Fig. 1.10. Tennessee State Capitol — 63
Fig. 2.1. Ward-Belmont Students, c. 1920 — 67
Fig. 2.2. 1905 Nashville Bible School — 72
Fig. 2.3. 1872 Advertisement and Ward Seminary Campus — 74
Fig. 2.4. 1910 Advertisement for Belmont College — 76

Fig. 2.5. Belmont College Sorority Clubhouse, 1905   76
Fig. 2.6. May Day Dance at Ward Seminary, c. 1890   81
Fig. 2.7. George Peabody College Social Religious Building, 1915   83
Fig. 2.8. Vanderbilt Medical Center, 1925   84
Fig. 2.9. Cartoon from Belmont College, 1910   88
Fig. 2.10. Vanderbilt University Nursing Students   89
Fig. 2.11. Ward-Belmont World War I "Flag Rally"   100
Fig. 3.1. Tennessee A&I President William Jasper Hale   124
Fig. 3.2. Fisk University Calculus Class, 1890   128
Fig. 3.3. Fisk University Campus, Late 1920s   129
Fig. 3.4. Fayette Avery McKenzie   130
Fig. 3.5. 1910 Meharry Medical College Groundbreaking Ceremony   133
Fig. 3.6. Meharry Medical College Operating Room   134
Fig. 3.7. Meharry Medical College New Campus   137
Fig. 3.8. First Graduating Class of Tennessee A&I, 1924   138
Fig. 3.9. Roger Williams University Collegiate Class, 1899   140
Fig. 3.10. Fisk University 1899 Graduating Collegiate Class   142
Fig. 4.1. The Arcade, Downtown Nashville, 1902   156
Fig. 4.2. State Fair Grounds, 1920s   159
Fig. 4.3. Mammoth Cave Trip, Vanderbilt and Ward-Belmont   163
Fig. 4.4. 1903 Ward Seminary Student Artwork   167
Fig. 4.5. Vanderbilt University Students, 1904   168
Fig. 4.6. Interior of Union Station   172
Fig. 4.7. 1922 Phi Delta Theta Members   178
Fig. 4.8. 1910 Belmont College "Manless Dance"   183
Fig. 4.9. Fisk University Chapel, 1902   186
Fig. 5.1. Vanderbilt vs. Ole Miss Advertisement   196
Fig. 5.2. Peabody College Football, 1920s   201
Fig. 5.3. Vanderbilt vs. Sewanee, 1930   203
Fig. 5.4. William Dudley   205
Fig. 5.5. Vanderbilt University Head Coach Dan McGugin
   and Assistant Coach Wallace Wade   208
Fig. 5.6. 1921 Vanderbilt University Football Team   210
Fig. 5.7. Dudley Stadium, 1922   212
Fig. 5.8. Vanderbilt University Yearbook Dedication, 1922   213
Fig. 5.9. 1921 Vanderbilt University Baseball Team   215
Fig. 5.10. Howard University versus Fisk University Football, 1919   218
Fig. 5.11. Original Ward Seminary Basketball Team, 1897   224
Fig. 6.1. Ryman Auditorium (1891) and the AT&T building (1994)   234

Acknowledgments

"Gratitude is the seed of gladness," according to the author and activist Lailah Gifty Akita. In writing this book many seeds of gratitude have been planted. I now have the opportunity to express and share my gladness. Truly, this project is a reflection of the unmitigated support I have received over the past two years from friends (new and old), family, and colleagues. Local historians generously provided feedback, chapter readings, and most importantly shared their unmatched areas of expertise without reservation. These goodwill ambassadors of academia include Linda Wynn, Reavis Mitchell, Jack May, Mary A. Evins, Ophelia Paine, and Ridley Wills II. I owe them all an enormous debt. In addition Ridley Wills II loaned his personal collection of historic images and maps, and Ophelia Paine connected me with others who were instrumental in fine-tuning the content. Ever the professional role model, Mary Evins offered much needed commentary during the revision process. Larry Youngs, who patiently supervised this project in its earlier iterations, was instrumental in helping me to expand and conceptualize the book's overarching themes and organization. This book would not be possible without his mentorship and friendship—both of which mean the world to me. I must also thank Wendy Venet who has inspired and encouraged me for years during and after graduate school. Also worthy of my deep appreciation is Judith Pierson who served as an editor and advisor throughout the writing and revision process. Her thoughtful and witty comments have made this book more intelligible and readable.

Mary Hofschwelle and Charles Holden, the outside readers for the University of Tennessee Press, offered crucial feedback that allowed me to reframe and transform the manuscript into its current form. Dr. Hofschwelle's poignant attention to detail, additional source suggestions, and clarifying questions and comments proved to be enormously helpful. My editor at UTP, Thomas Wells, is responsible for shepherding this book from its infancy. From our first conversation about the project at the Ohio Valley Historical Conference in 2014 to the final "approved for print," he has graciously endured my emails and questions—always responding promptly and with pragmatic reassurance. Thanks also to Gene Adair, who copyedited the book. Archivists and curators at local universities or colleges included in this study were always accommodating whether pulling a source, photocopying, or helping me navigate their school's rich history. Specifically I would like to thank Christyne Douglas at Meharry Medical College and Kelley Sirko at Metro Archives for going the extra mile. In addition the Tennessee Historical Society, American Medical Association, and the American Dental Association helped to track down elusive dates and documents. I must also thank Bobby Lovett, Joe Richardson, Paul Conkin, and Don Doyle for providing key institutional histories as well as narratives of Nashville's history in prior published works.

Good people bring out the good in others, and I am so grateful to have so many good friends, family, and colleagues. A few that I must mention include Stan Pethel, JoAnn Pethel, Rob Pethel, Joseph Pethel, Krissie Rigsby, Lynn Heath, Ali Hyrup, Polly Linden, Nicola Bullard, Jess Hill, Moe Hill, Lauren Finney, Carrie Owens, Ann Hamrick, Sally TerBeck, Amber Reece, Anne Stuik, Patricia Buttrick, Allen Karns, Susan Moll, Joanne Mamenta, Miller Callen, Tony Springman, Jack Henderson, Armistead Lemon, Lisa Keen, Jennifer Webster, Scottie Girgus, Susan Timmons, and Anna Stevens. These individuals checked in regularly, listened to me drone on about my progress (or lack thereof), and cared about this book not because of anything it might add to historiography but because it was important to me. Their interest in the *writer* superseded the writing itself, and they have been my metaphorical porch post. I have leaned on them all heavily over these many months. I extend my heartfelt thanks to each of you.

Several present-day Nashville leaders with deep connections to the community with respect to public policy, education, healthcare, and/or business gave freely of their time in order to answer questions related Nashville's commitment to higher education. These individuals are: Martha Ingram, David Williams, Karl Dean, Anne Davis, Megan Barry, Edie Carell Johnson, and Ralph Schultz. Nashville is so fortunate to have leaders across the spectrum (from business to the arts) that recognize and promote the value of higher education. Of course my students deserve a hearty thank you. They provided me with motivation and inspiration—most often without realizing it. In particular, students in the Belmont Honors Program who participated in my spring 2016 seminar entitled "Making the Modern City," offered insight and gave interviews that informed the book's epilogue.

Born in Rome, Georgia, my undergraduate adventure did not take me to Nashville, but it did bring me to Tennessee as I joined the ranks of the UT Vols. Georgia will always be on my mind, but I have come to call Middle Tennessee home these past ten years, and I am proud of Nashville's story and of its potential. It is my hope that this book will cement the city's legacy as the "Athens of the South" and inspire and embolden new generations of students and residents to come to Nashville to learn, work, and live. While I have done my best to be accurate and comprehensive, there are surely errors and omissions in the pages that follow. Any mistakes are unintentionally mine. As for my efforts, I hope they reflect the motto of the Ward Seminary Class of 1903. Alongside these college men and women of the past, I also strive, "To be, not to seem." My fondest hope is that all readers, whether in an office with papers piled high or at home on the couch, will find value in the voices and educational voyage of New South Nashville.

Introduction
Athens of the (New) South

> Just as Athens, Greece was recognized centuries ago as the center of learning, so Nashville was accredited from its very beginning as a community where the attributes of learning and the appreciation of the fine arts were reflected in the leadership of its men and women in all walks of life.
>
> —Henry McRaven, *Nashville, "Athens of the South"* (1949)

In 2013 the *New York Times* designated Nashville as the "it" city, a modern, new millennial hub of music, technology, business, and tourism, but Nashville's full-scale Greek Parthenon replica stands as a living monument to a city long recognized as the "Athens of the South." Nashville's reputation remains tethered to its enduring investment in, and the influence of, its institutions of higher education.[1] Local colleges and universities—their sweeping campuses, loyal alumni, ardent supporters, and the ever-present youthful vibe of students—are intertwined with Nashville's history and culture, dating back over 150 years.

Author Henry McRaven traced the origins of Nashville as a center for learning: "The 'Athens of the South' is the description given to Nashville by its early settlers in recognition of the educational and intellectual leadership manifest by its founders. . . . It is quite likely that Philip Lindsley was among the first to use the phrase. In 1825, he resigned his position as acting president of Princeton University to accept the presidency of Davidson Academy. In one of his early lectures he used the expression, 'Athens of the West'—Tennessee at that time being part of the western United States."[2] As the nation expanded West in the decades leading up to the Civil War, Nashville's title shifted to Athens of the South.

After the surrender of Forts Henry and Donelson to General Ulysses Grant early in 1862, Nashville became the first Confederate city to be occupied by Union forces. Thus, for most of the Civil War, Nashville remained in northern hands, and in many ways the city benefited. As other southern cities experienced burning, evacuation, and destruction of rail lines, Nashville escaped such devastation and was ready for New South boosters such as Arthur Colyar (chap. 2) to carry the banner of industrialization in the South. Nashville stood poised to follow this vision of transforming agrarian areas into industrial centers because of its demographic, structural, and cultural composition.[3]

Following the Civil War, the Lost Cause narrative also surfaced quite often in southern rhetoric. In a response to a Chicago magazine article entitled "Time to Call off Dixie?" the *Confederate Veteran* answered, "Time to call off Dixie? No! . . . Around Dixie turn our fondest memories. . . . The Lady of the South receives recognition at any convention she attends, because she stands out in any company, and shows by every word and deed, her superiority."[4] Even as leaders in the South selectively followed the models of northern cities such as Boston, Philadelphia, Chicago, and New York, they continued to maintain a distinctive sense of "southern-ness." These feelings represented the deep loyalty of white Tennesseans, despite having fewer slave plantations before secession and the state's union occupation during the war. Their pride in regional unity re-created a southern identity that promoted progress but revered tradition. This tension would bring change and contradictions, good intentions, and varied outcomes to Nashville from 1865 to 1930.

Nashville's population more than tripled during this era, growing from 43,350 in 1880 to 80,865 in 1900 to 118,342 in 1920 to 167,402 by 1940.[5] The city represented, as one writer termed it, a "blend of traditional Old South attitudes and the New South crusade to industrialize and follow the business policies of the North."[6] Tennessee had the highest number of Unionists and people opposed to the Civil War of any secessionist state, and it was less entrenched in the rigid social hierarchy of race. In other words, Nashville remained distinctive among other growing southern cities such as Atlanta, Birmingham, and Charlotte. The city industrialized on a larger scale in the 1870s and 1880s, but this characterized only part of its urbanization process. In the South, urban centers of commerce shifted because of their geographic position vis-à-vis the railroads. The cities of Atlanta and Nashville led the way as railroad centers with easier access to northern, midwestern, and West Coast markets. Tennessee's capital city also served as a major artery connecting the state to the rest of the nation with the Nashville, Chattanooga, and St. Louis Railway (NC&St.L).[7]

As early as 1885, Nashville received recognition in the *Memphis Ledger* for its role as a city and cultural arts center: "The village ... has grown to be a commercial emporium, the *entrepot* of a rich, wealthy, tax-paying division of the State, and the educational center of the South. ... It is a place of solid growth, the Athens of the South, the home of ripe scholarship and a generous and refined people."[8] A Vanderbilt University professor at the turn of the century also noted the trend toward urban living: "The most capable businessmen, lawyers, doctors, and preachers are practically all leaving the country for the town and city. [As a result,] the city is more and more setting the pace of and dominating Southern life and Southern thought."[9] Cities like Nashville could industrialize and urbanize in ways similar to northern cities, but southern pride and exceptionalism prevented cultural assimilation. The South would fashion its own version of modernity, integrating and reconciling northern ideas with southern realities.

Nashville, from 1865 to 1930, represented a hybrid of northern and southern ideas of progress that juxtaposed antebellum traditions and modern notions. The usual power players, older white men, continued to determine the city's direction, yet a new generation of historical actors began to shape the proverbial course. The people of Nashville were grappling with an evolving, collective identity throughout the Progressive Era. At the center of this socially constructed enterprise were young men and women, both white and black, who had greater access to higher education through the city's newly established schools, including Vanderbilt University, Fisk University, Ward-Belmont School, David Lipscomb College, Meharry Medical College, Roger Williams University, Peabody College, and Tennessee A&I.[10] With greater numbers of young people attending colleges and universities, these factors combined to influence the trajectory of Nashville's urbanization and distinctiveness as a regional center of learning.

Between 1864 and 1912 nine institutions of higher education opened their doors in Nashville. These schools were top-tier educational heavyweights in their respective areas. Vanderbilt debuted as one of the top three universities in the

South (along with Emory and Duke). By the end of the nineteenth century, "Vandy" was one of the country's premier private universities; Peabody College was a leading teacher-training college, in the South as well as the U.S.; Fisk University was one of the nation's most prestigious liberal arts universities for African Americans; Meharry Medical College stood as one of the only medical schools for African Americans, which also featured dental, pharmaceutical, and nursing schools; and Tennessee Agricultural and Industrial Normal School was the state's first public college for African Americans, which followed a vocational training model.

While a handful of females attended previously all-male universities before 1900, most women attended single-sex schools. The Ward-Belmont School in Nashville combined two regionally recognized schools, Ward Seminary and Belmont College. At its peak in the 1920s, with an enrollment of over twelve hundred students from thirty-six states, Ward-Belmont was well known as a music conservatory and the first accredited junior college for women in the South. Catering to more specialized educational niches, David Lipscomb College emerged as the premier parochial arm of the Church of Christ. Meanwhile, Roger Williams University trained African American men and women as preachers, missionaries, and teachers. Nashville was unique not simply because of the *quantity* of colleges and universities but also because of their *quality*.

For Nashville the demand for and supply of higher education yielded an increase in local students and young people largely from southern states who sought education beyond the primary and secondary level. The location of the campuses influenced the trajectory of Nashville's urbanization, pulling the city west. The colleges and universities of west Nashville made the area attractive for middle- and upper-class families as neighborhoods and suburbs provided an escape from the increasingly commercial downtown core. Vision combined with venture to fashion Nashville's reputation as a city of both culture and commerce.

Chapters in Context

Nashville, as a microcosm, is a city that deserves additional historical attention, particularly in the post–Civil War period. Nashville also invites a fresh analysis of the evolution of modern college life in a New South city. While historic periodization is always negotiable and nebulous, this book locates and defines the New South era in Nashville as the years between the end of the Civil War (1865) and the start of the Great Depression (1929). During this period, Nashville transitioned, emerging from a culture shaped by an antebellum heritage into a New South vision characterized by shifting expectations and educational developments.[11] Accompanying the establishment and accreditation of well-respected colleges during the period was the dramatic increase of women, African Americans, and sports/leisure in higher education.[12]

Chapter 1 examines the extent to which urban boosters, or business progressives, deliberately and consciously used higher education to create and control their vision of progress for Nashville particularly after 1890. Nashville was certainly southern, but a special sense of pride in its intellectualism and cultural offerings was decidedly different. Antebellum life in the rural South had little use for higher education and the arts, and many southern cities were slow to make them priorities. Local and outside businessmen and nonprofit organizations molded Nashville's New South image, but education stood at the forefront as a symbol of progress as well as a driving force that fashioned a particular vision of modernity. In other words, Nashville's colleges and universities served as both the benefactors of and the impetus for the developing urban ethos. The growth of commerce and manufacturing would steer the local economy, while institutions of higher education simultaneously softened and strengthened the city's image. To a large extent, higher education guided the how, when, and where of Nashville's development during this period.

As local colleges and universities grew and matured, so did Nashville. The city was heavily influenced by these schools, as well as by their locations, curricula, sports, social activities, student activism, and youth culture. Nashville businesses benefited from college students as customers and consumers. Following graduation, these young men and women would contribute to the local economy and city as employees, managers, business owners, lawyers, medical professionals, teachers, preachers, and social activists. Many graduates took their talents elsewhere, effecting change in the South and across the nation; however, many stayed in Nashville, whether originally from the area or not. This made all the difference.

Chapter 2 analyzes the role of higher education in the lives of middle- and upper-class white women attending single-gender schools and the influence of educated young women on New South society. Increased opportunities for women and experiences gained from a more autonomous and individualistic "college life" positioned Nashville's generation of educated women from 1865 to 1900 on a springboard into a southern version of the "New Woman." However, these women also emerged as a hybrid between the pre–Civil War southern belle and the liberated woman of the Progressive Era. In large part, these "modern belles" developed greater agency and more visibility as participants in public spheres because of their status as college students or alumnae. More accomplished than their predecessors, some women pursued individual and professional goals, while many others continued to enjoy their prosperity under the protective umbrellas of their husbands and fathers. Nevertheless, from 1900 to 1930 these educated middle- and upper-class women created new niches for themselves as "municipal housekeepers," social reformers, and clubwomen who contributed to society through their unpaid labor. In this way, women complemented the efforts of progressivism while remaining southern "ladies."

Chapter 3 explores the role of historically black colleges and universities (HBCUs) in Nashville. During this period, thousands of black women and men attended and graduated from Fisk University, Meharry Medical College, Tennessee A&I, and Roger Williams University to become teachers, doctors, ministers, lawyers, social workers, nurses, pharmacists, and entrepreneurs. As a result, local African American colleges helped fill the ranks of what would become the South's first formally educated, black professional class. Prejudice, segregation, and socioeconomic disparity continued to exist from 1865 to 1930; however, higher education and social activism made Nashville more bearable when compared to other southern urban centers.

Students attending local African American universities experienced "college life" in different ways from their white counterparts. Graduates from Fisk and Meharry largely constituted what W. E. B. Du Bois dubbed the "Talented Tenth," while others followed Booker T. Washington's model of racial uplift through skilled labor. Local black universities and colleges served to anchor the black community and established northwest Nashville as hub of black living, learning, and earning. Nashville thus maintained a vibrant African American community.

Chapter 4 explores the ways in which urbanization and education combined, resulting in a more modern youth culture, particularly after 1890. Mass entertainment merged with traditional forms of leisure, which allowed men and women to pursue recreation differently from the previously rigid courtship rituals practiced throughout the nineteenth century. By 1902 Nashville's downtown and surrounding areas provided new off-campus sites of interaction for young people; parks, theaters, athletic fields, and music auditoriums, all of which were connected by public transportation. These urban spaces further challenged previous boundaries of acceptable social interaction between men and women, white and black. Despite lingering Victorian notions, new on-campus sites of heterosocial activity (men and women socializing) also emerged in the form of fraternities, sororities, social clubs, and sporting events, both on and off campus. Such social interaction between male students and female "coeds" was more casual and would play an important role in the modern evolution of college life and college campuses. Local colleges and universities laid the cornerstone for an urban college youth culture.[13] In sum, Nashville's institutions of higher education and the students who attended them were instrumental to the city's new rhythm.[14]

Competitive collegiate sport was also at the heart of Nashville's burgeoning New South cityscape. Chapter 5 seeks to connect sports to changes in college life and leisure. The "school spirit" and southern pride generated by athletics acted as a bridge that connected Nashville's local culture and economy to its universities. The image of the refined academic collided with that of the rugged athlete—many southern men striving to be both. In particular, college football would bring together two unlikely allies: the ivory tower and the gridiron. And yet this unexpected coalition was a catalyst for increased student recruitment, school loyalty, and community and alumni support. Other popular sports included baseball, basketball, and track and field. In the South sports also symbolized notions of honor connected to the Lost Cause. This is especially ironic given the role of northern philanthropists and northern-based groups in establishing most of Nashville's colleges and universities. The collegiate "sports craze" paralleled a larger national movement resulting in a professional sports industry, which began in the 1870s.

In addition, African American and women's sports emerged during this period, albeit in different ways and with different results. College athletics at local HBCUs created similar patterns of school pride and loyalty, but black sports operated in a parallel universe that would not intersect with the white world of collegiate competition until after 1930. Unlike male sports, female athletic teams and programs (at HBCUs and traditionally white schools) developed and existed almost exclusively under the umbrella of education. Moreover, the development of competitive athletics for women accompanied other changes, including less restrictive and cumbersome clothing, growing health awareness, and commercialized leisure and recreation.

Chapter 6 will thread the needle through to the present, exploring the relationship between Nashville and its colleges and universities in the twentieth-first century. As higher education and urban living continues to evolve in the twenty-first century, Nashville could aptly be called "Athens of the New, New South."

Higher Education and Progressivism

The establishment of Nashville's major colleges and universities between 1864 and 1912 paralleled national movements of education reform, academic accreditation, and curricular development. Greater cultural acceptance of higher education for white women and African American men and women further democratized education. Cultural change and reform in Nashville did not occur quickly or drastically as social boundaries constructed by race, gender, and class were perpetuated by a hegemonic southern order. The South desired growth and improvement but feared that to fully embrace progress would disparage or betray deep-seated beliefs. In other words, the basic premise of the "game" had not changed, but certain new "rules" and "players" provided a more contemporary look and feel. Michael Dennis, in *Lesson in Progress,* argued, "Southern universities were at the forefront of the southern progressive movement . . . and Progressives in higher education represented the urban, commercial middle class that underwrote southern 'conservative modernization.'"[15]

White males entering college in the late nineteenth and early twentieth centuries constituted a new generation of southern men. Unlike their fathers and grandfathers, they were not tied to the same economic web created by land and slavery. Thus by varying degrees, these young white men envisioned a different southern society—one that increasingly valued higher education and urban commercial opportunities as the pathway to success. A generational shift was taking place that recognized *education* as a vehicle of social advancement from working- to middle-class and from middle- to upper-class. In addition to traditional university-level training in law, medicine, theology, and liberal arts, college curricula expanded to include engineering, social sciences, and business.

Laurence Veysey, in his seminal work *The Emergence of the American University,* identified two critical historical eras. Part 1 of the book, "Rival Conceptions of Higher Learning, 1865–1890," explores an era that witnessed an explosive growth in the number of collegiate institutions in the United States. This was accompanied by changes in curriculum and the ways in which men lived and earned a living, as well as by the increasing relevance of higher education for the industrial, urban world. According to one Williams College professor in 1888, "The varied attractions of city life restrain intellectual tendencies in the minds of many boys, and the variety of careers which they see opening before their older schoolmates leads to a strong tendency to follow business rather than classical courses."[16]

This shift in learning and living would lead to a second period Veysey discusses in part 2 of his book, "The Price of Structure, 1890–1910." During these years, Veysey contended, colleges adjusted curriculum and modified strict rules to meet modern needs. In return, the meaning of college also changed in society as Americans began to "see the academic degree as valuable in and of itself." As Veysey continued, "Formerly it had implied a distinction verging upon ascribed social status. Now it became a mark of the social mobility of one's parents and of the hope for further movement by their offspring."[17]

In *A Fierce Discontent,* historian Michael McGerr argued that colleges helped distinguish the emergent middle class from the working and immigrants classes. In a rapidly changing economy accompanied by growing urbanization, academic degrees provided leverage and a chance for upward mobility for those born into the middle class—neither poor nor privileged.[18] Arthur Cohen, author of *The Shaping of American Higher Education,* has labeled the period from 1877 to 1940 as the "University Transformation Era." The number of young white men and women entering college exploded during these years from 63,000 to 1.5 million. The percentage of white eighteen-year-olds entering college rose from a mere 2 percent at the end of Reconstruction to approximately 15 percent in 1930.[19]

The expansion of high schools, particularly in the South, created unprecedented demand for more teachers who needed additional higher education to fill the faculty and administrative positions for new primary and secondary schools. This was one reason for the dramatic increase in the number of female students in higher education. According to historian James Fraser, normal schools were institutions dedicated to teacher training. Such schools first emerged in Massachusetts in the 1830s and later spread throughout the country, particularly after the Civil War and the expansion of primary and secondary schools as well as of colleges and universities. "Normal schools," so named because students followed a basic educational curriculum designed to qualify individuals to teach a broad range of courses including history, English, foreign language, math, and science. In other words, it was a "normal," or general, curriculum—not specialized for the purposes of expertise but rather versatility in the classroom. Normal schools also focused on the art of teaching, referred to as pedagogy, which equally emphasized the academic mastery of content. In sum, students following the more generalized normal curriculum were capable of effectively teaching such subjects to younger pupils.[20]

The expansive movement that witnessed the birth of hundreds of new institutions of higher education across the country resulted in educational labels that, in many cases, bore little meaning. Terms such as college, junior college, senior college, university, and seminary were not always consistent with the level of instruction offered.[21] With the creation of the U.S. Office (later Department) of Education in 1867, the National Teachers Association in 1867, the Southern Association of Colleges and Schools in 1895, the Association of Collegiate Alumnae in 1882, the Southern Association of College Women in 1903, the National Colored Teachers Association in 1903, and the Southern Educational Association in 1888, educational reform began to take place in the South.[22] Such standardization helped create admission, course, faculty, and degree requirements at the turn of the century, but the uniform standards needed to define and assess the modern college would not truly begin until after World War I. The Southern Association of Colleges and Schools (SACS) emerged as the most widely recognized accreditation organization for schools in the South conferring bachelor's and master's degrees.

The Industrial Revolution, the growth of urban areas, and the increasing democratization of education greatly influenced the reform in education on a national level from 1865 to 1930.[23] Leading educators such as Charles Eliot at Harvard, Andrew White at Cornell, and John Dewey at the University of Chicago challenged classical education with a more progressive, pragmatic curriculum. Certain reformers argued that higher education should "broaden the scope of their curricula to incorporate more science, technology, non-classical languages and other modern subjects."[24] Others believed that education should shift completely to an industrial and skills-based curriculum.

The traditional European classical education in Nashville colleges and universities was reshaped with an emphasis on science, mathematics, medicine (including nursing), modern languages, engineering, physical education, and teacher training. Vanderbilt remained the most reputable university in the city, with most of its graduates going into law, medicine, dentistry, and engineering. At Peabody, Roger Williams, Meharry, Tennessee A&I, and Lipscomb, administrators adopted curricula designed to produce graduates who possessed a trade or provided a service, be it carpentry, teaching, nursing, or preaching. However, Fisk University resisted Booker T. Washington's call to make African American colleges primarily industrial or vocational instead offering a more traditional liberal arts curriculum. Ward Seminary, Belmont College, and later Ward-Belmont issued most diplomas in literature, music, and general education but added certificates in fields such as domestic science and secretarial work.

Not coincidentally, the Tennessee legislature passed a new education bill in 1903 to upgrade public schools in the state.[25] In 1909 the state passed the General Education Bill, drastically increasing the number of primary and secondary public schools in an effort to combat illiteracy and poverty. The bill also funded school and circulating libraries, established a teacher-certification system, and created four normal schools, three of them for whites (Middle Tennessee State, East Tennessee State, and West Tennessee State, today the University of Memphis), and one for blacks (Tennessee A&I, today Tennessee State University). In 1915, the state opened Tennessee Polytechnic in Cookeville (today Tennessee Technological University). The General Education Bill of 1909 laid a "real foundation for the development of public education in Tennessee . . . and influenced the educational legislation in other Southern states," according to Charles Lee Lewis.[26]

Philander P. Claxton led these state-level educational efforts in 1903 and 1909. Born in Bedford County, Tennessee, Claxton was to become the "Horace Mann of the South, and as a leader in the development of public schools was to make possible a New South," noted Lewis.[27] Claxton would also serve as a leader in several capacities with the Southern Education Association (SEA) after it separated from the National Educational Association (NEA) in 1888 following complaints of racial segregation and discrimination from northern attendees at the 1886 annual meeting in Nashville.[28] Personally Claxton was apolitical, desirous to improve education for all. Ultimately, he was appointed as commissioner of the Bureau of Education by President William Taft, who wanted "a southerner who would not mix in politics."[29]

His career as an educational activist, advocate, and administrator would span over half a century.[30] Claxton spoke to public audiences, lobbied state legislatures, and visited hundreds of small towns in Tennessee as well as in Kentucky, Alabama, Mississippi, South Carolina, Louisiana, Texas, Arkansas, and Georgia. His campaigns focused on educational reform and funding that would drastically expand the number of schools and implement curricular and attendance requirements. Charles Dabney of the University of Tennessee was also a major presence in the university-building process at the University of Tennessee as well as at other state institutions of higher education.[31]

In addition to public funding, northern industrialists turned educational philanthropists helped establish schools and endowments along with other wealthy southerners who sought to invest in their local communities. For example, southern education was one of John D. Rockefeller's favorite causes. From 1902 to 1909 the oil man put $53 million into the General Education Board, which in turn funneled resources to various campaigns in the South. More generally, northern philanthropic foundations assisted in the development of quality education in the South "by concentrating their money in a select number of promising schools" in the late nineteenth century.[32]

Before the South could establish great colleges and universities, it needed to give its students the intellectual skills and discipline necessary for higher education. Michael McGerr has argued that though the South was in dire need of primary and secondary educational reform to combat illiteracy and poverty; however, white southerners "worried about high taxes, Yankee interference, and the specter of African-Americans."[33] State and local campaigns, federal interest, northern philanthropy, and southern "buy-in" made a difference in the early twentieth century. The average number of school days in the South expanded from 144.3 days in 1900 to 155.3 days in 1909. Money per pupil also increased from an average of fourteen dollars to twenty-four dollars, and public secondary school enrollments grew from approximately 520,000 to 840,000.[34]

Aside from educational reform, the first quarter of the twentieth century produced a major period of reform known as progressivism. The movement included interest groups of all types—social, political, economic—who hoped to right certain wrongs caused by the industrial boom of the United States in the late nineteenth century. In larger cities such as Chicago, Boston, and New York, progressives sought better housing and sanitation, as well as labor and moral reform. While following some of the same patterns, the South laid claim to its own peculiar type of progressivism. "If southerners reformed at all," Glenda Gilmore commented, "historians judged their programs to be too little, too late."[35] But to say the South did not experience progress is a falsehood.

Slowly, the cultural heritage of the South would be transformed—but not lost—as urbanization, industrialization, and higher education expanded in the region. Arguably the South's greatest Progressive Era success, the growth of higher education helped promoted order, stability, and growth to a region long resistant to outside interference. The revolution in southern education, and specifically higher education in Nashville, involved many moving parts and actors. These included (1) government on local, state, and federal levels; (2) private philanthropy from organization and individuals in the North; (3) religious denominations that sought to firmly establish their place at the table of southern higher education and further "home" missionary work; (4) an industrializing and urbanizing South that slowly began to look forward to the future; (5) structural changes in higher education that included professional schools, attention to pedagogy, elective curriculum, university presidential presence, and professors as professional experts; (6) and a new Civil War–generation of students who viewed higher education as a positive good.[36] Nashville, as a city, provided the setting, the stage, and an urban identity that embraced the power of higher education.

Nashville's Colleges and Universities

Along with other southern cities, Nashville experienced the wave of new institutions of higher education. Some faltered and failed before 1930 for lack of funding, enrollment, or both; however, several of these schools not only survived but emerged as regionally and nationally recognized colleges and universities.[37]

Vanderbilt University

Vanderbilt University, founded in 1873 with a $1 million donation by railroad tycoon Cornelius Vanderbilt, was built just two miles from the heart of downtown Nashville. The Commodore, as he was known, donated the money to establish an endowment for a university in the South that would be "comparable to any in America."[38] Because of this philanthropy, the school was named after Vanderbilt; however, it was the Commodore's *only* major philanthropic gift. He was known as "a conqueror, not a benefactor."

This major gift was due, in no small part, to the perseverance and passion of Methodist bishop Holland N. McTyeire, who lived in Nashville. McTyeire's wife, Amelia Townsend, was a cousin of Cornelius Vanderbilt's second wife, Mrs. Frank Armstrong Crawford Vanderbilt. When McTyeire went to New York City for medical treatment early in 1873, he spent his recovery at the Vanderbilt mansion of his cousin-in-law. While there, he spoke with Cornelius Vanderbilt about his efforts to establish a Methodist university in Nashville, which had already been granted a charter.

Thus, the vision that ultimately became Vanderbilt University was first chartered as the medical school of Central University in Nashville, under the auspices of the Methodist Episcopal Church. In desperate need of funding and leadership, Cornelius Vanderbilt came to the rescue. Rather than donating money for the medical school and its proposed hospital, he opted to fund the larger university in order to train students in medicine as well as other subjects. Vanderbilt offered $500,000 initially and increased his gift to $1 million. After his transformational gift, Central University would be renamed Vanderbilt University. "If Vanderbilt University shall, through its influence, contribute to strengthening the ties which should exist between all sections of our common country," Vanderbilt stated, "I shall feel that it has accomplished one of the objects that led me to take an interest in it."[39] Cornelius Vanderbilt never visited the university that bore his name. After the Panic of 1873, his remaining years were devoted to saving his railroad empire.[40]

Bishop McTyeire supervised the university's planning and construction, and he also headed the Board of Trustees. Landon C. Garland was appointed as Vanderbilt's first chancellor and remained in this position from 1875 to 1893. Garland assisted McTyeire in establishing the curriculum, hiring faculty, and creating the policies and rules of the university. Historian Paul Conkin wrote that by 1893 the "Academic Department had what is arguably the strongest faculty in its history."[41] The Vanderbilt family did not manage or participate in the school's governance, and the Methodist church continued to manage the university through 1914. That year, formal and informal proceedings began that would separate the school from the Methodist Episcopal Church. The church's bishops and the administration had reached an impasse regarding the appointment of non-Methodist members to the Vanderbilt Board of Trust.[42] Vanderbilt formally parted ways with the church in 1915.

Leading the effort to separate the university from church control was James H. Kirkland, who served as chancellor from 1893 to 1937. He did so in order to make Vanderbilt an independent university, unfettered from denominational ties. The timing of Kirkland's appointment as chief administrator was crucial. The

Chance's Beard Transformation

FIG. 0.1. Vanderbilt University Chancellor (1893–1937) James H. Kirkland. Courtesy of Ridley Wills II.

university was at a crossroads with many of its professional and graduate programs, having phased out its Ph.D. offerings at the turn of the century. Kirkland was faced with serious choices, forced to choose between improvement and financial security or expansion and long-term investment in the school's academic programs. Kirkland chose expansion. Over his forty-year tenure he was instrumental in the development of Vanderbilt's reputation as a university that offered programs in the liberal arts and sciences on the baccalaureate and graduate level. He also chose not to eliminate fraternities, sororities, and football.

Kirkland's decision to broaden the university's academic and athletic appeal would affect student life and campus culture as well as the city of Nashville. Historian Helen Horowitz noted, "The trick [for administrators] was to harness college life, to limit its hedonism and more destructive elements, and to emphasize its relation to citizenship and service."[43] Despite the powerful influence of fraternities, football, and other changes in campus culture in the early twentieth century, Vanderbilt managed to increase its academic prestige and expand its reputation nationally. Proof of Vanderbilt's reputation was evident in the growth of its student body, campus, and departments. The student enrollment quadrupled from 307 in 1875 to 754 in 1900 to over 1,500 students by 1930.[44] A host of new buildings was completed during Kirkland's tenure, including Dudley Stadium and Old Memorial Gym, as well as new classroom buildings, a dormitory, and the original Vanderbilt Medical Center.

From the university's foundation, most assumed it would serve to educate young southern gentlemen; however, the board never passed any formal resolution restricting women. Thus, at least one female attended each term at Vanderbilt from its inception in 1875, although most were categorized as special or irregular students, meaning that they remained on a non-degree track. In the 1890s Vanderbilt women gained equality as students with the exception of access to the dorms.[45] As for competitive athletics, Vanderbilt's first football game was held in 1890. With eleven Southern Intercollegiate Athletic Association (SIAA) conference titles between 1897 and 1923, the new Dudley Field was dedicated in 1922. It was an era of Vanderbilt football dominance not seen since.

Vanderbilt had established its standing as a premier private university in the South. By 1889 it had reformed its academic program to mirror more closely the bachelor's, master's, and doctoral degree requirements of northern universities. Moreover, courses of specialized study expanded beyond the classical curriculum to include majors, electives, and general education classes. In 1895 Vanderbilt became the first Nashville school to be accredited through SACS. By 1915 it maintained a Law School, Medical School, Dental School, Nursing School, Pharmacy School, and College of Engineering.[46]

The Medical School, jointly operated with the University of Nashville until 1895, would become one of Vanderbilt's signature programs. In 1913 the department earned AMA accreditation as an "A+" school, and two years later, the newly renamed Vanderbilt Medical School formed a separate board, established a library, and began planning for a hospital. In 1925 Vanderbilt's new Medical School building and hospital opened, accompanied by expanded Nursing, Pharmacy, and

Dental Departments.[47] In 1927 the school reinstituted its Ph.D. programs and recruited accomplished academics for newly established professorships. By 1930 Vanderbilt had completed the vision laid out by New South supporters, educators, and reformers a half century earlier.

Throughout the New South period, Vanderbilt emerged as the leading private university and medical research center in the Southeast, rivaled only by Trinity (now Duke) University and Emory University. Despite its many programs and departments, Vanderbilt lacked a teacher's college. Emerging from the scattered histories of Davidson Academy and the University of Nashville in the early 1900s, Peabody College rose to fill that role.

Peabody College and the University of Nashville

Peabody College grew out of the University of Nashville, which was originally chartered by the colony of North Carolina and moved to Nashville in 1785 under the direction of Richard Henderson, James Robertson, and Thomas Craighead. The school subsequently divided into Davidson Academy in Nashville and Cumberland College, located in nearby Lebanon. Davidson Academy grew into the University of Nashville, and appointed Philip Lindsley, a Presbyterian minister and educator from New Jersey, as the school's first university president in 1824. Two years later Lindsley procured state financial support and changed the name of the school to the University of Nashville. He helped the school purchase 120 acres of land on the edge of then-downtown Nashville and expanded it into six associated divisions, including an Agricultural College, Medical School, Law School, Dental School, and Teacher's College.[48]

The departure of Philip Lindsley and the outbreak of the Civil War took their toll on the school's budget and student enrollment. Although the University of Nashville struggled from 1850 to 1875, the school was able to keep its basic programs afloat. To help with finances, in 1855 the university merged with the Western Military Institute, which, according to Paul Conkin, "offered both preparatory and college level instruction, but not up to the standards of the old university under Philip Lindsley."[49] This merger was the result of efforts by John Berrien Lindsley, Philip's son. During the war classes ceased except for those of the Medical School, which operated on a limited schedule. After the war the University of Nashville attempted a resurgence for its collegiate program but floundered, attracting fewer students and generating less money. Meanwhile, the Medical College flourished, and a new college preparatory school was established in 1867, Montgomery Bell Academy, following a $20,000 gift by industrialist Montgomery Bell. MBA, as it was called, replaced the Western Military Institute.

FIG. 0.2. University of Nashville new building in 1864 located in downtown Nashville. Library of Congress.

In 1875 a new School of Education, also known as a "normal" school, opened as the State Normal College of Tennessee and shared the University of Nashville's downtown campus. Several course programs were cross-listed as part of both schools. The normal school was established after a $1 million dollar gift from the Peabody Education Fund. The Peabody Education Fund had been founded eight years earlier with $3.5 million in funds for the purpose of providing "intellectual, moral, and industrial education in the most destitute portion of the Southern States."[50] The benefactor was George Peabody, who passed away two years after the fund was established and thus never saw the school that would bear his name. Peabody was born in Massachusetts in 1795 to a working-class family and became one of the wealthiest men in the United States through international trade and later as a financier.[51]

George Peabody was driven in part by a desire for sectional reconciliation and in part by a wish to invest in the educational and economic opportunities of the New South. Peabody wanted the South's "moral and intellectual development to keep pace with her material growth . . . and believed the duty and privilege of

Introduction 17

the more favored and wealthy portions of our nation [was] to assist those who are less fortunate."[52] In 1889 the school officially changed its name to the Peabody Normal College, although the University of Nashville concurrently operated as a college, controlled by a separate Board of Trustees.

Four-year graduates of Peabody Normal College could obtain a bachelor's degree through the University of Nashville. Thus, graduates of Peabody were actually graduates of the Literary Department of the University of Nashville as the state-chartered normal school had no authority to confer traditional degrees.[53] In addition, an arrangement was made between the Medical Department of the University of Nashville and Vanderbilt University in 1875. Vanderbilt students could attend medical classes at the University of Nashville, but Vanderbilt had no official role in the school's administration. This would change in 1895 when Vanderbilt University opened its own medical school.

To summarize and simplify: the University of Nashville was the only established liberal arts college in Nashville prior to the Civil War. Its charter was amended by the state legislature in 1875 suspending its college courses the same year Peabody Normal School opened on the university's old downtown campus. Peabody continued to offer several courses of study including education. The University of Nashville's medical school eventually closed, and its College Preparatory School continues to operate as Montgomery Bell Academy, still legally governed by the University of Nashville board of trustees. Nashville's white colleges and their partnerships and shared programs remained in flux from the 1870s through the 1890s.

Beginning in 1877, curriculum changes at Peabody occurred under President William Payne, who reorganized the school, requiring certain courses and electives in order to earn particular degrees. Previously, most graduates earned a teaching certificate, denoted as an L.I. (licensure of instruction). Payne, with educational experience and methodology training in Michigan, required work in Latin, physics, chemistry, and biology along with four courses in pedagogy. The new, reformulated B.A. (bachelor of arts) required Latin and Greek and several courses in the humanities and science. The B.S. (bachelor of science) degree also required Latin along with either French or German and several courses in math and science. The B.L. (bachelor of letters) was a mix of the traditional bachelor of arts and bachelor of sciences degrees. The B.L. course of study focused on Latin, Greek, modern languages, English, history, and pedagogy. Still, as Paul Conkin noted, these degrees rarely rose above the secondary level.[54] By 1894 Payne had ramped up the curriculum and instruction to match that of a four-year college.

Unfortunately, after Payne's resignation in 1901, Peabody Normal College experienced a tumultuous decade of instability and change. James Porter, his suc-

FIG. 0.3. The new campus for then named George Peabody College for Teachers in the 1920s. This site was the previous location of Roger Williams University until the early 1900s. Metropolitan Government of Nashville and Davidson County Archives.

cessor, hoped for early liquidation of the Peabody Education Fund's $1 million gift, but this did not happen until 1909, when it was decided that the campus would be moved from its downtown location to a new campus near Vanderbilt University.[55] After the decision to move to Twenty-first Avenue near Vanderbilt and the passage of the 1909 General Education Bill, the Peabody Education Fund made the commitment to distribute its remaining principal. Porter, along with many Peabody administrators, faculty, and students, fought the move west but to no avail. Porter resigned in 1909, realizing that the move was inevitable, but not without having fulfilled Payne's goal of making Peabody a four-year college with a highly decorated faculty, recognized degrees, and a sprinkling of graduate courses.

The school closed temporarily in 1911 for construction on the new campus. When the college reopened in 1914, it was renamed George Peabody College for Teachers, more commonly known as Peabody College. The school's mission was necessarily clear: to provide a premier private college for training white educators and administrators for the region's rapidly expanding educational system. The move also had mixed effects on other educational institutions, adding to the

Introduction

prestige of Vanderbilt but at a great cost to the University of Nashville, which formally ceased college operations in 1909. Although Peabody's administration recruited male students, the student body was predominantly female. Particularly popular were Peabody summer sessions that attracted non-traditional college students who were already teachers. Historian Mary Evins best summarizes the school's significance in early twentieth century, "Peabody served the South as an educational think tank, a gathering place for Progressive innovators and their stimulating perspectives, the gateway through which cutting-edge tenets of pedagogy spread into southern schools."[56]

David Lipscomb College

Church of Christ ministers David Lipscomb and James A. Harding founded Nashville Bible School, better known as David Lipscomb College, in 1891. They believed that no education was complete without dedicated training in the scriptures. The school's mission was to train male preachers and female missionaries. Lipscomb expanded its curriculum to include Hebrew, philosophy, German, French, natural science, music, and elocution by the 1896–97 school year. Cofounder, educator, and newspaper editor James A. Harding emphasized during the opening session that the school was not merely for training preachers but "designed to give musical, classical, and scientific courses, as well as Bible."[57] The school's enrollment and stability fluctuated. Acknowledging the need for a broader appeal, Harding declared, "We make no distinction between ministerial students and others; males and females, church members and non-church members . . . [they] are put in the same classes and taught the same way."[58] In 1896 Nashville Bible School had an enrollment of 110 students, with 26 women.

By 1914 Nashville Bible School offered B.A., B.S., B.L., and M.A. (master of arts) "certificates" in music, expression, and art.[59] The school had transformed from a meager Bible school to a school offering several degrees conferred on the authority of the Church of Christ. Most Lipscomb courses did not transfer to four-year universities, but the University of Tennessee and Peabody College accepted the school's general education courses for credit.[60] Many of Lipscomb's female students went on to other schools to complete requirements for teaching certification, which varied from state to state but rarely required a bachelor's degree until after 1930.[61]

H. Leo Boles, named head of the school in 1913, sought not only to ensure the recognition of degrees from Lipscomb but also to strengthen the faculty. By 1915 the faculty consisted of six men and six women, yet only three held any kind of college degree. Boles encouraged the faculty to take additional coursework at

FIG. 0.4. Nashville Bible School Faculty, 1914, with founder David Lipscomb center left. Metropolitan Government of Nashville and Davidson County Archives.

Peabody and Vanderbilt and hired new faculty with standard degrees and graduate degrees. For the first time, in the 1916–17 catalog, degrees held by faculty members were specified and included: B.L., B.S., B.A., M.A., and M.D.[62]

The school's location changed three times before 1893, when it purchased land and buildings on the Civil War site of the Battle of Nashville (an engagement that effectively ended the war in Tennessee in December 1864). The new campus was located on Granny White Pike in southwest Nashville and opened in 1903. After Lipscomb's death in 1917, the school also changed its name to David Lipscomb College. S. P. Pittman argued that the "change from 'school' to 'college' was evidently justifiable, for by this time the institution was recognized as a college."[63] However, SACS did not approve the high school and collegiate courses until 1954. Also, as an accreditation component of SACS, faculty members were required to have degrees from other accredited colleges and universities.

David Lipscomb College endured years of financial instability and growing pains from 1903 to 1920, which included leadership and name changes. Academically, there were also shifts in the curriculum that expanded course offerings and divided students into primary, college preparatory, and collegiate departments. By the end of the 1920s, Lipscomb had emerged as a legitimate institution of higher education, even though the school would not gain regional accreditation until after World War II.[64] While not a top-tier university during the New South era, the school attracted local students as well as young devoted Christians who sought a religious education in addition to collegiate coursework.

Ward-Belmont School

Ward-Belmont originated in the form of two schools: Ward Seminary for Young Ladies, founded in 1865, and Belmont College for Young Women, founded in 1890. In 1913 the two schools merged to become Ward-Belmont School and retained the name Belmont College until 1951, when the Tennessee Baptist Convention purchased the school and reopened it as a coeducational four-year liberal arts college.

With its founding immediately following the Civil War, Ward Seminary opened at precisely the right moment in urban and southern history. On September 4, 1865, Dr. William Ward and his wife, Eliza Hudson Ward, opened the

ELIZA HUDSON WARD   DR. W. E. WARD

FIG. 0.5. Founders of Ward Seminary Dr. William E. Ward and Eliza Hudson Ward. Harpeth Hall School Archives.

new school in the heart of downtown Nashville with six boarding students and forty day students. They began the school "with the idea of establishing a private seminary for girls, which would prove an honor to the South and would become a self-sustaining institution . . . [to] influence not only the lives of all the students . . . but the intellectual and cultural life of the entire city of Nashville."[65] Privately owned and governed, female seminaries emerged in the early 1800s and expanded throughout the nineteenth century. The term "seminary" became popular in the nineteenth century, referring to female schools whose curricula were more academically rigorous than those of finishing schools. Such educational institutions were seen as culturally acceptable alternatives to traditional male schools and curricula.

By the late 1880s Ward Seminary had garnered national attention as a reputable school offering instruction from the primary level through introductory college-level courses. The school championed the value of single-sex education and earned national acclaim from educators in the North. "[Ward] has educated a great many of the most prominent women of the present and previous generations. Thousands of its former students live in the city . . . [and] among these are the daughters of leading educators, clergymen, and numerous other citizens of the highest culture who esteem . . . the ideals to which [the school] clings," historians William Thomas Hale and Dixon Lanier Merritt wrote in 1913.[66]

In 1890 the number of educated women would increase in Nashville when a new school for females opened just west of downtown near Vanderbilt. Two female educators from Philadelphia, Susan Herron and Ida Hood, opened Belmont College for Young Women with ninety students the first year. The campus was located on the Belle Monte estate, which Hood and Heron purchased in 1889 after visiting Nashville to attend a National Education Association conference. This beautiful estate, once home to antebellum heiress Adelicia Acklen, was described as follows: "Like Rome resting on her seven hills . . . to the north can be seen the picturesque city of Nashville . . . to the south stretch the purple outlines of the Harpeth Hills; to the west the splendid spaces of landscape; and to the east the winding Cumberland River."[67]

Neither Ward Seminary nor Belmont College were accredited to confer bachelor's degrees. After the two schools joined forces in 1913, Ward-Belmont emerged as a college preparatory school, music conservatory, and junior college with a strong regional reputation. In 1925 the school's junior college was the first all-female school in the South to receive junior college accreditation by SACS. The school was located less than a mile from the campuses of Vanderbilt University and Peabody College. Nearly all of Ward-Belmont's students were young women from affluent families across the South, and they created a new image for southern

FIG. 0.6. Belmont College co-founders Ida E. Hood and Susan L. Heron. At the opening ceremony in 1890, Heron proclaimed that "girls brains were as deserving of development as boy brains." Harpeth Hall School Archives.

womanhood, partly based on custom and ritual and partly based on innovation and progress.[68]

The term "finishing school" has been used historically to describe all-girls schools devoted to the preparation of young women for lives in society. The term assumed a somewhat negative connotation in the twentieth century even as women's schools evolved to offer rigorous academic curricula on par with men's schools. The growth of college-level instruction and institutions established for the purpose of educating women created greater opportunity for individual expression and active involvement in the public sphere. This would play a major role in the creation of the "modern woman."

Fisk University

In 1866 the American Missionary Association (AMA) and the Freedman's Bureau chartered Fisk University. The school had as its mission "the education and training of young men and women irrespective of color" and was named after General Clinton B. Fisk.[69] Fisk was a former abolitionist and commissioned brigadier general of the Union army. After the Civil War, he was appointed an assistant commissioner of the Freedmen's Bureau and played a prominent role in aiding the AMA with the acquisition of land and the construction of early buildings. Other principal founders and organizers included AMA superintendent John Ogden, Reverend Erastus Cravath, Reverend Edward Parmelee Smith, and two prominent black businessmen, Nelson Walker and Richard Harris (who was also the first African American to serve on Fisk's board of trustees).[70]

In 1870, under the leadership of the school's principal Adam K. Spence, Fisk University relocated to north Nashville. The move was a good decision but one which further strained the university's finances. With the school on the brink of closure, Professor George L. White assembled nine musically gifted students, named them the Fisk Jubilee Singers, and the group departed for an international

FIG. 0.7. Jubilee Hall opened in 1876 and Livingston Hall was completed in 1881 at Fisk University. These buildings, along with the chapel, anchored the Fisk campus. Metropolitan Government of Nashville and Davidson County Archives.

fundraising tour. The goal to raise $20,000 was met and the university saved, but more important, the Jubilee Singers reached across racial lines and gained respect in both the black and white communities of Nashville.[71] Their efforts also helped to fund the construction of Jubilee and Livingston Halls. When the city marked its one hundredth anniversary in 1880, the Jubilee Singers marched and sang in a parade alongside white groups in an event meant to celebrate and highlight Nashville's best.

It would be fifty years after Fisk's founding before the General Education Board formed a Committee on Negro Education (1916) to address the inadequacies of funding through taxation for African American colleges. As for accreditation, there was no official certification for African American colleges by the Southern Association of Colleges and Schools (SACS) until 1928. In 1930 Fisk became the first African American institution to gain accreditation by SACS, and the school was also the first black college listed for approval by the Association of American Universities (1933).[72]

Even before Fisk's official accreditation, Thomas Jesse Jones published a study in 1917 for the Federal Bureau of Education. His study named Fisk and Howard Universities as the only two of thirty-two African American schools that offered college-level work.[73] It was President Fayette McKenzie (1915–1925) who raised the curricular standards and admission requirements after World War I, helping Fisk's standing as a four-year liberal arts college. He introduced new courses in science, music, mathematics, nursing, and medicine, and recruited highly qualified faculty who held traditional college degrees.

As a result, Fisk University was instrumental in the formation of an educated black middle- and upper-class. From 1865 to 1900 first-generation freed men and women emerged as college graduates, and from 1900 to 1930 a second generation, their sons and daughters, took advantage of increased opportunities for higher education at Fisk and other historically black colleges and universities.[74] These graduates not only contributed to Nashville but also moved to cities across the nation. Many would become pillars of their community as leaders and black professionals. Also of note, Fisk joined Vanderbilt and Peabody as the only colleges to establish endowments during this period.

Roger Williams University

Two other institutions of higher education for African Americans existed in Nashville as well. Roger Williams University first held classes in 1864, even before Fisk University. The school first opened under the auspices of the Nashville Normal and Theological Institute and grew out of the home of Reverend Daniel W. Phillips,

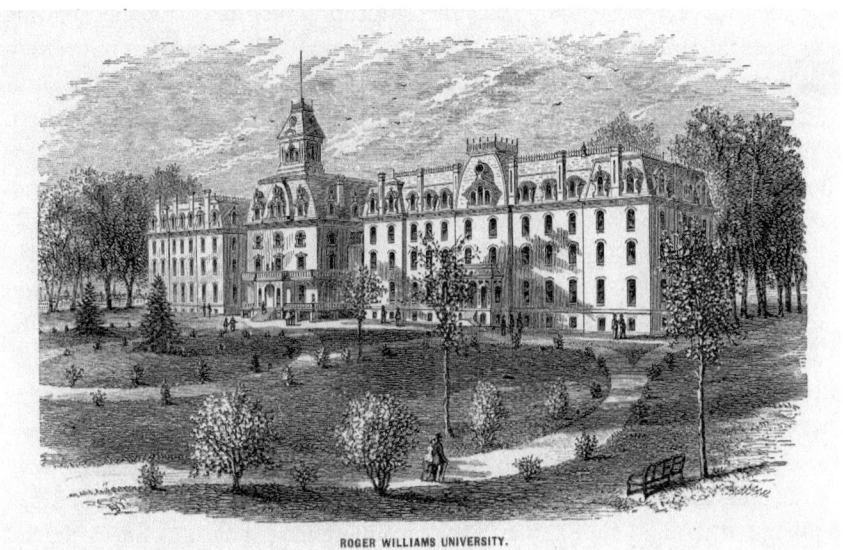

FIG. 0.8. Roger Williams University main building located on its original campus before the building's destruction in a suspicious fire in the early 1900s. The property became the home of Peabody College when it reopened on its new campus in 1912. Metropolitan Government of Nashville and Davidson County Archives.

an agent of the northern-based American Baptist Home Mission Society. Phillips, a white man from Wales, moved to the United States in 1831. He moved to Nashville in 1865, helped get the school off the ground, and served as president and chair of the Board of Trustees until 1890.[75] Other white Nashvillians on Roger Williams's board were J. P. Dake, a well-known doctor and homeopathic medical researcher, and W. P. Jones, who had practiced medicine in Middle Tennessee since the late 1840s.

Roger Williams University courses were the equivalent of a secondary school curricula with some college training. Its original mission was to "provide basic instruction for African American ministers and teachers, accepting any who could read, write, and do arithmetic at the fourth grade level."[76] By 1871 the school offered primary and secondary divisions as well as a "full collegiate curriculum" according to its catalog. Twelve years later the school was incorporated by the State of Tennessee as Roger Williams University. The school featured prominent black faculty members (such as John Hope) and trustees including the Reverend R. B. Vandavell—revered pastor of the city's preeminent black Baptist church.

The 1884–85 catalog shows 248 total students broken down into the following programs or departments: Theological (35), Normal or Teacher-Training (187), Collegiate (25), and High School or Preparatory (37). There were approximately thirteen faculty and staff members that same year. All students were required to take Bible classes, participate in daily chapel, and attend the church of their choice each Sunday. The university required twenty-five hours of service work per month, which reflected one of the school's mantras: "not to get but to give."[77]

Despite financial struggle and overcrowded classrooms, the school still produced hundreds of teachers for African American primary schools in the region and also trained African Americans in theology and practical subjects for the purposes of preaching and social work. After its campus, adjacent to Vanderbilt, was destroyed by a series of suspicious fires in 1905 and 1909, Roger Williams University moved to north Nashville in closer proximity to other black colleges. The university's former west Nashville location was sold to Peabody College, which moved there from its downtown campus in 1912. In 1918, at the invitation of Roger Williams, the American Baptist Theological Seminary moved to Nashville and occupied a portion of the Roger Williams's north Nashville campus.[78] However, enrollment at the university failed to recover from its peak in the late nineteenth and early twentieth centuries. In 1929 the school merged with Lemoyne Owen College in Memphis.

Meharry Medical College

Known as the "Saltwagon Story," the history of Meharry College is one of humanity, grace, and gratitude with overtones not unlike the parable of the Good Samaritan in the Bible. As the story goes, in the 1840s Samuel Meharry found himself lost, his wagon stuck in mud in Middle Tennessee. Desperate from hunger and fatigue, he happened upon the crude cabin of a black family recently freed from slavery. Still vulnerable to slave hunters paid to return free blacks to bondage, the family took a risk on the young Samuel Meharry, feeding and sheltering him for the night. When he departed the next morning, he prophetically turned to the family and said, "I have no money, but when I can, I shall do something for your race."[79] Samuel Meharry fulfilled his promise, and in 1875 he and his four brothers founded a medical school to meet the medical needs of African Americans for better healthcare. Meharry Medical College opened in 1876 under the auspices of Central Tennessee College as its Medical Department.[80] Central Tennessee was initially organized as a community school for freedmen, chartered by the state in 1867. After 1900 Central Tennessee College changed to Walden University and then Walden College in 1915. Funded largely by the Freedmen's Aid Society

FIG. 0.9. Central Tennessee College (later Walden University and the institutional base of Meharry Medical College until 1915) pictured here in 1894 in downtown Nashville. Metropolitan Government of Nashville and Davidson County Archives.

and Freedmen's Bureau, Meharry Medical College operated in conjunction with Walden, but the school quickly gained individual recognition as a separate entity.

It was the efforts of two unlikely friends that molded Meharry into a reputable school. George Whipple Hubbard was a white man from New Hampshire and a former Union soldier who attained his medical degree from Vanderbilt and the University of Nashville. Hubbard exhibited untiring devotion as a cofounder and lead administrator for the fledgling medical school serving on Meharry's faculty for over forty years. He was the longtime dean of the Medical School and Meharry's first president in 1915 after the school's separation from Walden. Hubbard was a "Yankee" but found friendship and common purpose with William J. Sneed, a white Tennessean and graduate of the University of Nashville, who served as a surgeon and physician for the Confederate army.[81] Sneed was a professor of surgery and taught anatomy on the faculty for over twenty years. Together, Hubbard and Sneed cofounded what would become Meharry Medical College and were instrumental in its early development.

In 1915 Meharry legally separated from Walden to form an independent medical college training African American doctors, nurses, dentists, and pharmacists. The Medical Department received a state charter in 1915, and Hubbard Hospital was completed in 1917 as a training hospital. By 1917 over five hundred students were enrolled in Meharry's programs. The school's graduates began to fill the void of medical professionals in the black community with these departments: Medicine, Nursing, Pharmacy, and Dental. In 1931 a new campus was completed in northwest Nashville adjacent to Fisk University's campus and less than two miles from Tennessee A&I. Meharry today remains one of only two predominantly and historically black medical schools in the United States. Howard University, typically considered the nation's most prestigious HBCU, is home to the other.[82] Along with Fisk alumni, Meharry graduates formed the backbone of Nashville's black elite.

Tennessee Agricultural and Industrial School
(Tennessee State University, 1968)

In contrast to the classical and professional curricula of Fisk University and Meharry Medical College, the State Agricultural and Industrial Normal School (a land-grant school) opened in 1912, offering training for the farm and factory.[83] Later known as Tennessee Agricultural and Industrial State Normal School (Tennessee A&I), it was the first African American school to be controlled and funded predominantly by the state. Before 1912 Tennessee was the only state to have legal and institutional segregation without providing a public college for its African American citizens. Tennessee A&I was one of four normal schools opened statewide as a result of P. P. Claxton's crusade for educational reform and state financial support for Tennessee's public schools. The school began with 245 students and enrollment topped 400 by 1916. "Think, Work, Serve" was the school's motto, which reinforced its mission as a trade and teacher training school.[84]

Tennessee A&I offered an array of training fields for men but only offered courses in home economics and teacher training for women until after World War I. A&I began as a school designed to train teachers, farmers, and skilled laborers, representative of Booker T. Washington's Tuskegee model. For the first ten years the school also maintained a high school division, in part because of the lack of secondary education for African Americans in Nashville. In 1920 the school admitted its first collegiate class in addition to those attending for industrial and vocational training. Two years later, Tennessee A&I officially became a four-year college, and in 1924 it granted eight bachelor's degrees to seven men and one woman.[85] Tennessee A&I's transition—from an industrial and normal school

FIG. 0.10. Tennessee A&I campus in 1930. Courtesy of Ridley Wills II.

with a high school division to a credible college with standardized curricula and entrance requirements—was not uncommon. Many such "trade" schools, white and black, followed this same path in the 1920s and 1930s.

Conclusion

New South scholarship has grown tremendously over the past thirty years, and many institutional histories have been written, particularly as colleges and universities celebrate centennial and sesquicentennial anniversaries. However, the relationship between southern urbanization following the Civil War and the establishment and growth of institutions of higher education remains largely unexplored. The emergence of southern colleges and universities in Nashville was one cornerstone of the city's progressive vision, but their development was not simply part of the Progressive Era. Rather, this particular development was what marked cities like Nashville as "progressive" and "New South." Their growth and modernization added dynamism, intelligence, and expertise to the changes taking place in the city and throughout the state.

Nashville, from 1865 to 1930, exemplified the reciprocal relationship shared between a southern city and its colleges. More broadly, the growth and modernization of colleges and universities were critical in shaping the South of the twentieth century. Students and graduates of these schools emerged as key players who utilized educational opportunity to their advantage. This new generation began to challenge certain aspects of a social system rigidly set along lines of race and gender.[86] The South, and in particular southern cities such as Nashville, would be forever changed by the determination of young adults to affect public policy and industry, participate in leisure and sports, and pursue higher education. This book will provide a better understanding of the context in which colleges and universities changed—succeeding or failing—and how they interacted with and affected the community and region around them.

Today's Nashville is a testament to the significance of this period and this subject. Country music may have turned Nashville into "Music City" by the mid-twentieth century and the "it" city in the 2010s, but as the full-scale replica of the Greek Parthenon bears witness, Nashville was first and foremost the "Athens of the South."

1
Southern Style
Urbanization and Higher Education

> The people of Nashville have learned the financial side of educational institutions as well as the refining influence of its colleges and schools.
>
> —*Birmingham Ledger* (June 1914)

In 1914, when asked to describe the most important development in Nashville's emergence as a southern city, a local businessman answered, "[We] have figured out that a university that has an average attendance of 1,000 is worth infinitely more to a city than a steel plant or an industry that gives employment to 1,000 men."[1] Higher education was a long-term investment that brought the promise of lasting benefits such as higher incomes, raised standards of living, and improved chances for upward social mobility. Nashville, and its leaders, intentionally invested in the power of higher education in order to bolster a particular vision of the city's future.

Prior to 1865 Nashville's self-proclaimed title as "Athens of the South" was debatable, but as the turn of the century neared, the city's manifest reputation as a regional center of higher education was undisputed. Visiting Nashville in 1884 the editor of the *Lewiston Journal* (Maine), E.L. Dingley, reported that "[h]e had never seen their superior, and they [schools] are a perpetual monument to the enterprising culture of Nashville's citizens.... An intelligent people must have intelligent institutions, and so the standard has been kept up."[2] In 1897, the *Official Guide to Tennessee Centennial and City of Nashville* also summed up the city's New South focus:

> [Nashville] is a center of Southern enterprises and projects, financial and commercial, ... And yet, it has an unquestioned prestige over all the sister cities of the South—its establishments devoted to higher education.... Among its eighty schools, public and private, every order is represented from kindergarten to university and from a military to a convent school. Its facilities for the schooling of youth are, in fact, so superior and comprehensive that fully 5,000 persons, it is estimated, are drawn to the city on that account... a figure indicating the value, in a business sense, of good schools.[3]

Nearly two decades later, in 1914, Birmingham reporters were sent to investigate and report on Nashville's educational institutions. Using Nashville as an archetype, their findings would be used to improve and increase colleges and universities in Birmingham. After several days in the city, the *Birmingham Ledger* reported, "Nashville well deserves the title of the 'Athens of the South.' This city is an educational center."[4] The reporter also noted that an estimated $25 million had

FIG. 1.1. Nashville's "New South prophet" Arthur Colyar. Metropolitan Government of Nashville and Davidson County Archives.

been invested in the various colleges and universities since the late 1890s.[5] The article clearly showed the acknowledgment, and perhaps envy, of other southern cities that desired the educational opportunities available in Nashville.

The *Birmingham Ledger* also stated, "Practically all of the other educational institutions of the city followed in the wake of Vanderbilt."[6] Undoubtedly, Vanderbilt University was the center of higher education in the city, with other colleges complementing the university's prestige as a school of "Southern Ivy League" status. Peabody College was noted as an institution known nationwide for teacher training, Fisk University and Meharry Medical College were nationally recognized black colleges, Ward-Belmont School attracted young women from across the nation, and Lipscomb College provided parochial and religious training.

The emphasis on education reflected local pride and garnered regional attention certainly, but more important, it signaled the priorities and foresight of southern urban boosters, business progressives, community leaders, and northern investors and philanthropists. Colleges and universities were not only advantageous elements of a progressive city but also a sound financial investment.

A shifting economy focused on industry and commerce rather than plantation economics and yeomen farming was the driving force behind what made the South "new." Those interested in promoting New South cities as desirable places to work *and* live are historically identified and defined as urban boosters. Henry Grady, the most famous New South booster and editor of the *Atlanta Constitution*, proclaimed in 1886, "We have sowed towns and cities in the place of theories, and put business in place of politics."[7] Lesser known, Nashville's Arthur Colyar was a Tennessee native who was a lawyer, school teacher, and newspaper editor. He opposed secession as a member of the Whig Party but ran and was elected to the Confederate Congress in 1863. Living in Nashville after the war, he became an ardent New South proponent who firmly believed that the path for the region's restoration was possible only through an embrace of industry and commerce. The owner of the Tennessee Coal, Iron, and Railway Company from 1858 to 1881 and a newspaper editorialist, Colyar made his New South case: "In ante-bellum days wealth flowed into the South, requiring little individual effort; but with the new order of things we find the people of the South fully realizing the necessity for individual effort, and everywhere industries of all kinds are springing up."[8]

A true urban booster, Colyar promoted Tennessee's commercial potential and abundant natural resources. He also stressed "moral living," industriousness, and higher education as tools to advance a new trajectory for Tennessee and Nashville specifically. Sarah McCanless Howell distinguished Colyar as Nashville's "Prophet of the New South" and concluded: "If he believed that society must be

FIG. 1.2. Union Station in 1931. Metropolitan Government of Nashville and Davidson County Archives.

built on solid economic foundations, he also thought that aesthetic and spiritual considerations must be an integral part of the structure."[9] Historian Jackson Lears argued more broadly that urban boosterism "promote[d] legitimate business, which was consistent with Christian morality and even Southern honor."[10]

This educational and urban revolution after the Civil War would begin downtown before pulling the city west. Former Tennessee State Historian Walter Durham noted that Nashville's downtown experienced growth under Union control during the war: "The hospitals were improved, storage facilities enlarged, and railroads furnished with additional locomotives, cars, and personnel."[11] After 1865 Nashville emerged as a railroad hub with a river connection extending as far as Pittsburgh and New Orleans. Residential white flight from Nashville's downtown began in the 1890s as businesses and entertainment venues in the urban core simultaneously increased. Access to transportation, expanded city limits, and new neighborhoods also contributed to the modernization of Nashville. As local and outside businessmen, politicians, and reformers molded Nashville's New South image, education stood at the forefront as a symbol of progress as well as a driving force that fashioned a particular vision of modernity.[12]

By the early 1900s, new moneyed families in Nashville were generally not transplants but rather a new generation of young men who earned and used their wealth in different ways from their fathers and grandfathers. While still committed to the "Lost Cause" mythos, New South men did so out of a sense of tradition. Dan Frost, in *Thinking Confederates,* argued, "Progressivist academics created a Lost Cause past capable of sustaining their hopes for a New South future. The means by which progress would be accelerated was higher education: scientific historical training to redeem the Old South, along with applied science training to bring about the New South."[13] It remains significant that the establishment or expansion of schools in the South, in particular Emory, Vanderbilt, and Trinity (later Duke) Universities, provided reputable southern alternatives to prestigious schools in the Northeast. This allowed a post–Civil War generation of young men the opportunity and choice to attend college in Nashville and other southern intellectual urban centers.

While many of these young white men benefited from family money, they used their affluent background to attend local colleges and universities and later ventured into various arenas of professional life in Nashville. On a parallel path, minority groups based on race, class, and gender had the most to gain as they moved away from large-scale disenfranchisement and toward greater opportunity for higher education, employment, and local activism. This included blacks and whites, women and men. Nashville's colleges served as both the benefactors of and the impetus for its developing urban ethos.[14]

These young men and women who came of age between 1865 and 1930 were vanguards of the New South. In Nashville, local colleges and universities served to educate and enlighten students, but they played a much larger role in shaping neighborhoods, public transportation, leisure, nonprofit activism and organizations, and the cultural arts. This collective emphasis on higher education and, subsequently, music and commercial leisure set Nashville apart from other southern cities (with perhaps the exception of Atlanta). According to Dewey Grantham in *Southern Progressivism,* "The development of the university was closely associated with the southern progressives' longing for economic progress, industrialization, and 'material uplifting,' . . . [and] the university would be an indispensable instrument in this economic transformation."[15]

Modern Notions

The Centennial Exposition of 1897 marked the midpoint in time between the end of the Civil War and the beginning of the Great Depression, an extended period of redevelopment and redefinition in Nashville. The notion of an international world's fair, operating for months with semi-permanent structures and large public crowds, first began in Europe during the mid-nineteenth century. Nashville's exposition followed the classic Greco-Roman style of Chicago's successful "White City" of 1893.

Author Bruce Harvey has argued that America's fairs "enacted a tension, or perhaps a genial competition, between city pride and national pride," but expositions in the American South added the layer of "regional loyalty" to its complex identity.[16] Southern urban leaders utilized the nineteenth-century phenomenon of world's fairs to relaunch their cities with an eye toward progress. In particular, Nashville's civic leaders hoped to use this opportunity to fashion its image as an urban example of southern progressivism and modernity. However, according to Don Doyle, "symbols of technological and social progress were juxtaposed against a model slave plantation. . . ."[17]

FIG. 1.3. Tennessee Centennial Exposition. Metropolitan Government of Nashville and Davidson County Archives.

FIG. 1.4. 1897 Centennial Exposition Board of Directors. Metropolitan Government of Nashville and Davidson County Archives.

In the wake of the U.S. economic Panic of 1893, Nashvillians attempted to restore vitality to the city's commerce while preparing to host the state's centennial celebration and the Centennial Exposition. The national economic depression played a large role in the boosters' decision to cultivate business and tourism using the fair. As the secretary of the planning committee, J. B. Killebrew, stated: "This exposition will bring people from all over the country who will see the progress and development that is going on in Tennessee. Do these expositions pay? They most assuredly do. Atlanta, Philadelphia, Chicago, San Francisco, Paris, Vienna, and others have paid and increased the population and manufacturing industries of these places."[18] But it was Nashville's reputation as a center of intellectual culture, by the mid-1890s, that moved the planning committee to choose the Parthenon as the exposition's epicenter.

As a member of the Old South order, J.B. Killebrew was able to transition successfully from a reliance on rural-based economics to a life and career that emphasized both agriculture and urban commerce as evidenced by his leading role in the exposition's planning.[19] In other words, he was equally devoted to the countryside as well as the city. His son, George Waverly Killebrew, would represent a New South order. After attending Vanderbilt University from 1913 to 1915, he joined the Bransford Realty Company and quickly expanded his business interests in Nashville. By 1919 his professional title was "Phosphate Manufacturer, Banker, and Capitalist."[20] George Killebrew would also serve as a trustee at Ward-Belmont in the 1920s. As historian Edward Ayers explained: "The direction of their [New South men] movement was more lateral than vertical, a shift from a relatively comfortable way of life built on land ownership to a relatively comfortable way of life built on more fluid capital."[21]

The Centennial Exposition of 1897, as an event, also provided historical insight into the South's adaptive interpretation of progressive reform. Southern progressives continued to view society through a paternalistic lens, and solutions to social problems were many times met and addressed by community leaders who acted as "guardians" of the city. Dewey Grantham noted, "It is significant that progressives sometimes coupled education, which they emphasized as an instrument of material progress and social control, with the need to cleanse the political process and limit participation to those who were prepared for responsible citizenship."[22] In *Thinking Confederates* Frost added to Grantham's line of reasoning: "Although Southern adherents of progress generally believed in its inevitability, they also believed that society needed to work actively to attain it."[23]

As the seat of state government, Nashville's industry built upon the city's commercial networks, central location, and rivers—all present prior to the Civil War. Indeed railroads would play a major role in Nashville's ascension from small city to regional urban center before and after the war. Certain New South cities such as Durham, Roanoke, Charlotte, Birmingham, Chattanooga, and Knoxville were born out of new commercial industry centered on tobacco, machine works, lumber, textiles, and railroads.[24] Memphis grew in large part because of its intersection with the Mississippi River and railroad connections; Birmingham became a center of iron production in the South; and Chattanooga also grew in industry and population through iron manufacturing. Atlanta grew because of north-south and east-west railroads as well as burgeoning cotton and textile industries. Moreover, Atlanta had hosted three prior expositions: the Atlanta International Cotton Exposition in 1881; the Piedmont Exposition in 1887; and, most significantly, the Cotton States and International Exposition in 1895.

Most southern cities during the eras of Reconstruction and the New South fought political battles over commerce, urban development, and race relations. Higher education was an indicator of this new era of modernity and expansion, but not a driving force in the trajectory of most southern cities. Nashville, however, was different: higher education was part of the very fabric of the city and, in turn, an essential part of the whole cloth of the city's image, reputation, and appeal.

Urban Development and Movement

In 1890 the city added a new ward to its jurisdiction. A city report exclaimed, "What may be the future of this fifteenth child of Nashville! Let us call her Progress."[25] In fact, the *Nashville City Directory* proclaimed in 1890 that "we can call Nashville a city."[26] In 1905 the city annexed four new areas that included what would become west Nashville, Waverly Place, Lockeland, and Eastland. With these additions the city expanded from seven to fifteen square miles. The census of 1890 reported Nashville to be the third largest city in the South, with a population of 76,168 behind New Orleans (242,039) and Richmond (81,388) and ahead of Atlanta (65,533). However, the city's rate of growth did not match that of Memphis, Birmingham, or Atlanta (which passed Nashville's population in 1900). By 1920 New Orleans was still the most populous city in the Deep South, but Atlanta's rapid growth earned it a second-place ranking, followed by Memphis in fifth place. Nashville's urban population continued to grow, but the city fell to ninth in total population.[27]

The symbiotic relationship between the spatial organization of Nashville's urbanization and educational institutions helped solidify and designate the urban spaces occupied by New South men and women. The location of Nashville's colleges and universities played a large role in the direction of downtown outgrowth and the subsequent suburban movement. Vanderbilt students first attended on-campus classes in the fall of 1875 and by 1912, all of Nashville's white colleges had moved into the western perimeter of the city, closer to Vanderbilt than to downtown. After buying the former property of Roger Williams University, Peabody College for Teachers relocated across the street from Vanderbilt. Ward-Belmont was situated literally around the corner from Vanderbilt and Peabody, while Lipscomb College moved its campus to its present location in 1903, two miles further west of Belmont (Ward-Belmont after 1913). Just as higher education drew the city westward, the changing cityscape would, in turn, mold the emergent college culture. College life for New South students was dependent on the city, but students (and the success of local colleges) equally influenced the spatial parameters and urban design of the greater Nashville area.

Edgefield, Nashville's first suburb, earned its name because it was on the border of the Cumberland River and east of Nashville's city limits. Until 1880 it remained a separate city, booming during the 1870s to become a neighborhood for Nashville's elite, who built "flamboyant examples of Victorian and Queen Anne styles of architecture."[28] When Nashville annexed the area, many of Edgefield's residents were in favor of receiving additional public services and the possibility of a new bridge. After the annexation, Edgefield maintained a reputation of prestige; however, by 1900 Nashville's growth shifted from east to west. This occurred in part because of the growth of Vanderbilt and, to a lesser extent, Peabody, Ward-Belmont, and Lipscomb on the southwestern edge of the city.

In addition, a 1916 fire hastened the decline of Edgefield, or east Nashville, as an area of prominence. The fire started in a lumberyard and spread quickly as a result of high winds, destroying nearly 650 homes and businesses with damage estimated at $1.5 million at the time.[29] Nevertheless, east Nashville retained an important role in Nashville's urbanization, increasing the population of the city as well as extending public transportation and private business. The annexation of Edgefield pushed Nashville beyond the definition of a "walking city," a development necessary to join the New South city movement.

As white downtown businesses continued to deny black residents full participation as consumers, a thriving black commercial district developed near Fisk, Meharry, and Tennessee A&I (after 1912). This north Nashville area also served as the primary residential neighborhood for middle- and upper-class blacks. Prior

FIG. 1.5. 1894 Belmont Mansion and early students. Metropolitan Government of Nashville and Davidson County Archives.

FIG. 1.6. The neighborhood west of Vanderbilt University and Belmont College was an outgrowth of white middle and upper-class growth connected to the expansion of higher education and business in Nashville. Pictured above is Belmont Boulevard in 1901. Metropolitan Government of Nashville and Davidson County Archives.

to 1920 most African American businesses were located along Charlotte Avenue between Fourth and Tenth Avenues North, which ran west from downtown and parallel to West End Avenue and Twenty-first Avenue South/Hillsboro Road. After 1920 the black commercial center shifted a bit north to Cedar and Jefferson Streets. While these streets were near Charlotte Avenue and still close to downtown, this shift occurred because of the importance of Fisk, Tennessee A&I, and Meharry—all of which bordered the Jefferson Street corridor.

The Belmont area is perhaps the most deeply entrenched in Nashville's higher education heritage. In 1905 the Belmont neighborhood was annexed into the city, with developer George Blair of the Belmont Land Company subdividing much of the former Acklen and Montgomery estates. It was the beginning of the suburbanization west of downtown Nashville and would be followed by Richland, West End, and Belle Meade. The Acklen estate was owned by Adelicia Acklen (1817–1887). During her adult life, Acklen was one of the richest women in the United States. Born into a wealthy family, she married three times, the second time to Colonel

Joseph A. S. Acklen, who tripled his wife's fortunes by 1860.[30] After her death in 1887 part of her estate, including the Belmont mansion, was converted into a school for girls. This was the origin of Belmont College, which would merge with the more widely known and prestigious Ward Seminary (located downtown) to become Ward-Belmont School in 1913. The remainder of Acklen's estate was partitioned and sold as residential lots. The resulting Belmont neighborhood quickly became home to many in the white middle class, including teachers and businessmen.

Although close to downtown, Belmont was considered a suburb by 1910, and its design reflected antimodern sentiments, with open lots that gave the neighborhood a "park-like aura."[31] The college campuses in Nashville between 1873 and 1930 all contributed to that aura; Vanderbilt (with 75 acres), Ward-Belmont (with 35), Peabody (with 50), and Lipscomb (with 65) added up to over 225 acres, all within walking distance of Centennial and Sevier Parks. The campuses also featured impressive green space, such as Peabody's Magnolia Lawn and Peabody Esplanade, as well as Vanderbilt's Alumni Lawn and Bishops Common.

Also in west Nashville, the Richland–West End neighborhood originated when land was purchased in 1904 from the former estate of John Craighead. The area was known as "Craighead Corners," and as lots were sold in 1905, contracts restricted buyers, stating that they could not use the land for a "store, factory, saloon . . . hospital, asylum . . . but the said property shall be occupied and used for residence purposes only."[32] African Americans were restricted from owning property in the area, reflecting efforts by middle-class whites to control urban growth along lines of class and race.

The Belle Meade suburb served as more than a neighborhood; it was created as an outlet and haven for the Nashville elite. Luke Lea bought the majority of the Belle Meade Farm estate in 1904 and developed two-acre plots for residential use with a club at its center. Belle Meade was marketed as a spacious neighborhood with extensive opportunities for leisure largely via the Belle Meade Country Club, which featured golf, tennis, riding, and social events. Over the next fifteen years, more and more of Nashville's new moneyed families relocated from the increasingly crowded and polluted downtown area into this new section on the edge of town. The accessibility of Belle Meade also remained a key factor in the development of this elaborate and elite suburb as streetcars were extended into the western part of the city.

In 1901 many residents in *Dau's Society Blue Book,* which listed prominent members of local society, still lived downtown or in Edgefield across the river in east Nashville. As the first two decades of the twentieth century passed, these areas no longer provided an escape from traffic and people.[33] Belle Meade residents successfully fought the city's attempts at annexation, creating a permanent buffer between it and the city. As historian Lawrence Levine has suggested, neighborhoods and clubs such as Belle Meade became synonymous with wealth. These wealthy areas made possible the erection of new boundaries that separated the lives and leisure activities of upper-class whites from other working-class whites and blacks.[34] Neighborhoods such as Belle Meade also insulated elite whites from the "undesirable" characteristics of downtown living and urban growth.

As residential trends shifted away from city districts and wards, many downtown residential areas were demolished, leaving few affordable housing options for urban residents until the National Housing Act of 1934. Areas such as Black Bottom, Hell's Half Acre, Elizabeth Park, Fisk-Osage, Buena Vista, Salemtown, Cab Hollow, and Germantown in north and east Nashville served low-income and working-class residents, largely immigrants and African Americans. Fisk, Meharry, and Tennessee A&I anchored these minority communities in north and northwest Nashville. Vanderbilt, Peabody, Ward-Belmont, and Lipscomb were centrally located in west and southwest Nashville neighborhoods. By 1930 the transformation was complete; Nashville neighborhoods were effectively identifiable according to race, ethnicity, and socioeconomic rank.[35]

Social registers also reflect interesting residential patterns from 1896 to 1920. First published in 1896, Crozier's *Nashville Blue Book: Selected Names of Nashville and Suburbs* provided the names, addresses, and professions of prominent families. *The Wayne Handbook of Nashville* of 1897 was compiled for the Centennial Exposition and listed over one hundred clubs, societies, and related organizations, including music, literary, and professional groups. Finally, the *Nashville Society Blue Book* of 1907 revealed an updated list of prominent families in a similar fashion to Crozier's *Nashville Blue Book*. These sources uncover subtle efforts to distinguish between "old" (rural, planter) and "new" (urban, commercial) money by noting family ancestry and marriages.[36] Nashville's new elite relied on higher education as well as business to gain position and prominence on a local and, ultimately, a national scale.

In *Philadelphia Gentlemen* E. Digby Baltzell shows that members of the national upper class "were more likely to live in the more fashionable neighborhoods, to attend [certain] churches, to have graduated from the right educational institutions, and to have grown up in the city."[37] Nashville's equivalent to Baltzell's model included early suburban neighborhoods such as Richland Park, Belmont, Hillsboro, Sylvan Park, and Belle Meade. It is also important to note that just as Nashville participated in the making of a new national upper class, their cultural values as southerners created a certain dichotomy between North and South.

In the North, universities such as Yale, Princeton, Harvard, and Columbia served as the "right" schools to attend if one wanted to join elite networks. In the South, the upper class remained loyal and supportive of schools such as Vanderbilt, Duke, and Emory because they wanted a southern equivalent. Many prominent families in Nashville did not want to send their children to "Yankee" colleges and instead sought to create their own elite institutions.[38] Instilling southern culture and pride became part of the college experience in Nashville and other southern cities. This made colleges in the South different from institutions of higher education in other parts of the country.

Transportation also played a major role in Nashville's urbanization. In 1866, the city's first horse-drawn-trolley system allowed for greater mobility throughout downtown. Nonetheless, until 1880 Nashville was still considered to be a "walking city" with very few developed neighborhoods outside the city limits.[39] The first extension of public transportation westward would prove instrumental in the development of middle- to upper-class suburbs to the west of downtown in

FIG. 1.7. 1897 Ward Seminary students on their way to the Centennial Exposition. Harpeth Hall School Archives.

1889 when the McGavock and Mt. Vernon Horse Railroad Company acquired six electric streetcars that ran out West End Avenue. By 1890 the company ran lines completely powered by electricity.[40] In 1893, Mary Hamilton (Thompson) Orr, one of the first females admitted to Vanderbilt (under a "special student" status), reflected on the convenience that public transportation afforded college students: "From Broad Street, I took the electric car and rode out to Vanderbilt."[41]

By 1898 the city streetcar system helped expand city boundaries and allowed better access from the suburbs in the west to and from downtown. Public transportation also linked downtown businesses and entertainment venues, clubs, and theaters to the campuses of Vanderbilt, Peabody, Ward Seminary, Belmont, Roger Williams, Fisk, and Lipscomb. All the schools except Lipscomb were located on one of the main arteries that flowed out of downtown: West End Avenue, Twenty-First Avenue/Hillsboro Road, and Charlotte Avenue.[42] Ward Seminary and Meharry were both located downtown until 1913 and 1915, respectively. By 1915 trolleys carried more than one hundred thousand people into and out of the city each year.

The permanent shift from street trolleys to private automobiles occurred as World War I ended. By 1920 many cars cost less than $400, making them affordable for the middle class. For example, the cost of a Model T was only $300.[43] As a result, cities experienced a new wave of modernism in the 1920s and 1930s because of the automobile industry, along with all the byproducts and problems created by the latest technology of travel and convenience. As James Powell noted, "Not only would cars change the face of the city's maneuverability but also further reinforce the effect of transportation, and who could afford it, in the formation of white suburbia to Nashville's Western sector."[44] In 1926 diesel engine buses were introduced in Nashville to supplement existing street railway services. Over the next decade, trolleys began to fade from the city's landscape, and by 1941 streetcars had disappeared altogether. Public transportation was largely privatized, creating a commuter middle class by 1940. In *Sorting Out the New South City,* Thomas Hanchett argued that the redefinition of Charlotte, North Carolina, was driven by economic change that "propelled the reorganization of the urban landscape." This included changes in transportation and residential living, with neighborhoods identifiable by class and race and the function of its downtown shifting "solely to business."[45] Nashville also followed this pattern.

The Parthenon from the Centennial Exposition, Vanderbilt's Kirkland Hall, Fisk's Jubilee Hall, and the Belmont Mansion in all of its antebellum glory were central landmarks in the city's expanded landscape and highlighted Nashville's emphasis on learning and culture. The growth of higher education and commercial ventures mutually benefited one another, and local colleges and universities generated much-needed patriotism and "city spirit." To add to the city's prestige, all local institutions (until Tennessee A&I) were private and, therefore, more competitive and selective in certain respects. There were conscious efforts on the part of public and private leaders to promote the academic programs, athletics teams, professional training, and other extracurricular activities available to students attending Nashville's college and universities. Administrators and boards of trust, which included many business leaders, also worked together to highlight the city's impressive collegiate campuses and facilities as the best in the South.

Boosterism and the Commercial-Civic Elite

The expansion of power of the municipal government and community leaders provided an array of modern services for its citizens and represented a key component of southern-style progressive reform. "Urban boosterism" or "business progressivism" describes a new class of commercial and civic-minded elites that emerged in northern and southern cities during the late 1800s and early 1900s. Politicians and leaders of railroads, publishing companies, apparel manufacturers, banks, insurance companies, law firms, hospitals, and other members of the professional class represented this group of commercial-civic elites in Nashville. Instead of amassing agrarian fortunes, many of these men gained their prestige through the accumulation of wealth via industry.[46] While not traditional urban boosters of business, university presidents and chancellors such as James Kirkland, Bruce Payne, and Fayette McKenzie also had many civic-commercial ties and played highly visible roles in shaping local policy.

This new generation of commercial-civic elites, business progressives, and municipal government officials did much to modernize Nashville as an attractive New South city in which to live, go to school, and do business. Expanding its power throughout the 1880s, the municipal government granted franchise rights to the newly formed United Electric Railway (UER) to operate streetcars on specified streets in the city, and in doing so, the company acquired the "properties of twelve street railroad companies, including the McGavock and Mt. Vernon."[47] In 1896 the UER was acquired by the Nashville Street Railway. Within a few years, Percy Warner, a prominent local businessman, had purchased the street railway company, merging it with his own electricity company in 1903.[48]

Historian Judy Sealander, in her book *Grand Plans,* explained the complex relationship between state and local businesses and social reform efforts. Sealander explained, "The business sector may have been the enemy of progressivism or the genius behind it. . . . Crucial to progressivism may have been a complex business-led reorganization of the public and private institutions of society."[49] Such public-private interests did accomplish reform within the city; however, much was determined by a profit-based vision of progress: better public transportation, more efficient labor and production, and increased railroad routes.

The congruency between prominent families, associated with commercial interests, and local colleges and universities remains evident in Nashville. Many of these families had supported higher education as trustees of the University of Nashville before the Civil War and Peabody, Vanderbilt, Ward-Belmont, or Fisk after the war. For example, Felix Robertson, son of Nashville founder James Robertson, not only served on the board but also became the University of Nashville's president after Philip Lindsley resigned in 1850. Felix accomplished a great deal during his lifetime (1781–1865): he served as a mayor of Nashville, held a long tenure on the medical faculty at the University of Nashville, and was Andrew Jackson's personal physician.

Another example of someone who benefitted from and contributed to higher education in Nashville was John Thompson. Thompson attended Kentucky Military Academy and was later a member of the first graduating class of Vanderbilt's School of Law in the 1870s. He was a board member of the University of Nashville for several years, practiced law, and lived on his family's estate at Glen Leven just outside of downtown Nashville.[50] Families such as the Robertsons and Thompsons represented "old money," but they were also active participants in a professionalized and rapidly changing southern economy. Historian Paul Conkin noted that "membership was a social and political asset, for such families."[51]

Others, such as the Ingram family, established roots in Nashville during the New South era. Orrin Henry "Hank" Ingram, a transplant from Wisconsin, came to Nashville in 1928 to run a yarn factory owned by his family. After a few months he returned north with his wife, Hortense Bigelow. During a midwinter snowstorm he purportedly said to his wife, "Only a damned fool or an Eskimo would live here when you could live in Nashville."[52] The couple moved back, and the family quickly joined the ranks of Nashville's commercial-civic elite. The Ingram family emerged as an ardent supporters of Vanderbilt University in several capacities. Three generations of Ingrams have served on the Board of Trust, multiple family members are university alumni, and several transformational gifts have allowed Vanderbilt to build new facilities and endow scholarships and professorships (see chapter six). The value placed on higher education can also be seen through the Ingram's support of Belmont University, Fisk University, and Meharry Medical College.[53]

Additional New South success stories tie together Nashville businessmen who linked local colleges to the larger community. In 1908 the May Hosiery Mill opened, representing just such growth. Jacob May, a German-born Jewish man, emigrated from Europe and moved to Nashville. He founded the Rock City Hosiery Mill in the former Church Street penitentiary in 1895 before moving it to a newer location downtown and becoming sole owner of May Hosiery Mill in 1901.[54] Jacob May's son Daniel May would be a member of the New South generation, combining industry with educational and civic reform. A 1919 graduate of Vanderbilt, Daniel May served as a chief executive at his father's mill, a trustee on the boards of Vanderbilt University (1951–82) and Fisk University (1950–59), and a member of the Nashville Board of Education (1943–53).[55]

Another family that played an important role in the development of twentieth-century Nashville and Vanderbilt University was the Wills family. Ridley Wills was a successful New South businessman who cofounded the National Sick and Accident Association in 1901, after purchasing the company's stock at auction. The other founding members were C. A. Craig, E. B. Craig, T. J. Tyne, and Newton H. White. The company was renamed the National Life and Accident Insurance Company, best known as National Life.[56] While based in Nashville, the business expanded coverage to regions outside the South and to larger pools of people, with many new customers coming from the rising middle and professional classes. Vanderbilt alumnus and Fugitive poet Jesse Wills joined the family business and was a longtime executive of National Life. Ridley, his son Jesse, and his grandson Ridley Wills II (board member emeritus) served on the Board of Trust at Vanderbilt University.

By 1925 National Life was headquartered in a building downtown off of Seventh Avenue and made famous by its motto "We Shield Millions." In perhaps a twist of fate or a stroke of genius by Edwin Wilson Craig, son of one of the founders and a Vanderbilt alumnus, the company began a radio station based on an acronym of their motto, in part to advertise and in part to entertain. In 1922, John H. DeWitt, who later served as WSM's station president, built the first radio transmitting tower in Nashville. In its first year of live radio (1925), the station broadcast a "barn dance" program nicknamed the Grand Ole Opry. The Grand Ole Opry quickly became one of Nashville's most recognizable symbols and would forever cement the city's claim as the home of a new mainstream musical genre: country music.[57]

The family behind the Cheek-Neal Company also actively supported higher education through several different roles over multiple generations. The business began with their coffee blend. Their coffee received rave customer reviews at the prestigious Maxwell House Hotel in 1892, after which the hotel sold the coffee exclusively. As a result, cousins Joel and Christopher Cheek, owners of the company, renamed their product Maxwell House Coffee. Christopher Cheek's son, Leslie, inherited Maxwell House Coffee as part of C. T. Cheek and Sons and built Cheekwood Estate from 1929 to 1932. Leslie Cheek served on the Board of Trustees at Ward-Belmont in the 1920s. Leslie Cheek's daughter, Huldah Cheek Sharp, a 1922 graduate of Ward-Belmont's preparatory class, and her husband, Walter, continued the family business and maintained strong ties to higher education and the city's cultural arts. Walter Sharp chaired the Vanderbilt Department of Fine Arts and Music, served as a trustee at Fisk University and as the first president of the Nashville Arts Council, and was the founding director of the Tennessee Commission on the Performing Arts.[58] Other local corporate owners who shared a civic-commercial mindset included Jakes Foundry (iron), Neuhoff Packing Company (meat), Lanier Mill Company (flour), and H. G. Hill Company (grocers). Specifically, H. G. Hill and his son H. G. Hill Jr. provided leadership as longtime members of the Board of Trustees and invested donors to Peabody College.[59]

Not all New South men were corporate owners; in fact, most became small-business entrepreneurs after graduating from local colleges and universities with degrees in newly specialized fields. James William Warner (not to be confused with James C. Warner) graduated from Vanderbilt in 1881 (Pharm.D.). His son and grandson would also graduate from Vanderbilt in 1913 (Pharm.D.) and 1945 (B.A.), respectively.[60] James William Warner established a successful multigenerational pharmacy business in Nashville called the Warner Drug Company. In total, the Warner family served Nashvillians for 128 years, from 1881 to 2009, when James W. Warner III retired.[61] The Warner men represented a different version of New South success. They were not extravagantly wealthy, but they emerged as men of means who served the city that provided them with college and graduate training. From 1875 to 1930 Vanderbilt (and to a lesser extent the University of Nashville and Peabody) produced hundreds of graduates who stayed in Nashville and formed the bulk of the city's professional, white-collar class as doctors, lawyers, pharmacists, dentists, and the like.

In the political sphere, no individual was more visible in the early twentieth century than Hilary Howse. Howse was Nashville's "progressive" mayor, serving for twenty-one years from 1909 to 1938. He was not a college graduate, but he was a businessman and a self-made man who moved to Davidson County from neighboring Rutherford County. His long, sporadic tenure represented the city's best-known political machine. Howse was the "city boss"—manipulating politics and business to serve a public and sometimes personal good.

Shortly after Howse's election, he sponsored a cleanup campaign in 1910 and again in 1911, making many public trips to lower-income neighborhoods, including Black Bottom and Hell's Half Acre. Black Bottom, as it was called, was located near the Cumberland River and therefore prone to flooding, which left black muddy residue on its streets.[62] One local citizen described the area as a "conglomeration of dives, brothels, pawn-shops, filthy habitations . . . accompanied by the daily display of lewdness and drunkenness on the sidewalks and redolent with the stench of every vile odor."[63] Hell's Half Acre was another seedy downtown area, a red-light district on the north slope of the capitol near an immigrant area later known as Germantown.

Reform during his tenure included establishing free health clinics and public milk stations (to reduce infant mortality), expanding the city hospital, raising salaries for city employees, and the promotion of a new city high school, later named Hume-Fogg High School.[64] He helped lead the effort to establish Hadley Park in 1912, the South's first designated park for African Americans. Howse also lobbied for Nashville as the home of the state's only publicly funded school for African Americans (Tennessee A&I). The Tennessee A&I campus was located in northwest Nashville near Fisk University but less than two and a half miles from downtown.[65] He was otherwise disconnected from most local colleges or universities.

Howse would run for mayor again in 1917, losing by a narrow margin. Historian Don Doyle summed up the next decade of local politics: "Between 1915 and 1923 Nashville's city government came under the control of the downtown business elite, but instead of good government efficiency and moral reform, a period of chronic factionalism and spotty leadership ensued."[66] Aided by women and African American voters hoping for additional municipal reform, Howse won the mayor's office again in 1923, serving until his death in 1938 (for a total of eight nonconsecutive terms). His brand of urban liberalism left Nashville "wide open for illegal saloons, bootleggers, gamblers, and petty political corruption, [but also] with an emphasis on health, schools, hospitals, slum cleanup, and other human welfare policies."[67]

The "downtown business elite" referenced by Doyle was made up of white New South men, most of whom had capitalized on a combination of family money and commercial ventures. Local institutions benefited from their success as many of their sons and daughters attended local white schools: men to Vanderbilt, the University of Nashville, and Peabody; women to Ward Seminary (and later Ward-Belmont) and Peabody, along with a handful to Vanderbilt. Attending these schools secured and reinforced their position in local society and provided professional and academic training for their children. These factors motivated many families to send their sons and daughters to local colleges, serve as trustees, and/or to provide financial support.

There existed direct connections between urban boosters and higher education in other southern cities, but the New South men of Nashville fashioned a unique relationship. Members of the civic-commercial elite decidedly and consciously used higher education to create and control their vision of progress for Nashville. This combination of power and interest certainly played a large part in the urban order of Nashville during the late nineteenth century. In 1907–1908 the Board of Trade laid out their objectives, which maintained a tone consistent with business progressivism and urban boosterism: "to promote the commercial, manufacturing, and industrial interests of Nashville; to advance its sanitary conditions, educational and transportation facilities; to advertise Nashville and its advantages, and to advance the general welfare of Nashville and its people."[68] Higher education became the "angle" from which business progressives would make their pitch that Nashville was the ideal New South urban center. Moreover, this angle softened the image of an industrial city by equally focusing on culture and learning.

Club Women and Power Couples

Accompanying Nashville's growth were new and complex urban ills demanding new types of social reform. White women would play a major role in the New South as many younger women gained greater access to higher education, the workforce, and public service. Education afforded opportunity and experience in the public sphere, and young women often used their education as a springboard for greater change. However, many women, both young and old, ultimately sought change through the powerful men in their lives, perhaps because it was more effective or perhaps because many still believed in the southern order of things. Anne Firor Scott has argued that women in the New South shifted from a quest for personal piety to a more communal cause of religious and social work. In fact, reform issues such as Prohibition used the banner of social improvement as well as that of moral development.[69]

Popular perceptions of women in the workplace and their marital status also shifted and normalized. By 1914 the *Nashville Banner* reported, "A business woman doesn't have to fib about her age nowadays, says the *New York Sun*. . . . This is the day of the intelligent well equipped woman in the business world."[70] In truth, many Nashville businesses and institutions preferred older and unmarried women because of their dedication to welfare work, office work, and employment as teachers and nurses. Although many jobs available to women continued to exist in fields that remained of little interest to men seeking employment, the proclivity of women holding fulltime jobs outside the home continued to gain acceptance in Nashville. Yet, marriage and unpaid labor remained the norm for middle- and upper-class women. The prevailing motivation for working women and paid employment outside the home was one of necessity, not choice.[71] Moreover, Nashville's married female leaders such as Anne Dallas Dudley and Elizabeth Keith maintained the support of their husbands.

Organizations like the Young Women's Christian Association (YWCA) combined church women, working women, and ladies from high society. A letter to the editor published in the *Nashville American* in 1898 first prompted the call to action. Within a matter of months, three rooms on Fifth Avenue became the headquarters of Nashville's YWCA. In 1909 the YWCA broke ground for a new building on Seventh Avenue, with over one hundred rooms for residence. In *Women Helping Women,* historian Carole Bucy argued that "the intersection of the lives of women from different backgrounds and different social classes became a distinctive characteristic of the YWCA."[72] By 1906 college campuses had established local YWCA established clubs, including Vanderbilt, Peabody, Fisk, Ward Seminary, and Belmont. In 1921 the YWCA established Blue Triangle Branch in order to provide services for African American women. The YWCA was not a charity but an organization dedicated to civic reform, with an emphasis on the education, job skills, housing, recreation, and moral living of young working women. The YWCA even offered classes through Peabody College for Teachers in foreign languages, English, psychology, and history that carried transferable college credit.[73]

Historian John A. Simpson noted that at the time, "Nashville women in tune with the growing social and economic needs of their city left the literary clubs in growing numbers for agencies that promoted 'municipal housekeeping.'"[74] The Centennial Club was organized specifically for "public-minded" middle-class and elite local women in 1905. Their stated purpose was "the cultivation of higher ideals of civic life and beauty; the promotion of city, town and neighborhood improvements; the preservation and development of landscape; the promotion of hygiene and sanitary conditions."[75] In the written history of the community-oriented Centennial Club, the ladies of Nashville proclaimed, "We shall never have clean cities until the women undertake the job, nor shall we know how to be good national housekeepers until the private housekeepers of the nation extend their hereditary function to public needs and duties."[76] The Centennial Club was established with over five hundred members, required a fifty-dollar membership fee, and was "reputed to be the first women's civic club in the state."[77] The Women's

Civic League of Nashville would join the Centennial Club, with many overlapping members and causes, as a major urban reform organization in 1927.

The Centennial Club worked both independently and in conjunction with the Board of Trade and other local service clubs. Allison Isenberg, author of *Downtown America*, argued that the turn-of-the-twentieth century City Beautiful movement, led predominantly by female "municipal housekeepers" and clubwomen, allowed women to "define work as civic and public, rather than political."[78] Women played a significant role in Nashville's urban metamorphosis, many of whom were graduates of Ward Seminary or Belmont College (Ward-Belmont after 1913). The role of women and social, benevolent, and civic clubs increased dramatically in the 1890s, many times combining several functions—that is, literary meetings, service projects, and social functions. Organizations such as the Centennial Club, as well as the Relief Society, Junior League, Ladies' Hermitage Association, Belmont Civic Federation, and many others, offered white women a more public and visible role in Nashville. Many of these efforts resulted in community service or fundraising campaigns in order to preserve southern tradition, yes, but also to preserve propriety in the midst of progress.

Historian Maureen A. Flanagan has shed light on this phenomenon in Chicago, where female activists, reformers, and clubwomen—who were from the middle and upper classes—pursued an "alternative vision of the good city."[79] Chicago activist women played a role in pursuing and implementing an expanded role of government that included public health efforts and quality of life for all. Nashville women played a similar role in downtown and surrounding neighborhoods. The height of the "municipal housekeeper" movement lasted for nearly thirty years before downtown business areas entered a period of decline in the 1930s and female consumers moved from the urban core to suburban shopping centers.

Elizabeth B. Keith and her husband, Samuel J. Keith, perfectly illustrate the combination of urban boosterism and the women's club movement. Samuel J. Keith, the president of the Fourth National Bank of Nashville and a trustee of Vanderbilt University, served in several capacities for the Centennial Exposition of 1897, including its Executive Committee and Board of Directors, and as its Finance Committee chairman.[80] Meanwhile, his wife, Elizabeth, helped to establish a new organization called the Old Woman's Home. By the late 1880s many Civil War widows and elderly women needed additional support in an era with few social safety nets or community organizations. For two years the home operated in partnership with the Nashville Relief Society, which later dissolved. On December 17, 1891, the State of Tennessee granted a charter establishing the Old Woman's Home. A Board of Directors was organized to operate the home and provide care to the residents, who were known as "inmates." Elizabeth Keith served as the president of the Board of Directors for over twenty years.[81]

Another power couple was Guilford Dudley Sr. and Anne Dallas Dudley. Guilford Dudley Sr. was one of the founders of the Life and Casualty Insurance Company. The L&C, as it was known, would change the downtown skyline in 1957 with the building of Nashville's first "skyscraper." Guilford Dudley Jr., a Vanderbilt alumnus and board member, headed the project and opened the L&C Tower. Dudley Jr. was also a prominent member of Belle Meade's country club, and he helped bring a high-profile equestrian event to Nashville in 1941—the Iroquois Steeplechase.[82] Steeplechase would emerge as the annual party for Nashville's elite, as the wealthy (new and old money) attended the event to see and be seen. Both father and son were part of the emergent civic-commercial class, invested in the city's downtown core but attending school and living in west Nashville. The Dudley men literally reshaped the cityscape as the business grew from its humble start in 1903 with Guilford Dudley Sr. to its imposing new downtown headquarters under the leadership of Guilford Dudley Jr.

The elder Dudley's wife, Anne, was equally accomplished. Historian Margaret Wolfe described her as a woman with "a distinguished family name, . . .

FIG. 1.8. Anne Dallas Dudley and children as part of the campaign for women's suffrage. Tennessee State Library and Archives.

good wit and a healthy sense of humor . . . an attractive matron but a suffragist all the same."[83] Anne Dallas Dudley was a descendant of Confederate and national leaders, a graduate of Ward Seminary, a founding member of the Nashville Equal Suffrage League, president of the Tennessee Equal Suffrage Association (1915–1917), and vice president of the National American Woman Suffrage Association (NAWSA). As a young child, her son Guilford Dudley Jr. accompanied her to many suffragist marches, meetings, and rallies. In 1914 Dudley and her children led the way in a landmark suffrage march from the state capitol to Centennial Park.

Anne Dallas Dudley perfectly defined and articulated the complexities of the New South for women. She was able to reconcile progressivism with southern ladyship. Her language and image as a mother of two disarmed many of her critics. She once remarked, "the cradle will still be rocked, the dishes washed, and still by feminine hands, even if women should take thirty minutes of their time a year for casting a vote."[84] After the Nineteenth Amendment was ratified in 1920, Dudley turned her efforts to urban and social reform as a founding member of the Woman's (later Women's) Civic Club of Nashville in 1927, and in the 1930s she served as president of the Maternal Welfare Organization of Tennessee.[85] Dudley exemplified the power of women in the public sphere so long as it was shrouded within concepts of Republican Motherhood, "municipal housekeeping," and as clubwomen counterparts to the commercial-civic elite.

Women well known in Nashville's social circles were not limited to Dudley and Keith. Other prominent women included Margaret Weakley, Margaret Lindsley Warden (Ward-Belmont, Peabody, B.S.), Sadie Warner Frazer (Ward Seminary), Ada Scott Rice (Ward Seminary graduate and society editor for the *Nashville American* by 1904), and Sara Conley Ward (daughter of Ward Seminary founders Dr. William and Eliza Ward and Ward Seminary alumna). Sara Conley Ward was also the architect of the Woman's Building at the Centennial Exposition.

Black Business Progressivism and Social Reform

As the twentieth century began, African American men and women would seek a seat at the table of municipal policy and urban reform, further defining southern progressivism. Prominent African American leaders such as James Napier and Richard H. Boyd supported the principal tenets of order, unity, morality, and productivity in their vision for the city. A chorus of women such as Minnie Lou Crosthwaite and Nettie Napier also joined as visible participants and leaders of urban-related reform.

In *The City in Southern History,* Blaine A. Brownell and David R. Goldfield traced the evolution of the emerging city within shifting definitions of southern identity. They explored the "twoness" of many cities such as Atlanta, Nashville, Birmingham, and Memphis, arguing that there existed a "mixture of old gentility and new dynamism" that typified the best of nostalgic idealism with progressive notions of expansion and development. This "twoness" represented a selective use of "hospitality and violence, racism and tolerance, and ingenuity and fatalism," all of which fell under the banner of southern culture without any serious charge of inconsistency. African Americans in the South were faced with new challenges as freed men and women sought a more legitimate place in society while facing racial disenfranchisement, prejudice, and segregation. Nashville's African Americans experienced the same discrimination and inequality. And yet, because of black business and exceptional institutions of higher education in Nashville, African Americans were able to transcend certain disadvantages experienced by those in other southern cities.

Public pressure to segregate public transportation had mounted in Tennessee in the late 1890s, and such efforts clearly served to further stigmatize and polarize African Americans in the city.[86] For African American men and women, the state's Separate Car Law of 1905 officially brought government-sanctioned racial segregation to Nashville. The new program went into effect in July 1905, and immediately black leaders such as R. H. Boyd, owner of the *Globe* newspaper and head of the Baptist Publishing House, issued a call for "those of the race who are able to buy buggies, and others to trim their corns, darn their socks, wear solid shoes and walk."[87] Fifty years prior to Rosa Parks and the Montgomery Bus Boycott, Boyd organized a boycott of Nashville's streetcars with the help of other members of the black elite. The *Nashville Banner* reported that African Americans, both young and old, including some local students of Roger Williams and Fisk Universities, chose to walk rather than ride.[88] Subsequently Boyd formed the Union Transportation Company, a short-lived black-owned streetcar company. After the Union Transportation Company dissolved, the boycott also lost its fervor.[89]

Nashville and other urban areas illustrate the prevalence of southern racism and disenfranchisement. The African American community had neither the political nor the socioeconomic power to defeat discrimination during this period. Still, Nashville differed in several ways from cities such as Atlanta, Memphis, and Birmingham because of its materially prosperous and culturally affluent black community.[90] These men and women used their economic success to invest in other businesses and venues that catered to their black constituents. Thus,

Nashville's African Americans could still enjoy time for recreation and leisure in Hadley Park, patronize businesses off the Jefferson Street corridor, and/or attend Fisk, Meharry, or Tennessee A&I without severely threatening their white counterparts.

At the time, African Americans could look to the *Globe* for vital information concerning their community. Owned and distributed by African American leaders James C. Napier (namesake of Napier Park) and R. H. Boyd, the publishing company originated in 1905, and the newspaper circulated from 1906 to 1913.[91] These two men were also instrumental in the founding and advocacy of the Negro Business League, which began in 1900 with the help of Booker T. Washington. In fact, both Napier and Washington served on the Board of Trustees for Fisk University for many years. In 1912 the Negro Business League transformed itself into the Nashville Negro Board of Trade, which included men connected to local HBCUs such as Napier, Preston Taylor, and Boyd.

The Negro Board of Trade helped increase public space as well as programs aimed at improving the recreation and health of the black community. The board worked with white city officials to open a new city park, promote outdoor carnivals and fairs, support booster clubs for young businessmen, and hire black nurses at the Nashville Health Department. Moreover, fundraising events were planned to raise money for continued health reform as well as relief committees for those hit by disease, fire, or flooding. Thus, in many ways segregation in the 1890s solidified the need and place for what historian August Meir called an African American "bourgeoisie of business and professional men who depended on the Negro masses for their livelihood and [which] was gradually assuming upper class status."[92] Likewise, this new black bourgeoisie was responsible for providing effective leadership in social reform, higher education, banking, and other businesses.

From 1865 to 1930, local institutions of higher education not only trained hundreds African American men and women to join the professional and working classes but also trained thousands of teachers, doctors, nurses, social workers, preachers, and public servants (see chapter three). Reflecting the rise of a black middle and elite class, the *Globe* proclaimed in 1913:

> True Nashville Negroes can boast of their publishing houses, banks, furniture factories, undertaking establishments, drug stores, also an up-to-date men's furnishing store and a high class ladies' millinery, but these do not cover the field: no, not by far . . . there is not a single shoe store, book store . . . others might be mentioned but these are sufficient to show that there is an abundance of room for Negro business enterprises in the city.[93]

As for white businessmen, Nashville's Chamber of Commerce acted in a manner similar to those in other southern cities such as Atlanta, which promoted the positive aspects of urban and industrial growth while not admitting to the realities of black slums, racial violence, and segregation. Mayor Hilary Howse extolled the progress of municipal reform, focusing his efforts on improving conditions for Nashville's black community, but his local initiatives were small victories in a system mired with systemic economic and political inequality. In his address to the National Negro Business League in 1917, President James C. Napier declared, "Mob Law, the Jim Crow system, poor housing, poor and short-term schools, inadequate educational advantages, disenfranchisement and a general abbreviation of citizenship, are the things with which none of us are satisfied in this Southland."[94] In certain ways Napier's statement was an indication of the sense of legitimacy of Nashville's black community. In other words, black leaders felt powerful enough to publicly criticize the status quo.

Black and white female students and graduates were propelled into the public sphere and became agents of change through local organizations, where they engaged in social work, taught classes, and provided their community with much-needed services and resources. For example, "Mother" Sallie Sawyer, a black woman, first proposed a Nashville settlement house in 1907, and the Bethlehem House opened downtown in the fall of 1913 offering housing, health services, and community classes. Modeled after Jane Addams's Hull House, both black and white women governed the Bethlehem House in Nashville, and the interracial staff included volunteers, social workers, teachers, and students from Fisk University (African American), George Peabody College for Teachers (Caucasian), and the CME Church (African American), as well as the National Urban League (African American) and Woman's Missionary Union (Caucasian). Those involved in its creation gave it the name "Bethlehem" because they turned a dilapidated building into a comfortable and clean facility and hoped its light would beckon those in need to come. Not only did the facility help the young and the poor, but Fisk's involvement with Bethlehem House, in tandem with the biracial Nashville League on Conditions Among Negroes, also "supported the reality of whites and African Americans working together to provide social services."[95]

Historian Cynthia Neverdon-Morton has noted that "Nashville was among the first [southern cities] to attempt to remedy social problems by involving both white and African-Americans directly."[96] In part, Nashville was best poised to lead efforts of interracial cooperation because of the nonprofit organizational infrastructure created by local colleges and universities and new generations of college-educated citizens who believed in progressive ideals.

Conclusion

In 1877 President Rutherford B. Hayes visited Nashville to lay the cornerstone for a new U.S. customs house. In a speech at the state capitol, he announced, "Nashville's importance as a strategic point during the Civil War forecasted her importance as a commercial center, and I believe you will live to see her a city of half million population."[97] Census reports show that Nashville maintained just over eighty thousand people in 1900, less than other leading southern cities.[98] Yet, Nashville's inimitability arose from a variety of factors that brought the city national recognition as "Athens of the South" during the New South era.

Just as local colleges and universities were shaped by the growing city, the city was substantially influenced by the augmentation of higher education. Nashville's colleges and universities, along with the students and faculty connected to them, did not exist in a vacuum. Rather, they appeared on the larger stage of the changing city surrounding them. Nashville would have experienced growth and change *without* local colleges and universities, but these schools played a key role in determining just how the city grew and expanded. Nashville's modern notions did not suddenly appear after the Civil War. Instead, the establishment of higher education was a key manifestation of the city's political, commercial, and social sectors.

Nashville emerged as one of the premier cities in which to live as well as a center for culture and commerce. Nashville's urban vision, and stress on education and progress, continued to expand through the Roaring Twenties. Although the city would not avoid issues of poverty, racism, and political corruption, its urbanization played a pivotal role in statewide and regional progressive movements. Most important, the growth and development of Nashville represents a microcosmic model that helps to understand southern progressivism with regard to layered issues of education, gender, race, and leisure. The city served as the stage for a new host of actors in Nashville—young women and men attending local colleges and universities.

This younger generation—more idealistic and more tolerant—would join New South society with a different vision from that of their parents. Formally educated and more readily accepting of the South's defeat, New South men welcomed industrialization and tacitly recognized the elevated role of women and blacks in the public sphere. White men who graduated from local colleges and universities, particularly between 1880 and 1930, were more capably trained and qualified to contribute to a changing southern society. These men certainly benefited from greater opportunity to attend accredited colleges and universities offering a mix of classical liberal arts and professional studies. However, black men, black women,

FIG. 1.9. View of downtown Nashville from Capitol Hill in 1864. Metropolitan Government of Nashville and Davidson County Archives.

white women, and other minority groups had a great deal to gain from both urban reform and higher education. These self-made groups used education to their advantage to effect change in Nashville while remaining within a white patriarchal structure.

From 1865 to the Centennial Exposition in 1897 Nashville searched for its place in the postbellum South. From 1897 to 1930 Nashville completed its New South city makeover. Downtown Nashville shifted almost entirely to industry and business after the turn of the century, leaving only the very poor as full-time residents who lacked the means to move. Thanks in large part to streetcar tracks and institutions of higher education, Nashville's prominent suburbs developed to the city's west. Yet there were other factors that led to the urbanization of Nashville: the expansion of the city's limits, political reform, public-private partnerships, creation of city parks, growth of women's clubs and activism, an influx of new

FIG. 1.10. Tennessee State Capitol, War Memorial Building Complex, and downtown core in the 1930s. Metropolitan Government of Nashville and Davidson County Archives.

business and people, and railroads. All of these factors also symbolized the ideal southern city.[99]

Men such as Atlanta's Henry Grady and Nashville-based Arthur Colyar, James Napier, Christopher Cheek, Percy Warner, and Guilford Dudley Jr. led the way for new industry and investment in a region ripe for change and commerce. While some viewed the city as a place of vice, extravagance, and greed, others saw opportunity and excitement.[100] Urban boosters in the New South promoted an idealized metropolis, which combined commerce with culture to inject new life into a war-torn but proud region. Nashville's urbanization from 1865 to 1930 represents a story of modernity—southern style.

2

Modern Belle

Gender and
Higher Education

The fair ones came, saw, and conquered.

—*The Hustler* (Vanderbilt student newspaper, March 9, 1900)

In 1903 *The Iris,* the annual of Ward Seminary for Ladies, revealed an intriguing dichotomy in an editorial entitled "The Ideal and the Other." Agnes Amis, treasurer of the senior class, stated, "My ideal is, like the other, preparing for college; but—O, the difference between them!"[1] Her submission documents the shifting self-perception and self-projection of many women attending institutions of higher education in the Progressive Era. Amis described two very different models of femininity, but in truth, most educated southern women emerged as a hybrid between the two—a "modern belle" of sorts. Part of this shift in the South was made possible through greater social acceptance of women's work and intellectualism. And yet, notions of southern gender, deeply embedded by time and tradition, circumscribed and undercut the educational and professional potential of women. In her editorial Amis captured this tension, viewing herself as the ideal college student exhibiting pride as a more autonomous and independent woman:

> "Miss Ideal" is quite a studious girl, who is very fond of her books; stands high in her classes; and scorns with a "pooh!" any mention of or allusion to a boy as a beau.... She takes any caller she happens to have out and plays tennis or ball or runs races with him. She is very proud of her prowess in athletic sports; and, in fact, is fond of telling how she distanced one of her "beaux" in a foot race. She spends much time on books, and likes nothing better than to dream of Wellesley, herself, in cap and gown, as part of the landscape. In personal appearance, she almost approaches the masculine; she wears her hair parted and pulled (or slicked) back; she has an entire disregard for "style"... yet she has a distinct style of her own. In school, her manner is entirely polite, though cold and forbidding; while out of school, she is a jolly, good fellow all around.[2]

In contrast, Amis described "Lady Other," with undertones of reverence, as the traditional southern young woman seeking propriety through marriage and moral (feminine) character.

> [She] is entirely different, for she is a graceful feminine creature; cares much for style—not "Miss Ideal's" sort, however.... Her desires and also herself are entirely opposite from "Miss Ideal's." The delights of her heart are [dancing] balls, beaux (really truly ones), and to be a real young lady.... She is the same in school as she is out.... She is seemingly very frivolous and light, but beneath that runs a strong current of the good and the noble though to the casual acquaintance she shows no good quality whatever. Taken all in all, they are very different, yet each quite attractive in her way; still, they form a striking contrast.[3]

Amis characterized a new twentieth-century generation of women and a youth culture that preferred tennis courts over courtship and fraternity parties to dancing balls (see chapter four). For Nashville's young white women, behavioral expectations reminiscent of antebellum culture shifted to a more active "Gibson Girl" in the early 1900s, which evolved into the independent woman of the 1920s. From 1865 to 1900 most all-female seminaries, academies, and colleges had been safe places where parents sent their daughters to live and learn under the watchful eye of teachers and housemothers. Caught between conflicting goals, Amis represented the paradox of what many females from 1900 to 1930 regarded as ideally "modern" with that of older generations and "traditional" standards. From Nashville to New England, higher education provided women with the tools to

FIG. 2.1. Ward-Belmont students circa 1920. Harpeth Hall School Archives.

break with conventional notions of femininity—or at least gave them the choice.[4] As a result, the social and professional mobility higher education provided was not only valuable but increasingly in vogue after 1900.[5]

By 1925 this image was in full force, with short-styled hair, neckties, hats, and exposed knees. As historian Mary Evins has argued, most southern women were not "feminists, but many were very active agents of change nevertheless," and their actions made them "New Women even if they themselves might have rejected the term."[6] In Nashville, girls at Ward-Belmont were allowed to bob their hair or cut it short, a punishable act before 1923; Vanderbilt women openly smoked in the late 1920s. These educated young women were neither defenseless debutantes nor militant suffragists. They were "Steel Magnolias"—women who exemplified both femininity and fortitude.

The increasing enrollments of Nashville's single-sex schools throughout this period reflected the South's preference for "separatist institutions" and "were part of a larger cultural ideal that both limited and extended women's educational opportunities."[7] In addition, Vanderbilt's reluctantly admitted women who constituted over twenty percent of the student body by 1915. Other private institutions in Nashville witnessed sizable increases of female students after 1900. From 1917 forward at least half of all students enrolled at Peabody and Lipscomb, as well as local HBCUs (Fisk, Roger Williams, and Tennessee A&I) were women.

According to historian Barbara Solomon, the educated white woman of the late nineteenth century was an enigma, and "female collegians (unlike male) were caught between the attraction of using their education in professional ways and keeping in mind that a woman's usefulness was not equated with [male] professionalism."[8] Sarah Stage and Virginia Vincenti identified the "female professional" as a contradiction in terms—an anomalous, gendered term that incorporated male objectivity.[9] However, Solomon concluded that an "increasingly industrialized society not only created new demands for the university training of professional men but generated needs in service fields that trained women could fill."[10] Home economics, nursing, education, and social work filled such new industrial demands as women joined the workforce in greater numbers; even as these professions reinforced traditional feminine roles. Amy McCandless concluded: "Although the emphasis on feminine domesticity and docility stifled the aspirations of some Southern women, it led others to employ the protective mantle of ladyhood to effect change in their communities."[11]

Moreover, the advancement of education for both men and women created an advantageous association between Nashville and its schools. Several trustees, such as George Killebrew (son of J.B. Killebrew), Leslie Cheek (son of Christopher Cheek), and William Ward Jr. (son of William Ward Sr.), were business leaders, women's education advocates, and New South men. Educational institution building was an integral part of New South business boosterism and urban growth, and this symbiotic relationship carried with it unintended consequences for gender relations as it galvanized and empowered the young women attending local colleges.

During the New South Era administrators of both single-sex and coeducational colleges in Nashville generally erred on the side of caution in regard to their promotion of women's higher education, paid labor, and political participation. Nonetheless, female graduates would contribute more visibly in the public sphere. In Nashville, for example, white female graduates of local colleges led urban organizations such as the Centennial Club, Nashville Relief Society, Woman's Club, Hermitage Society, and Young Ladies' Auxiliary Club. Others, such as Anne Dallas Dudley, a graduate of Ward Seminary, were leaders in the suffrage movement on the local, state, and national levels.

Higher education did serve as a springboard for upper-class women in the South; however, the means and ends of their inclusion in higher education reflected an ongoing struggle. In Nashville, Vanderbilt, Peabody, David Lipscomb, Ward, and Belmont (later Ward-Belmont) exemplified both the momentum and inertia of change experienced by white women wrestling with new roles and opportunities. Such cycles of challenge and reaction would continue to reveal a shift from antebellum and Victorian values to a more modern, progressive vision of acceptable behavior for southern women.

Convention versus Compromise

Southern educators and leaders continued to debate the merits of women's intellectual capacity, the usefulness of collegiate training, and the consequences of educated females in male-dominated spaces. Throughout the United States most private and public universities had begun to admit small numbers of female students by the late 1890s, although many were classified as "special students" or "irregulars." Specifically, 410 of the 451 colleges in the country were open to women in 1898.[12] More dramatically, the number of girls' schools exploded in the South from a handful in 1865 to 142 in 1910.[13] In 1912 there were approximately 24 schools offering "collegiate work" for women in Tennessee alone.[14] These numbers are unintentionally misleading by present-day standards. In truth, there were 4 southern women's colleges that offered courses and degrees recognized by other schools as well as by the professional world before 1915: Agnes Scott College (Georgia), Goucher College (Maryland), Randolph-Macon College (Virginia), and Sophie Newcomb Memorial College (Louisiana).[15]

The historiography on women's education in the nineteenth and early twentieth centuries reveals the peripheral, influential, and fluid role of women in higher education and society; the place of southern women is particularly complex. Historian Amy McCandless argued that "social regulations, physical education programs, extracurricular activities, student government . . . created a campus climate that both reinforced and challenged regional gender, class, and racial stereotypes." She continued, "Yet these same factors created bonds of sisterhood that encouraged women to unite with other like-minded women."[16] As McCandless concluded, "Southern colleges and universities were among the most vehement opponents of coeducation in the first decades of the twentieth century."[17]

Nashville's institutions of higher education carefully weighed convention versus compromise on issues of women's education. Traditionally male-dominated schools resisted and feared the "feminization" of university study and life. As a result, all-female schools emerged as a viable alternative. At the University of Nashville, in operation since 1826, female students had never been considered until the school was forced to address it with Peabody's establishment in 1875. As Paul Conkin noted, the university Board of Trustees had trouble coping with the new, radical, coeducational reality.[18]

Vanderbilt University had never barred the admission of women, and at least one woman attended each year as a "special student" beginning in 1875. However, female enrollment did not significantly increase until the twentieth century. As more middle- and upper-class women sought education, certain previously all-male colleges began to accept limited numbers of females. In the 1908–1909 Vanderbilt catalog, issues of gender were directly addressed under the "Requirements for Admission": "Young women will be admitted upon the same conditions as young men."[19] It is evident that qualified women were the equals of their male counterparts but with different rules, housing accommodations, and limited access to physical education and sport.[20]

Vanderbilt's female students encountered direct and indirect expressions of doubt and animosity. In a rare glimpse of that environment, an editorial by Lois Godbey, a standout female graduate of the class of 1908, offers a defense of Vanderbilt women. In her junior year, Godbey wrote:

> In the last issue of *The Observer* was an editorial on co-education which states the case fairly from a boy's point of view. But I would like to present it as it appears to a co-ed. We agree that co-education at Vanderbilt has, under the existing state of affairs, many disadvantages. But the statement that it is not imperative that a girl go to Vanderbilt is debatable. It is understood that a girl has the right and also the need of education, and of as good an education as she can get.[21]

In this statement, intriguing phrases and words loaded with complex meanings point out the dichotomy of the coeducational institution. Beneath the accolades, the tension generated by women's success in higher education continued to perplex a society that welcomed certain progressive ideas but resisted them in practical terms.

There existed a subtle hostility toward women on campus in the 1890s and early 1900s. In many cases women were not treated as serious students, discouraged from taking classes in math- and science-related fields, and at times, simply ignored. For example, when selecting courses, women could only take classes with remaining slots after the regular registration period (for men). In fact, when speaking to the entire student body, Kirkland regularly addressed them as "the gentlemen" or "Vanderbilt men" from 1893 through much of the 1920s. Despite women having access to most buildings (which came in 1895), the presence of the "coeds" in the gymnasium, library, and study rooms irritated many Vandy men who resented restrictions that impeded their dominion on campus while "protecting" a woman's morality.

Vanderbilt student publications did acknowledge the positive influence of increased female enrollment in 1895, the same year that women officially gained more equitable access to buildings and courses. As Vanderbilt's newspaper, the *Hustler,* reported on the female freshman class, "The class of Ninety-nine is already famous for its Co-eds."[22] Some early coeds were not just "famous" but excelled. In April 1898 the *Hustler* recognized senior Celia Rich, who earned the prestigious Founder's Medal for graduating first in her class from Vanderbilt's dental school.[23] Two months later, graduating senior Marion Palmer Kirkland was also noted as the class "historian, poet, prophet . . . and treasurer."[24] Moreover, the Vanderbilt *Commencement Courier* acknowledged that "she has at all times been the inspiration of the class, urging on to higher and better things, sharing in its triumphs, and making less bitter its failures, and . . . one who always stood . . . first in her classes and first in the hearts of '98."[25] Marion Kirkland also held membership in the Campbell Chapter of the Daughters of the American Revolution as well as Phi Beta Kappa, earning a master of arts from Vanderbilt in 1899.[26]

Yet, the Vanderbilt community, along with other middle- and upper-class Nashvillians, continued to struggle with the effect of women's education on antebellum notions of femininity within the dominant patriarchal structure. For example, in 1900 the number of honors received by females gained attention in Vanderbilt's *Commencement Courier*. The article complimented female achievements while touting the educational standards originally set by male students:

> It is with a great deal of pleasure that we see such an increase among the co-eds. They were first admitted to Vanderbilt with fear and trembling on the part of the faculty, and the question was asked, "Would they be able to successfully cope with young men in their classes?" for on no other basis could they enter. But that fear has passed away, and now we tremble lest we be left behind in the race for distinction. Not only have they shown themselves equal in brain and endurance, but they have outstripped us in the contests for two medals this year. In the Pharmaceutical Department Miss Hunnicut won Founder's Medal, while in Third English Miss Pierce won the prize over some thirty strong intellectual men. This shows what they are capable of doing in the way of higher education, and the doubt that formerly existed has rightly passed away. All hail then, to the co-ed of the future . . . we will welcome without prejudice such worthy foes.[27]

Such examples of praise for female students were rare and often laced with a thin layer of resentment through the 1920s. By the 1930s, the number of Vandy women and their academic accomplishments garnered greater and more frequent recognition.

David Lipscomb College stood in stark contrast to Vanderbilt's approach to growing numbers of female students. The student body was almost exclusively male from 1890 to 1895, but by the school's thirteenth anniversary, over 33 percent of the student body was female. Alumnus and faculty member S.P. Pittman stated that the school's policy on women "was not out of harmony with the wishes of the founders nor did it run counter to the popular trend in education."[28] The 1903 catalog confirmed the school's commitment to coeducation: "Mixed schools when properly conducted are much better for both males and females; each has a refining power and strengthening influence upon the other. Still, the young ladies are not allowed to receive calls from the young gentlemen nor will any association of the sexes be permitted out of the classroom except in company with the member of the faculty."[29]

In 1885 the administration at the all-women's Ward Seminary offered a different interpretation of educating males and females together. The 1885–86 *Annual Announcement* stated that "co-education of the sexes has been tried in many places, but it is on the decline and we do not believe it best."[30] The announcement defended this position by claiming that the commonly held argument for

FIG. 2.2. 1905 Nashville Bible School, later David Lipscomb College chemistry class. Harpeth Hall School Archives.

coeducation as a tool for making male students better behaved was an invalid point: "They say it refines boys. . . . But what parent wishes their daughter to be put to such a use as refining boys, at the risk of the loss of their own delicate and feminine qualities?"[31]

Such arguments reinforced the idea that coeducation would expose young women to the chaos and danger of a "man's world" and risk the female virtue and innocence so highly valued by middle- and upper-class families. This also applied to the perceived "moral chaos" of Tennessee's emerging public school system, which made private schools attractive as well. Even as more traditionally male institutions such as Vanderbilt admitted a handful of women in the 1890s and early 1900s, many educators, parents, and community members continued to believe that single-sex education provided the best alternative for women.

One such educator was Edward Clarke, a Harvard professor and medical doctor, who published *Sex in Education* in 1874. He argued that "women should not attend college even though they were capable of doing so; if they did attend, their education should be different as to protect their fertility."[32] Like Dr. Clark, proponents believed that all-female academies or seminaries allowed women to pursue education beyond basic reading and math, trained them in the "art of living," and provided new avenues for courtship without risking their health. Such institutions were also called *finishing schools,* a term used historically to describe schools devoted to the preparation of young women for lives in society.[33]

Ward Seminary in the late nineteenth century boasted of its challenging curriculum, which included courses in Latin, Greek, French, trigonometry, elocution, history, geography, philosophy, physiology, literature, music, art, geology, government, physical science, chemistry, and even mythology. It was considered a finishing school by some but an academy by others, as a significant number of its college preparatory graduates continued on at four-year universities. By 1886 the school offered "post-graduate" courses in poetry, elocution, voice culture (singing), and English. Moreover, at a time when schools often opened and closed for lack of funds or students, the seminary maintained solid numbers with over 200 students by 1880. After its merger with Belmont College for Young Women in 1913, enrollment tripled to 591 students for the 1917–18 school year with pupils from thirty-eight states as well as the Alaskan territory and Canada.[34] From 1925 to 1929 the student body swelled to 1,200 students, both part-time and full-time, with more than eighty faculty members before its steady decline during the Great Depression.[35]

Ward Seminary did not abandon the idea of women ultimately finding satisfaction with the home, family, and community. However, the school recognized more modern goals of women's education and the desire of many students to

FIG. 2.3. 1872 Advertisement for Ward Seminary Campus located on present-day Rosa L. Parks Blvd. in downtown Nashville. Harpeth Hall School Archives.

continue their higher education in 1910: "The courses of study are adapted to meet the requirements of the present ideals of education.... Students completing the [college preparatory] course are admitted without examination to Randolph-Macon Woman's College, the Woman's College at Baltimore, Wellesley, Vassar, Chicago University, Vanderbilt University, and other institutions."[36]

Ward Seminary kept pace with certain new academic disciplines in the social sciences as the new millennium ushered in modern notions of education and school facilities and equipment. In 1902 Ward Seminary awarded certificates or diplomas to thirty-eight students from its "Seminary Course," four students in "Elocution," seven students in "Piano," and four students in "Voice."[37] Certificates and diplomas did not transfer to reputable colleges or universities, but Ward Seminary did award several "College Preparatory" certificates that resulted in the admission of four women to Wellesley College and two students to Vanderbilt University. With one student from Illinois, the remaining women who went to four-year schools came from Tennessee. In the early 1900s Ward Seminary also added a certificate of English as well as practical cookery and maintained an average of approximately thirty graduates in their "Seminary Course," with smaller numbers graduating from Piano, Voice, and College Preparatory Departments.[38]

Many schools such as Ward Seminary retained the title "seminary," which resonated better with southern culture. In contrast Belmont College for Young Women opened thirty-five years after Ward Seminary at a time when schools increasingly preferred the more modern title of "college" over that of "seminary." However, while Belmont chose to advertise as a college, the lines remained quite blurry for educational institutions until after the turn of the century because of a lack of accreditation agencies, educational requirements, and faculty training. An early prospectus admitted that the Belmont's mission was to combine "all that was good in the old-fashioned finishing school . . . with every worthy thing in twentieth century education of mind and heart."[39]

The opening of the Belmont College for Young Women in 1890 was a day of excitement both for its female founders and for the city. The *Nashville Daily American* proclaimed, "Yesterday was a red letter day in the educational annals of the city, the opening of the Vassar of the South, Belmont College."[40] Belmont's student enrollment grew from nearly 100 in 1890 to nearly 150 in 1905. As the school's reputation as an elite boarding school for young women broadened, so did the geographical diversity of students—representing twenty-eight states during the 1904–5 school year.

Most of the students were from southern states; Tennessee topped the list, averaging 33 percent of the student body at the turn of the century. Beyond its home state, Belmont consistently attracted students from other southern states, such as Arkansas, Mississippi, Alabama, Louisiana, and Kentucky. Texans represented approximately 15 percent of the student population from 1900 to 1912.[41] Beyond traditional southern states, a handful of students ventured to Tennessee from other regions. Charlotte King, class of 1906, came to Belmont from

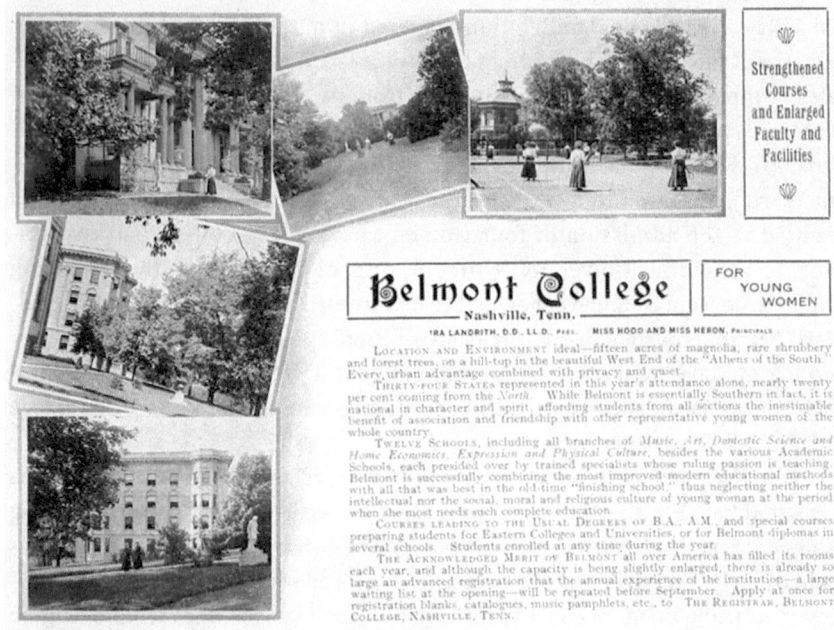

FIG. 2.4. 1910 Advertisement for Belmont College. Harpeth Hall School Archives.

FIG. 2.5. Belmont College Sorority Clubhouse, 1905. Harpeth Hall School Archives.

Iamogordo, New Mexico. Georgine Reid, who was in the "irregular" class, hailed from "Muscogee, I.T.," a city located in what was then Indian Territory—present-day Oklahoma.[42] And sisters Mary and Sara Geers came from Buffalo, New York; Mary entered as an "irregular" student, and Sara joined the class of 1909.[43]

Classes at Belmont were also divided into several interesting groupings that included "irregulars" or students not seeking a specific course of study. These students typically received the "Special Diploma" upon graduation and often represented a sizable portion of the student body. For example, in 1906, with just over 350 enrolled students at Belmont, 101 of them were "irregulars." Many young women who came from rural areas had little opportunity for preparatory work for college. Boarding schools such as Belmont that offered "irregular" admittance provided for these types of students.

Ward Seminary also had "irregulars," but they were far outnumbered by students in the College Preparatory, Fine Arts, and Collegiate Departments. For those in the world of higher education, the heavy enrollment of "irregular" students was an indicator that the school provided primarily college preparatory work or fine arts training and was not truly a college. In 1912 Elizabeth Colton, a leading women's educator, reported: "Irregular pupils affect the standard of a college ... [and] constitute the leading characteristic, and, at the same time, the leading weakness of southern colleges for women."[44] Stereotypically, irregulars were young women who attended institutions of higher education to gain a firmer grasp of academic subjects but were more likely to leave school once they entered courtship or were married.

Ward Seminary merged with Belmont College for Young women in 1913. From the beginning, the union allowed the schools to offset their weaknesses and build on their strengths. Ward Seminary enjoyed a national reputation as an academically rigorous school for girls, whose graduates could continue on to four-year universities. Belmont College for Young Women was a school at a crossroads with an expansive camplus but a declining enrollment. To meet and conform to accreditation standards, Ward-Belmont was divided into two distinct entities after 1925: a College Preparatory Division and a Junior College Division. Previously, from 1913 to 1925, a student was classified as a freshman, sophomore, junior, junior-middle, senior-middle, or senior.[45] Those pursuing college courses were deemed either senior-middle or senior. A student's designation was based generally on age but also on previous education and level of skill. In short, the system may have allowed for greater flexibility, but the lack of standardization and consistency further muddied the waters for Ward-Belmont's institutional status before 1925.

As a whole, single-sex education emerged as the preferred, most viable option for white southern elites and those in the rising middle class. In fact, this was part of the shifting national educational landscape. Of the 451 white colleges and universities in the United States in 1929, 143 were exclusively designed for females. In other words, over 30 percent of all institutions of higher education were all-girls schools. Parents were more likely to encourage their daughters to attend all-girls seminaries or "colleges" than male-centric schools such as Vanderbilt University, the University of Nashville, or the state's flagship institution, the University of Tennessee. However, normal (teacher-training) schools emerged as a second option for young women. Such schools were an acceptable cultural compromise for most southerners. If women were to enter the white-collar workforce, then they should do so as educators.

Peabody's predominantly female student body from 1900 to 1930 reveals the cyclical effect of public education expansion in the South. As schools were established, teachers were needed, which resulted in greater numbers of female teachers in the workforce and larger numbers of women attending institutions of higher learning. In Tennessee 68 percent of teachers were men and 32 percent women in 1887. By 1896 the numbers stood at 56 percent male teachers and 44 percent women. By 1903 48 percent of teachers were men and 52 percent women, and in 1912, 34 percent were male and 66 percent female. In twenty-five short years, the ratio of male to female teachers had completely reversed in the Tennessee.[46]

In 1900 Peabody's student enrollment hovered around six hundred, mostly female and mostly from Tennessee. Peabody did confer legitimate bachelor degrees through the University of Nashville (1880–1909), but B.A. graduates were relatively few and almost exclusively male. Most women prior to 1914 did not graduate, and those who did were mostly awarded an L.I. (licentiate of instruction)—also viewed as the equivalent of a teaching license. Peabody added a graduate program as well as Industrial Arts, Physical Education, and Home Economics Departments, and enrollment soared to nearly thirty-two hundred students (77 percent female) by 1924.[47] Peabody required fifteen high school course units for its degree programs, but none were specified. Instead, early catalogs noted, "Peabody gives as much weight to individual aptitude and demonstrated ability as to formal academic requirements."[48] In other words "Peabody rejected very few applicants," according to Paul Conkin.[49] Some Peabody graduates went to Vanderbilt to earn bachelor's or master's degrees. More often, Ward-Belmont women came to Peabody to complete their studies in education, physical education, or home economics.

Bruce Payne (president from 1911 to 1937) believed much like William Payne (president from 1887 to 1901 and no relation) that too many females would tarnish the reputation and prestige of the college.[50] Instead of limiting the number of females admitted each term, Bruce Payne's goal was to attract more young men to the profession of teaching—and thus to Peabody. He did so by recruiting male faculty and developed a school administration program, which was more likely to attract male students.[51] Despite his best efforts, the number of women on-campus increased in the 1920s and 1930s while the recruitment efforts of would-be Peabody men never gained the momentum sought by Payne.

Until the 1910s a lack of reliable, reputable primary and secondary schools was a major reason southern higher education lagged behind that of the North. In the 1870s and 1880s, much of the blame was placed on the lack of college preparatory schools for girls that would truly equip them for college work. An 1899 report on the nature of southern preparatory schools acknowledged this fact.[52] According to the article's findings, the lack of female students was largely due to the dearth of quality education received at the secondary level. There were many more options for young men to receive a college preparatory–level education, as private academies or military–style schools were prevalent throughout the country. Many such schools for men were established prior to 1865, or soon after, and did not admit women. In addition, it was common for colleges and universities to maintain college preparatory divisions, also largely closed to women.

As a southern university able to confer bachelor's degrees, Vanderbilt's faculty and administration explained, "While our [southern] universities have been opened to girls, there have been no schools in which they could get the necessary training for a collegiate course . . . [with] the result that they [are] very much handicapped, and many have been prevented from taking full courses for degrees because of a lack of preparation."[53] In fact, evidence presented in the 1899 article credits the success of the few female graduates from southern colleges with their earlier academic training at boys' schools.

In a regional comparison, northern schools for women provided a more advanced level of instruction and a larger number of college preparatory courses, enabling graduates to continue on in traditional bachelor programs. Schools such as Vassar, Smith, Mt. Holyoke, Bryn Mawr, Barnard, Radcliffe, and Wellesley had long offered curricula that prepared female students for advanced study in four-year universities. In fact, several of these schools, better known as the "Seven Sisters," boasted the accreditation to confer bachelor's degrees by the end of the 1890s.[54]

Daughters of the Rich

In *The Education of the Southern Belle,* Christie Farnham wrote that education gave southern white women some empowerment prior to the Civil War, even if only more control over dating and marriage.[55] From the 1860s through the 1880s, most colleges and universities in the Northeast, Midwest, and South encouraged women to use their education for work related to domesticity, teaching, or at most a marginal role in the public sphere.[56] In *Gender and Higher Education in the Progressive Era,* Lynn Gordon noted that while more women attended colleges and universities after 1865, most educated young women still married within five years after matriculation and continued in large part as subordinates to their husbands' interests.[57] However, the increasing significance of women's education and its evolution from 1865 to 1930 reveals a broader trend. It was not that women could not find happiness in the home; it was that they had greater agency. And gradually, more female graduates chose to pursue activities outside the home, paid and nonpaid—and most of those in addition to motherhood and marriage.

Overall, and in relative terms, few of Nashville's white female students came from poor families or hardscrabble farms. However, it is important to note that the "whole South was poor," with "typical incomes in the eleven former Confederate states only half the national average."[58] Still, a new symbiotic relationship emerged for the middle and upper classes in the 1890s that increased southern wealth in Nashville as the city industrialized. As a result, the solidification of an existing class mixed old money from the plantation economy with new investments in transportation, shipping, printing, and other business sectors.

Public versus private education grew to be one of the defining issues in southern education from 1865 to 1930.[59] Like most southern states, Tennessee supported very few public state institutions of higher education. In fact, the system of publicly funded and regulated secondary schools remained in the developmental stages until the first decade of the twentieth century. (Nashville's first public university would be Tennessee A&I, designated as a coeducational college for African Americans.) A 1904 article in the Vanderbilt *Observer* reported on an assembly held on campus where students presented written essays. Student Charles Gray Burkitt, in an essay entitled "Progress in the Education of Women," narrated the history of women's education from the Middle Ages to 1904 and advocated for the "advanced education for both sexes at the expense of and under the supervision of the state."[60]

Despite Burkitt's argument in favor of publicly funded post-secondary education for women, all of Nashville's institutions of higher learning that included women in its student body were private. Thus, educated women in Nashville came from families who had the means to send them to school. This plainly and clearly distinguished those who could afford private education from the many who could not. Certainly higher education for women was not judged as a necessity (nor would it be for much of the twentieth century), therefore, the women who attended college enjoyed a "luxury" made possible by their family's finances.

Ward Seminary served as a prime intersection of education, gender, and class. From its inception, Ward Seminary catered to women from prominent families, both in Tennessee and other southern states. The school was located on Spruce Street before moving two miles west of downtown. Its purpose and level of instruction for its middle- and upper-class students were first outlined in the mid-1880s in its *Annual Announcement:*

> In 1865 it was conceived that the want of the country was a more thorough preparation of *our* daughters for the duties of life. To this end a free classic course was inaugurated, and a full course in all other departments. . . . [Ward Seminary] has surpassed all other schools in the South in numbers and facilities, as shown by the report of the Commissioner of Education, at Washington, for years past. There are many excellent schools for girls in the United States, but we believe they do not offer a wider range of instruction and observation, nor greater attention to accomplishment and good manners, than this Seminary.[61]

Themes of class pervade not only Ward Seminary but are also revealed in other schools in Nashville, particularly Belmont College for Young Women. Belmont students were referred to as "Belmont Belles." Many upper-class parents saw postsecondary training for their daughters as a launching pad for adulthood. As such, higher education beyond basic schooling became part of a new "coming out" ritual for society women, and the commencement exercises provided a ceremonial setting for the traditional May Day festival. Like its predecessors, Ward-Belmont School also participated in May Day festivities with graduation

FIG. 2.6. May Day Dance at Ward Seminary, c. 1890. Harpeth Hall School Archives.

weekend culminating in a performance by college seniors (typically ages twenty to twenty-one) around the May Pole, complete with streamers, white gowns, and dancing. At Ward-Belmont the "court" included a May Queen, College Maid, and (high school) Prep Maid. The 1929 *Milestones* celebrated the event's pageantry and history: "Among the traditions of Ward-Belmont, one of the loveliest is the celebration of May Day. The south slope of the lawn fairly calls for dancers, sprites, and elves. . . . The happy array of past May Days passes in review in a stream of blended colors gently blown along by soft breezes and graciously led by all the ancient traditions."[62]

Ilana DeBare, author of *Where Girls Come First,* noted, "Many girls' schools and women's colleges instituted annual May Day celebrations that involved an elaborate pageant with gowns and flowers, and the selection of a May Queen and her court. These rituals celebrated spring, but they also celebrated and promoted the southern ideal of woman as delicate, graceful, pure, and virtuous."[63] The May Festival paralleled similar debutante and cotillion exercises for the daughters of the upper class. More broadly, historian Joan Marie Johnson noted, "Formal education marked class, refinement, and—surprisingly—marriageability" for many southerners after 1865.[64] Johnson also pointed out that marriage rates at southern liberal arts female colleges were close to 70 percent.[65] In other words, all-female schools in the South turned out nearly as many brides as graduates, reinforcing the finishing school reputation.

Though Vanderbilt University had no May Day equivalent, cultural expectations for alumna were apparent. In 1906, the *Hustler* wrote that fourteen of the forty-nine Vanderbilt female graduates in 1907 were already married by the following fall and added, "The student body joins *The Hustler* in the heartfelt wish that many more will go and do likewise. Here's success to the Co-eds."[66] Although the comment is masked in a congratulatory tone, traditional roles are the main object of applause as the predominantly male student body reaffirmed the primary role of women as wives and equated success and desirability with marriage as a young adult. It remains quite clear that southern society continued to encourage prominent young women to use their education to enhance their primary position as wives and mothers of prominent men.

As a whole, the issue of class seemed particularly sensitive for middle- and upper-class families in the South in the early twentieth century. In addition to single-sex institutions, most Vanderbilt women were either the daughters of faculty, administrators, or prominent Nashville families. Annie Paschall was the first woman to receive what was known as an "entering scholarship" at Vanderbilt in 1891. However, most women received no financial aid, and there remains no evidence to suggest that scholarships existed for women.

Some students were valedictorians or highly motivated graduates from reputable college-preparatory schools who desired a traditional university degree. Vanderbilt's female students were likely more driven to achieve academic success than were the majority of students at all-girls schools during this period.

An article in Vanderbilt's newspaper entitled "Daughters of the Rich" reflects the consternation and yet conflicted views regarding higher education (and the supposed autonomy gained) for women of the middle and upper classes:

> No class of women are more to be pitied than the daughters of rich men, who, having real force and energy of character, have no vent for it, because fashion requires them to sit still and fold their hands. It does not require this of their brothers.... [But] the daughter of the millionaire must still her pulses and close her eyes and ears to the possibilities, and think of nothing but husband-hunting. We never can know how many real heroines are behind the wall of restriction 'till what is called "adverse" fate sets them free to stand upon their own feet, and to use their own hands, and know their own powers, which had been dwarfed almost to extinction by inaction.[67]

In another article, Lois Godbey, Vanderbilt class of 1908, did not deny the ultimate goal of middle- and upper-class women as prominent members of the community and as wives and mothers of prominent men. However, she defended the desire of women to attend Vanderbilt:

FIG. 2.7. George Peabody College Social Religious Building was completed in 1915 and anchored the main campus quadrangle. Courtesy of Ridley Wills II.

FIG. 2.8. Vanderbilt Medical Center, 1925. Metropolitan Government of Nashville and Davidson County Archives.

It is true that there are many good women's colleges in the United States, but there are only two first-class colleges for women in the South. . . . They offer us no subjects that Vanderbilt does not, but Vanderbilt offers many that they do not. And the elective system of Vanderbilt gives us an opportunity to consult our individual tastes. It is true that we could go to Vassar or Wellesley, which are as the [Ivy League] colleges for men, but we do not go to them for the same reason that the Vanderbilt boys do not go to Harvard and Yale.[68]

Issues of class and gender were also apparent at Peabody College—a school with subcollegiate status, training mostly women to enter the fields of primary or secondary education. Although Peabody's total enrollment would skyrocket after 1918, enrollment during the tenure of President Eben Stearns (1875–87) included only twelve women, several of whom were prominent daughters of Nashville families.[69] In addition to Stearns's daughter, other women from powerful families included the daughter of University of Nashville's chancellor John Berrien Lindsley, who was also a descendant of John Sevier, Tennessee's first governor.[70] Overall, Peabody mostly attracted young women (as well as men) from middle- to upper-class families. It is important to note that these original students "were not poor girls seeking a chance to teach, but young women from affluent Nashville homes seeking a secondary-level education and a profession."[71] However, Peabody scholarships were available to reduce or cover tuition for need- and merit-based students. In contrast, there were no significant financial aid or scholarship programs at Vanderbilt, Ward, Belmont, or Ward-Belmont.

David Lipscomb College, or Nashville Bible College, did not advertise for or attract the same type of student that Vanderbilt, Ward Seminary, Belmont College, or even Peabody did. With three teachers, thirty-two male students, and two female students, the school charged approximately $30 for instruction and room and board throughout the 1890s. By comparison, Ward Seminary's 1885 tuition was approximately $150 for the same services. By 1900 Lipcomb's tuition had risen modestly, but female students were required to pay additional funds for supplies, clothing/uniforms, and linens that were deemed "unnecessary" for male students. Females who attended Nashville Bible College were not seen as a part of or even an extension of the social elite. Instead, the "college" remained a second-tier school compared to other colleges in Nashville. In large part, this was because of the different nature and purpose of David Lipscomb College as a Church of Christ school intent on training missionaries, preachers, and teachers.

In 1916 Jeanette Rankin of Montana became the first woman elected to the United States House of Representatives, Woodrow Wilson declared his support for a woman's right to vote, and Margaret Sanger opened the Brownsville Clinic in New York City. At the same time, Ward-Belmont junior Damaris Smith wrote a poem clearly emphasizing a preference for "Lady Other," as described by Agnes Amis in 1903:

> Genus homo is charmed by smiles,
> And often caught with wanton wiles,
> He's often enticed with laughter and wit,
> But more substantial things his appetites fit.
>
> Mrs. Herbrick, who is both charming and wise,
> Does teach us in the art of pies,
> So that when we go out in quest,
> Our future fortunes will be the best.
>
> Then Miss Cooper with wonderful skill,
> Does teach us how our homes to build,
> For there is no greater success in this life
> Than keeping a man in love with his wife.
>
> To the scholar of Latin, Greek, and of Math
> We admit that she great knowledge hath
> But when it comes to the Diploma giving
> I'll take mine in the art of living.[72]

Nashville's well-to-do young women remained conflicted. As the women's rights movement gained momentum on issues ranging from suffrage to birth control, many men (and women) in the South sought a softer version. Nashville's female graduates emerged as the compromise—an amalgamation that rested symbolically between Scarlett O'Hara and Clara Bow.

"Genderfication"

From 1865 to 1930 educational reform, accrediting agencies, and professional associations established standard admission, course, faculty, and degree requirements. However, these developments and standardizations also created gendered tracks for women. In other words, as higher education expanded, the culture and curricula grew differently for men and women. Divided along lines of gender, particular classes designed for women included domestic science/home economics, teacher training, physical education, social work, and an emphasis on music. As such, curricular reform defined and, in many ways, limited women's education to degree tracks focused on "soft subjects" ranging from piano to literature while deemphasizing classical majors, engineering, law, medicine, and science.

Even as opportunities to attend college and join the workforce expanded, an increasingly tracked collegiate curriculum created a different lane for women on the highway of higher education. Fine arts such as music, dance, theater, and art were still popular, but new courses of study were designed to match traditional notions of domesticity and femininity with those of the modern world. However, from 1900 to 1910 many colleges, both single-sex and coeducational, had created home economics courses and, in some cases, departments. Lipscomb, Ward-Belmont, and Peabody followed this trend. First called domestic science or domestic art, "home economics" became the term of choice by 1920. Perhaps more than any other field of study, home economics created a gendered curriculum for women—a practical science to be used in the home and community. In a curious way, this curriculum better fulfilled the "art of living" motive than the curricula offered to men in preparation for fatherhood or careers in business.

Linked to Republican Motherhood and the cult of domesticity, home economics combined several historic roles for women: municipal housekeeper, teacher/educator, social reformer, and "queen of the home."[73] As Megan Elias has noted, instead of being a product of the conformist culture of the 1950s, the era most commonly associated with the subject, "home economics began as an organized social movement at the end of the nineteenth century"; it was led by Ellen Richards, the first woman to attend (1870–73) and later teach at the Massachusetts Institute of Technology.[74] This new academic subject emphasized physical health and connected morality with healthy living. Indeed, early home economists were progressives who wanted to provide greater training and opportunity for social reform but also for women's role in the workplace. It was a mixed-message movement, according to historian Mary Hoffschwelle: "Early home economists expounded . . . the importance of home life for inculcating moral and social values, yet they taught mostly cooking, sewing, and classroom methods. These contradictions mirrored conflicts within southern progressivism."[75]

Ward Seminary first introduced a domestic science class in 1907. In 1910 Belmont College offered domestic science and domestic art under the umbrella of home economics, which was listed as one of twelve departments in addition to the traditional academic departments. Belmont claimed that the school and its programs "successfully combine[d] the most improved modern educational methods with all that was best in the old-time 'finishing school,' thus neglecting neither the intellectual nor the social, moral, and religious culture of young women at the period where she most needs such complete education."[76] The home economics instructors at Belmont were both from the North: Grace Frysinger, a graduate of Oread Institute and Drexel Institute, and Margaret Dismukes, a "household arts" graduate of Teachers College at Columbia University.[77] After the merger, the home economics instructor at Ward-Belmont was Edna Atwood, a graduate of Carnegie Institute of Technology and Teachers College at Columbia University.[78]

Highly trained at progressive schools, these instructors capitalized on the growing trend of home economics not only as a course but also as an academic discipline or major. However, many women's schools fought the movement despite the cultural acceptance of this comfortable hybrid that lay between the professional and domestic spheres. In 1905 the Association of Collegiate Alumnae (later the AAUW) would deem home economics "an inappropriate topic for women's college education" because the organization "believed it would further lower the 'mediocrity' of women's schools struggling for credibility."[79]

Neither Ward Seminary nor Belmont College promoted home economics as it did other courses of study, and the "Seven Sisters" schools denounced its legitimacy as an academic subject. Perhaps these schools believed domestic science diluted their otherwise strong liberal arts curriculum, or perhaps because it did not provide a skill set that was essential for prominent women who often had domestic help for household cleaning and cooking. Either way, both schools slowly came to the proverbial table—which began offering domestic science courses in the early 1900s. Incredibly, the femininity attached to home economics was equated with the masculinity of men's sport at Belmont. The 1910 *Milady in*

FIG. 2.9. Cartoon depicting the evolution of college life from Belmont College 1910 yearbook. Harpeth Hall Archives.

Brown yearbook proclaimed proudly, "She took Domestic Science at BELMONT. He took Football at VANDERBILT."[80]

After 1913, Ward-Belmont and Peabody College legitimized home economics with both schools creating departments for the subject. Historian Mary Hoffschwelle identified multiple purposes of the home economics program at Peabody that "sprang from the Progressive impulse" of social reform in the South. In particular, Hoffschwelle argued that from 1914 to 1939, "the college was a self-appointed agent of reform, with special interest in southern education, home life, and agriculture."[81] Thus the development and growth of Peabody's Home Economics Department was a reflection of the changing roles of women in the south, and the social roles they filled in the home, school, and potentially the workplace.

The Ward-Belmont catalog also described the school's ultimate embrace of home economics as part of the southern progressive movement in 1924:

> The lifting of the homemaker's work to its proper place among the sciences is perhaps one of the most significant recent educational reforms. Domestic Science and Domestic Art are now regarded as essential in a well-rounded education for women. Responding to this *Progressive* movement, Ward-Belmont maintains a thorough department for the study of the home and its varied problems.[82]

In 1898 Ellen Richards, a prominent chemist and national pioneer for home economics, called for the subject to be "put on par with the other sciences" and believed that chemistry, physics, and biology were "only the stepping stones of sanitary science."[83] Although home economics did not create the gender-specific alternative to male-dominated fields in science as advocates had hoped, domestic science did train women for professional careers outside the home that extended beyond volunteerism.

Another gender-specific field for female college students was nursing. Meharry Medical College and the Millie E. Hale Hospital both offered three-year nursing programs for African American women (see chapter 3) that produced a new career-path and professional network for black graduates who trained in Nashville and worked throughout the country. For white women, Vanderbilt offered nursing classes as early as 1909 but primarily to train the staff for the Medical School's small downtown clinic. As nursing professionalized, shifting

FIG. 2.10. Vanderbilt University nursing students. Metropolitan Government of Nashville and Davidson County Archives.

from basic care of patients and housekeeping to rigorous training and academic study, Vanderbilt and Peabody both established more legitimate (three-year) nursing programs in 1912. Student enrollment increased and local nursing programs gained a respectable reputation throughout Middle Tennessee, but nursing did not yet attract socially prominent young women.

The Vanderbilt yearbook, *The Commodore,* first pictured eighteen nursing students in 1918, reflecting at least a tacit acknowledgement that nursing students were part of the Vanderbilt community. Seven years later G. Canby Robinson, dean of medical department, appointed a director of nursing and petitioned to enlarge and improve the nursing program as the hospital planned its expansion and new facility. As Paul Conkin wrote, Chancellor Kirkland "was peeved" about the high costs and "was not very sympathetic to the [nursing] school."[84] Vanderbilt's program coordinated for several years with Peabody's public health nursing program to allow course credits and hospital training hours to transfer between the two. After northern non-profit organizations bestowed several grants, it was clear that these philanthropic groups believed that Vanderbilt was the logical choice as a model nursing school in the south.

In 1930, one such group, the Rockefeller Foundation raised its annual support of Vanderbilt's nursing school to $35,000 on several conditions: the creation of a dean of nursing, the admission of nursing students on par with other medical students, a legitimate degree program, and the structural reorganization of the Medical School to include nursing education. These changes did not happen overnight, but Vanderbilt's nursing program did reflect a passive concession by the university to offer a curriculum specifically for women. From 1909 to 1930 nursing students were still considered as hospital staff rather than as college students. But developments in nursing helped to complete the program building that would be instrumental to today's modern Vanderbilt University.

Women may not have worked in traditional professions, but they carved out new niches for themselves including home economics and nursing. Women trained in these fields often used their talents to affect change through social reform efforts. These were gender specific and certainly did not bring about equality in the workplace, but they did create new professional opportunities for college-educated women. Thus, women's schools as well as coeducational institutions developed and adapted curricula to provide training for particular jobs, and consequently, women attended college to enter such professions.[85]

In contrast, the study of music—particularly voice, piano, and violin—was not a new niche for women. However, the renewed emphasis on music or music-related studies represented yet another distinct lane for young women seeking higher education. This was most prevalent at Ward-Belmont. In the 1920s the school shifted from a music department to a semi-autonomous Conservatory of Music that operated within the Junior College. In 1927, the Conservatory of Music published its first catalogue independent of the school's academic catalogue, and a year later the name was officially changed to the Ward-Belmont Conservatory of Music. This title was thought to bring more prestige to the previously separate departments. Even through 1935 the Conservatory of Music was authorized to confer only certificates. While diplomas could be issued, certificates held more legitimacy—in part because they were typically awarded for mastery of a particular instrument or in voice.

Music diplomas remained an "in-house" distinction that carried little weight and were not the equivalent of an associate's or bachelor's degree. As the 1930 music catalogue noted, "Students intending to enter the music profession as teacher or performers, or those desiring a broad training, making possible the acquirement of true musicianship, are advised to enter the certificate course."[86] This complicated process of classification reflects the broader process of modernization.

By the 1940s certificates and special diplomas would yield to traditional degrees, and names such as seminary faded from the educational lexicon except for ministry training. The titles given to classes also changed in the 1940s to include three versions of a "senior": a high school senior was a senior-prep; a first-year college student was called senior-middle; and a second-year college student had the stand-alone title of senior. Although these groupings seem confusing today, to those at Ward-Belmont these distinctions were apparent. Within each division, day students were largely separated from boarding students, and college prep students rarely interacted outside of class with those in the collegiate department. Moreover, young women who were part of the school's Conservatory of Music and other separate departments spent much of their daily schedule apart from those seeking a general education degree.

Notwithstanding the development of Vanderbilt's nursing program, many connected with the university continued to fear the "feminization" of the school. By 1913 the Vanderbilt student body had seventy-eight women or just over 20 percent of the academic enrollment, compared to single digits at the turn of the century.[87] In 1915, after the establishment of a YWCA chapter at the university, Vanderbilt women began pushing for more equitable treatment. The spark that led to the formation of a committee to evaluate the status of women at Vanderbilt was the issue of whether the women's basketball team should be allowed to travel to distant colleges to play games.

Despite Chancellor Kirkland's concerns, the committee recommended a women's dean, a separate residential house on campus (previously there was no on-campus housing for women), and equality in all facets of curricular and extracurricular activities. The committee did recommend that women's athletics should not be intercollegiate but intramural only. Intercollegiate competitive sports teams were disbanded, but otherwise, not much would change for women over the next few years. In 1923 the newly established Alumnae Council and University Woman's Club raised enough money to hire their own dean and designate two additional houses as dormitories.

The period from 1916 to 1929 also brought many firsts for Vanderbilt women: entrance into the School of Religion, Dental School, and Law School (1916), class president (1918), entrance to the Medical School (1926), a female athletic association (1929), and the first Ph.D. (1929). In 1927 Vanderbilt women finally earned membership in the American Association of University Women, granting them formal recognition and forcing the school to do so as well.[88] Following World War I and the passage of the Nineteenth Amendment, observed Paul Conkin, "they were numerous enough, and self-conscious enough, to organize and to battle for their rights."[89]

By 1903 David Lipscomb College had constructed a new campus on Granny White Pike in southwest Nashville, three miles from Vanderbilt and two miles from Belmont College. As with many private institutions without an endowment, the school relied on fundraising, tuition, and resources from the Church of Christ. Female students were necessary to keep Lipscomb afloat financially. Lipscomb not only accepted women but also taught young men and women together for general education classes. Superintendent James A. Harding declared, "We make no distinction between ministerial students and others; males and females, church members and non-church members . . . [they] are put in the same classes and taught the same way."[90]

However, Lipscomb's curriculum extended along gendered tracts beyond general education requirements. Girls took classes in sewing, home economics, and French, as well as additional courses in literature, while males were encouraged to take advanced classes in science, mathematics, and Latin. Not surprisingly, most females attained degrees in either the arts or literature. The introduction of a home economics course further gendered the curriculum in 1914. Three women were awarded degrees out of fifty graduates in the class of 1899. With the establishment of domestic science, the number of women at Lipscomb rose to twelve out of thirty-three students (over 36 percent) who graduated with the class of 1909.

In addition to Lipscomb, Peabody maintained large numbers of female students who attended classes in a coeducational setting. For African Americans, Fisk University, Roger Williams University, Meharry Medical College, and Tennessee A&I continued to emphasize the enrollment and achievements of male students; however, steps toward a curriculum more tailored for women were underway. As institutions of higher education for African Americans, these schools played a prominent role in the education of black women (see chapter 3).

Black women faced a different set of circumstances from their white counterparts. Middle- and upper-class white females attended local colleges and universities for various reasons. Higher education at such institutions secured their place in "society," and although many used their education in the workplace, many did not. For white women, working in the public sphere was less about necessity and more about individual fulfillment and self-sufficiency. African American women in the Progressive Era South would never have such options; instead, they led their sector of "society" by seeking to improve the living conditions of the black community. Black female students and graduates would help fight illiteracy, health problems, and inadequate municipal services in Nashville, the South, and the nation.[91] They were instrumental in shaping an emergent black middle and upper class, but unlike their white sisters, they were not "belles."

For both black and white women, Nashville could be considered a place of relative opportunity as the city offered more choices for higher education than did most southern cities. All of the city's colleges and universities accepted women, even if they were assigned "irregular" or "special" status or steered toward certain courses of study. In terms of single-gender schools, Ward-Belmont (and its predecessor schools) was a leading college preparatory school, music conservatory, and junior college in the South. In addition, several other women's schools operated in Davidson County during part or all of this period including Buford College (1886–1920), Boscobel College for Ladies (1889–1914), Mrs. M.E. Clark's Select School (1885–1896), and Nashville (formerly Price's) College for Ladies (1880–1899).[92] By 1915 female students represented at least 20 percent of the student body at Vanderbilt, and women represented at least 40 percent of the student body at Peabody, Fisk, and Lipscomb. These percentages would rise even higher by 1930.

Faculty and Administration

In 1895 an article in the periodical *Bachelor of Arts* offered a compelling but curious case for women's education by citing the potential profit to be made in all-girls schools. It noted that women's colleges were sound investments and a better financial speculation than men's colleges. In addition the article noted lower faculty budgets and higher tuitions because "women professors, it seems, get lower salaries than men professors, while the yearly bills that students pay the college are usually much larger when the students are girls than if they are men."[93]

Ward Seminary quickly rose as a premier school for girls after 1865, with a higher enrollment and tuition than smaller and more rural girls' schools. Although individual salary records do not exist, the 1885–86 annual announcement reported only $160,000 paid to faculty in its first twenty years. With an average of approximately thirty-five faculty during these years, the average salary was just over $200 per year, although these figures do not reveal discrepancies in pay between male and female faculty members.[94] At Peabody College, board members prudently offered male teachers almost double the salaries of female teachers. This included award-winning faculty such as Julia Sears, a prominent professor of mathematics and rare academic appointment who taught at Peabody for thirty years.[95] Overall at Peabody, according to Paul Conkin, "women teachers were not equal to men, for they never held an administrative position or received comparable salaries, at least in the early years."[96]

Although there are no statistics revealing pay discrepancies at David Lipscomb College, there are other undeniable realities regarding female faculty. At Lipscomb the ratio of male to female faculty averaged 4–1 throughout the period. Moreover, from 1891 to 1925, no female held a teaching position in math, science, history, or religion. Instead, women such as Effie Anderson (1903–10), Lydia Burcham (1914), and Ida Noble (1908–14) taught instrumental music, French, and voice culture, respectively.[97] The closest academic position held by a female was in language, English grammar, literature, or foreign languages (French typically). By 1914 David Lipscomb College also offered courses taught by women in domestic science, but the subject was not considered part of the Science Department.

In 1921 the Association of University Professors published a report of women faculty in colleges and universities. Of the schools that participated, twenty-nine were all-male, and of those colleges and universities only two women served as faculty members, one in the Harvard Medical School and the other in the Yale School of Education. In the fourteen women's colleges surveyed, men still represented more than 25 percent of the faculty. In sum, there were 12,869 faculty members in the United States, with women representing 13 percent.[98] The majority of these women taught courses in education, home economics, English, or the fine arts; and most colleges and universities had no dean of women position. Thomas Woody, writing in 1929, cited the fear of "further weakening the masculine tradition" as one of the reasons for the lack of female faculty.[99]

As all-girls schools, Ward Seminary and Belmont College maintained higher numbers of female faculty, particularly in English and the fine arts. By 1910 Ward Seminary had a School of Expression, School of Elocution, Conservatory of Music, Collegiate Preparatory Department, and Collegiate Department. One faculty standout was French-Canadian Edith Margaret Smaill, who joined the faculty in 1910. Smaill represented one of many faculty members who came from the North. She studied at McGill University in Montreal and the Curry School of Expression in Boston, and completed graduate work with voice and drama teachers in the

United States. Smaill, also a vocal supporter of women's suffrage, came to the school highly recommended having made impressive tours throughout North America and Europe, including performances for British royalty.

Smaill infused the Ward School of Expression with a new sense of purpose and enthusiasm. During her tenure the mission statement for the department was "to help the student to 'find herself' and realize her powers and possibilities; to give such training as will develop her individuality; to train the voice and body to act in co-ordination with the mind; to learn to how to think and what to do to become [independent] and strong."[100] In 1915 she left Nashville to take a position at Wellesley College, where she would remain until the 1930s.[101] Ward Seminary's faculty included many other faculty members with impressive résumés as well.

Belmont College also maintained an outstanding faculty, particularly for a small, private all-girls school in the South. In the final five years before its merger with Ward Seminary, teachers' résumés included bachelor and master's degrees from Columbia University, the University of Wisconsin, Cornell University, Mary Sharp College, Vassar College, and Vanderbilt University. The "presiding teacher," or presumably "academic dean," Wilhelmine E. Key, received her Ph.D. from the University of Chicago, and history instructor Virginia Wendel graduated from Harvard University with "special student" status. Belmont was certainly attracting highly qualified and credentialed faculty to Nashville.

Belmont College founders and co-presidents Ida Hood and Susan Heron were also formidable, driven women. Neither Heron nor Hood was from Nashville or the South. Both women were born in Pennsylvania; they met as classmates at the Shoemaker School of Oratory, also called the National School of Elocution and Oratory, in Philadelphia. Hood graduated in 1880, and Heron graduated soon afterward. Following graduation, the two began looking for work. Hood wrote about a conversation that would shape the rest of their lives:

> One perfectly beautiful moonlit night we were sleeping in my country home near Philadelphia, and not being willing to be separated we then and there determined we would have a school of our own. Some weeks later the State Teachers' Association was meeting in Washington, Pa. [There] we met an old professor . . . and we told him of our plan to start a school of our own. He said, "I will not say 'Go West, young women,' but I will say 'Go South.'"[102]

After a short stint at Martin's Female College in Pulaski, Tennessee, the pair took out a loan and purchased the Belle Monte estate after visiting Nashville for the annual meeting of the National Education Association in 1899. They would lead the school for twenty-three years and help set in motion the merger before their retirement. They remained prominent members of Nashville's clubs and social organizations. Other than Hood and Heron, there were no female presidents or top-level administrators at any of Nashville's colleges or universities.

In 1922 Anna Mary Bowie became the first female faculty member in the Vanderbilt School of Medicine, and three years later Ada Belle Stapleton was named dean of women and became the first woman appointed as a full-time academic professor (in English). Prior to Bowie and Stapleton, alumna and faculty member Stella Vaughn was the first to campaign for issues of equal access, equal opportunity, and pay equity for women. Vaughn was either directly or indirectly a part of two official policy changes, first in 1895 to affirm the admission of women and again in 1915 to allow women more freedom on campus. A native of Alabama, Vaughn moved to Nashville with her family after her father, William Vaughn, took a position as a professor of mathematics at Vanderbilt. After attending Ward Seminary, Vaughn was admitted "by courtesy" in 1892, and she was allowed to earn a degree despite women's murky status at the university.

After graduation in 1896, Vaughn assumed a more permanent role at Vanderbilt as the school's first female instructor of the newly formed Physical Education Department. Surprisingly, Vaughn held this position for nearly a decade without pay, living on-campus with her family. From 1905 until 1913 she earned $100 per year. Although not a proponent of coeducation or women at Vanderbilt, James Kirkland proposed a pay raise: "I recommend that Miss Stella Vaughn be given $200 instead of $100 for her work. It is of great value to the young women studying at the university, and she has not measured her services by the time demanded of her according contract. She has not only taught them in the gymnasium, but has supervised their sports and in a general way has acted as advisor and friend."[103]

Vaughn founded the Vanderbilt chapter of Kappa Alpha Theta sorority and was the club's advisor for decades. For over five decades, Vaughn housed female students in what was later renamed the Vaughn House. She continued to coach, teach, and serve unofficially as the first dean of women. Vaughn's achievements as a student, athlete, and faculty member did not come without many personal frustrations. Kirkland continued to question the role of women and coeducation in general. As late as 1925 Kirkland stated that Vanderbilt's "general tone and atmosphere is that of a college for men and will probably so remain."[104] But he could not disparage the important role and legacy of Vaughn, spanning more than sixty years. Stella Vaughn earned her title as the "Grand Old Lady of Vanderbilt University" with undoubted sacrifice and devotion, yet little recognition.[105] Posthumously, fifty-six years after her death, Stella Vaughn was inducted into the Vanderbilt University Athletic Hall of Fame in 2015.[106]

Dr. William Ward was a prominent figure in Nashville as well as the world of higher education following his founding of Ward Seminary six months after the Civil War ended. Ward's views reflected the larger regional and national perspectives of many educational institutions regarding a rising new class of educated women and notions of acceptable behavior for elite women. In his 1885 commencement speech entitled "The Coming Woman," Ward revealed his anxiety and reservations about the growing autonomy and independence of women. His most direct attacks focused on trends related to the shifting role of prominent women in society, although he seemed to reluctantly acknowledge that throughout the country and in the South certain trends were already in motion:

> The coming woman ought not to be, but I fear she is aiming to make herself, independent of man. Just as far as she does this she contravenes the law of the Almighty, who made her for a help-meet for man. . . . Woman is dependent on man; she is weaker; she ought never to be educated out of that idea. Independence perforce destroys sympathy, and sympathy is the subtle, all-pervading, and omnipotent energy that binds all mankind together. If the coming woman is to come to that, let her never come.[107]

Ward's comments reflect the still-prevalent ideology that women should seek education solely to better themselves for ultimate roles in the home and as agents of social benevolence and service. In presenting a postbellum vision for an "improved" southern belle who still knew her place in the home and in society, Ward's words are not atypical of southern society in the late nineteenth century. Ironically, he acknowledged that the coming woman would be more autonomous and use her education for her own betterment. Ward feared that higher education would indeed enable women to become more dynamic individuals within political and professional arenas. Like many, he believed that distinctively male and female characteristics were mutually exclusive. In other words, such views precluded women from being both independent and sympathetic. Ward's views were common, confirming the role of Nashville's colleges as sites of social and cultural change.

Throughout his forty-four year tenure, Chancellor James Kirkland, questioned the merits of coeducation and female students at Vanderbilt. Ideally, his solution was the creation of a women's annex or *coordination,* which would segregate women from classes, campus organizations, and university events while still allowing them to "attend" Vanderbilt. As author Lori Bateman argued, "Somewhat of a compromise between a separate college for women and full-fledged coeducation, coordination became a viable option for the education of women, which consisted of a men's and women's college under a single administration and board of trustees."[108] After the failure of Kirkland, educational leaders, and urban boosters to secure ownership of Price's College in 1898, Kirkland continued to pursue the idea of coordination. However, national trends moved away from this organizational model.

Kirkland changed his strategy but not his cynicism about women at Vanderbilt. Like William Payne (1887–1901) and Bruce Payne at Peabody (president, 1911–37), he believed that if numbers of female students continued to rise, the status of the university would be jeopardized.[109] On the other hand, qualified women who met entrance requirements could pay full tuition and came from well-respected families. This reality created a conundrum for Kirkland and other college administrators across the nation.

While female students performed well in the classroom, their status on campus faced renewed resistance and isolation in the 1920s. Kirkland's 1923 semi-centennial address noted that "Vanderbilt was founded as a university for men" and seemed resentful of "Peabody's feminine atmosphere" next door.[110] Perhaps practicing what he preached, Kirkland's only child and daughter, Elizabeth, attended the all female Wellesley College.[111] Perhaps it was just as well. Kirkland had long referred to Vanderbilt women as an "agitation" and still viewed them as guests more than as students. It was not just Kirkland who sought to minimize the so-called "feminine atmosphere." As late as 1929 nearly all student references in the *Hustler* were to males, women were segregated to the chapel balcony for assemblies, and the alumni association's publication remained the *Directory of Vanderbilt Men*.

At Peabody College, President William Payne never stated that he maintained a bias against female students or their enrollment at Peabody Normal College; however, according to Conkin, "gender entered into his analysis."[112] The L.I. (licentiate of instruction) degree that granted teacher certification was designed specifically for women. The few men who did receive an L.I. did so in lieu of a bachelor's degree.[113] With required courses in pedagogy, these women were well prepared for teaching but not administration or leadership positions. Payne also believed that "because of the nurturing aspects of their gender, they were the best teachers in grades one through five."[114] He also held the position that females need not be trained to take or teach higher levels of math or science because "women's minds were not fitted to such abstract subjects" and that their careers would only last until they married and began families.[115]

Despite William Payne's disposition with regard to females and education, both as students and educators, female students continued to dominate class rolls and serve prominently in the faculty ranks. This would continue through the tenures of the successive presidents during this period, James Porter (1901–9) and Bruce Payne (1911–37). It is true that most female Peabody graduates ceased to teach after marriage and children, but many remained single, following the "path of their mentors—Miss Sears, Miss Bloomstein, Miss Jones, and Miss Carpenter."[116] Although these lifelong educators dedicated their lives and careers to "teaching teachers," few ever reached an administrative position or were viewed as part of the social elite of Nashville. In the south marriage and family still seemed to be a prerequisite for admission to select circles.

In sum, many administrators and faculty feared the feminization of the university and viewed female students as endangering the school's reputation. Even male administrators at all-female institutions sought to mute the full engagement of women in the public sphere. As a whole, college and university leadership from 1865 to 1930 evolved to include women (as students or faculty) but struggled with their role as intellectuals. Administrators sought to provide all students with the academic tools needed for success but carefully avoided the appearance of promoting gender equality or empowerment in ways that might challenge the southern order of things.

World War I and Suffrage

World War I and the Nineteenth Amendment produced many advantages for young women attending colleges. As their brothers, beaux, and male friends served at home or overseas in the military, women rose to fill the leadership and student enrollment quotas left empty by their absence. Although male students returned from the war to resume most positions, the war years were pivotal for women on campus. During 1917–1918 female students asserted greater leadership and visibility in classrooms, student organizations, and athletics. Moreover the suffrage movement gained real traction in the early 1900s. And while many women voted in line with their fathers and husbands, their political and public participation was historic. These trends would continue into the 1920s and 1930s.

In the summer of 1917, Vanderbilt formed a Student Army Training Corps (SATC) as did many colleges and universities throughout the United States. This transformed the university into a military campus. Nonmilitary students continued classes full-time, which included a record number of women, along with men who did not qualify for military service. In fact, the senior class had but one male, and women made up the majority of both the sophomore and junior classes as well. Senior class president Ednelia Wade served as the first female class president in 1918–19. By the time of World War I, female students already

FIG. 2.11. Ward-Belmont World War I "Flag Rally," was held in April 1919. The celebration welcomed home Colonel Luke Lea and the Tennessee troops. Ward-Belmont girls dressed in crepe paper replica of the American flag at the foot of the Tennessee State Capitol. Tennessee would be the final state legislature needed to ratify the Nineteenth Amendment, granting women the right to vote, in this very building less than a year later. Harpeth Hall School Archives.

outpaced male students with an academic average of 81.72 percent compared to 71.47 percent, respectively.[117] Women continued to serve as class officers and in other student organizations after 1918; thus, the war actually increased equity between the sexes on campus. As a result, Chancellor Kirkland set a quota for female students for the first time in 1921. Greater gender equity from 1915 to 1927 also separates Vanderbilt from other southern (and local) colleges during the period because women attended the same courses and followed the same curriculum as the men.

Like the coeds at Vanderbilt, women became the majority of the student body at Fisk University during World War I when six hundred African American men mobilized much of the campus as a military base. The number of females attending the university during the war caused many African American families to question the standard of safety for their daughters at Fisk. In a *Fisk University News* article entitled "Is Fisk Safe for Girls?" the university addressed the inquiries regarding the level of supervision and protection afforded female students, especially as the United States Receiving Camp began to welcome soldiers bound for training and/or service.

World War I directly affected Ward-Belmont and Peabody College less, as their student populations were already predominantly female. The male students who did attend Peabody were mostly older than thirty and married with children. Although no current students of Peabody died in World War I, five Peabody alumni were killed in action. Ward-Belmont student publications are filled with references to eating "war bread," which was made with substitutes for wheat and sugar (or reduced amounts of those commodities) to provide for military food production. In 1918 freshman Ruth Gresley lamented in a short poem: "A plate of war bread before her, at first she did sigh, and then with a cry. I'll eat it for [Herbert] Hoover [director of the U.S. Food Administration]."[118] Ward-Belmont students also contributed to the war effort through fundraising, knitting, preparing Christmas boxes for soldiers, book drives, selling and buying war bonds, and joining the "Eyes for the Navy" letter campaign and citywide collection of binoculars and field glasses.[119] After the war, students participated in a World War I rally for veterans at the state capitol.

There are glimpses of women's rights and pro-suffrage groups in the records of Nashville's colleges and universities, but they remain buried beneath sports scores, social announcements, and other tidbits of campus news. The earliest mention of suffrage, in print, comes in the form of a denouncement: Dr. Ward's speech "The Coming Woman." In listing things that "the Coming Woman ought not to be," he contended that "she ought not to seek to come to the political arena, where the rougher man contends, quarrels, and fights. She ought not, therefore, to want the ballot."[120]

Ironically, Anne Dallas Dudley, a Ward Seminary graduate, led the local and statewide suffrage movement as the first president of the Nashville Equal Suffrage League. In 1915 she served as the president of the Tennessee Equal Suffrage Association, a post she held until 1917, when she became the third vice president of the National American Woman Suffrage Association (NAWSA). She was also actively involved in World War I efforts on the home front as an officer in the National Woman's Liberty Loan Commission and state president of the Tennessee Woman's Liberty Loan Commission, both of which were involved in selling war bonds. In 1920 Dudley served as a delegate to the Democratic National Convention. She challenged New South men to "embark upon a new knighthood, a new chivalry, [in which] men would not only fight for women, but for the rights of women."[121]

Shortly after the matriculation of women at Vanderbilt in the mid-1890s, the student newspaper noted the growing interest of women regarding the question of political enfranchisement. Male students did not know quite how to react, as an item in the *Hustler* made clear: "It is rumored that a Woman's Rights Club has been organized by the co-editor with special regard to the Gymnasium [and other issues]. We understand they have carried their point . . . we'll not tell on them, but we admire this display of co-ed pluck."[122] Although most suffragists were middle- and upper-class women who had the time and money to engage in nonprofit activities, most Vanderbilt alumnae did not directly participate in the movement. In 1907 one student stated, "A large percent of the women alumnae are mistresses of their own homes, and many of the others . . . do much to raise the standard of culture in their own communities. . . . As for 'women of the world,' I have not been able to find in the roll of Vanderbilt alumni the name of any woman who is a participant in any political movement."[123]

Arguments used by anti-suffragists were of the usual variety: women's minds were not capable of such important decision making, the southern family would be disrupted, and the enfranchisement of black women would lead to "colored rule." Most white men and women agreed that women's suffrage was less important than white supremacy; in the South race would continue to trump gender. Many African American women favored women's suffrage but realized that their political voice would not be heard until all African Americans were legitimately included in the political process. Unlike black women in the North, African Americans in the South faced higher levels of racism and sexism. As Rosalyn Terborg-Penn argued in *African American Women in the Struggle for the Vote*, "African American, not white, suffragists continued to use strategies in support of universal suffrage, whereas white women for the most part campaigned for their own enfranchisement."[124] White women achieved their goal with the Nineteenth Amendment.

In 1920 an anti-suffragist rally entitled "To Save the South" was held at the Ryman Auditorium in downtown Nashville. Attendees claimed that suffrage would lead to racial and gender disruption, eventually destroying southern culture and social roles.[125] White women in favor of suffrage rarely included black women in the movement. Certain southern suffragists preferred state legislation so that the issue of race could be controlled without federal intervention. The meeting at the Ryman focused on the fears of whites in regard to greater political participation by African Americans, as evidence in a 1920 broadside, entitled *The Truth about the Negro*:

> For the sake of southern civilization, for the sake of womanhood, and for the sake of the welfare of the Negro race as well as the white race, the Susan B. Anthony movement should be defeated.... This amendment will not only hurl women into political competition and battle with men, but it will and must involve political warfare between the races—a thing that no thinking American, black or white, should advocate.[126]

Couched in paternalism, such commentary reflects the attitude of many white men (and some women). Nashville may have been progressive—southern style—but its white citizens did not intend to bring equity to the black community.

Regardless, many black women proactively advocated suffrage on their own behalf. Most African American women active in the suffrage movement were part of the middle- or upper-class who had attended institutions of higher education. Interest in women's rights surfaced at Fisk University three decades before the passage of the constitutional amendment. The *Fisk Herald* wrote of the Ladies' Reading Room, reporting its frequent and intense use by female students. The article also makes subtle connections between the activism and personal growth of women in education with eventual political empowerment. The 1889 article also states: "Some do not have a chance to learn the news of the day, and as the day is coming when women will vote, it is well for the young ladies to be well posted on all important political questions."[127]

Conclusion

Prior to the Civil War, few adult women maintained more than the equivalent of an eighth-grade education. After 1865, even without a comprehensive classical education or a bachelor's degree, educated women modified meanings of motherhood and spousal duty to include "work" outside the home. Higher education represented a convenient strategy whereby women could propel themselves into otherwise restricted public spheres and help mold new definitions of acceptable behavior in New South cities like Nashville by 1930.

Females attended colleges and seminaries in greater numbers throughout the United States after 1865 for several reasons. Many institutions of learning opened after the Civil War, particularly in the South, and upper- and middle-class women and their families increasingly valued and pursued education beyond the elementary level. Private or independent schools remained preferable for middle- and upper-class families in order to insulate their daughters from the "moral danger" and chaos of urban public schools and to ensure that their education properly prepared them for marriage and life's work. Women's education beyond the secondary level remained a controversial issue, especially in the South, where cultural expectations upheld "Lady Other" as the preferred model of femininity.

As girls' schools evolved to offer rigorous academic curricula equal to that of boys' schools, the concept of a "finishing school" assumed a somewhat negative connotation in the twentieth century. While Ward Seminary from 1865 to 1912 and Belmont College from 1890 to 1912 fit the traditional finishing school description, women who attended and graduated from these schools did set and meet a range of personal and professional goals. They also reinforced traditional coming-out rituals such as May Day festivals. Women's colleges were viewed as less threatening in the South—as the majority of graduates fulfilled their roles as wives and mothers. Most would not complete four-year degrees or enter professions; however, they laid the groundwork, as did the institutions they attended, for future generations of college women. The Great Depression, coupled with the growth of coeducation, would lead to a declining enrollment at Ward-Belmont through the 1930s and 1940s. After World War II many women's colleges closed or merged with other schools as higher education models permanently shifted to coeducation. Reflective of this pattern, Ward-Belmont closed its doors as an all-female junior college in 1951, but reopened as a four-year coeducational liberal arts college—today's Belmont University.

In the early twentieth century, all-girls schools and junior colleges like Ward-Belmont served as experimental laboratories of sorts, combining greater freedom, intellectual stimulation, allowances for individual expression, and active involvement in the public sphere. Nashville's all-female institutions served as gateways to top-tier traditional universities and sites of social awareness and communal activism. These schools also searched for the middle ground between training women for a vocation, the "art of living," or an alternative that produced graduates capable of both. The cross-pressure between these competing goals remains at the very core of a subtle yet certain shift for southern women and culture.

From 1865 to 1910, the education profession for primary and secondary schools shifted permanently and predominantly to women. Female teachers needed collegiate and pedagogical training, and institutions of higher education were needed to train them. The transformation from Peabody Normal School to the George Peabody College for Teachers is evidence of the demand for better-trained teachers. Ultimately, women gained degrees in primary or secondary education, pedagogy, physical education, and home economics. Mary Evins concluded that Peabody emerged as "a dynamic nucleus for ideas, scholarship, and educational reforms," which was "nourished by a broad student body and nationally recognized faculty."[128]

As Nashville urbanized in the late 1800s and early 1900s, the city's growth and modernization paralleled evolving cultural views of education and gender, despite the slower pace of southern progressivism. As the city's major university, Vanderbilt played an important role in defining the scope and spectrum of women's education. Throughout this period, Vanderbilt continued to struggle with the issue of women's education in regard to admission, leadership positions, degrees allowed, and athletic functions; yet the school took great care to keep abreast of regional and national trends. Vanderbilt was significant to Nashville because it was the sole four-year university conferring nationally recognized bachelor's, master's, and doctoral degrees. An exception for this period (1865–1930) and for the South as a region, Vanderbilt did not participate in the "genderfication" of its curriculum as did other schools by offering degrees in education, home economics, or the fine arts. (The exception was nursing, which was not considered a part of Vanderbilt's traditional undergraduate curriculum until after 1930.)

The number of female graduates at Vanderbilt remained relatively small from 1873 to 1920. Nevertheless the percentage of female students increased incrementally, as well as the respect, recognition, and achievement of many Vandy women. After lobbying for greater equity on campus, women represented over 20 percent of the student body by 1920. Most impressive is that female graduates from Vanderbilt earned their degrees based on the same standards as those for males but with much less prior preparatory education and less administrative/faculty support on campus.

World War I, women's suffrage, progressive reform, and an industrialized urban economy served as the biggest catalysts for female students who gained legitimacy as measured by their own distinction and achievements rather than through relationships determined by dating and domesticity. Nonetheless, women as a whole entered public and professional arenas as more visible participants after 1865. The strength of traditional gender roles in the South undercut and circumscribed women's college educations in ways different from those in the North. However, women created new niches through emergent fields that bridged the divide between public and private life.

As a result, Nashville's colleges and universities, both single sex and coeducational, created an adapted curricula to provide training for those jobs. Consequently, women had to go to college to enter those professions. As education developed through the 1920s and beyond, women pursued majors and specializations in areas beyond the prescribed training intended for females. This accompanied the nationally recognized system of educational accreditation and the standardization of curricula, programs, and degrees. Some used their degrees in niche-specific professions, such as teaching, nursing, and music, while others contributed to Nashville through social work and urban reform via volunteerism and civic clubs.

Nashville reflected larger trends found in other southern states and growing cities. As Amy McCandless has noted, the "traditional image of southern womanhood and the accompanying stereotypes of race, class, and gender continued to be pervasive, affecting . . . academic and professional choices."[129] Nashville, like other local southern communities, maintained and reinforced southern notions not of a "modern woman" but rather of a "modern belle."

3

Beyond the Talented Tenth

Race and Higher Education

> Nothing awakens desires and creates want like educational institutions. ... They are fountain heads that send forth streams of influence ... refreshing [new] generations.
>
> —G. D. Pike, *The Jubilee Singers* (1873)

In 1903, fifteen years after graduating from Fisk University, W. E. B. Du Bois stripped away the politics of race, gender, and class to capture the essence and ethos of higher education in his seminal work *The Souls of Black Folk:*

> I sit with Shakespeare and he winces not. Across the color line I move arm in arm with Balzac and Dumas, where smiling men and welcoming women glide in gilded halls. From out the caves of evening that swing between the strong-limbed earth and the tracery of the stars, I summon Aristotle and Aurelius and what soul I will, and they come all graciously with no scorn nor condescension. So, wed with Truth, I dwell above the Veil.[1]

Du Bois, the first African American to earn a Ph.D. from Harvard University, viewed institutions of and opportunities for higher education as the hand that would lift the veil for newly emancipated African Americans. Rightfully so, the creation and sustainment of black colleges would be "southern higher education's most rapid and visible accommodation to the new order of postwar life," according to Clarence L. Mohr.[2] But white southerners, even those considered progressive, had no real interest in African Americans lifting the veil. As Michael Dennis noted in *Lessons of Progress,* the white "objective was to improve, not disrupt, the social order."[3] In contrast, for Du Bois education was the key that would eventually open previously closed doors: "Education and work are the levers to uplift a people. Work alone will not do it unless inspired by the right ideals and guided by intelligence. Education must not simply teach work—it must teach Life."[4]

Booker T. Washington, a Fisk University trustee, offered a somewhat different version of racial uplift, which he believed to be more palatable to whites and more practical for blacks. He spoke publicly in Nashville on several occasions, most notably in 1909 when he delivered an address to more than seventy-five hundred people in the famed Ryman Auditorium. At the 1909 event, Washington was introduced as "the advocate of Negro industrial education" and said:

> Nashville presents a noteworthy example of what education has done for the Negro. Nowhere in the South is the average of intelligence and literacy among them higher than here . . . [including] Fisk University, Walden University, and Roger Williams University. With Walden is connected Meharry Medical College, the pioneer Negro medical school, which has turned out about one-half of all Negroes who practice medicine today.[5]

Washington recognized that Nashville was a different kind of New South city, precisely because of its educational institutions. He returned to Nashville in 1913 to speak to the Negro Baptist Convention: "There is in the city of Nashville by reason of the liberal spirit shown by the White people and the unusual opportunities for education of our race perhaps the most advanced group of our people, all things considered, to be found anywhere in the South."[6]

Washington calibrated the region's racial tension by appealing for white approval to advance black education, as he made his case throughout the South:

> I am sure that every white man in Tennessee will agree with me that if this is true, the Negro should have the same chance of preparing himself for life, so that he may understand the law and how to obey it. This can only be brought about by proper methods of education—I mean education of the head, heart, and hand, that education which will teach every member of our race the dignity of labor and

at the same time will teach every member some trade or occupation by which a living can be made.⁷

Historian Crystal deGregory believes that Washington was "principally committed to exploiting white paternalism to win both ideological and financial support for black colleges by any means necessary."⁸ Because whites were also more comfortable with Washington's conservatism, his industrial model came to be dominant in the South from the 1870s through the 1930s.

These two leading figures would frame the higher educational and professional debate for African Americans as institutionalized discrimination and segregation burrowed into southern society. They also both maintained strong ties to Nashville's HBCUs. Booker T. Washington served not only on the Fisk University Board of Trustees but also as principal of Tuskegee Institute in Alabama. He was a prominent symbol of African American higher education touting self-improvement and industrial education. W. E. B. Du Bois was a graduate of Fisk University, served as a trustee, was the catalyst of a student revolt at Fisk against a white administration (1924–25), and established the Department of Sociology at Atlanta University (now Clark Atlanta University). He unabashedly advocated for social, political, and economic equality and feared that white control over black education would shortchange the potential for black self-determination. Despite differences in tone, philosophy, and approach, Du Bois and Washington sought the same basic goals and shared far more in common than not. For both, higher education was the foundation for the incorporation and acclimatization of African Americans into an interracial model of urban American culture.

Nashville experienced less racial violence, lynching, and hostility because the city's black leaders chose to follow Washington's accommodationist approach as opposed to confrontation or protest. That is not to say that African American leaders in Nashville did not criticize, resist, or boycott when faced with Jim Crow politics. But as a whole, Nashville's black community chose to create "a world-within-a-world."⁹ However, local black elites were instrumental in the success of the city's HBCUs, and in turn, students and alumni emerged as new members of a professional/middle class. Mutually reinforcing, these two groups created a powerful cycle that distinguished Nashville from other southern cities with less educated, less prosperous black populations.

In response, the white community tacitly acknowledged, and even took some pride in, the national attention garnered by local black colleges—which largely played by "white rules." Nashville's African American schools, one white city leader boasted in 1909, were a "noteworthy example of what education has done for the Negro.... Nowhere in the South is the average of intelligence and literacy among them higher than here."¹⁰ In other words, race was a major part of southern modernization, and modernization was messy.

From 1865 to 1930 Nashville served as a prominent center for a different brand of African American opportunity and community development. Fisk University was the most prestigious African American university south of the District of Columbia. Meharry Medical College, which began as part of Central Tennessee College (later Walden University, 1865–1925), was one of the only schools in the nation to offer advanced training in medicine, dentistry, pharmacology, and nursing to African Americans. Roger Williams University trained black teachers, preachers, and missionaries before merging with a Memphis college in 1927. Tennessee A&I Normal School (now Tennessee State University) was the fourth of Nashville's four HBCUs, opening in 1912 as the first and only public institution of higher education for blacks in Tennessee. The school offered basic education courses, K–12 teaching licensure, and mechanical/agricultural certificates until after 1922. Crystal deGregory has referred to Nashville in the nineteenth century as "Black Athens" and the city's major HBCU colleges as a "quartet." These four schools would offer primary and secondary schooling, training for the classroom and pulpit, and bachelor degrees for advanced study. But also of great distinction were the medical and graduate programs at Fisk and Meharry.

From the end of the Civil War until after World War I, most black "colleges" or "universities" had self-assigned titles. This was not unlike many white, single-gender, and private coeducational institutions before standardization or accreditation. A report from 1895 revealed that only 11 percent (1,020) of all African American students (9,066) enrolled in so-called colleges supported by private northern missionary and denominational groups were actually pursuing collegiate-level work. Twenty years later, statistics had modestly shifted to 29 percent (3,750 out of 12,894) of students enrolled in college courses.¹¹ Clarence L. Mohr suggested that "notwithstanding their frequent 'Industrial' or 'A&M' designations, the real mission of black colleges, apart from providing elementary and secondary classes, was training teachers, and to a lesser extent ministers, who would return to educate the children of black communities across the South."¹² These numbers would significantly improve in the 1920s with the expansion of land-grant colleges, but it would take a second civil rights movement and school desegregation to fully implement black higher education in the American South.

The African American community in Nashville experienced positive change during this period. However, attitudes toward sociopolitical equality, and greater professional opportunity, moved sluggishly in the South. John Hope, an African American professor at Roger Williams University and later president of Morehouse and Atlanta Universities, took an aggressive tone as he addressed the Negro

Debate Society of Nashville in a rebuttal of Booker T. Washington's model of self-improvement and industrial education:

> If we are not striving for equality, in heaven's name for what are we living? If money, education, and honesty will not bring to me as much privilege, as much equality as they bring to any American citizen, then they are to me a curse, and not a blessing. . . . If we cannot do what other freemen do, then we are not free. Yes, my friends, I want equality. . . . Now catch your breath, for I am going to use an adjective: I am going to say we demand *social* equality. . . . If equality, political, economic, and social, is the boon of other men in this great country of ours, then that . . . is what we demand. Why build a wall to keep me out? I am no wild beast, nor am I an unclean thing.[13]

Black leaders presented sometimes complementary and sometimes conflicting visions of the best path forward for blacks—in modern America generally, as well as in the transitional New South.

Alumni of Fisk, Meharry, Roger Williams, and Tennessee A&I were also New South men and women, leading the way for industrial and commercial growth in Nashville through the establishment of black schools, hospitals, publishing houses, pharmacies, insurance companies, banks, parks, entertainment venues, and law firms. Although men led the way, women also played important roles both as active agents in the community and as wives of prominent black men. From 1865 to 1930 Nashville did not attempt to integrate white and black worlds of work, study, or play. However, Nashville's educated class of African Americans created alternatives that allowed for greater growth and success than did those of other major southern cities, with the notable exception of Atlanta.

In particular, Fisk and Meharry produced professionals and intellectuals, despite the dark cloud of Jim Crowism that had fully developed by the turn of the twentieth century.[14] They authenticated Du Bois's message designating the need for a "Talented Tenth." Du Bois did not coin the phrase, but he was the first to popularize it. In 1903 Du Bois published his signature essay "The Talented Tenth," in which he declared, "The Negro race, like all races, is going to be saved by its exceptional men."[15]

Nashville maintained a black professional class that exceeded the "Talented Tenth"—perhaps more accurately the "Fantastic Fifth." Not all who came to Nashville for an education stayed in Nashville, but they did influence black intellectualism, healthcare, and social reform in the city. This new generation would make significant gains in improving and serving the black community within a racially segregated but increasingly urban society. Higher education would also help create a thriving black commercial district, inspire black cultural and community pride, provide central and safe spaces for African Americans, and soften the sharp edges of racism within the city.

Nashville's "quartet" of black colleges would serve as incubators for civil rights well before the civil rights movement following World War II. In addition to this "quartet," the American Baptist Theological Seminary, which formally opened in Nashville in 1924, was the institutional home of student-leaders such as civil rights icon John Lewis. In this later movement, Nashville played a leading role, serving as the model and training ground for the sit-in movement and institutional desegregation. But the significance of Nashville HBCUs began with translating opportunities for higher education into opportunities for racial uplift and activism during the Reconstruction and Progressive Eras.[16]

Context and Subtext

The Centennial Exposition of 1897 held in Nashville featured a Negro Building that white organizers proclaimed the most "beautiful building on the grounds" and urged those "interested in the progress of the Negro since the days of slavery" to visit.[17] Originally the committee was chaired by Nashville's most prominent black citizen, James C. Napier, who resigned citing health reasons but was likely frustrated by exposition organizers. Napier was an admirer and personal friend of Booker T. Washington, but his vision for the Negro building was not accommodationist enough for the all-white executive planning committee. Napier was succeeded by Richard Hill, a black businessman and strong advocate of industrial education.[18] Hill asserted that black Tennesseans were "on trial . . . as to what we have done, and are now doing since our emancipation."[19] The exhibition building was filled with displays of African American–produced goods and educational achievements. By replacing the moderate Napier with the conservative Richard Hill, the exposition organizers ensured that the message conveyed to visitors was one of racial cooperation, progress, and harmony.

White southerners and urban boosters preferred Washington's vision for black life in the white South—gradual improvement through practical training that would elevate the African American community and, more important, the entire region. Many African Americans also agreed with Washington's approach, but some felt that the price of progress was too high to move so slowly. Those who wanted greater inclusion in white society, politics, and commerce followed the lead of W. E. B. Du Bois. These competing visions would play out at this world's fair-style event in 1897—a midpoint between two game-changing events in American history—the Civil War and the Great Depression.

Nashville's exposition opened with a speech from W. H. Councill, the black principal of the Agricultural and Mechanical College for Negroes in Alabama. He proclaimed, "This kind of higher industrial education is the only kind the Negro needs now. . . . Will the white man continue and enlarge the work of encouragement to the struggling race; or will he use the shotgun instead of the Holy Bible; the bloody knife instead of the spelling-book? These are problems for Caucasian brains."[20] Just hours later, John W. Thomas, the fair's president delivered a speech that day from the white perspective: "I address you as fellow citizens for though the colored race may have a different complexion and differ in intellectual attainments from the white race, we are still fellow citizens of one, great nation under one great flag."[21] Though they acknowledged equality in theory, such messages from southern white leaders like Thomas were clear examples of goodwill paternalism.

White organizers touted the exposition's Negro Building, with its three hundred exhibits, as proof that "the South [had] been misunderstood and grossly misrepresented." The prominence of the building and participation of black elites and the state's HBCUs would also demonstrate, according to the exposition's official history, "that the white and black people of the South understand each other perfectly and do, if left to themselves, get along as pleasantly and peaceably as any two races that ever dwelt together"[22]

And yet the Tennessee Centennial Exposition was technically a segregated space. John Edward Bruce, a black journalist, published an account of his visit to Nashville's fair:

> I visited every building on the grounds, especially those to which the local kickers said negroes would not be admitted, viz, the Woman's building and the Auditorium. At both I was treated courteously. . . . It was said also that Negroes could not buy refreshing drinks. . . . [But] I went over there, bought soda water and drank it on the spot. The roof didn't fall in, and nobody called me "negra" either. I had similar refreshment in the Machinery building, where I also partook of some delightful sweet cider, which was served to me by a white woman of tender years and prepossessing face, who politely requested me to call again.[23]

African Americans surely experienced racial discrimination and segregation at the exposition as they did on public streetcars, parks, and white-owned businesses in Nashville. Laws that created separate restrooms, seating requirements, and schools normalized segregation. At other times, as with the exposition, segregation was largely unspoken and unenforced. These were the realities of "Jim Crow modernity." Historian Nathan Cardon has argued that the lack of formal segregationist policies ultimately served white interests who wanted to "convince northerners of the South's harmonious race relations [and] also to bring in much-needed revenue."[24] This was the New South answer to the debate on race: to talk of racial harmony without including African Americans in the conversation.

Exposing this tension was Adelene Moffat, a white woman, who spent most of her childhood in Nashville and returned as a young adult to teach at Howard Female College in Gallatin, Tennessee, just outside of Nashville.[25] The most defining and enduring moment of Moffat's public career occurred at the 1911 NAACP Conference. In her speech "Views of a Southern Woman," she revealed an atypical version of southern progressivism.[26] Moffat argued that "caste prejudice" defined the social order in the New South era:

> On this race question we seem to be unable to reach real issues because we are to so great a degree governed by phrases rather than by facts. We think we have race prejudice in the South, but we have not; we have only caste prejudice; the race prejudice is in the North. . . . The artificiality of the barrier between the two races creates the problem. . . . The problem is a common problem of humanity—bad housing conditions, bad sanitary conditions, bad political conditions, bad industrial conditions, insufficient education, of both white and black.[27]

Much of the South lived in poverty with limited chance of upward social mobility. Middle-class and white elites, many of whom were connected to local white colleges and universities as alumni, trustees, or boosters, were less overtly racist. However, they exhibited prejudice and discrimination by ignoring and isolating African Americans and nearby HBCUs. Thus, the "artificiality of the barrier" remained the color of one's skin, and whites from all socioeconomic classes used this measure as the most basic mark of their social status.

In 1889 a *Fisk Herald* editorial reiterated the troubling paradox that lay before southerners of both races. The editorial contrasted antebellum and postbellum culture:

> A New South with old ideas, old customs, [and] old prejudices . . . is one of the inexplicable problems of the age. . . . Old wines should not be put into new bottles. . . . Records of enmity and hatred should not be refreshed in the hearts of the present generation. . . . Here and there a desperate blow is aimed at every attempt to educate and thus raise to a higher plain the moral, social, civil, and political standard of the masses. . . . All liberty loving and law abiding citizens among us are puzzled to see the application of the assumed name [New South].[28]

In fact, most African American colleges such as Fisk University and Tennessee A&I, enforced military-like rules and strict discipline to deter students from worldly temptations. The 1904–1905 *Fisk Catalog* states: "No profanity, betting and gambling, use of ardent spirits as beverages, and the use of tobacco; also card-playing and dancing. No weapons or fireworks, no traveling on the Sabbath."[29] Such rules were common on both black and white college campuses but hard to enforce. At Fisk, president Fayette McKenzie (1915–1925) was known for holding students to strict standards and dismissing students who violated such rules. Though a passionate educator, Tennessee A&I's president William J. Hale (1912–1943) was also authoritative. He required faculty members and students to adhere to strict rules, including a dress code, curfew, and class attendance. He also prohibited students and faculty from participating in political activity. Yet, even as the black community attempted to follow the guidelines of good citizenship, they lived under the constant threat of racial violence.

Issues of race also led to violence between white and black communities that reinforced racial hierarchies in the South as well as in the North. Ironically, *lawfulness* was a key component emphasized by and for blacks in their effort to achieve full citizenship. Historian Grace Hale, in *Making Whiteness,* documented the "deadly amusements" of spectacle lynchings carried out by whites, exposing perhaps the most unlawful acts occurring in southern states during this period.[30] Lynchings were set in public, attended by thousands, and reported widely in papers and photographs. Some whites sought souvenirs or a ticket for the "lynch train" and events were promoted and sold as a form of spectator entertainment. In fact, W. E. B. Du Bois called lynching the new "white amusement."[31]

According to historian Kathy Bennett, lynchings in former Confederate states claimed the lives of 2,805 people, without trial, from 1882 to 1930. During this period 217 Tennessee victims were brutalized at the hands of civilians and non-state actors. Of this number 81.5 percent were African American. Tennessee's murder-by-mob numbers ranked sixth in the South behind Mississippi, Georgia, Texas, Louisiana, and Alabama and took place primarily in Middle and West Tennessee.[32]

As proof of Nashville's comparatively moderate racial climate, the city recorded three lynchings from 1882 to 1930, compared to eighteen in the Memphis–Shelby County area, where local newspapers disturbingly described such events as "an outstanding lynch success" or the "greatest lynch carnival." Victims were often tortured and sexually mutilated postmortem.[33] Fisk alumna and trustee Minnie Lou Crosthwaite recounted the Nashville lynching of Ephraim Grizzard in April of 1892:

> They went thru Nashville without question at 2 p.m. in the day, marched to the jail, battered down the door, took the prisoner to the bridge leading from Cedar St. and lynched him. My husband stood in the rear of the O'Bryan Bros. Store on

the [downtown] square, and saw it. Two of my white neighbors, both young lads, came home and told me about it, and exhibited a bit of his clothing as a treasured souvenir. And, if the people who do those things want to come on the campus of Fisk and do the same thing, they will.[34]

Anti-lynching crusades were launched by liberal whites and African Americans. One notable leader was Ida B. Wells, a summer session student who attended Fisk University in the 1870s. Wells went on to become one of the leading anti-lynching advocates in the nation and wrote often about the subject in Memphis newspapers. Perhaps as a sign of New South social and criminal justice reform, Tennessee passed legislation that made lynching a felony in 1897. There is no direct connection between this legislation and the Centennial Exposition of 1897, but it surely benefited those who sought to show that Tennessee, and specifically Nashville, was more progressive than other southern states. The last recorded lynching victim in the state was in 1940. Elbert Williams, living in Brownsville, one hour east of Memphis, was murdered for attempting to establish an NAACP chapter in the town and registering to vote.[35]

Nashville was overall less involved in the wicked hysteria and vigilante white "justice" connected to lynching than were other urban areas in the South. Living in Nashville, Kate Herndon Trawick, a white woman and Fisk trustee, spoke to the issue of lynching. In a 1917 speech, she explained and critiqued its criminal and cultural motivations, pointing out the argumentative inconsistencies of those who supported lynching. First, she debunked the notion that African Americans were the dominant group of men who committed acts of sexual assault. She noted that in 1917, there were 620 rapes in the South, and of that number, "450 [were] white and 170 colored."[36] However, her most intriguing argument challenged the perception that lynching prevented crime. Instead she argued that it provoked greater tension and criminality: "For every black criminal put to death at the hands of a mob, hundreds of white criminals are made. It is resorted to terrorize and restrain, but instead, it arouses race prejudice and deepens race hatred."[37]

One white southern official commented in 1900, "To bring about better relations between the races we need more education, both of the whites and the blacks. Men must be educated to broader views of the relations they bear to each other."[38] There were white Tennesseans who supported some level of education for their black counterparts. Yet, white southerners across the region, as well as in Nashville, vigorously opposed the integration of blacks into their world. In other words, educating younger generations of African Americans eased the conscience of white southerners while preventing blacks from becoming either a burden or a threat.

Census records show African Americans in Nashville represented 26 percent of the city's population in 1867, while the black populations of Knoxville and Memphis stood at 30 and 50 percent respectively.[39] By 1910 the population of Nashville's Davidson County was just over 110,354 with 73,831 Caucasians (67 percent) and 36,523 African Americans (33 percent). Out of these totals, there lived 12,119 whites between the ages of six and fourteen and 5,538 African American children.[40] Nashville maintained twenty-two primary and secondary schools for whites, compared to twelve for black students, which was proportionate to the numbers of school-age children. Still, the limitations of African American education remained clear—9.7 percent of whites were illiterate while 27.3 percent of all African Americans could not read or write.[41] Moreover, 1910 census data reveal that monies spent per student (based on Davidson County teachers' salaries) for public education was $16.98 for whites and $9.37 for blacks.

The Bureau of Education (established in 1867) conducted a national survey of African American education and published its report in 1917. It concluded the following about Tennessee: "The inequalities between the appropriations for white and colored schools are probably not as great in Tennessee as in states where the Negro population constitutes a larger percentage of the total."[42]

Funding, Accreditation, and Black Boosterism

Higher education for African Americans was dependent on cooperation between several groups: white northerners, white southerners, southern state governments, southern local governments, and southern blacks. In theory, lawful and productive African Americans would contribute to southern society as a whole. However, most of white society was skeptical, if not downright suspicious, of black higher education despite its potential mutual benefits. This nuanced reality prevented African Americans from participating in the democratic system as outlined by the Bureau of Education:

> Democracy's plan for the solution of the race problem in the Southland is not primarily in the philanthropies and wisdom of northern people; nor is it in the desires and struggles of the colored people; nor yet in the first-hand knowledge and daily contacts of the southern white people. Democracy's plan is in the combination of the best thought and the deepest sympathy and the most abiding faith of these three groups working with mutual faith in one another.[43]

The differences among each group made it difficult to devise or implement a unified plan. Any consensus reached involved the money of northern organizations, the ambition of African Americans, and the limited tolerance of white southerners. As such, southern schools for African Americans struggled with questions of "ownership, administration and boards of control—white or black, southern or northern, philanthropic or denominational," according to Thomas Jesse Jones, author of *Educational Adaptations* (1916).[44] In truth, leaders of the white community (from the North and South), would dictate nearly every aspect of African American education, from funding to accreditation to curriculum. The only thing beyond their control was what graduates would do with their education.

All African American higher education institutions in Nashville received financial support from Christian churches or organizations, as did many white colleges, during this period of educational growth. However, for many black colleges and universities, religious affiliations provided essential funding and were viewed as "missionary work" by many church denominations.[45] As a result, many religious organizations, both white and black, felt a civic obligation and Christian responsibility to help fund African American institutions of higher learning.

Nonetheless many in the South, including some white religious leaders, believed that African American college graduates would lead to social disorder in the public sphere. Atticus Greene Haygood, an educator, minister, author, and president of Emory University (1875–1884), sought to reassure his white audience with subtlety: "Do not, beloved white brother, care at this word 'elevation.' Let me whisper a secret in your ear, *'That cannot be done unless you get below him.'"* Haygood actually accepted the idea of higher education for African Americans because he believed it would improve southern society. However, as Clarence Mohr noted, Haygood, like many progressive white southerners, "promoted black education while simultaneously calming white fears of educated blacks as political actors and economic competitors who would eventually seek 'social equality.'"[46]

Drawing a sharp contrast to the condescending tone of men such as Haygood and other white southerners was James C. Napier. Napier, an African American and register of the U.S. Treasury under President William Howard Taft, served on three of Nashville's HBCU boards of trust, and cofounded Tennessee A&I. A successful businessman and community activist, he declared in 1912 at a congressional hearing: "We aspire to be not ornaments, not puppets set up to look at, but useful, law-abiding, industrious and productive citizens. As such we are trying to grow into that usefulness . . . and we only ask that assistance that all others have [for fair distribution of federal funds for public higher education in Tennessee]."[47]

As historian James D. Anderson pointed out, "From the Reconstruction era through the Great Depression black higher education in the South existed essentially through a system of private liberal arts colleges . . . [and] involved largely a study of the interrelationship between philanthropy and . . . black leaders."[48]

Many schools were funded by multiple financiers and nonprofit organizations. For example, the budget for Fisk University included monetary support from the American Missionary Association, endowment funds, Slater Fund, Phelps Stokes Fund, tuition, and periodic fundraising campaigns conducted by the Jubilee Singers. Fisk president George A. Gates (1909–12) was the first administrator to reach out to white southerners to serve on the Board of Trustees when he realized that all white members were from the North. A New Englander himself, Gates understood that to have white southern men on the board, in particular men from Nashville, was important as most Fisk graduates would work and live in the region.[49]

In addition to tuition, Meharry Medical College received its primary funding from the Freedmen's Aid Society and the Methodist Church. Meharry also received philanthropic contributions. For example, the General Education Board of the Rockefeller Foundation donated $88,000 to Meharry to enlarge and renovate Hubbard Hospital, which was one of two hospitals for African Americans in Nashville. Roger Williams University obtained much-needed, yet inadequate, funding from the American Baptist Home Missionary Society.

By 1890 nine land-grant colleges for African Americans had been established in the United States. As educational reform swept the South, several public colleges opened for both white and black students to provide more practical agricultural, industrial, and teacher training. P. P. Claxton, leader of the state's educational crusade, found support in Governor Malcolm Patterson, who garnered the reluctant approval of the state legislature in 1909. Nashville secured its bid as the site of the only public state "college" for blacks through several sources of funding in 1911, which resulted in the opening of Tennessee A&I a year later. Davidson County promised $80,000, the city of Nashville provided $20,000, and the Tennessee legislature appropriated $75,000. Private pledges totaled $40,000 after a door-to-door fundraising effort in Nashville's African American community.[50]

Leading the effort to locate the school in Nashville were black urban boosters such as James C. Napier, Richard Boyd, Benjamin Carr, and Preston Taylor. Black boosterism operated much like white boosterism—as businessmen sought to "boost" (or promote) a town, city, or organization to attract business and recruit employees. However, black boosters in Nashville focused specifically on promoting African American organizations, including educational institutions. Napier, Boyd, Carr, and Taylor formed the Colored Normal School Association and used their influence as members of the Negro Board of Trade, Davidson County Negro Republican Club, and Nashville's chapter of the National Negro Business League.[51] According to historian Bobby Lovett, most of these men embraced Booker T.

Washington's "conservative racial philosophy and emphasis on industrial (and mechanical arts) manual labor education for the black masses."[52] In fact, State Superintendent of Public Instruction R. L. Jones assured Governor Malcolm R. Patterson and the state legislature that "the Negro school would be like the existing private Negro colleges that prepared Negro students to be no more than discontented propagators."[53] While a bond issue was passed in Davidson County, most white voters were wary of opening a school for African Americans funded primarily with tax dollars.[54]

Among Nashville's colleges there existed an inexplicit relationship between black and white schools and vice versa. Although recognition and marginal relationships existed, there were no true partnerships between black and white institutions. One exception was the Bethlehem House where white Peabody and Vanderbilt students volunteered alongside Fisk students. Moreover, black faculty members did not teach courses at white colleges or universities as some of their white counterparts did at black schools. Vanderbilt professors would serve as guest lecturers or commencement speakers at Fisk, Meharry, and Tennessee A&I, and administrators often attended major events at other local schools.

Specifically, Tennessee A&I president William J. Hale worked to cultivate good relations with the administrators at Peabody and Vanderbilt.[55] In 1929 Vanderbilt's Dr. Alva W. Yalor, a professor of social ethics, was invited by Hale to address the students of Tennessee A&I. Yalor stressed the need for greater "preparation for service," lauded students for following Washington's industrial model, and encouraged "other races to appreciate and adopt it."[56] He also spoke highly of the students and work being done at Tennessee A&I, but his message was not an appeal for interracial cooperation or an indication of Vanderbilt's interest in partnering with Tennessee A&I.

Accreditation was the other issue vital to the success or failure of African American schools. In truth, the creation of accreditation agencies was a major concern for all institutions claiming to offer collegiate work or confer legitimate degrees regardless of race, gender, institutional-religious affiliation, or other defining characteristics. In the South, the Southern Association of Colleges and Schools (SACS) was formed in the late nineteenth century. As standards, requirements, and evaluations became more uniform and consistent, many African American "colleges" and "universities" were stripped of their titles because they did not meet the collegiate standards set by the all-white SACS agency.

In 1900 W. E. B. Du Bois performed an unofficial study of black schools and generously determined that thirty-four schools (out of approximately fifty) could be considered colleges, with a total enrollment of 726 students.[57] In a more prudent evaluation ten years later, Du Bois concluded that only Fisk, Howard,

Atlanta University, Morehouse, and Virginia Union were "First-Grade Colored Colleges." Two organizations formed to help support, regulate, and improve African American schools: the National Association of Teachers in Colored Schools as well as the Association of Colleges for Negro Youths, which aimed to encourage the maintenance of college standards, administration, and curriculum.[58]

Prior to 1920 the Bureau of Education assigned a respective "status" to each African American school, ranking them on a spectrum ranging from a true college institution to a special school. As such, the report served as "not only the 'Who's Who' in Negro schools, but ... also a 'Domesday' book showing who is not who."[59] The report's main author, Thomas Jesse Jones, provided a harsher evaluation and classification of African American schools, claiming that only Fisk and Howard were worthy of the claim "university."[60] However, in one sector of the report, Meharry was referenced with Fisk and Howard as a college. In reality, Meharry was still not on par with the two schools; however, it remained distinctive in nature because of its role as a medical college.[61] The Bureau of Education noted the special circumstance of Fisk University with its proximity to the so-called black belt and "the progressive educational ideals of the large white institutions of Nashville with which Fisk maintain[ed] friendly relations."[62]

Roger Williams would never gain SACS accreditation while operating in Nashville, while Meharry University gained an "A" rating in 1923, according to the two-tiered SACS accreditation model for black colleges. Fisk University would earn full SACS accreditation in 1930, the first HBCU to receive such sanction. Not surprisingly, from 1865 to 1930 African American institutions in Tennessee and the entire South were compelled to seek collegiate accreditation on terms defined by all-white regional and national rating agencies.[63]

In the 1920s several northern philanthropic groups, including the General Education Board (GEB) of the Rockefeller Foundation and the Julius Rosenwald Fund, would contribute millions of dollars to help Tennessee A&I achieve true collegiate status. In 1927 "Normal," which indicated teacher training, was dropped from the school's name; the campus added new facilities and faculty; and the Primary and Secondary Divisions were phased out. Still, it would be nearly twenty years before the college was fully accredited by SACS in 1946, three years after the death of William Hale (president, 1912–43). SACS did this under pressure from northern philanthropic agencies, like the GEB, that controlled large amounts of money flowing into southern education.[64]

Education was the great equalizer and a key factor in the creation of an elevated class of African American leaders. Whether to follow the educational philosophy and vision of Booker T. Washington's "Atlanta Compromise" (see below) or W. E. B. Du Bois's "Talented Tenth" would prove to be another matter. Nashville served as a sort of testing ground where these opposing philosophies would be introduced and implemented. The end result would show that each was successful in its own right and played an important role in shaping New South Nashville.

Industrial and Vocational Education

Louis Holmes attended Tennessee A&I Normal School from 1920 and graduated with a bachelor's degree in 1926, just before the school's name was changed to Tennessee A&I State Normal College. He was described by his classmates as "an athlete and a mechanic [who] can build anything from a mousetrap to an aeroplane."[65] Determined to work their way up in a white world, graduates of Tennessee A&I's class of 1926 asserted, "Never cease until we conquer."[66] In 1928 the opening commencement hymn was the "Negro National Anthem," and the senior class motto was "Deeds Rather Than Words."[67] The school was Nashville's only true industrial school, which also produced thousands of teachers from 1912 to 1930.

Booker T. Washington's Hampton-Tuskegee model, articulated in his "Atlanta Compromise" speech before a biracial audience at the Cotton States and International Exposition in 1895, had gained cultural approval by the turn of the twentieth century. W. E. B. Du Bois continued to extol the higher virtues of a liberal arts training and a desire for more immediate social, economic, and political equality. However, Du Bois could not deny the forward motion and empowerment afforded African Americans operating within the Hampton-Tuskegee educational model. Industrial training was certainly preferable to the denial of educational opportunity altogether. In fact, in southern states it seemed the only acceptable (and immediate) option.

In the first quarter of the twentieth century, Thomas Jesse Jones emerged nationally as a leading voice for the industrial/vocational educational model for African Americans. A white man with a Ph.D. in sociology from Columbia University, Jones accepted a position at Hampton Institute in Virginia. He was later appointed to compile and publish his research as the author of the "Negro section" of the United States Census of 1910. In 1913 Jones became the educational director of the Phelps Stokes Fund and was also assigned to a leadership position within the Bureau of Education's Division of Racial Groups.[68]

Jones's research and recommendations for African American education were more widely read by government entities, private individuals, and religious/secular groups than any other such studies in the country. He believed that primary and secondary education should be provided for children as well as industrial/vocational training for young adults. Jones's reasoning rested on the idea that vocational education would allow blacks to assimilate into society as part of the working class without upsetting the social hierarchy. Once again, the direction of education would largely be influenced by a white man's definition of the purpose, scope, and expected outcome of education for blacks. After Jones's death in 1950, the *Journal of Negro Education* stated, "To say that Jones did not accomplish some good . . . would be far from the truth. [But] he would have achieved greater success if he had not been so narrow-minded [and] short-sighted."[69]

Although many African American graduates pursued industrial or vocational careers, the city did not fit neatly into the Hampton-Tuskegee model followed by many southern states. Specifically, Fisk did not subscribe to this model and instead maintained a liberal arts curriculum that largely mirrored white four-year universities. In 1889 the university clarified its mission: "Fisk University, since its first days, has steadfastly had as its chief aim the higher education of the colored people. . . . It believes in industrial education but chooses to leave that work to other institutions which have that as their end."[70]

However, Fisk did offer some courses and certificates in "practical" training.[71] The school created an Industrial Department that offered training in printing, carpentry, mechanics, nursing, hygiene, cooking, and sewing. Students were required to devote an hour a day "to such manual work as may be required of them."[72] As early as 1882 the university had erected Livingstone Hall—a library as well as laboratories for industrial education. However, in the administration's words, "The College work is first, industries second."[73]

The major institution associated with vocational training was Tennessee Agricultural and Industrial State Normal School, founded in 1912 as the first and only African American school to be controlled and funded predominantly by the State of Tennessee.[74] The school opened with 230 students; enrollment topped 400 by 1916; and by 1929 the student population had exploded to over 2,000.[75] Tennessee A&I's secondary curriculum centered on a four-year "academic" set of courses with the option of continuing with additional coursework as a "junior" or "senior." It is important to note that the majority of students were not enrolled in a degree program but rather in summer sessions that provided teacher training. Lovett summarized the school's significance in *A Touch of Greatness*: "Students at Tennessee A&I came from all walks of life and often returned to their home towns, spreading black college graduates throughout Tennessee's rural counties."[76]

William J. Hale was a shrewd and successful administrator, guiding Tennessee A&I through its first thirty-two years. Described as the school's "First President, Educator, Business Executive, Friend to Mankind, Christian Gentleman," Hale worked his way out of poverty and through Maryville College in East

Tennessee. After a short stint as a teacher, Hale was appointed principal at a black grammar school in Chattanooga. The next year Hale led a fundraising campaign to make Chattanooga the home of the state's first African-American college, but Nashville's local government outbid Chattanooga by $9,000. The Tennessee legislature was so impressed with Hale during the legislative and funding process that it appointed him the new president of the college and in 1911 moved his family to Nashville, where he would oversee construction.[77]

Hale carefully selected the first faculty members, a total of thirteen instructors, and all of them graduates of Atlanta, Fisk, or Howard Universities. He visited comparable industrial schools in the South, adopted a precollegiate curriculum, and fought for greater state funding and federal funding related to the Morrill Land Grant. Hale was a pragmatic accommodationist who sought to work within an antagonistic system that both supported and suppressed his efforts. Students "liked and feared" Hale but most respected him because their success depended on his ability to maintain the school's viability. Hale also had to appease white state and local officials such as Governor Ben Hooper, Governor Austin Peay, Mayor Hilary Howse, education officials, and state legislators.

FIG. 3.1. Tennessee A&I President William Jasper Hale (1912–1943). Metropolitan Government of Nashville and Davidson County Archives.

But he was often reminded that no matter how great his accomplishments, he would always be seen as a second-class citizen. According to Bobby Lovett, "Hale knew firsthand the deep racism held by most white officials in Tennessee. A soft-spoken mulatto with wavy brown hair streaked with white, a strong chin, and cold gray eyes, Hale looked like a 'white' man. He often endured the insults directed against blacks by state officials before they realized that the pale-skinned Hale was African American."[78]

Hale may have ruled with an iron fist, but he rolled out the red carpet when visitors came to campus. He often invited important guests to Tennessee A&I, hosted elaborate dinners, offered tours and performances by well-mannered students, and sent guests home with a turkey from the school's farm or handicrafts made in one of the school's shops. While he wined and dined white visitors and potential donors, he nickel-and-dimed the students and faculty, creating a monopoly on transportation to and from Union Station and requiring faculty members to sign checks face down while he paid them in cash—shortchanging teachers to help the school's monthly balance sheets. In 1927 the National Association of Teachers in Colored Schools elected Hale to its presidency. He remained active in the community as well, serving on the local Citizens Bank board and the Tennessee Commission for Interracial Cooperation (1919–21). He was recognized by the Harmon Foundation for Distinguished Achievement among Negros, receiving the organization's Gold Award for outstanding achievement in education in 1930—the first Tennessean to win this prestigious honor.[79] Though not himself a black urban booster, Hale made sure he operated in the same social and professional circles as men such as Boyd, Napier, and Taylor.

The growth in student enrollment at Tennessee A&I signaled the affordability and accessibility of industrial education for young black men and women. Although the school taught traditional academic subjects, vocational training remained at the fore. Tennessee A&I offered courses in bookkeeping, masonry, woodworking, and construction-related fields for the men and sewing and cooking for women. The school, audited annually by the state government, operated on a budget of approximately $40,000. Tuition for Tennessee students was free, although students paid for room, board, books, and registration. What tuition the school did receive accounted for less than 10 percent of the budget. Funds also came from the federal government as well as African American and white churches.

The school would eventually offer college courses in addition to industrial and vocational training but not until 1922. Tennessee A&I gained recognition as a college by the state government and Board of Education in 1922 (but not yet by SACS) and the American Association of Teachers' Colleges in 1933, and A&I's faculty also reflected a higher level of instruction. By 1930 the faculty had thirty-eight members, with twenty-four (63 percent) holding at least a bachelor's degree. Nearly 50 percent of the faculty was female, many of whom were instructors in the school's "normal" course to train teachers. Student enrollment within the Collegiate Department also rose steadily from forty-five seniors in the class of 1930 to just over one hundred students enrolled as part of the class of 1933.[80] President Hale's efforts to raise the bar at Tennessee A&I was not an effort to discredit technical training but rather to meet educational standards needed to achieve accreditation and attract new students. By the time Tennessee A&I State College celebrated its twenty-fifth anniversary, the institution and property were valued at $3 million.[81]

In the minds of many, industrial education offered both social justice and social control. As James Anderson has suggested, "The needs of the South's racially segregated society were to determine the scope and purpose of black higher education, not the interests and aspirations of individual students or the collective interests of black communities."[82] For whites in the North and South, this seemed a comfortable solution that allowed African Americans to be good workers and citizens without fundamentally disrupting notions of race and class.

Historically, efforts to increase vocational and industrial training remained noble, and Tennessee A&I enrolled and/or graduated thousands of African Americans from 1912 to 1930; however, the Hampton-Tuskegee model played a secondary role in Nashville. The leading role was played by schools such as Fisk and Meharry, which attracted students from the local community and across the United States. Nashville was a mecca and a magnet for black liberal arts and professional education as it carried with it the hope of ultimate participation in a new black middle and elite class.

Liberal Arts and Black Professionalism

In 1896 Henry L. Morehouse coined the phrase the "Talented Tenth" to describe a plan that would produce new middle and upper classes of African Americans.[83] In 1900 W. E. B. Du Bois bolstered the term "Talented Tenth" when he provided statistics that revealed the exponential value of education. College-level institutions in the South had, according to Du Bois, "trained in Greek and Latin and mathematics 2,000 men; and these men trained fully 50,000 others in morals and manners, and they in turn taught the alphabet to nine millions of men."[84] Education gave thousands of poverty-stricken blacks in Tennessee the tools to become economically self-sufficient, healthier, and more productive members of society. As a byproduct, higher education also moved a small minority of African Americans into leadership positions that brought individual success and benefited the collective whole. In large part, the "Talented Tenth" grew from the ranks of institutions in Nashville, Tennessee.[85] In particular, Fisk University and Meharry Medical School produced leaders instead of laborers.

Many progressive reformers in the North and South acknowledged that education for African Americans could help alleviate urban ills. In 1875, 188 of 228 African Americans attending college in the state were students at Fisk. Because of the Tennessee capital's advantage as an already established educational center, the Bureau of Education believed that Nashville, as a southern city, was best poised to form a "cooperative relationship with the progressive southern people in the improvement of the condition of the colored race."[86] In *Educational Adaptations*, Thomas Jesse Jones wrote, "More and more, the leadership of the race is devolving upon its strong and capable men and women. Successful leadership requires the best lessons of economics, sociology, and education."[87] Nashville provided the urban backdrop for many who would serve as leaders in black communities across the region.

Nashville's most recognized HBCU offering liberal arts university training did not begin as a university. First established in 1866 and chartered the following year, the school opened as the Fisk Free Colored School with over nine hundred enrolled students by the end of the first term. By 1871 the school had ramped up instruction to include collegiate coursework and teacher training. The university's curriculum included multiple years of study in Latin, Greek, calculus, English, history, sociology, psychology, and literature to obtain a bachelor's degree.[88] Its theological curriculum included additional courses intended to give instruction and credentials to future ministers. Like many colleges of its day, Fisk also instructed younger students in its College Preparatory and Grammar Schools. But perhaps most impressive was Fisk's offering of a master's degree as early as the late 1890s.[89] Under President E. M. Cravath, Fisk enjoyed relative stability and growth from 1875 to 1900, aided by the fundraising efforts of the Jubilee Singers, who by 1900 had received worldwide acclaim. Cravath, along with school treasurer and choir director George L. White, organized the Fisk Jubilee Singers to raise much-needed funding for the fledgling school.[90]

Founded by white missionaries, the school implemented strict rules for behavior and required Bible study, prayer, and chapel services. Moreover, the repertoire of the Fisk Jubilee Singers consisted mainly of black spirituals, evangelical arrangements of hymns, and other popular anthems of the Protestant church. Prior to his tour as a member of the Jubilee Singers in the 1870s, student Thomas Rutling was nearly expelled for writing "romantic notes" to a female classmate, followed by a second offense for which he had to sign a confession promising

FIG. 3.2. Fisk University calculus class, 1890. Library of Congress.

"with the help of God and the aid of man I will never be guilty of such a thing again."[91]

Despite the success of Fisk's enrollment and the fundraising provided by the Jubilee Singers, the school struggled financially in the early 1900s. President James Merrill (1901–8) resigned in frustration. Booker T. Washington, ironically a proponent of industrial education and a critic of liberal arts curricula, was elected to the Fisk Board of Trustees in 1909. Washington and his wife, Margaret Murray Washington, a Fisk alumna, campaigned for the school and secured funding from Andrew Carnegie for a new library. Also in 1909, George A. Gates was appointed Fisk's third president. Gates's experience as an administrator stabilized and expanded the school's curriculum and raised academic standards as he worked with other black colleges to establish uniform admission requirements. According to the Bureau of Education's 1916 report, Fisk's "geographical location and progressive management are unusually favorable to the development of a strong central institution for college training and social service."[92] By 1920 Fisk had an endowment of $1 million.

Fisk also began to attract students from other southern states as well as other regions. Perhaps the university's most famous graduate remains W. E. B. Du Bois, who came to Fisk from Massachusetts, and graduated in 1888. Du Bois, while

FIG. 3.3. Fisk University campus in the late 1920s with the construction of a new Meharry Medical College building to the West. Metropolitan Government of Nashville and Davidson County Archives.

living in Nashville and attending Fisk, formed many of his ideas as a thinker and writer.[93] Not only did he gain knowledge in the classroom, but he also gained an education outside of the classroom—as a black man living in the South. He was able to experience firsthand the regional differences that distinguished the South from New England. These experiences were crucial to solidifying Du Bois's philosophy that social equity for blacks could only be achieved through racial elevation made possible by education.

Despite the calls for industrial training, the Fisk administration and faculty continued to promote a classical education that would produce students with critical thinking skills, self-confidence, individual ambition, and community spirit. President Fayette Avery McKenzie noted in 1915, "Let us dare to be big! . . . Let us commit ourselves to the task set before us. Let us dare to expect large resources,

FIG. 3.4. Fayette Avery McKenzie, President of Fisk University (1915–1925). Library of Congress.

to plan large things. Let us say, not pleasure but achievement, not comfort but power, not ease but struggle! Let us dare to be a university!"[94]

Fisk would "dare to be big" in expanding the work of its Department of Sociology to address the social ills affecting the health and well being of African Americans. First established in 1910, the department was headed by George Edmund Haynes. Haynes's wife, Elizabeth Ross Haynes, would also be instrumental in the department's work, although as a black woman Ross Haynes had fewer opportunities for pay, publication, or professional advancement. Both George and Elizabeth were Fisk graduates, class of 1903, and struck an "ideological middle ground" between Du Bois's "race leaders" and Washington's "obedient, productive laborers."[95] George was from Arkansas and Elizabeth from Alabama, a testament to the regional draw of Fisk. After George received a Ph.D. from Columbia University (the first African American to do so), the couple returned in 1910 to Fisk, where George became a professor.

Fellow Fisk professor Cornelius Wortendyke Morrow "reminded Fisk faculty members who proudly boasted of George Hanes's accomplishments that Elizabeth Ross had been his intellectual equal, or better," according to historian Francille

Rusan Wilson.[96] Elizabeth went on to complete graduate work at the University of Chicago and received a master's degree from Columbia. She was also the first African American woman to serve on the national board of the YWCA. Ross Haynes was a force in the Nashville community and at Fisk University. Leading education programs on tuberculosis, typhoid, and pneumonia, she taught classes, managed and trained Fisk students, and supported her husband's research while pursuing her own. This power couple connected the university to the local white community in meaningful ways while serving the needs of the black community. As Joe Richardson concluded, "Fisk had always emphasized community service, but its fame for training social workers began with the Haynes, who became international experts on racial affairs."[97]

George and Elizabeth Haynes brought further distinction to Fisk and drew a new generation of black students to the university, those who desired a liberal arts foundation but sought to affect society through progressive reform and social work. This formidable couple also provided leadership on a national stage through organizations including the National Urban League (cofounded by George), the Association of Negro Colleges and Secondary Schools, the Department of Labor, the YMCA, and the YWCA. George and Elizabeth Haynes's tenure at Fisk reflects the close association and, at times, interdependent relationship between the black college and the black community.

Fisk's Department of Sociology worked in areas outside of Nashville as well. Charles Spurgeon Johnson, chair of the department by 1928, worked with his students on projects across the South, including an "intensive community study of Macon County [Alabama] to search for the environmental sources of infection" of venereal disease, which exceeded 25 percent for African Americans ages fifteen to forty.[98] Johnson would later become Fisk's first black president (1946).

Fisk alumni effected change in small waves, whether teaching behind a podium, preaching from the pulpit, or engaging in social work or health-related fields.[99] By 1900 Fisk claimed over four hundred graduates, though most were males.[100] According to Richardson, "This record sounds even more impressive when . . . only 1 percent of blacks in the United States, or less than 23,000 persons, were in professional service in 1900."[101] Fisk's 501 enrolled students in 1900 included: 85 from Nashville, 150 from Tennessee beyond Nashville, and an astounding 266 came from out of state or abroad. Such numbers spoke to the prestige of the university as well as to the appeal of Nashville as an accommodating city for African Americans.[102]

The *Reports of the Freedmen's Aid Society* of 1869 foreshadowed the next half-century for aspiring African Americans, stating, "The halls are crowded with students preparing to teach school, *practice law or medicine,* or teach the glorious Gospel."[103] From the 1870s onward, Fisk graduates entered many professional fields such as social work, law, religion, politics, education, and medicine. However, most received additional education or training at other colleges before entering law or medicine.

In many ways, Fisk and Meharry grew as partners, with many medical graduates coming from the ranks of Fisk alumni. The two schools were located between Charlotte Avenue and Jefferson Avenue. Fisk University was situated on Seventeenth Avenue and Meharry Medical College on Eighteenth Avenue (renamed Dr. D. B. Todd Jr. Boulevard), both of which intersected Charlotte and Jefferson. In *Educating Black Doctors*, James Summerville noted, "The goal for Fisk and Meharry was to produce graduates who would attack the vestiges of slavery, poverty, and excess morbidity" with both schools seeking to close the gap and "make up for years of education lost, to catch up in a rapidly moving industrial society, and to adjust to an ambiguous status assigned them."[104]

Meharry began as a separate Medical Department in 1876 within the already-established Central Tennessee College (later Walden University).[105] In 1915 Meharry was separately chartered as an independent college, formally separating from Walden. Meharry College sought to fill a pressing need as, "[b]lack communities across the South realized that their communities were in need of other kinds of black professionals in addition to teachers and preachers," according to Crystal deGregory.[106] deGregory concluded, "Nowhere was this need more obvious than in Nashville, a city that straddled the line between begrudged black advancement for some and black suffering in mass. . . . Central Tennessee and Fisk embodied these challenges, as well as the many contradictions inherent in the rhetoric of the New South."[107] The need for African American doctors, dentists, nurses, and pharmacists remained great as black were disproportionately affected by poverty and disease, particularly tuberculosis.[108] As a general rule, white doctors did not take black patients, and white hospitals did not admit or treat African Americans.

From the outset, Meharry's purpose was to train African American medical professionals. It would become the premier medical school for blacks in the South, training both men (doctors, pharmacists, dentists) and women (mostly nurses).[109] The school's Dental and Pharmacy Departments began in the late 1880s, and in 1910 the Nursing Department was officially established. In 1916, the Bureau of Education reported that the school, operating on a budget of only $8,400 a year, lacked adequate equipment, furniture, and instruction.[110] A year later, the report noted improvement: "[There are] 505 professional students at Meharry Medical College. . . . The professional training given in Meharry Medical College is valuable."[111] It remains significant that the term *professional* was used to describe Meharry's purpose.

FIG. 3.5. 1910 Meharry Medical College groundbreaking ceremony for new building as part of Walden University. The famously bearded Dr. George Hubbard (president 1876–1921) center left, and Nashville urban booster James C. Napier in crowd on right. Meharry Medical College Library Archives.

In many ways, the urgent necessity of healthcare was a clarion call for black women pursuing higher education who desired a profession other than teaching. Meharry's coursework in nursing dates back to 1892. The George W. Hubbard Hospital's Training School for Nurses opened in 1910 one year after Vanderbilt established its first nursing program. One member of Meharry's inaugural nursing class, Hulda Lyttle-Frazier, a native Nashvillian, ultimately spent much of her professional career improving healthcare in Nashville. After graduation in 1913 and work in New York, Lyttle-Frazier returned to Nashville and was appointed head nurse of Hubbard Hospital on the recommendation of George W. Hubbard. She made many improvements to the school, hospital, and nursing program.[112]

While nursing provided an avenue of professionalization, Darlene Hine has argued that black nurses not only were subjected to pervasive racism and sexism in the male-dominant medical profession but also suffered discrimination at the hands of white nurses' associations.[113] In 1896 the Nurses Associated Alumnae of the United States and Canada was formed, which later became the American Nurses Association in 1911. The group barred black women from membership. In

1908 a parallel organization was formed and named the National Association of Colored Graduate Nurses (NACGN). Lyttle-Frazier would serve as vice president and president of NACGN.

Black nurses from Meharry also completed their training and residencies at the Mille E. Hale hospital, a second hospital serving local African Americans and operated privately by Dr. John Hale and his wife, Millie. John Henry Hale graduated from Walden University with a B.S. in 1901 and earned his M.D. from Meharry in 1905. "Big John," as he was called by those who knew him, first practiced medicine in Dr. Robert Fulton Boyd's Mercy Hospital and in many ways continued Boyd's legacy after his sudden death in 1912. Established in 1916, the Millie E. Hale Hospital became a training facility for Meharry doctors and nurses along with Hubbard Hospital. By 1922 the Millie E. Hale Hospital had served over four thousand black patients and expanded the number of beds from twelve to fifty while maintaining an average of twenty-five nursing students in its three-year program.[114]

Millie E. Hale completed the Fisk University teacher's program and later graduated with a B.A. from Fisk in 1927. Although Mrs. Hale passed away in 1930, the Millie E. Hale Hospital continued to operate under the direction and

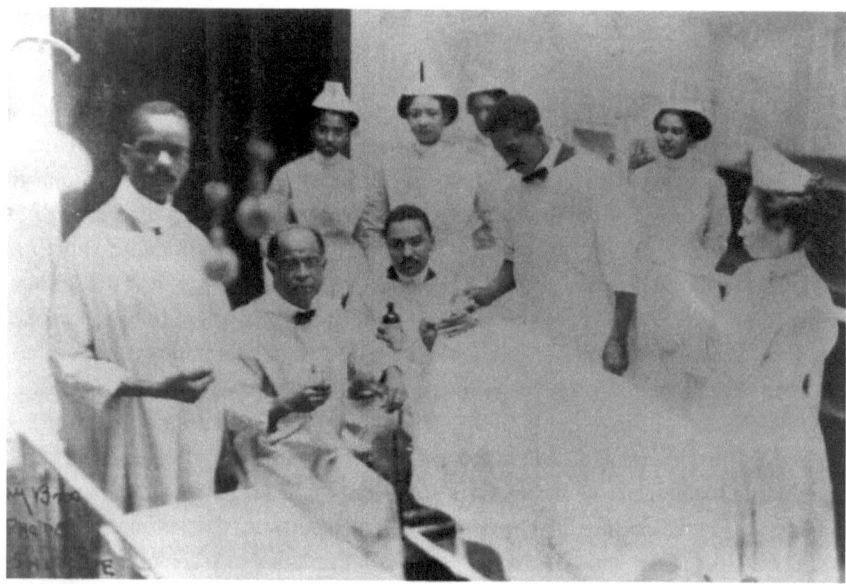

FIG. 3.6. Meharry Medical College Operating room with Dr. Robert F. Boyd holding presumably a bottle of chloroform in 1910. Meharry Medical College Library Archives.

leadership of her husband until 1938. Dr. Hale became the chairman of the Surgery Department at Meharry, chief of surgery at Hubbard Hospital, and associate director of Meharry's Tumor Clinic. Throughout his career as a renowned surgeon and hospital administrator, Hale performed over thirty thousand surgeries while also teaching full-time at Meharry and serving in part-time capacities at Hubbard Hospital.[115]

When Meharry Medical College opened the Hubbard Hospital in 1917 it did so with the help of northern philanthropic foundations and local fundraising. The hospital was designed to meet the local community's medical needs and to serve as the Meharry's teaching hospital. Efforts to establish Hubbard Hospital were led by Dr. George Hubbard and Dr. Robert Fulton Boyd (of no relation to Richard Henry Boyd). Born in Giles County, Tennessee, Robert F. Boyd moved to Nashville as a young man and began night classes at Fisk University. Dr. Boyd was one of Meharry's earliest graduates, earning degrees in medicine (1882) and dentistry (1887) and a certificate in pharmacy. After postgraduate work at the University of Chicago, Boyd joined the Meharry faculty, specializing in gynecology and clinical medicine.

According to Dr. Axel Hansen, Boyd was "the first Negro to earn a living by the practice of medicine in Nashville."[116] Boyd headed the Nashville Anti-Tuberculosis Association, and established the privately run Mercy Hospital in 1900 on Fourth Avenue downtown.[117] He also ran for mayor of Nashville in 1893, not because he believed he would win but because he wanted to draw attention to issues within the African American community. Dr. Boyd often held public forums and gave lectures on health and hygiene in an effort to educate blacks in Nashville and decrease the mortality rate caused by tuberculosis and other diseases. He founded what would become the National Medical Association because the American Medical Association (AMA) consistently barred black physicians from membership. In addition to medicine and politics, Dr. Boyd was elected the first president of the People's Savings Bank and Trust Company in 1909, the city's second African American bank.

Robert Boyd, John Henry Hale, and Millie E. Hale were proof that Fisk and Meharry produced graduates who formed the backbone of a new black elite class in Nashville. Fisk and Meharry largely drove this new professional class of educated men. As Axel C. Hansen concluded, "To be talented, but not Caucasian, during the first quarter of the twentieth century presented unique and overwhelming challenges that only a select few African Americans could transcend."[118] Together, these educational institutions and black businessmen formed a partnership, aided in large part by women who also served in professional roles as social workers, teachers, and nurses. Bobby Lovett noted that "the change in local black leadership was already noticeable by the mid-1880s. . . . By the 1920s, the elite class persons' domination of black Nashville's leadership ranks and its society and culture was infused with more middle- and professional-class persons."[119]

Meharry's student body grew throughout the 1920s and included students from Fisk as well as Tennessee A&I, thus beginning a long, mutually beneficial relationship between the three schools. For example, Reginald C. Neblett and Herbert Harrison (of the Tennessee A&I classes of 1924 and 1925, respectively), both continued their educations as medical students at Meharry. Many aspiring physicians obtained their undergraduate education at Fisk or Tennessee A&I and later graduated with their medical degrees from Meharry.[120] (Meharry gained full accreditation from the AMA by 1943, the ADA by 1945, and SACS by 1972.)[121]

By the end of 1920s, Meharry was in desperate need of new facilities. According to Reavis Mitchell, "With contributions from the General Education Board and the Rockefeller, Rosenwald, Eastman, and Carnegie foundations, together with assistance from the City of Nashville and Meharry alumni, the college moved in 1931 from First Avenue to its present location in Northwest Nashville, one street west of Fisk University."[122] The new campus and Hubbard Hospital complex were adjacent to Fisk University.[123] In late 1931 President Herbert Hoover wrote to Meharry president John J. Mullowney to express his interest in the continued work of the college on its new campus:

> I am interested to learn that the new Meharry Medical College and Hospital will be dedicated tomorrow. This institution with its record of years of service has contributed splendidly to Negro professional education. I trust that the enlarged modern plant made possible by generous benefactors will enable it to enter upon a new era of usefulness. Protection of the public health is one of the most constructive forces in the nation, and I congratulate you on the opportunity which the institution now has to train professional workers in the field of medical practice and public health.[124]

Despite the accomplishments of Meharry and its graduates, most African Americans attending some type of college entered the teaching profession, not medical-related fields. In 1911 the *Crisis* reported that of the approximately five thousand African American college graduates, 54 percent served as teachers, 20 percent were ministers, 4 percent practiced law, and 7 percent entered the medical profession.[125] In particular, females entered the teaching ranks in staggering numbers. By the end of World War I, nearly 80 percent of all African American teachers were women, despite discouraging conditions and wages. (The national average for white teachers was $156 and $107 per year for black teachers.)[126] In

FIG. 3.7. Meharry Medical College new campus adjacent to Fisk University in Northwest Nashville, 1940. Library of Congress.

Reading, Writing, and Segregation, Sonya Ramsey argued that by the 1930s the majority of black professional women in Nashville were teachers, which "demonstrated their belief that becoming educated, middle-class community leaders would help them adapt to—and sometimes overcome—the economic and social obstacles of a racially inequitable system."[127]

Fisk University served as a major training center for African Americans who sought to become primary or secondary educators. The most common scenario involved a rural community or small town writing to Fisk and expressing their need for a teacher. Many students who accepted positions in such areas became much more than classroom teachers. Upon accepting a position in south Georgia, one Fisk graduate found herself as the "Sunday school Superintendent, janitor, and moral leader of the community as well as an instructor."[128] Over seven hundred Fiskites served as teachers by 1900 even though they were unable to complete degree requirements at the university.[129] Both whites and African Americans could teach without a college degree, and state certifications had not yet been formalized. However, collegiate and teacher training courses increased the chances of gainful employment and provided the content and skills necessary for successful classroom instruction. By 1915 roughly 50 percent of graduates served as teachers

FIG. 3.8. First graduating class of Tennessee A&I and the school's band pictured in 1924. Metropolitan Government of Nashville and Davidson County Archives.

or administrators in schools across the nation, and an estimated seventy-five thousand children in the South learned under the tutelage of Fisk graduates.[130] In fact, among African American institutions, Fisk was second only to Howard University in Washington, D.C., in producing teachers during this period.[131]

From 1865 to 1912 Fisk and Roger Williams led the way in training teachers and administrators, but Tennessee A&I would quickly become a force as a normal school for African Americans after 1912. Tennessee A&I State Normal School became Tennessee A&I State College officially in 1927, three years after the school graduated its first college class with seven men and one woman. The first class of graduates received B.A. degrees, although subsequent graduates would receive B.S. degrees until after 1940.[132]

By the mid- to late 1920s, Tennessee A&I's faculty and student body reflected a school in transition but one with an upward trajectory. In 1925 a student wrote "A. and I. is young enough to be progressive and modern yet old enough to have stability."[133] Of the nearly twenty-eight faculty members (sixteen men and twelve women), the majority held bachelor degrees. Approximately three-quarters of the faculty had graduated from Fisk, Meharry (Walden), or Tennessee A&I—or had earned diplomas or degrees from other southern black colleges such as Howard, Morehouse, or Tuskegee. Interestingly, graduate work at Columbia, Harvard, and the University of Chicago was also listed for several faculty members.[134] Black teachers who wished to pursue graduate education of any sort from 1865 through the 1920s had to leave the South.[135]

The curriculum in the 1920s provides insight into the transitional nature of Tennessee A&I and illustrates the tension between the industrial/agricultural and liberal arts educational models. Core coursework included English, biology, physical education, physical science, history, and psychology. Students also attended courses in art, music, and language (unspecified). However, the majority of courses still focused on practical training, with courses offered in sewing, domestic science, dressmaking, agriculture, carpentry, stenography, printing, and shoemaking.[136] The program that experienced the greatest increase was the normal school, training teachers for new black schools in Tennessee and throughout the South. The school's yearbook, *The Radio,* noted, "The State requires from one to two years of college work to teach in a first class elementary school and four years of college work to teach in a first class high school. . . . Judging by the number [of students] . . . pursuing four years of college work there will be a much larger number of graduates."[137]

Indeed, the enrollment of students seeking educational certification through the Normal School Department increased. Five of six graduates from the class of 1925 pursued teaching; twelve of sixteen graduates from the class of 1926 became teachers; and the class of 1927 produced nearly thirty teachers.[138] In addition to graduates who followed a traditional college curriculum, attendees in summer sessions received enough training to begin or continue teaching in K–12 classrooms, mostly in rural areas, as the number of schools in Tennessee exploded from 1909 to 1930. Tennessee A&I noted in 1925, "In fact the school . . . has grown to be the largest Summer School in the world for Negroes, with an enrollment of more than 1,200 teachers from Tennessee and adjoining states."[139]

Roger Williams University was to African Americans what David Lipscomb College and Peabody College were to whites, training students to teach, preach, or perform mission work.[140] The school conferred its first bachelor's degree in the mid-1870s and relocated to a new campus largely purchased by the American Baptist Home Mission Society (ABHMS) after a local white Baptist minister led the $30,000 fundraising effort. Land to build a permanent campus was purchased in 1874, on Hillsboro Road in west Nashville, next to Vanderbilt University. Roger Williams University's catalog announced a master's degree program as early as 1886. Neither the bachelor's nor master's degree was the equivalent of a tradi-

FIG. 3.9. Roger Williams University collegiate class of 1899. Library of Congress.

tional degree but certain courses *did* transfer to other black colleges. As previously mentioned, the school temporarily closed after several buildings were destroyed by fire.

Roger Williams reopened in north Nashville in 1908. Eight years later the school continued to operate on a shoe-string budget of roughly $5,000. Its new property, including land and buildings, was valued at an estimated $98,000.[141] Roger Williams offered an academic curriculum with limited college training and included the study of Latin and English for four years and at least one year of mathematics, science, history, Greek, Bible, and foreign language. The majority of female students followed a general education program that qualified them to teach. In addition, the school offered several courses in industrial education including cooking, sewing, millinery, construction, theology, and bookkeeping.[142]

The Bureau of Education reported that after its reopening in 1908, Roger Williams University primarily offered secondary education with a few "ministers of meager education" studying theology.[143] Though Roger Williams was more accurately a high school than a university, Davidson County needed the city's black colleges to offer secondary training. Not until the 1930s, with the infusion of money from the Rosenwald Fund of Chicago, would additional black high schools open in the county. Other than Pearl High School, located near downtown Nashville, there were no black public high schools outside the Nashville city limits in Davidson County.[144]

Women and "Municipal Mothers"

In the 1895–1896 *Catalog of Fisk University,* the administration and faculty officially took a position on women's education: "Fisk University has from the first recognized the absolute necessity of the *right education* of the girls and young women of the race, whose elevation and advancement it was founded to promote. . . . In the classroom they have equal advantages with the young men and can pursue any one of the courses of study established in the University."[145] The following year Meharry College's Bellina A. Moore graduated as valedictorian of her pharmacy class in 1897. At commencement she declared, "[H]ome [was] the best and highest field for women, but not for all women. Men [had] held the heights so long that they were selfish and wanted women to stay on the lower levels . . . [but] women [were] entering every profession and succeeding in all."[146] Nashville's black colleges and universities were a home base for African American women's activism and education. Female graduates of local colleges worked as agents of change within black communities and as public advocates for Nashville's African Americans in particular.

FIG. 3.10. Fisk University 1899 graduating collegiate class. Library of Congress.

Women were a part of Fisk from the outset. Female students were in attendance on the first day of classes, although they were severely outnumbered for the school's first thirty years. Worthy of note, the first group of Jubilee Singers, organized in 1871, included seven women and four men. Within the student population only three women, out of nearly fifty students, graduated from class of 1889. As historian Sally Schwager commented, "[C]oeducational schools for southern blacks had proliferated after the War, and black families placed extremely high value on the education of both their sons and daughters," but black college men outnumbered college women in the U.S. until World War I.[147] Women's studies scholar Linda Perkins noted that in 1890 only thirty black women held B.A. degrees, compared to over three hundred black men and twenty-five hundred white women.[148]

Although both white and black women enjoyed greater opportunity for higher education and professional prospects to some extent, the colleges they attended often perpetuated conventional female roles (see chapter 2). Particularly in the

South, women were expected to serve and nurture in an effort to create a clean and healthy home environment and to use their time outside the home in service to the community. By 1889 the Industrial Department of Fisk boasted that the sewing class consisted of one hundred young women, including boarders and day pupils, who devoted an hour a day to the "art of making and mending linens" for the kitchen, bed, and bath using the university's sewing machines.[149] In 1890, an article entitled "Training Our Girls for the Responsibility of Life," applied the cult of domesticity to black women: "Evidently, God intended woman to be queen of the home. . . . Man's power is to determine, not so with woman's; her power is not active, progressive, and defensive, but to guide, direct, and teach. . . . Her past condition and training have been such that her training is a very vexed question."[150]

The year 1895 marked the first official instance whereby Fisk outlined the purpose of its newly established Department of Domestic Science: "Fisk University aims to properly qualify its students for the duties and responsibilities of home and social life, as well as for those of the school-room. Hence the establishment of this special department for the supplemental education of young women."[151] When the industrial kitchen was completed, black female students received lessons in cooking, nursing, and hygiene so that they might "render great service to society by teaching truer and healthier ways of living, and more rational methods of caring for the sick when they enter upon their life's work among people."[152] A decade later, the Fisk catalog of 1904–1905 emphasized the responsibilities of black women at home as well as in employment fields of service: "[Whether] scrubbing a floor, or washing a dish thoroughly [women] should be taught and compelled to do everything well, even the very smallest thing. Life is made up of small things, and these done well make life a success. . . . The mother of the father of this Country was not an educated woman, but she was plain and ordinary."[153]

Even with the nearly 50 percent female-graduate rate by 1910, Fisk's emphasis on black men over women was apparent. In 1908 university president James Merrill announced the school's mission: "The development of Christian manhood in an education for service."[154] Meanwhile Roger Williams University offered similar coursework and maintained an average of one hundred students from 1908 to 1916 (60 percent male, 40 percent female). Tennessee A&I also maintained a significant female enrollment, but once again, most were in domestic departments or teacher training. On May 27, 1924, Lora A. Myers of Nashville was the first woman to earn a bachelor's degree from Tennessee A&I, after the state authorized the school's collegiate status. While the number of female students increased at Fisk, Roger Williams, and Tennessee A&I, women were generally placed into the gendered curriculum that resulted in a clear-cut set of professions.

Despite certain disadvantages, young female graduates played a vital role in the improvement of their communities not only as actors but as mediators within a racial hierarchy less threatened by black women than by black men. The efforts of African American women remained necessary for the improvement of their community as they endeavored to raise it out of poverty. Institutions of higher education for white women developed feminine resourcefulness and refinement and served as "finishing schools." For black women, higher education taught practical and necessary skills and served as "survival schools." Both models of education for women provided academic training and intellectual stimulation in an institutional setting—a positive development for women of any race or class.

The term *municipal housekeeper* refers most often to progressive middle- and upper-class white women who believed that city conditions were an extension of the home, and therefore part of a private sphere over which women had domain. Thus, to preserve and protect their families, reform-minded white women argued that it was their responsibility, if not their duty, to maintain the health and welfare of the wider public through "cleanup" sanitation campaigns, milk drives, disease prevention, and the like.[155] The charitable and community service of white women remained more philanthropic: raising money for good causes but with less direct engagement with efforts on the ground.

Black women were generally not included in the municipal housekeeper movement, but that does not mean they did not play an essential role in urban improvement. They were progressives in their own right, participating in social reform and health education campaigns, teaching in one-room schoolhouses, organizing church functions, and taking care of the home. They were more than municipal housekeepers: they were *municipal mothers,* invested members of their communities who sought to preserve and protect the black family. Barred from membership in the political and social club movement of white women, these women formed parallel groups such as the National Association of Colored Women's Clubs (NACW), Day Homes Club, and the Phyllis Wheatley Club.

Another organization that operated in a similar capacity in Nashville was the Woman's Missionary Union, with many female students and faculty wives from Fisk University and Meharry Medical College as members. The establishment and strength of black women's clubs and service organizations confirm Glenda Gilmore's findings in *Gender and Jim Crow*: "Black women discovered fresh approaches to serving their communities and crafted new tactics designed to dull the blade of white supremacy."[156]

Several educated black women in Nashville used their college training for individual and collective gain. However, most did so with the help of their husbands' support and status in the community. Before Lugenia and John Hope arrived in Nashville, Lugenia worked and taught under Jane Addams at Kings Daughters and the Hull House in Chicago. When John accepted a faculty appointment at Roger Williams University in 1897, Lugenia taught local community classes in Nashville.[157] After moving to Atlanta, Lugenia Burns Hope established and led the Neighborhood Union in 1908, an educational and service organization that became a model of urban southern progressivism.

In addition to the Hope family, Roger Williams also enjoyed the leadership of Arthur and Willa Townsend—a formidable husband-and-wife team. Arthur, a physician and professor, was the president of Roger Williams from 1913 to 1918. Willa Townsend taught at the university and directed the music and choral programs; she also served on the Sunday School Publishing Board that produced the *Baptist Standard Hymnal*. Townsend was active in the community as a member of the National Baptist Convention, the Women's Auxiliary of the Nashville Medical Association, and the NAACP.[158]

Two of the original Fisk Jubilee Singers joined the black educated elite, forming strong partnerships with their husbands while also making individual contributions. Georgia Gordon Taylor volunteered her talents in the black community until her death in 1913. She joined her husband, local black businessman Preston Taylor, in an effort to establish Greenwood Cemetery for African Americans (1888), a mortuary (1888), and the Greenwood Recreational Park for Negroes (1905). Prior to 1888 African Americans had been buried in Mt. Ararat (1869), which later became part of Greenwood Cemetery (1989) and known as Greenwood Cemetery West.

Ella Sheppard Moore was the de facto leader of the Jubilee Singers during their final two tours in the late 1870s. She married Reverend George Moore (also a Fisk graduate) in 1882. After living in Washington, D.C., the couple returned to Nashville in 1892 and reestablished their relationship with their alma mater—even building their house next to the school's campus. In addition to assisting Fisk's various choirs and sometimes singing herself, Moore began delivering public lectures and publishing articles on African American and women's issues. She worked for the American Missionary Association, NACW, and Tennessee Women's Missionary Union. Additionally, the Moores were friends with Booker and Margaret Washington, as well as with Frederick Douglass. George Moore was also one of the first black men to be appointed to the Fisk Board of Trustees.[159]

In 1865, Minnie Lou Scott (later Crosthwaite) watched as Fisk's white founder, Erastus Milo Cravath, and his wife first rode onto campus, arriving in a carriage also carrying Tennessee's governor, William G. Brownlow. Just six years old, Minnie Lou became one of Fisk's earliest and youngest students, attending the primary school from 1866. She later enrolled in Fisk's Teacher Training Department and graduated in 1877 at the age of seventeen. In 1884 Minnie Lou Crosthwaite passed the teacher's examination for Nashville schools and became one of the first of four black public school teachers in Nashville.[160] Her husband, Scott Crosthwaite, later became the city's first African American principal.

James C. Napier, the first black man to be elected to the Nashville City Council, led the effort to pass a resolution allowing black teachers in local primary and secondary schools for African Americans. Napier's efforts to secure positions for black teachers, such as Crosthwaite, succeeded. But it must also be noted, as Howard Rabinowitz wrote, that "this early display of black power had its costs, ... [as] blacks accommodated themselves to the system of segregated schools and produced a group with a vested interest in its continuation."[161]

After teaching for twenty years in Nashville and Knoxville, Minnie Lou Crosthwaite returned to Fisk and completed her bachelor's degree in 1903. She later joined the faculty at Fisk, holding several positions that included math instructor, advisor, registrar, and alumni trustee representative. She also served in many community groups, including the YWCA's Blue Triangle Branch (for black women, 1919), City Federation of Colored Women's Clubs (1911), and the Day Homes' Club (1907). Crosthwaite spent her life serving others as an educator and activist for nearly sixty years before her death in 1937.

A small number of African American women from Nashville's HBCUs would reach elite professional status as physicians. Georgia Esther Lee Patton completed the normal course at Central Tennessee College (later Walden University) in 1890. She immediately began taking courses in the Meharry Medical Department that same year. Upon graduation, she became the first African American woman in Tennessee to receive a license to practice medicine and perform surgery. Patton's career took her to Liberia in Africa before she returned to marry in 1897 and practice medicine in Memphis.[162] In 1905 Emma R. Wheeler graduated from Walden University's Medical, Dental, and Pharmaceutical Colleges. Following graduation, she and her husband, Dr. John Wheeler, moved to Chattanooga to practice medicine and later opened Walden Hospital in 1915.

Not all female graduates went on to such significant careers, but Patton and Wheeler remain proof that African American women could do exceptional things given the opportunity for higher education. Glenda Gilmore summarized the contrasting goals of race, gender, and power: "White middle-class women lobbied to obtain services *from* their husbands, brothers, and sons; black women lobbied to obtain services *for* their husbands, brothers, and sons."[163]

Conclusion

In 1895 Booker T. Washington called for cooperation between the races, but as one of his contemporaries noted, "His message, like the seed in the parable, fell on good ground and brought forth much fruit; elsewhere the ground was stony and the seed was choked. The South heard, but the South was divided."[164] Over sixty years after the passage of the Thirteenth (1865), Fourteenth (1868), and Fifteenth (1870) Amendments, southern blacks were still denied equal treatment and political participation. The threat of violence, racial profiling, and lynching also remained a constant source of fear for blacks who sought recognition as American citizens rather than second-class subjects. In a compelling 1917 article entitled "Do Not Rock the Boat," one Fiskite attempted to cloak problematic racial issues with national patriotism: "The United States is at war. . . . It is not the white man's war; nor is it the black man's war. All of us are together in the same boat on the sea of war; [and] . . . every American is under the highest obligations to his country to say to those who think not, 'Do not rock the boat!'"[165]

Yet throughout the period, Nashville maintained a unique urban role as a center of African American education. When Booker T. Washington visited Nashville in 1909 he had noted that Nashville's black community maintained higher literacy rates and a greater "average of intelligence" than those in other southern towns and cities.[166] Washington attributed much of this progress to the existence of Fisk University, Roger Williams University, and Walden College (which then included Meharry Medical College). Washington promoted an industrial model for black higher education, and Tennessee A&I (which opened three years after his visit) was certainly a success story given the goals of many black leaders and the fears of many white leaders before 1930.

Like Washington, Du Bois also applauded Nashville and its black colleges and universities, arguing that at Harvard "he found no better teachers, only teachers better known."[167] He was not satisfied with industrial education and described the need for schools like Fisk, Howard, and Atlanta Universities: "It can thus be seen that the work of education in the South began with higher institutions of training, which threw off as their foliage common schools, and later industrial schools, and at the same time strove to shoot their roots ever deeper toward college and university training. That this was an inevitable and necessary development, sooner or later, goes without saying."[168]

In contrast to Tennessee A&I's emphasis on service and technical training, Fisk sought to train the mind but did not discount service. In his inaugural address, Fisk president Dr. Fayette Avery McKenzie (1915–25) argued that culture and service were the ideals of the university. McKenzie further articulated the meaning of these ideals: "There are those who are inclined to throw cultural education into contrast with industrial education—the education of the mind rather than the hands, the education for thought rather than for earning, the education for a life rather than for a living, for divinity and eternity rather than for existence and the present."[169] Fisk and Meharry intentionally trained African Americans to ascend into a professional class. For example, by 1920 there were approximately 3,855 black doctors in the United States, most of whom were graduates of either Howard or Meharry.[170] Fisk and Meharry attracted bright and motivated young blacks from across the south, many of whom would contribute to the city long after their matriculation.

Additionally Nashville produced more black teachers than did any other southern city with a comparable population. Black teachers, after Reconstruction and in the first decades of Jim Crow, were community leaders and interracial diplomats. According to Adam Fairclough, "Teachers made up the backbone of the black middle class, and were, along with ministers, the most important source of black leadership."[171] The link between education and personal empowerment was clear. Fisk, Tennessee A&I, and Roger Williams produced thousands of teachers who would proudly serve on the front lines in primary and secondary schools throughout the south and the nation.

With institutionalized segregation, black urban boosters worked to develop their corner of the Nashville community. The black commercial district that ran parallel to the campuses of Fisk, Meharry, and Tennessee A&I provided a sense of identity and promoted African American businesses while also emphasizing higher education. Most of Nashville's black businessmen were directly and actively involved in affairs at Fisk, Meharry, and Tennessee A&I. Many were trustees, and some were part- or full-time members of the faculty. By 1915 Nashville had the state's second largest black population, and the city also featured African American–owned banks, dozens of black businesses, four HBCUs, and a prosperous black elite class.[172] Washington made note of the economic and social gains:

> [Education] has made the Negro population stable, law-abiding, and industrious. They are respected by the white inhabitants, and racial friction is rare. Property and commercial interests of the Nashville Negroes are large, and rapidly increasing.... The total of all the taxable property held by Negroes has a value of several millions. They have two banks, a hospital, and several publishing houses.[173]

During this period, education was the common thread weaving together the fragile strands needed for racial uplift and stability. Black men and women who attended local colleges and universities used their education, in turn, to benefit those around them. For some it meant taking their new skill set to another city or state. For the majority it meant living and working in Nashville, setting in motion reform and commercial efforts that would have a prolific effect. The city's African American students gained visibility for themselves and used education as a tool for self-determination, social activism, and racial uplift. Many alumni used their education and talents to become paid professionals, breaking cycles of ignorance and destitution.

As the number of graduates increased from 1865 to 1930, so did organizations, businesses, agencies, and schools for African Americans living in Nashville. The symbiotic relationship between the city and its black colleges is clear in Booker T. Washington's appeal to Nashvillians, "for justice on the part of the whites, industry and reliability on the part of . . . their black neighbors . . . and cooperation on the part of both."[174]

4

Pursuit(s) of Happiness
College Youth Culture, Campus Life, and Leisure

> First floor full . . . Gallery gorgeous with gala galaxy of girls. Balcony bristling with blustering boys . . . Vendome Theater the place . . . It was an audience full of college spirit.
>
> —The *Hustler* (December 21, 1910)

On her way to school, in 1902, a young woman from Ward Seminary met a young man from Vanderbilt's medical school who was also on his way to class. They talked as they walked along their shared path before parting ways. This chance meeting sparked a romance, and after several weeks, the two found themselves leaving class early so that they might spend more time together. The day after a squabble, the young man ran into the young woman getting off the streetcar, and as she dropped her books in the rain, he began to apologize for his recent behavior. Five minutes later, the "smiling Senior and the beaming Sophomore were blissfully unconscious of the mud beneath and the water above. . . . For two people, at least, the weather prophecy was incorrect for that day. The weather was perfect."[1]

Young white men and women born *before* the start of the Civil War who attended colleges and universities in the 1860s and 1870s were constrained by antebellum expectations. Social events were still based on literary societies, town-and-gown affairs, glee clubs, and debate teams. In other words, extracurricular interaction remained under administrative control and largely academic. Those born *after* the Civil War who entered higher education in 1880s and 1890s were key players in the formation of modern college and city life in New South Nashville. College life created a new developmental stage between adolescence and adulthood that afforded greater freedom and less accountability. Thus, the significant rise in the number of men and women attending colleges and universities from 1865 to 1930 paralleled a shift in social norms and acceptable behavior among students on and off campus. For them, the "weather was perfect" to mix the business of school with new forms of recreational pleasure. By the turn of the century, college life included a burgeoning of public spaces where young men and women could pursue relationships without the traditional restraints of strict chaperonage or rules of courtship. Men and women interacted more *because* of the outlets provided by education.

New pursuits of happiness were determined by divided spaces and unwritten rules that created artificial boundaries for and between white men, white women in coed settings, white women in single-gender settings, black men, and black women. In addition, this period witnessed the advent of now-familiar labels such as "geeks," "jocks," and "preppies." Young people found themselves simultaneously freer and more pressured to conform. The intersectional roles of administrators, faculty, students, and community leaders also sheds light on the diversity of experience for college students. At the heart of cultural and collegiate change was greater autonomy and choice. Student choice was influenced and redefined by three consistent forces: the creation of new spaces (both public and private), leisure as a commodity to be consumed, and the participation of college students and young adults in unchaperoned leisure activities.[2] Schools and students reacted to cultural and educational changes in different ways: resistance, rejection, suppression, acceptance, or active promotion. There was no singular pursuit of happiness; rather, there were multiple paths at varied paces.

After the turn of the century, college life included much more than college coursework. In 1909 Woodrow Wilson, then Princeton University president, wrote that college men could be made to study and perform on examinations, but their spirits were elsewhere: "The side shows are so numerous, so diverting—so important, if you will—that they have swallowed up the circus, and those who perform in the main tent must often whistle for their audiences, discouraged and humiliated."[3] Vanderbilt chancellor James Kirkland gave a series of chapel talks in 1910 that echoed the concerns of many administrators and faculty. Kirkland went even further than Wilson, fearing the long-term consequences of cultural change:

> The temptations of college life of to-day are much greater than ever before. The dangers are greater and the freedom is more complete and the men, therefore, should either be made stronger or else go down entirely. All education ought to result in character or else its failure. . . . The college waste-heap is worse than the commercial waste-heap. It is very sad; it is incurable. There are over 100 college graduates in Sing Sing prison. One-third of men seeking beds in the Bowery missions in New York City have been to college.[4]

In the late nineteenth century, new forms of entertainment were generally viewed by administrators as distracting at best, and dangerous at worst. This is not to say that supervision, strict rules, and chaperonage ceased to exist at the college-level institutions, including those in Nashville. However, free time and new outlets and forms of entertainments notably increased. College administrators fought to keep their footing on shifting cultural sands without negatively affecting student recruitment. Historian Helen Horowitz believes that most did so with some success: "However alien the fraternity and club world from academic purposes, by the early twentieth century college administrators understood it and believed that they could contain its potentially destructive elements."[5]

College men and women lived by increasingly complex rules based on setting and circumstance and, in turn, learned to navigate between curricular and extracurricular worlds. This grew even more complicated for young African Americans. The differences among the campus cultures of Nashville's HBCUs and Vanderbilt, Peabody, or Ward-Belmont were stark. As extracurricular offerings increased and Victorian discipline and decorum eased on white campuses, black colleges and black students faced generational and racial roadblocks that sought to discourage frivolity.

Colleges and universities were still places of scholarship and solemn study, but intellectual pursuit was only one component of the broader experience sought by New South men and women. By the 1920s most schools had implemented competitive athletic programs and permitted a Greek (or alternative) system of sororities, fraternities, and social clubs. The constructs of modern college life as we know them today, with students' lives intersecting in and out of the classroom, were firmly in place by 1930. Because of the richness and variation of local institutions and students of higher education, Nashville provides a window through which the evolution of the southern college experience can be viewed, examined, and better understood. For better or worse, this emergent college culture in Nashville became a symbol of New South modernity.

More broadly, higher education expanded sites of interaction for young people with less formality than antebellum courtship and also reflected new ideas about homosocial and heterosocial interaction.[6] The terms *homosocial* and *heterosocial* are relatively new to academic language; they describe social relationships and groupings that were prevalent in the Gilded Age/Progressive Era. Homosocial simply refers to single-sex groups (for example, athletic teams and sororities), while heterosocial refers to groups of men and women who intermingled more freely and casually (for example, at club dances and sporting events). The terms are intended to describe social groupings with heterosocial involving social (nonsexual) relationships between members of the opposite sex and homosocial relating to social relationships based on single-sex membership or participation.

New spaces for college interaction ranged from gymnasiums and theaters to parks, from football stadiums to country clubs. This transformation also, at times, challenged authority. Historian Paula Fass has argued that the premise is oversimplified: "The youth of the twenties did not reject the authority of their nurture, nor were they symptoms of the irrelevance of the society's norms. On the contrary . . . the young translated the changes in nurture into new behavioral norms which continue to organize our lives."[7] Many middle- and upper-class adults and reformers worried that young people would only associate "a good time" with cheap thrills and vices such as alcohol and sex.[8]

College students were but one ingredient that constituted New South Nashville. The advent and development of leisure as a product to be bought, sold, and consumed created a new industry in the 1890s. The leisure industry was naturally suited to young, single men and women, independent of parental supervision, who sought a break from the rigor and monotony of academic study. Moreover, leisure and mass entertainment in Nashville grew at a faster pace than in many similarly sized southern cities.

Nashville had served as a cultural reservoir in the South before, during, and immediately after the Civil War. The city was connected by river or rail to other major cities, regularly hosted famous performers and opera/theater companies, and claimed antebellum presidents Andrew Jackson and James K. Polk as hometown heroes. At the Tennessee Centennial Exposition in 1897, local residents and visitors alike marveled at the electric lights, Memphis pyramid, and exhibition buildings that surrounded the Athenian centerpiece. Below, a manmade lake swarmed with gondolas giving guests rides, while others enjoyed the wonder of the Streets of Cairo and Chinese Village. The 1.8 million total visitors also enjoyed the Vanity Fair section offering rides and exotic animals.

Located less than three miles from all of Nashville's colleges, this world's fair-style event gave the city's leisure industry a modern jumpstart, and college students took full advantage of the momentum.[9] Students from Vanderbilt, Ward-Belmont (and predecessor schools), Peabody, and Lipscomb, and to an extent African Americans at local HBCUs, explored new on- and off-campus activities as they molded college life into its modern form.

Urban Identity and Fun in the City

The commercialization of leisure reimagined what it meant to rest and relax. Leisure was commodified, becoming an industry in and of itself. The idea was that if leisure cost money, then the more money spent, the more "fun" experienced.[10] In turn, new forms of entertainment helped to redefine meanings of class, gender, and race in the public sphere. Cities represented modern outlets of freedom that reinforced the capitalist machine of maximum production and increased consumption. By 1890 such trends trickled down to growing urban centers in the South. The role(s) of and reactions to the emergent youth culture would shape new notions of community. College students, with more money and free time, were a driving force behind the evolving urban identity of Nashville.

Lawrence Levine added an instrumental piece of historiography in his study of northern cities in *Highbrow/Lowbrow: The Emergence of Cultural Hierarchy in America*. In the late 1800s and early 1900s, a shift in demographics occurred in many cities, particularly in the North with its influx of immigrants and the dramatic increase in industrialization. Upper class families reacted by erecting cultural boundaries that defined acceptable and unacceptable behavior reflected in recreational choices. However, another defining feature of labor production and cultural consumption, according to Levine, was the emergence of a new middle class. This "middlebrow," if you will, participated within public spaces both as the more privileged arm of the labor class as well as an agent of reform for the social ills and immoral leisure activities of urban areas.[11] It was precisely this "middlebrow" that would also transform white universities.

From 1865 to 1930, Nashville reflected the shift of wealth with old-money families and businesses challenged by the rise of a new middle class, both white and black. As the leisure industry expanded, many in the middle class found neutral ground whereby some forms of recreation were acceptable (certain social clubs, parks, and so on) while certain other behaviors were not, such as gambling and drinking. These changes were set in motion by industrialization and the rise of consumer capitalism. While Levine focused on northern cities, on many levels, Nashville also mirrored this leisure revolution and its effect on social class hierarchy.[12]

In Nashville the reputation of certain streets and establishments allowed only limited interaction between social classes. Part of the 1915 Ward-Belmont rules stated that students could go shopping in pairs on weekends, but they could not pass through certain parts of the Arcade, which was an area known for shopping but also known for its nearby bars, pool halls, and gambling. Likewise, "Printer's Alley" and "Jack's Alley" grew from an alleyway behind Broadway (what would be called Nashville's Main Street) into a backstreet full of music bars and beer dives.[13] Several billiard halls catered to the middle and upper classes, such as the Olympic Bowling Alley and Billiard Parlor, which an advertisement described this

FIG. 4.1. The Arcade, which opened in downtown Nashville in 1902, was modeled after an arcade in Italy. It served as a hub of social activity and consumerism in the early twentieth century and remains standing today. Metropolitan Government of Nashville and Davidson County Archives.

way: "Gentleman's Place of Amusement, Vanderbilt men must come see us as we have six tracks and seven tables."[14] As a whole, privileged white men at Vanderbilt were free to move about Nashville's downtown as they pleased.

Wealthy whites anxiously sought to create a space away from the disorder of downtown's rowdy club and music scene. Social, business, and service clubs, as well as private parks for golf and other activities, separated those with means or privilege from the working class. Such boundaries were artificial because they were largely determined by who could pay, who was invited to apply, and who had the unspoken connections necessary to gain social access to certain circles and organizations. In Nashville middle- and upper-class whites began moving away from downtown with many settling in new suburbs west of downtown. This was aided by the extension of streetcar lines, electricity, and public transportation prior to 1920. With these new developments, residents had more land and more room, for preferred leisure activities not connected with the general public.

By 1890 two prominent businessmen, James C. Warner and Overton Lea, each had a golf course on his estate. Warner's course was located at his home, called Renraw, on Gallatin Pike in east Nashville, and Lea's eight-hole course was located in west Nashville at his family home, called Lealand, on Granny White Pike near what was then Nashville Bible School (David Lipscomb College). The Nashville Golf Club was organized at the Maxwell House Hotel in 1900. After the clubhouse was built on part of the Whitworth estate on Harding Road in west Nashville, both white male and female members could mix and mingle informally or officially socialize at planned party events.[15]

The Nashville Golf and Country Club ventured west when Belle Meade developer Luke Lea convinced his fellow club members that the move was advantageous, both as an outlet for leisure and a haven for residential living. In 1914, 144 acres of the Belle Meade development were transferred to the club, which was renamed the Belle Meade Country Club in 1921.[16] Many members of the New South generation were associated with Vanderbilt or Ward-Belmont and entertained regularly at Belle Meade Country Club, the Hermitage Club, the Centennial Club, and others.[17] Thus, Nashville's elite controlled, to an extent, who had access to high society.

The leisure industry blossomed throughout the growing city and its colleges, creating a symbiotic relationship that permitted young men and women to enjoy camaraderie off campus. The 1896 Ward Seminary Annual Announcement stated, "Young ladies pursuing their education in a large city enjoy many advantages that cannot be obtained elsewhere . . . [because] cities are becoming more and more the centers of culture and refinement."[18] College activities transitioned from guest lectures and formal receptions to those more closely associated with the glitz and glamour of the Gilded Age—dance halls, amusement parks, and variety shows. Such "cheap amusements" were largely outside of administrative control. College rules and regulations forbade bad behavior but were difficult to enforce off campus. Regardless of administrative efforts to regulate forms of social interaction, the promise of freedom and fun increasingly attracted college students regardless of socioeconomic background. And students at all of Nashville's colleges and universities benefited from the growth of entertainment venues, local parks, and off-campus events.

One such popular seasonal activity was roller skating at the Hippodrome Skating Rink, which opened February 5, 1906 and was conveniently located just west of Vanderbilt on West End Avenue.[19] Many school clubs and societies held skating parties, but the rink also attracted many single men and women who came in homosocial groups as well as couples. It was a typical sight at the rink to see a "large and jolly crowd skat[ing] to the music of a brass band."[20] The *Hustler* gives an insightful account into the intersection of commercialized leisure, new urban space, and male/female relationships: "From the number of boys that are seen leaving the campus going in that direction every afternoon and after supper there certainly must be a fascination with a pair of skates on that one does not get from any other source of pleasure. . . . It is worth going over to see the crowd and the girls, even if a fellow has not the nerve to put on the seemingly uncontrollable wheels."[21]

Other nonschool-sponsored entertainments offered "fun in the city" outside the classroom. Cumberland Park opened in 1891, and a racetrack and grandstand, named the Coliseum, was built to seat over five thousand people. The Coliseum operated as a racetrack approximately two miles outside of downtown on the Nolensville Turnpike. Although racetracks attracted some unsavory patrons, many families and young adults visited to watch horse, bike, and foot races.[22] The Cumberland Fair and Racing Association was formed and sponsored harness racing from 1891 to 1894. Foot races (or running events) were held on the track from 1893 to 1906, including some events sponsored by Vanderbilt's track team and field day competitions. In 1904 the first automobile race took place, and two years later the first Tennessee State Fair was held on the grounds. From 1906 to 1930 the fairgrounds expanded their offerings to include a large swimming pool called Cascade Plunge, a variety of on-site restaurants, an amusement park called Fair Park, and car races.[23] Races and other attractions made Cumberland Park and Sulphur Dell (an athletic ball park located just behind the state capitol) the most popular outdoor sites of mass entertainment in town.

It was also during the late nineteenth and early twentieth centuries that Nashville became a center for theatrical and musical performances in the South. Male

FIG. 4.2. State Fair Grounds in the 1920s. Metropolitan Government of Nashville and Davidson County Archives.

and female students alike enjoyed the performances and tours that frequently passed through Nashville.[24] Students from local colleges and universities either rode streetcars or sometimes loaded up on horse-drawn wagons to go downtown to visit one of the city's theaters. Not only did college students patronize artists and groups who came to Nashville to perform, but students from local colleges also attended school-sponsored events held at local venues. For example, Ward-Belmont School and Vanderbilt University sponsored a musical series for several years and hosted events at the Ryman, which featured prominent lecturers and extended an open invitation to the public.

The number of performances held in large auditorium spaces continued to increase dramatically in the late nineteenth century. As a result, new theaters and venues opened and existing spaces were expanded to meet this demand.[25] The Adelphi Theater first opened in 1850 and was later renamed the Grand Opera House. The Grand Opera House boasted one of the largest stages in the nation, and the *American* described its grandeur as "a temple to the muses clothed in the splendor of Aladdin's Palace."[26] Others included the Olympic Theater (renovated in 1875), Masonic Theater (also renovated in 1875), the New Park Theater (1884), and the Vendome Theater (1887).[27] The Vendome Theater also reflected the latest technology of the day with steam heat and electric lighting. On January 8, 1894, the well-known opera singer Adelina Patti performed at the Vendome and according to the *Nashville American,* "Every seat was taken, every box, and there were five hundred to six hundred standing in various parts of the theatre. It was a triumph of the greatest sort."[28] By 1890 Nashville's combined indoor venues could hold over six thousand people. As Martha Ingram documents in *Apollo's Struggle,* the number of theaters was impressive for a city whose population hovered at only seventy-six thousand during a time when large venues were not common.[29]

No theater shaped the trajectory of Nashville's urban identity more than the Ryman Auditorium. Lula C. Naff, manager of the Ryman from 1915 to 1955, once asked, "Who wanted to see [evangelist] Billy Sunday when they could go see [actress] Mary Pickford for a dime?"[30] Her question was timely. During the first two decades of the twentieth century, mass entertainment in the South reflected a distinct shift from the religious to the secular. The Ryman Auditorium was no exception, first opening as the Union Tabernacle Auditorium in 1892. The stated purpose of the building was to be "strictly religious, non-sectarian, non-denominational and for the purpose of promoting religion, morality and the elevation of humanity to a higher plane."[31] The auditorium, situated in the heart of downtown, was instantly popular and featured preachers like Sam Jones, who held revivals and delivered powerful sermons widely attended by Nashvillians and people from surrounding areas.

At the turn-of-the-century the Ryman's emphasis shifted from religious revivals to secular entertainment. Religious events at the Ryman did not disappear; in fact, the interior space still looked more like a church than a theater—which later led to the Ryman's nickname "The Mother Church of Country Music." With a new stage (built in 1901) and balcony (1897), Ryman Auditorium quickly became the premier downtown venue with greater space for audiences and performers.[32]

As Nashville grew as a cultural and intellectual center in the South, college students helped add "Music City" to Nashville's "Athens of the South" reputation. Throughout the first quarter of the twentieth century, they enjoyed new venues and took advantage of new-found freedoms away from campus. Attending events at the Ryman mixed entertainment and education in a socially acceptable way, even though female and male students were often seated in separate sections.[33] College students were a large part of Nashville's audience base, making the city an attractive stop for artists, politicians, musicians, and other performers who could cater to a young audience.

The notoriety associated with the Ryman as the "go to" place for entertainment was due, in large part, to local colleges and their students who regularly attended events. As Rosalyn Kirsch, a student at Ward-Belmont, recalled in 1916: "Whenever we went to the Ryman, the whole school went on special streetcars. . . . We didn't have to wear hats or gloves when we went, and you can imagine what a bunch of roughnecks we looked like. As soon as the car stopped we all jumped out and dashed at full speed to the Ryman a block up the street."[34] Such comments also reveal the trickle-up nature of commercialized leisure. Ironically, upper-class women dressed down to go out in public, a marked shift from twenty years prior, when their attire and comportment was critical to their high-society status and reputation.

Other notable events and performances (1900-1930) held in Nashville and attended by college students included: the Italian baritone Giuseppe Campanari, president William H. Taft, Booker T. Washington, the "world's greatest violinist" Jan Kubelik, the virtuoso pianist Ignace Jan Paderewski, the American Ballet Theater in *Swan Lake,* comedian Will Rogers, and the great Irish tenor John McCormack. When Theodore Roosevelt delivered a speech at the Ryman in 1907, he complimented the Vanderbilt football team on their successful season. In response, students in the Vanderbilt section "whooped" and hollered for over a minute, leading Ryman officials to intervene.

What would become the Grand Old Opry first began when the WSM radio station launched a weekly Saturday night program entitled "Barn Dance." The new name was born in 1925 when the radio program host, Judge Hay, commented, "For the past hour we have been listening to music taken largely from Grand Opera, but from now on we will present 'The Grand Ole Opry.'"[35] The Ryman would serve as the home of the Grand Ole Opry from 1943 to 1974. As the Grand Ole Opry made musical history at Ryman Auditorium, neighboring Honky Tonk Row on downtown's lower Broadway became a creative breeding ground for hopeful performers, musicians, and songwriters yearning to make it in "Music City."

In addition to live entertainment theaters, Nashville's first moving picture theater opened in 1907. However, movies were largely seen as unacceptable for unchaperoned college students until after 1915. In 1918 actor and comedian Charlie Chaplin came for a visit to tour the city. While visiting, he found the time to go to Ward-Belmont, and students fawned over the movie star. As one student commented, "He is nice looking isn't he, and didn't he seem to enjoy himself? You are not accustomed to having a gentleman bow twice and then fall down in the midst of five hundred girls are you?"[36] Doubtless, Chaplin fell as a stunt to entertain, typical of his on-screen personality and comic style, but his celebrity status reflected the power of movies as a more affordable and accessible alternative to live theater and performances. The *Nashville Banner* addressed the topic in 1914: "There is nothing pernicious about moving pictures—any more than there is about grand opera. In fact, a good, well-ventilated moving pictures theater would be a decided asset in a place like this."[37]

By 1925 movies and celebrity culture had infiltrated college life and perhaps most affected young women seeking love and romance, who also grew more bold when interacting with men. As Rosalyn Kirsch, a Ward-Belmont student who graduated in 1921, admitted in her memory book:

> This is about the most lovesick bunch of girls I have ever known. Their motto is undoubtedly, "Anything for a man!" In the movies on Saturday night, in the exciting love parts . . . they yell and scream and clap and stamp. And when the final close up is flashed on the screen, the shouting back and forth would certainly make the hero's ears burn. . . . Most of the girls' favorite expression is "He could have me in a minute." (Like every man on earth is just dying to have them.) They sit up in the windows and flirt with the men who pass in cars.[38]

In the early 1900s dances and parties were also commonplace, although those connected with colleges still included chaperones or faculty sponsors. Particularly curious were "nutting parties," where young college students and young adults met in wooded areas to search for tree nuts. David Lipscomb College often hosted nutting parties after which students finished off the night with fellowship around a campfire, roasting and eating chestnuts, walnuts, and pecans. Such picnics and holiday events were common at all of Nashville's colleges. These forms of socializing cost very little but allowed young people to flirt, date, court, and form friendships—as participants rather than spectators. Even the bicycle craze of the 1890s allowed men and women in Nashville to actively interact in ways unthinkable a decade earlier: "To the ladies, *Chat* would say adopt the wheel. It brings roses to the cheeks and a sparkle to the eye, and the devotions of many a cavalier have been won by just these simple attributes. They need not be startled by the fiery bloomers which the pretty girl of our frontispiece has donned . . . for this is merely her holiday attire and on week-days she sports a milder variety."[39]

Male and female interaction could occur formally and informally, as couples or as groups, through traditional dates, clubs, dance halls, sporting events, and amusement parks. Dance halls, historian Randy McBee argued, led to disorderly behavior in streets and amusement parks and challenged progressive goals of morality and self-control in regard to drinking and promiscuity.[40] Nashville's downtown did feature a few dance halls; however, most college students were strictly prohibited from going to dance halls because they were deemed unsuitable or even dangerous.

That is not to say that Nashville's college men and women did not dance, but dances varied based on the group and its purpose. Vanderbilt and Ward-Belmont students attended debutante and youth society balls at local country clubs.[41] Quite often larger events such as music concerts or theater productions were held in the Vendome Theater or Ryman Auditorium. Moreover, Vanderbilt's sororities and fraternities regularly joined forces to cosponsor activities and dances. When petitioning for permission to hold a dance, college students were resourceful and creative, making use of holidays, sports events, or themes to justify a party.

Specifically, themed dances were very popular and permitted students to dress up, role-play, or venture to an exciting off-campus location. At Vanderbilt one of the highlighted spring trips taken by students was an annual "Mammoth Cave Party." In 1911 nearly fifty students took the L&N train to Glasgow, Kentucky, for a weekend of "Subterranean Wonders," which featured a trip into the cave and the Annual Mammoth Cave Ball. The *Hustler* reported that "the music was fine and dancing was the order of the day and was highly enjoyed."[42] For many years, Ward-Belmont's F. F. Club hosted a matinee costume dance at the Belle Meade Golf and Country Club on the outskirts of town.[43] From theaters to country

FIG. 4.3. Mammoth Cave trip was coordinated annually between Vanderbilt and Ward-Belmont. Pictured here are Ward-Belmont students, c. 1920. Harpeth Hall School Archives.

clubs to themed parties, Nashville's college students played an important role in normalizing casual interaction between men and women, as well as the cultural acceptability of modern dating.

T. J. Jackson Lears has argued in *No Place of Grace* that there existed an antimodern alternative to the emerging cultural order ushered in by the industrial revolution.[44] Antimodernists sought to reform problems brought on by industry and new forms of behavior, including leisure, through such means as the pastoral atmosphere of parks. The creation of public city parks established, in theory, space for recreation and leisure that encouraged good health and social interaction in a natural settings—an escape from urban and industrial sprawl.[45]

Nashville followed the model of many other cities, albeit on a smaller scale. Nashville's park system developed through a seemingly unlikely source: the railroad. The initial interest in creating parks and playgrounds throughout the city started with the end of the Centennial Exposition of 1897. The NC&St.L Railroad Company had been the celebration's biggest contributor, and many of the men on the executive committee maintained ties to the railroad industry. The motivation for railroad companies to invest in public space for recreation and leisure was not altogether altruistic, as railroads and trolleys earned a great deal of profit from fares going to and from public parks.

After the success of the Centennial Exposition, community leaders and railroad executives agreed that the Parthenon replica should be made permanent. In 1901 Mayor Head appointed members to serve on the Board of Park Commissioners.[46] Over the next fifteen years, the board succeeded in acquiring the exposition grounds as a city-owned park and also established new parks in each major residential sector of Nashville. In 1903 the Park Board built a swimming pool, stocked Lake Watauga with fish, planted flower gardens and shrubs, built walkways, and opened Centennial Park to the public. Athletic fields and tennis courts were added in 1911. By 1915 there were eighteen parks across Nashville covering 450 acres. This number included some private parks such as Greenwood Park, designated for blacks and owned by prominent African American politician Preston Taylor, and James E. Caldwell's Glendale Park, leased by baseball star Jake Wells in 1904 and used to stage vaudeville, drama, and comedy theatrical productions.[47]

The parks quickly became sites of mass entertainment hosting annual Easter egg hunts, Groundhog Day celebrations, and group picnics. In addition, for several years the park sponsored free summer opera performances, and in 1914 park officials hung a screen to show free outdoor movies. For example, many of the social functions sponsored by colleges and universities were held in Warner Park, Centennial Park, or Shelby Park.

Other parks maintained a more specific purpose with profits in mind. Glendale Park operated as an amusement park from the 1880s until Percy Warner, president of the Nashville Railway and Light Company, purchased it in 1907. Warner had long been an animal enthusiast with eccentric tastes, and he quickly moved his flock of pheasants onto the property. Over the next year, Warner purchased many animals, including a buffalo from Buffalo Bill's Wild West show, and opened Nashville's first zoo. A trip to the zoo cost fifteen cents, five for the trolley and ten for a ticket. In the 1910s and 1920s, college students flocked to the zoo on weekends, often times for a date or in homosocial groups. Open only during the day, young men and women mixed and mingled freely.

There was no official law or rule that barred African Americans from the city's parks; however, there existed an unspoken understanding that blacks should not visit parks that served predominantly white areas. Nashville's Board of Park Commissioners recognized the need for parks designated primarily for African Americans. As a result, Hadley Park was dedicated in 1912 specifically for the use of the city's black community. Commissioner F. P. McWhirter, a white man, stated that the park was not created "because of any law prohibiting anyone of whatever race or color from visiting any city park," but because African Americans had "never visited or shown any desire to visit the public parks."[48] While one could easily argue with his statement, the establishment of black parks provided African Americans with safe spaces in which to socialize without the threat of discrimination. On the other hand, a "separate but equal" park system perpetuated local segregation.

Geeks, Greeks, and Agrarians

In the spring of 1900, Vanderbilt University held its Annual Oratory Contest on campus. Early in the day, the invitation committee received a phone call from a faculty member at Ward Seminary stating that one hundred young ladies would be in attendance for the contest. As the contest hour drew near, the young men anxiously awaited "the fair ones" whose presence "stimulated the speakers almost to the point of intoxication."[49] Vanderbilt's newspaper, the *Hustler,* provided insight on the developing relationship between men and women enrolled in local institutions of higher education:

> The point on which we desire to lay stress is the interest manifested by Ward's in Vanderbilt affairs. They do us the honor to attend both our athletic and forensic contests.... Wherever a Vanderbilt man goes he should be unstinted in his praise of Ward's, who have been so enthusiastic in their loyalty to Vanderbilt. Ward's is unquestionably in the forefront of female education in the South, and richly

merits the splendid prestige and patronage that it maintains. . . . Here's to them, three cheers and a tiger![50]

This passage precisely illustrates the evolution of a youth culture grounded in higher education. Although Ward Seminary and Vanderbilt University existed as separate institutions, students knew one another and supported their activities and events. There existed a special bond between Ward (later Ward-Belmont) and Vanderbilt because of the similar socioeconomic backgrounds of most of its students' families. It was also not uncommon for students from David Lipscomb or Peabody to attend a lecture sponsored by another school or to mix and mingle at the city-wide tennis tournament or other athletic events. Collectively, college students were bound by two shared experiences, the challenge and opportunity provided by higher education and an urban environment that fostered social interaction through sports, clubs, and cultural arts.

Such opportunities for recreation varied as greatly as the shifting social norms that characterized the last quarter of the nineteenth century. From the late 1890s through the 1910s, many social events continued to maintain a heightened sense of propriety and order. The newly formed Woman's Club at Vanderbilt University hosted one of its "entertainments" in 1900:

> The ladies of the campus, always having the happiness and pleasure of the students at heart, have for years given one or more entertainments during each year especially for the students. . . . It will be in the Chapel . . . and the principal feature will be the reading of "Esmeralda" by Professor Merrill. . . . After the chapel entertainment all are expected to adjourn to the society halls for a social time during the remainder of the evening . . . Every student has the privilege of bringing any young lady whom he chooses—with her consent.[51]

By 1909 the Woman's Club no longer existed, but a new club arose to fill its void. Members of the Girls' Club were a stark contrast to their predecessors, holding meetings on topics such as suffrage, politics, coeducation, and college life and hosting at least two theatrical plays per year. Ten years prior, as the above passage suggests, club members could only attend with a date if invited. Women were not allowed to invite men as dates even to their own club event.

Nationwide, the Victorian concept of the separation of the sexes had begun to crack after 1900, and restrictive gender and recreational roles began to loosen. In the first decade of twentieth century, men and women alike began attending events alone or with a casual group. Once there, men and women could informally socialize with the opposite sex in large and small group formats. This shift in social interaction was met with enthusiasm by college students. In 1907 one Vanderbilt student said that "the excitement was apparent" after a Phi Delta Theta dance. He credited this to the "delightful ease and informality of the occasion that added greatly to the charm."[52]

College life for women changed dramatically, but in what ways and to what extent depended on the institution. Prior to the 1930s, most Vanderbilt men dated women from one of the nearby girls' schools. Perhaps this was because there were fewer women at Vanderbilt. Or perhaps Vanderbilt's female students were more intimidating as they challenged gender norms head-on, entering the previously all-male world of a top-tier university. In contrast, students from Ward Seminary (1865–1913), Belmont (1890–1913), and Ward-Belmont (1913–51) were women who sought to challenge themselves academically but ultimately were far more likely to enter society life than professional life. Some college prep graduates went on to four-year universities, and some completed teaching certification at Peabody, but many attended these schools as part of a coming-out ritual and as preparation for society and club life.

Women were a small minority at Vanderbilt until World War I. After 1920, Vanderbilt's coed population crossed the 20 percent threshold, and college life began to settle into a recognizable routine of classes, athletic events, Greek

FIG. 4.4. 1903 Ward Seminary student artwork. Harpeth Hall School Archives.

FIG. 4.5. Vanderbilt University students in 1904. Metropolitan Government of Nashville and Davidson County Archives.

activities, and other school functions. Vanderbilt men continued to date women from Ward-Belmont and Peabody after 1930, but the social life and the university community were more or less self-contained by the end of the 1920s. In other words, as women became a greater percentage of the student body, Vanderbilt was less dependent on other schools for coed social interaction. By 1930 Vanderbilt had become a university of men *and* women who shared a common identity and sense of school loyalty.

In addition, the emergence of fraternities and sororities and the expansion of college coursework precipitated new categories by which "students created their own standards of success," resulting in five general categories of students. The "swells" consisted of "big men" or "all-around girls" who were associated with "money, clothes, contacts, and a fun-loving spirit."[53] The "grinds" or "digs" were students from modest backgrounds who largely refrained from challenging the "swells." They were more often ignored than bullied. The "freaks" or "outsiders" were ostracized; the labels were based primarily on socioeconomic background rather than on social awkwardness. They were outsiders and treated as such. The "brains" or "geeks," a fifth category, were intellectually sharp students who could float throughout the four categories depending on their social skills and socioeconomic status.

Particularly at Vanderbilt and Ward-Belmont, a student's college reputation was as dependent, if not more so, on family background as academic achievement. Moreover, a student's positive or negative college experience was often determined by one's peers. The "swells" were active in the Greek system, sat atop the collegiate clique pyramid, and were visible and active participants in events that "punctuated the calendar."[54] Chancellor James Kirkland recognized similar student groupings at Vanderbilt, categorizing students as Fraternity Men, Non-Fraternity Men, Athletes, and Biblical Department Men. Deemed "moral" by Kirkland, Biblical Department Men were likely "freaks" or "outsiders" to fellow students, as most were scholarship students and not part of the general education curriculum. Kirkland barely recognized the women at Vanderbilt, even though one in five students were female after 1920 (see chapter 2).

These student-devised social categories, along with newly introduced general education course electives, bred mediocrity in the minds of many educators. Writing in 1915, Henry Seidel Canby, Yale professor and *Saturday Review* editor, argued that increasing enrollments, endowments, and elective courses were detrimental to higher learning:

> When circumstances are favorable, the forcing of a needle into soft iron is not more difficult than to push one really new idea into an immature brain. But if there are thirty brains of all ranges of capability to be manipulated, the difficulty is multiplied. The lazy millionaire's son, the earnest child of an uncouth immigrant, the able inheritor of sufficient brains—must come forward, all of them, or the year's work is wasted.[55]

Kirkland likely agreed with this sentiment but made his case carefully so as not to offend alumni or donors:

> We can trace many of the great changes to the expansion of the curriculum and ... the elective system. . . . The average college graduate of to-day can converse lightly on nearly every subject but deeply on none. There are so many outside interests, which distract a student's attention that ... there is nothing left but the multitude of side shows. . . . [Even] the college professor is glad to get rid of the mass of students who are uninterested in his work.[56]

During the first two decades of the twentieth century, sororities and fraternities laid the groundwork, along with varsity sport, for the modern collegiate experience. Historian Helen Horowitz recognized that by the end of the first decade of the twentieth century, in "certain universities, the Greek system commanded the loyalty of a significant part of the student body."[57] The Greek system of fraternities and sororities remained instrumental in the shift of increased acceptability for social interaction between male and female students. Paula Fass argued that "fraternities and sororities dramatized the mechanisms of peer selection and conformity" that were deliberately designed to build up students' self-esteem through the fall rush season, only to give way to purposeful humiliation during initiation after new members were accepted.[58]

Embedded into the very meaning of higher education after 1915, fraternities and sororities provided acceptance and ritual that grew, alongside athletics, as perhaps the most formative aspect of college life. Although Greek organizations were not coeducational and limited membership based on gender, their homosocial nature turned heterosocial when they hosted parties, dances, and other events. Membership dues and entrance fees to events reflected the high cost of leisure—and even friendship.

In the decades following the Civil War, fraternities (more so than sororities) at white colleges were "increasingly defined by class and academic laziness." "Fraternities were for men of means," concluded historian Nicholas Syrett.[59] Prior to the Civil War, attending college had been one indicator of social class in the South; as higher education democratized and expanded in the postbellum era, fraternities provided a new way to separate the gentlemen from the men. This Greek phenomenon emerged as an important factor in the formation of a modern hierarchical structure that distinguished privilege and reaffirmed socioeconomic advantage.

No local college campus was more obsessed with Greek life than Vanderbilt University. Early on, the faculty and administration fought fraternities, referring to them as secret organizations and "evil." Vanderbilt's first chancellor, Landon Garland (1875–93), "thought fraternities worse than every other youthful indulgence or vice" and attempted to prohibit them noted Paul Conkin.[60] Perhaps worse, secret societies emerged to fill student demand. Phi Delta Theta operated as a sub-rosa (underground) group in 1876 and requested permission to form an open, legal chapter, only to be denied by the Board of Trust.[61] The rising power of modern youth culture and the persistent demand of students won out, and there were eight fraternities by 1886. Immediately they became competitive, and hazing incidents pushed the administration to second guess its decision. But it was out of their control; fraternities remained popular, generated school spirit, and offered a different kind of loyalty on campus. At the same time, "fraternities gained prestige through exclusion . . . [and] during the post-bellum period they primarily excluded men on the basis of 'social class,' according to Syrett.[62]

From the 1880s through the early 1900s, fraternities and the old literary societies coexisted with equal prestige, but increasingly fraternity men dominated student life. Fraternity members were seen as "big men" on campus; however, the nature of fraternities and their relationship to the academic side of university life would change. No longer were fraternity men the regular winners of academic awards, such as Vanderbilt's coveted Founder's Medal. Between 1910 and 1930 academic awards and medals noticeably shifted to women and "outsiders." Universities such as Vanderbilt split into two camps, those already wealthy and those who hoped to be. As a result, students more or less self-segregated, with each group holding decidedly different views of college and its purpose. Horowitz noted, "What outsiders held in common was the perception of college as preparation. Whatever pleasure the four years might hold were incidental to the primary pursuit—an education to lead the advancing in the world. Outsiders sought to succeed in the classroom, not in the extracurriculum."[63]

On the female side, Vanderbilt's Phi Kappa Upsilon sorority formed in 1897–98 and Theta Delta Theta appeared two years later.[64] These two organizations began locally but later joined national sororities. Phi Kappa Upsilon became a branch of Kappa Alpha Theta in 1904 (the first in the South), and Theta Delta Theta affiliated with the national Delta Delta Delta in 1909. As a whole, sororities were more tame and less rowdy when compared to fraternities.

In the fall of 1900, Kappa Alpha Thetas hosted a party where the "lawn was a sea of brightly colored Japanese lanterns and in the absence of the harvest moon, cast their mellow light upon the young people beneath." Party attendees included "Vanderbilt's handsomest men . . . and with oodles of charming girls."[65] Meanwhile, Delta Delta Delta sponsored an annual coed "tallyho ride," in which students loaded up in cars for an afternoon drive out to the country. In another instance, thirty-five Vanderbilt men and their dates left Union Station on a private train car chartered specifically for the Kappa Alpha Theta party. They traveled to "Craggy Hope" (a station in the mountains), visited the city, hiked, picnicked, spent the night, and returned the next day. The overnight trip included faculty sponsors, but it is clear that Vanderbilt men and women socialized with more freedom and less oversight.[66] The role of faculty members in extracurricular activities would continue to decrease in the 1920s and virtually disappear after World War II.

Illustrating the enthusiasm for Greek life at Vanderbilt, the totals for fraternities and sororities in 1909 are as follows: Phi Delta Theta, 35; Kappa Sigma, 33;

FIG. 4.6. Interior of Union Station located on the western end of Broadway in 1902. All of Nashville's colleges and universities were less than three miles from Union Station. Metropolitan Government of Nashville and Davidson County Archives.

Sigma Alpha Epsilon, 34; Kappa Alpha, 26; Beta Theta Pi, 20; Delta Tau Delta, 13, Sigma Nu, 22; Alpha Tau Omega, 29; Delta Kappa Epsilon, 31; Sigma Chi, 41; Phi Kappa Psi, 18; Phi Kappa Sigma, 29; Kappa Alpha Theta (sorority), 14; and Theta Delta Theta (sorority), 11. These numbers show that over half of male and female students were members of a fraternity or sorority, a trend that continued throughout the 1920s and beyond.[67] From 1910 to 1930 Greek organizations selected many of its members from the old money crowd rather than from the New South's rising middle class. The desire to have the "right" men and women dictated membership invitations, rush rituals, and dues.

In less than twenty years (1883 to 1900), fraternities had gone from prestigious groups that competed for the smartest, "ablest" men with an active on-campus presence to "often self-indulgent little communities" that "retreated from active involvement in the campus."[68] Freshman initiation—or spiking, as it was sometimes called—also involved severe and violent hazing, which included paddling, "scalping" (shaving one's head), kidnapping, false imprisonment, theft, and fistfights. In one instance, a Vanderbilt freshman was tied to a tree and abandoned in the woods, forced to find his way back to campus in the darkness of night. Syrett argued, "Hazing within fraternities was another way for fraternity men to test the manly mettle of their prospective initiates." Perhaps more disturbing was the fact that "prestige was so well established that freshmen were increasingly willing to undergo humiliation and torture for the privilege of membership."[69] While the proposition of individual degradation in exchange for collective dignity appears counterintuitive, the practice of hazing and the popularity of rushing signaled the increasing power and independence of fraternities and the new youth culture that drove them.

University control over social events and student life diminished with the rise of off-campus fraternity and sorority houses. At Vanderbilt most fraternities and the two sororities operated off-campus houses by the 1920s. The rise of fraternity houses, in particular, had a significant effect at Vanderbilt as well as at major universities nationwide. "Frat" houses allowed Greek men to separate themselves and reinforced the notion of wealth as fraternity houses were expensive and only college students who could afford such living were invited.[70] Thus, fraternity houses further "perpetuated the class hierarchy."[71] Off-campus Greek housing also led to new levels of bad behavior with members concentrating far more on throwing parties than on their studies.

Kirkland conceded that fraternity life was damaging the larger reputation of the university. Ironically, the university had severed ties with the Methodist church in 1915, in a move instigated largely by the university (and Kirkland). Even while under Methodist governance, compulsory daily chapel had been reduced in 1905, with most students excused at least three days per week. Even the Glee Club faced charges of gambling and sexual promiscuity on their 1912 tour.

Kirkland called for a "moral crusade" which would roughly last from 1910 to 1915, and he sought the participation of a group of administrators, faculty, non-Greeks, women, and even a few fraternity men.[72] In 1911 the group concluded an institutional evaluation, and its findings revealed disturbing trends for the fraternities. Over half of all males with membership in a fraternity had poor grades. Kappa Phi's average was the equivalent of a D (63.9), which led the faculty to impose a delayed rush until after November and required freshman to live in the on-campus dormitory, Kissam Hall. Fraternity members signed pledges of morality, faculty sponsors were assigned, and Greek/non-Greek student alliances were created. The university also passed or stiffened rules on drinking, gambling, and sex; set a midnight curfew; and limited dances to two per year, with required chaperonage. Academic-standing requirements for freshman rushes and members living in fraternity houses were also established.[73]

Historian Paul Conkin contended that new rules "incensed the fraternity men on-campus, who claimed they were being treated like children. The faculty felt they had been acting like children."[74] Fraternities responded by printing a parody mocking the new regulations with "rules" of their own, which included the following:

> No ladies shall be admitted to any fraternity house, at any time, without being chaperoned by their mother and father and the Faculty Supervisory Committee or, in case of the death of one or both parents, without the first regiment of the Tennessee infantry accompanied by the President of the Board of Trustees of Vanderbilt University.
>
> The number of entertainments at which there is played checkers, parches, or puss wants a corner given by a fraternity, either in the morning, afternoon, or evening, shall be limited to one each scholastic year, with the generous exception of one afternoon tea during the Christmas holidays.
>
> The fraternity men in college may attend the entertainments of fraternities other than their own, provided . . . that their scholastic record shall show perfect attendance on all classes and an average of not less than 99.2, and that they have a doctor's certificate signifying their physical ability to stand the grueling strain of such entertainment, and that their invitation be signed.[75]

Efforts to reform fraternities were largely unsuccessful, and despite suspensions and expulsions, Greek life continued to encourage the impulsive behavior of young, single men who felt entitled to live the good life.

More ominous than fraternities, a handful of secret societies also existed at Vanderbilt. Of course, all fraternities were "secret" until 1883, when they were approved by the Board of Trust. As Greek life developed over the next fifty years, "Vanderbilt's paucity of residential life made student groups extremely unstable, and amid the volatile, extracurricular froth, small and elite groups of extremely well-connected men began to form outside of traditional Greek channels," noted a 2013 article in the *Hustler* on the history of Vanderbilt's student societies.[76] These included Alpha Sigma Sigma, also known as the Jackass Club, whose group seal included liquor bottles "at various stages of emptiness" and the motto "work hard, play hard." The club was last mentioned in the 1893 *Commodore*.[77]

By 1903 the Jackasses were replaced by the Commodore Club (for seniors) and the Owl Club (for juniors); and an invitation to join either organization was one of the highest student-designated accolades a Vanderbilt man could achieve. These clubs were not secret, practically speaking, but "carried with them a certain mystique." The Owl Club's reputation had a notoriously intense hazing process: "One 1930s Owl Club initiation required visits to multiple Nashville movie theaters, where initiates ran down the aisles and yelled 'Fire!'"[78] (The Commodore Club morphed into Vanderbilt's current chapter of Omicron Delta Kappa in 1934.) The Owl Club, tarnished by scandals in the 1930s, including unflattering pictures in *Life* magazine, was shuttered in 1947 after "administrative blowback from a series of 'risque and off-color' skits performed by initiates at a banquet."[79]

On the opposite end of the spectrum, the period from 1910 to 1930 also witnessed a religious revival, a renewed YMCA presence, and social reform, which was a reaction no doubt to the moral decline associated with the growth of Greek societies. Conkin noted that social life at Vanderbilt consisted of "fraternities and sororities on one hand, the YMCA on the other, with a certain tension between the two extremes."[80] Filling the gap, new organizations at Vanderbilt included a student association (1910), social science club (1901), spectator club (1912), and pep band (1905). On the cusp of World War I, Vanderbilt's student body had grown more diverse, with more than eleven hundred students, but most still came from affluent or middle-class southern families. New departments such as Sociology (1913) and scholarships brought students of more humble means. Biblical Department students were nearly all on financial scholarships, and many in the College of Engineering and general academic departments also worked to pay for tuition ($150 per year from 1918 to 1923). These students were less likely to join fraternities and sororities.

In addition, the university removed the word *dance* from the commencement program, organized evangelical "gospel teams," and held a religious revival on-campus that resulted in two hundred signed cards of commitments to Christ in 1912. Vanderbilt students also participated in urban reform efforts as professors of the Department of Sociology enlisted students to "help clean up downtown Nashville," including gambling halls and the "tenderloin district," known for prostitution.[81] These efforts at Vanderbilt coincided with the height of the Progressive Era. While student organizations and behavior endured a reckoning of sorts, the tide of modern college life and notions of fun outside the classroom would overcome cultural backlash. The 1920s saw the death of the once-prestigious literary societies and other older groups such as the Glee Club and Dramatic Club. Instead, social life revolved around fraternities, football games, and dances in the gym.[82]

In addition to Greek and club life, Vanderbilt's campus culture also swirled around a strange but coveted "honor" each year. The university continued to recognize students for academic honors, but a new award emerged that reflected the intersection of student achievement and student popularity. It began with James William Dodd, better known as "Uncle Billy" Dodd, who joined Vanderbilt's faculty in 1879. In 1885 he established an enduring tradition: the naming of the

Bachelor of Ugliness, abbreviated B.U. Despite its name, it quickly became the "most sought-after honor for Vanderbilt men, an honor bestowed after a hotly contested election."[83] The process to elect a winner was both ritualistic and chaotic:

> About May 1 [1905] a preliminary mass meeting is held, and each department of the University names its candidate and selects its "Hustling Committee," whose duty is obviously to hustle for votes. On Founder's Day, May 27, the B.U. election is held in the University chapel. The [student] chairman, having been elected, is installed in the midst of a shower of green plums, peaches, rubber balls and much that isn't so nice by half, and sundry freshmen . . . are placed upon the rostrum as targets for the assemblage. They make formal nominating speeches devoted to describing the ugliness of the respective candidates in the most elaborate and convincing manner.[84]

The award was given annually from 1885 through the 1970s.[85] The winner was awarded the "B.U. degree" during commencement weekend. The B.U. was largely co-opted by fraternity men and/or athletes after 1910. Women also added their own version, awarding the "Lady of the Bracelet," beginning in 1929. Today the award is simply called the Outstanding Senior Award.

Student culture at other Nashville colleges developed differently from Vanderbilt University, although similar patterns exist. As part of the Church of Christ, David Lipscomb College required chapel services, and student coursework relied heavily on theology and Bible studies. The school did not have an official Greek system or national social club affiliations. That said, by 1906 Lipscomb's literary societies and clubs operated more or less like organized fraternities and sororities. Similarly, Peabody College featured several literary societies but no national fraternities or sororities. Peabody men were members of clubs such as the Agatheridian and Erosophohian Societies, which operated as debate teams. Peabody women formed their first club in 1880 and added the Peabody Literary Society in 1889. In 1896 women formed a third literary society, the Adelphi. These groups were essential to the extracurricular activities of students.[86] Peabody's students had choices of participating in gym exhibits, dramatic and musical performances, and the *Peabody Reflector,* the school's student-run newspaper. The YMCA and YWCA also maintained a strong presence on Peabody's campus. Worthy of note, female students from Peabody often accompanied Vanderbilt men to their fraternity functions.

Inclusion distinguished Lipscomb and Peabody's clubs from Vanderbilt. Clubs and societies maintained, as a whole, open policies for membership, a stark contrast to the exclusivity of Vanderbilt's societies, fraternities, and sororities. In fact, David Lipscomb College went to great lengths to control students' extracurricular interests. The school required all its females to join Sigma Rho, which later split in 1913 into Kappa Nu and Sapphoneans. All male students were required to join either Calliopean or Caesarion; the latter was renamed Lipscomb.

Not all clubs at Nashville's colleges were serious in nature. More jovial groups existed, such as the Old Maid's Club and Lunch Pail Club at Ward Seminary, the Sewing and Skillet Club at Ward and David Lipscomb, and David Lipscomb's Red Headed Club. Ward, Belmont, and Peabody also maintained state clubs whereby students joined according to the state where they lived before coming to Nashville. It was a way to meet new people while also establishing common bonds. State clubs were prevalent in colleges throughout the U.S. through the 1910s. More generally, clubs and societies were either all-female or all-male. However, there are examples of coed clubs as early as 1905 at both Peabody and Lipscomb.[87]

Despite the explosion of fraternities, sororities, and athletics on campuses in Nashville and nationwide, many universities simultaneously enhanced academic programs. For example, Vanderbilt greatly improved its standing as a regional university with the successful expansion of the Medical Department, the reinstatement of the Ph.D. program, and the creation of Schools of Economics, Engineering, and Sociology. However, the most significant intellectual movement at Vanderbilt between 1873 and 1930 was not in these developments but rather two overlapping groups of young men and faculty, known as the Fugitives and the Agrarians, who would lead a southern literary and philosophical revolution. These men would epitomize what T. J. Jackson Lears referred to as "antimodernism."

The Fugitives' original core, led by fifteen students and faculty members, first met in 1914. The faculty leader was Vanderbilt graduate-turned-professor John Crowe Ransom. Born in Pulaski, Tennessee, Ransom graduated from Vanderbilt in 1909 at the top of his class. He was also a member of the Phi Beta Kappa honor society and editor of the *Observer,* a literary periodical, in 1908–9. From 1910 to 1913 Ransom studied in Oxford as a Rhodes Scholar and joined the Vanderbilt faculty as an English professor in 1914.[88] Walter Clyde Curry (of the English Department faculty, 1915–55) was also a leading voice within the group.

Prominent student members of the Fugitives included Alec Stevenson (editor of the Vanderbilt *Observer,* class of 1916, and later a Nashville businessman), Stanley Johnson (class of 1917, B.S.; 1921, M.A.; faculty, 1921–25), Jesse E. Wills (class of 1922, B.A.), Donald Davidson, and Robert Penn Warren. Davidson began as a student in 1909, then left, and returned in 1914. Earning his B.A. and M.A. from Vanderbilt, he joined the faculty and remained a teacher from 1920 to 1968, maintaining a long and influential academic career.[89] It was Davidson who invited fellow students to join the Fugitives, including John Allen Tate (class of 1922, B.A.). Tate, in turn, helped recruit two other intellectuals: Ridley Wills

PHI DELTA THETA

Bottom Row—Robert Knight, Joe Clark, McNeilly, Dantzler, "Tobe" Woodroof, Wills, G. E. Adams, Tate, James Waller, Tom Zerfoss, McDonald.
Second Row—Embry, Orr, R. Waller, Beard, C. B. Street, Warterfield, Thomas, Currey, Craig.
Third Row—C. T Woodroof, E. Sperry, Sid Keeble, Barham, Leslie, Landess, W Woodroof, Creveling, Godchaux, Coleman.
Fourth Row—Griscom, Fletcher, S. Clark, Sanders, Webb, Ed Keeble, Shapard, D. Street, Knight, Brockman.

FIG. 4.7. 1922 Phi Delta Theta members in front of their fraternity house including Jesse E. Wills and Allen Tate, members of the Fugitive literary group. Courtesy of Ridley Wills II.

(Vanderbilt alumnus and cousin of fellow Fugitive Jesse Wills, class of 1922) and Robert Penn Warren, both of whom boarded with Tate. Warren (class of 1925, B.A.) would become a preeminent American author and poet and the winner of three Pulitzer Prizes. Arguably, noted Paul Conkin, these men composed "the most important single chapter in a now widely recognized renaissance of literature in the South and stimulated the most extended twentieth-century debate about the cultural identity of the South."[90] College "rebels" of a different sort, these young intellectuals also articulated an antimodern view in opposition to the industrial urban boosterism in the New South.

On campus, many of these students and faculty were members of the Calumet Club and various fraternities; however, the group mainly met off campus for discussions ranging from the literary to the metaphysical. In 1922 the group began the three-year run of a literary periodical called the *Fugitive*. The publication's seventeen issues received much literary and critical attention. Its editors, Ransom, Davidson, and Warren, developed their talents, publishing their own poetry as well as works from hundreds of submissions across the region. As Conkin noted, "The *Fugitive* was by far the most influential publication ever tied in any sense to Vanderbilt University."[91]

After the original group broke up in 1925, a new alliance with many of the same members emerged in its place. The Agrarians, or Southern Agrarians, were led by Tate, Ransom, Davidson, and Warren, who edited and published essays on southern politics, culture, and life in 1930. Their work culminated in a landmark book entitled *I'll Take My Stand,* a manifesto that "condemned the industrialization and capitalism that many saw as the struggling South's salvation and defended many southern traditions and ways of life."[92] The Southern Agrarians, or "Twelve Southerners," as they were also called, sought to reconcile the rapid industrialism, commercialization, and consumerism associated with the New South. They promoted a simpler version of living, labor, and self-determination based on an antimodern philosophy, as they believed that modernity had stripped the region of its exceptionalism. Stark Young, one of the authors of *I'll Take My Stand,* summed up the sentiment, also expressed by Warren and Tate: "In the shifting relation between ourselves and the new order lies the profoundest source for our living. . . . That a change is now in course all over the South is plain; and it is as plain that the South changing must be the South still. . . ."[93]

The Southern Agrarians asserted that the South's best future entailed a return to its past and that for the region to lose its identity in the name of profit-based industrialism would be a disastrous choice. Ransom's essay "persuaded southerners to fight back, not blindly and belligerently as in the war, but by forming alliances with like-minded people all over the country" to fight Yankee industry, preserve order, and prevent the destruction of nature.[94] The essays touched on many topics, contextualized by southern history and culture; however, *I'll Take My Stand* largely avoided issues related to race or social justice. In that sense, it reflected the perspective of white society and specifically New South men—whether Southern Agrarians or not.

Chancellor James Kirkland never supported the Fugitives and was, at times, embarrassed by the more politicized Agrarians. Indeed most of the university's board members and major donors were very successful industrialists. But even Kirkland could not deny that both groups added to the intellectual prestige of the university and brought national and international attention to Vanderbilt.

In some ways, the Fugitive Poets and the Southern Agrarians worked against the school's efforts to prove it was a national university. These men and their publications also contradicted many local Nashvillians who embraced southern urbanization and even southern progressivism. In other ways the Fugitives and "Twelve Southerners" did more to make Vanderbilt a national university than did any other development, apart from its sports successes and Greek societies. The writings and distinguished careers of the Fugitives and Agrarians illustrate the symbolic pressure point between the rural South and its cities in the early twentieth century. Poems from the *Fugitive* and essays from *I'll Take My Stand* did not affect daily college life for most students at Vanderbilt, but ideas connected to the Agrarian movement brought a shift in college culture, further dividing those seeking to join a philosophical movement from those seeking to join a fraternity.

Single-Gender Campus Culture

Collectively, white women at single-gender schools were less aggressive in seeking or achieving greater freedom on or off campus. Female students did have some agency, but their ability to decide what to do and when to do it was contested and controlled from 1865 to 1930. Meanwhile, white college men "lived with long formal lists of rules, but they did so with little oversight and in the relative freedom of dispersed surroundings," noted Horowitz.[95] In contrast, white women's schools remained heavily supervised, required compulsory daily chapel, and maintained a strict disciplinarian regime intended to preserve the innocence of young women living away from home.

In regard to the goals and desired outcomes of college women, a subtle but significant shift took place. First-generation college women (1860s–1880s) were "forthrightly serious, single-minded and conscientious," while second- (1890s–1900s) and third-generation (1910s–1930) college women desired higher education for the purpose of learning but also to socialize and network. And yet, a connective force linked women on single-gender campuses despite generational differences—what Barbara Solomon called "the common enterprise of being college bred."[96]

Nashville's Ward Seminary, Belmont College, and later Ward-Belmont fit this model of administrative and faculty control on campus, coupled with deliberate efforts to protect students from the temptations of the outside world. Ward Seminary founders Dr. and Mrs. Ward, personally enforced rules that ensured the moral virtue of each student throughout their tenure (1865–1887). Dr. Ward, as an ordained Presbyterian minister, even led most chapel services. Examples of his actions reflect the tone and tenor of campus culture at Ward Seminary. In 1866 Professor Ward, as the girls called him, put his book down during a lesson to remind a Miss Clark to "preserve her dignity" as she sat on the front row of class with her "feet protruding from the hem of her floor-length skirt."[97] In another instance that year, Ward caught several of his students on the first-floor parlor in their nightgowns as they listened to the serenade of their Vanderbilt beaus. One female student recounted, "It was the fashion for our boyfriends to serenade us with guitar, banjo, and their fresh young voices. . . . Suddenly Dr. Ward walked in. . . . We got up those steps quicker than we had come down!"[98]

In the 1870s the Wards instituted policies that focused on Victorian notions of modesty, humility, and restraint. In the 1880s students were required to wear maroon or dark-colored dresses.[99] Simple dress was expected, and one source reported that student Annie Chadwell nearly cried "when the many dainty bows which held the fluffy tarleton drapery of the whole front of her dress had to come off."[100] Early catalogs proclaimed the school's moral outlook: "It is our purpose to avoid extravagance in dress. . . . Positively no low neck or short sleeve dresses will be permitted on our school platform."[101]

Ward prohibited visitors on Sunday and closely supervised the students during recreation and off-campus trips. Other ritual traditions during his tenure as principal served to inculcate discipline and reinforce notions of southern chivalry and decorum. For example, students filed into the daily chapel two by two and followed a similar pattern as they marched in pairs into the dining hall. At lunch some students sat at a designated "French table," where no English could be spoken, while Latin students sat with their instructors.[102] Another custom initially grew out of respect for the school's founders as students curtsied to Dr. and Mrs. Ward while entering and exiting the dining hall. The school's founders opened the school to promote greater academic achievement for its female students, and yet it remains clear that antebellum notions of southern propriety and gender endured as a centerpiece of Ward's overall student culture from 1865 until his death in 1887. Unlike Vanderbilt and other predominantly male schools, Ward Seminary experienced change at a much slower pace.

Just three years after William Ward's death, a new single-gender school opened just west of downtown on the former antebellum estate of Belle Monte. Led by Ida E. Hood and Susan L. Heron and and later by Dr. Ira Landrith as regent, Belmont College for Young Women also maintained strict regulations designed to protect the virtue of young women. In its first decade, chapel was required twice a day, six days a week. After 1900, as Helen Horowitz noted, "While founders of most of the women's colleges meant them to be 'non-sectarian,' but distinctly Christian, college life became increasingly secular."[103] The first published *Announcement and Prospectus of Belmont College* in 1890 articulated rules regarding promptness, daily exercise, tidy rooms, neat dress, and reverence for the Sabbath. Students were not allowed off campus without a chaperone, and "gossip [was] discouraged." Girls were not permitted to wear "silk dresses or dress with low necks and short sleeves on campus."[104] Instead, boarding and day students donned brown uniforms—hence the yearbook's title from 1905 to 1912, *Milady in Brown.* The "Milady" refers to the chivalric notion of "My Lady," suggesting a reverence for Victorian concepts of the behavior expected of upper-class young women, as well as codified notions of modesty and morality.

According to regulations published in 1895 "Gentlemen callers" were required to bring letters of introduction, and the young ladies could not receive dates on Saturday afternoons. Moreover, students were punished if they were caught "burning lights after the last bell," and they could not receive packages containing "eatables," except for "boxes of fresh fruit."[105] All mail first passed through the school's office, and the administrators reserved the right to open suspicious letters in the "presence of the student" or to forward inappropriate correspondence to the student's parents. Finally, day students attended classes in a separate building and were forbidden to enter the dormitory room of a boarding student.[106]

Though not accredited, Belmont certainly appeared to have an active college atmosphere. Students were young women mostly between the ages of seventeen and twenty-one; the campus offered classroom space, a dining hall, and dormitories; and students participated in school-affiliated clubs, sports, and sororities. While Ward Seminary did permit some sororities, Belmont College allowed sorority houses on the edge of campus. Early sororities included Beta Sigma Omicron, Theta Kappa Delta, Tau Phi Sigma, and Chi Omega.[107] Apparently, Hood and Heron hoped to avoid "secret sororities," but despite their efforts, "there was a time when [secret societies] threatened to be disturbing elements at Belmont."[108] Several properties near the campus were available for purchase, and because of increased enrollment in the 1890s, the school obtained four nearby houses and "offered them to the four sororities which had arisen in the college on condition that each would become responsible for the protection of their chapter-houses."[109] An adult female resided in each chapter house and acted as a chaperone and hostess. The girls of the four sororities "accepted this opportunity for community life with avidity, and not only gave the guarantee asked for, but made good their pledges with true womanly fidelity."[110]

The school year featured many annual social events, including an all-school picnic, Halloween carnival, Thanksgiving dinner, sorority-sponsored Valentine's Day dance, Colonial Day Tea, Tally-Ho party, May Morning Breakfast, "Park Day" (held at nearby Centennial Park), Senior Luncheon, Alumnae Banquet, and the Principals' Reception Day (similar to an Awards Day).[111] The Halloween Carnival was a particularly exciting event that students anticipated from the start of the school year. Student Willye O. Smith provided a detailed account of the evening in 1904:

> It was an ideal night for ghosts and goblins. The air was charged with mystery, and the college stood like some haunted mansion. . . . Suddenly the bell pealed

forth a loud summons, and almost instantly the campus became alive. . . . From one tent came the sound of the banjo . . . from another came the muffled voice of a fortune teller. The girls marched round the fires, forming a large circle, [and] sang. . . . After this everyone enjoyed a general feast, roasting apples on long sticks over the fires and popping corn."[112]

From the 1870s through the early 1900s, "smashing" (a term used to describe intense best-friend relationships between women), all-girl parties, and all-female dances were not only common but the only socially approved option for well-to-do young women who hoped to marry well. For example, the girl's club Sigma Rho at David Lipscomb College performed a "man-less wedding" in 1912. Another "man-less" event was the special dinner and dance held each year at Ward-Belmont on

FIG. 4.8. 1910 Belmont College "Manless Dance" located in main hall of Belmont Mansion. Harpeth Hall School Archives.

George Washington's birthday. Students dressed as members of colonial society and performed several musical and dance numbers. One student recalled that "those who did the leading most of the time had a rather hard adjustment to make when they went on to coeducational institutions and found themselves dancing with boys rather than girls."[113] This notion was completely turned on its head between 1900 and 1920, so much so that the idea of women dancing together and "smashes" were considered taboo by the end of the 1920s. Even after 1930 certain traditions were simply modified and continued, reflecting the value of nostalgia and the enduring image of the strong but ultimately submissive southern belle.

From the beginning, clubs were a major part of the college experience at Ward, Belmont, and Ward-Belmont. These included "State Clubs," athletic clubs, and music clubs and ensembles. Although the school regularly advertised and emphasized the school's nonsectarian status, religious overtones were ever present in school culture. The largest religious club, the Young Women's Christian Association (YWCA), began in 1892 at Belmont, emphasizing moral character, community service, and healthy living. Belmont's YWCA fluctuated in size, but regardless of numbers, "the faithful few met, sewed, sang, read and prayed."[114] By 1904 the club had 135 members, nearly 75 percent of the student body at the time. The growth of the YWCA on college campuses reflected national trends related to "muscular Christianity," which included women and emphasized moral living, hard work, and physical/mental strength.

Modesty and propriety remained important values at Ward-Belmont through the 1920s and 1930s. Institutions such as Ward-Belmont were determined not to let the sexual revolution of the 1920s upset the notions of proper behavior, dress, and decorum needed to become a true "lady" and, in particular, a "southern lady." However, girls at Ward-Belmont were allowed to bob their hair or cut it short in 1923. By 1933 sailor tops, bloomers, long stockings, and lace-up boots had been traded in for tennis shoes and lighter clothing, including navy blue wool shorts and white shirts. Students were also allowed to wear skirts that revealed their legs, but they were strictly forbidden from smoking on campus. Although students did sometimes smoke when off campus or out of town, girls could be expelled if alcohol consumption was reported. There was not a formal dress code at Ward-Belmont, but students were expected to dress plainly, and makeup was allowed only for dinner and off-campus excursions. When going out in groups for nonschool activities, girls were required to wear long dark dresses, gloves, and matching dark hats.

Certain rules regarding chaperones also changed for young women who boarded and were part of the junior college (accredited in 1925). From 1913 to 1930 students were still required to have an adult or faculty chaperone whenever they left campus. In the early 1930s students were allowed to travel into downtown Nashville or make other short excursions provided they were, at a minimum, in groups of two or three and traveled by either taxi or streetcar.[115] However, dates with young men were still chaperoned and required written parental permission through 1935. If a young man came to visit a student on campus, the girls could "entertain their dates in the parlors just off the recreation hall where the chaperone on duty would wander back and forth like a sentinel guarding his post."[116]

Alumnae Sarah Bryan Benedict, Sarah Colley Cannon, and Mary Elizabeth Cayce wrote: "One wonders if all this procedure was worth a two-hour visit in a Victorian parlor equipped with full length mirrors at strategic points, hard horsehair sofas, and a gliding chaperone who somehow floated through the rooms continually making her presence known by clearing her throat!"[117] While women made strides in higher education, at southern all-female colleges students were still largely bound by tradition and gender roles through the 1930s. Men at Vanderbilt joined fraternities that included rushing, hazing, and drinking; women at Nashville's all-girls schools hosted tea parties, wore white gloves, and generally followed rules of formal courtship.

A Tale of Two Campuses

With most of Nashville's white and black college campuses separated by less than three miles, the college experience of Nashville's black students remained markedly different from that of their white counterparts. African American students at local HBCUs benefited from Nashville's growth and new recreatoinal outlets but remained confined to a segregated system of leisure.

Nashville's most established and exclusive undergraduate black college was clearly Fisk University. Students and student life on and off campus faced intense scrutiny from the faculty and administration as well as the larger black and white community. For example, students were restricted from going to the bars and pool halls in black neighborhoods such as the notorious Bucket of Blood Saloon, as reported in the *Fisk Herald*. From the late 1800s through the first two decades of the 1900s, students at Fisk lived and learned within the confines of white leadership and a racially divided society. Spurred by cultural change on a national scale and the end of World War I, Fisk students finally rebelled in 1925. College life did shift after the infamous 1925 student riot, but changes remained incremental until after World War II.

For African American male students at Fisk prior to 1927, most extracurricular activities were academic. In addition to the Jubilee Singers, perhaps the most accomplished and well-known club was the debate team. This highly competitive group participated in the annual "Triangular Debate" with Atlanta and Howard Universities, which carried with it a great deal of school pride and, of course, bragging rights for the year.[118] There were several literary societies, including the Union Literary Society, the Dunbar Club, Extempo, and the oldest, Excelsior, founded in 1894. Many of these clubs would transform into fraternities as the Greek movement finally reached campus after 1927. One other club was Fisk's black chapter of the YMCA. The well-respected professor Adam K. Spence brought the YMCA concept to campus as early as 1887, and author Rodney T. Cohen contended that "Fisk was likely the first black college in the country to host a YMCA group."[119] With a YMCA chapter and strong student participation, Fisk was invested in the "muscular Christianity" movement as a way to bring moral uplift to the black community as well as gain respect within the broader Nashville community.

For black females, opportunities and venues for leisure represented a different definition of recreation. While white female students primarily used their free time

FIG. 4.9. The famed Fisk University chapel pictured here in 1902. Metropolitan Government of Nashville and Davidson County Archives.

outside of class for fun and fellowship, "African American women transformed recreation and leisure experiences into a vehicle for social change based on race and class issues," according to M. Deborah Bialeschki.[120] For example, there were no Fisk-sponsored sororities until 1927–28; however, many female Fiskites were members of city sororities or organizations as early as 1900. The primary work of such organizations was not to sit and socialize but rather to discuss and plan how best to serve the community. These young women formed the backbone of the black clubwoman's movement dedicated to urban reform and health campaigns. Even female members of the Jubilee Singers found themselves in a position of service as their entertainment provided funding for the university.

On campus, Fisk women could join one of three club societies. The Decagynian Club was the oldest literary club, founded in 1899, where members discussed important issues both "literary and practical."[121] Athlea Brown, a Fisk student, began the DLV Club in 1900. The name stood for *Duodecem Literae Virgines,* representing twelve young women studying the classics as well as science. By 1917 the club expanded membership and changed its focus to preparing women for service and leadership. In 1905 the Harmonia Club was established as a women-only musical club that studied music history and composition and also sang at special events. So, while Fisk maintained a club life on campus, these organizations were academic or service oriented—quite different from the clubs and societies that flourished on white campuses.

The ground shifted under Fisk University in 1915. Three years earlier President George Gates resigned after a nervous breakdown, and Richard Harris, one of Fisk's black founders, passed away. After three years of uncertainty and transition, the Board of Trustees appointed Fayette McKenzie as president in 1915. Also that year James C. Napier, the prominent businessman, succeeded the late Booker T. Washington on the board. McKenzie's vision for a modern Fisk University brought hope and stability, but his subsequent obsession with discipline and order would result in conflict and volatility.

From 1915 to 1925, Avery McKenzie played a necessary and essential role in raising the educational and curricular standards necessary for Fisk's competitive academic standing in an age of accreditation and standardization. But third-generation post–Civil War African Americans entering colleges and universities were unsatisfied with the status quo on black campuses. Demands for changes in campus culture and student regulations would open new wounds as white administrators, including McKenzie, rubbed many young African Americans the wrong way. Student revolts against white administrators at HBCUs were common in the 1920s, reflective of the broader rebellious youth culture sweeping the nation. Specifically, Fisk students protested against wearing school uniforms, prohibitions against smoking, almost total separation of the sexes, and regulations "more appropriate for 1866 than 1925."[122]

McKenzie vigorously opposed racial discrimination in Nashville. For example, he protested local discrimination and signs for "whites only" at local parks and drinking fountains. However, as a member of the Kiwanis Club and Chamber of Commerce, he seemed more interested in fostering relationships with white urban boosters and conservative black businessmen such as James C. Napier and Richard Henry Boyd. McKenzie's efforts paid off as he raised significant funds and financial pledges toward Fisk's $1 million endowment goal.

Since its founding in 1866, Fisk had worked to build racial pride and solidarity in the black community while also maintaining good rapport with white society in Nashville and New York (where most board members and benefactors lived). In many ways McKenzie's efforts paid off as white business leaders spoke highly of Fisk, boasting of its success and pointing to the school as a source of local pride. In fact, important visitors to Nashville were regularly given a tour of the campus, but some alumni and Fisk students believed that the price of white goodwill came at the cost of the school's founding principle.[123]

The growing tension over student policies was racial but also generational. Certain student clubs, literary societies, and debate teams had been established early on, and McKenzie did not disband these organizations. However, he dissolved the student government association, suspended the student newspaper, the *Fisk Herald,* and suppressed student and faculty opposition. He ruled with an iron fist, enforcing rules that strictly prohibited cigarettes and alcohol, required study hall, forbade intercollegiate athletics, and punished men and women from eating or walking together, even during daylight and without physical contact. McKenzie also refused to support the newly established NAACP branch in Nashville and barred the group's recruitment of students.[124] By the summer of 1924, Fisk University was ripe for revolt.

Small-scale student demonstrations, petitions, and letters to McKenzie and/or the Board of Trustees were effectively ignored. If anything, campus dissent strengthened McKenzie's resolve. His President's Report in 1924 stated, "Wild voices increasingly fill the air with lamentation over the chaotic motions of modern college youth, but rare is the courage that dares to profit by the wisdom of the centuries."[125] Though well-intentioned and sincere in his approach to strict discipline, his actions provided "fuel for revolt and W. E. B. Du Bois supplied the spark."[126] As a Fisk alumnus and board member, Du Bois delivered an address to an alumni meeting on Fisk's campus in June 1924. He called for McKenzie's removal, an alumni boycott, and student action. He said that while the university had raised considerable money, it had become "a place of sorrow, of infinite regret; a place where the dreams of great souls lay dusty and forgotten."[127]

After Du Bois's speech and subsequent editorials in the *Crisis,* tensions rose between students and the administration and between the Board of Trustees and alumni. Lines were drawn, sides were chosen, and a standoff ensued. At the heart of the matter were two issues: (1) whether Fisk should accept the confinement of a Jim Crow society in Nashville and train their students accordingly or risk losing northern funding and existing local white support, and (2) whether Fisk students should have a liberating, modern "college experience" or submit to a militaristic-style college culture that most local and educational leaders believed best. The two issues were interconnected but reflected a clash in the battle between continuity and change: one on a campus level but with implications that could affect southern culture more broadly.

The final answer came on February 4, 1925, when student protestors were dispersed outside McKenzie's office. Chanting "Du Bois! Du Bois!" and "Before I'll be a slave, I'll be buried in my grave," protesters turned riotous, breaking over forty windows, purportedly firing pistols, and stirring violence on campus.[128] McKenzie called the police, who stormed through dormitory doors and assaulted several students in their "zealous efforts" to arrest the protest's ringleaders.[129] Ultimately seven students were arrested and expelled. The community response was swift but divided. With over twenty-five hundred people in attendance, a meeting at a nearby church "reflected the transition of upper middle class blacks [who largely supported the students] into the elite ranks and the declining influence of the old Negro elite," who supported McKenzie despite their outrage over police brutality.[130] Student strikes over the following weeks also severely disrupted university life.

Older black leaders such as Napier and Dr. John Henry Hale tried to diffuse the situation, but only McKenzie's resignation, which he tendered in April 1925, would temper the flames of unrest in the black community. The student riot also stoked unrest and fear in the white community, particularly between older whites and younger African Americans. Prior to his resignation, McKenzie lamented, "Not only will the white citizens and the money of Nashville be turned in other directions, but the same will be true of a considerable part of the North."[131] Fisk students ran an advertisement in the conservative *Nashville Banner* assuring white Nashvillians that "they believed in law and order, and no pistols were fired on the campus" and were simply asking "for new rules, fair regulations, and the good will and respect of the community."[132] Historian Bobby Lovett articulated this bigger picture: "The Fisk student strike and similar ones at Howard University and other Negro colleges during the 1920s signaled the slow death of northern white paternalism in southern black educators.... Fisk University never regained a strong financial base of support from Nashville's colored aristocracy or its white plutocracy."[133] McKenzie's policies had instigated a standoff that pitted students and alumni against many of Nashville's black elites, middle- and upper-class whites, and northern philanthropists. As a result of the student revolt, many individuals and groups in the white community (both North and South) withdrew their financial pledges.

The new university president, Thomas Elsa Jones, a white man from Indiana, would reestablish good relationships with local whites, reignite a successful fundraising campaign, dramatically increase faculty salaries, and continue to improve curricular instruction. His initial efforts to restore trust and provide stability built upon McKenzie's work but with a very different approach. Jones's strategy successfully led to SACS accreditation in 1930, New York State Board of Regents' approval of the B.A. degree in 1931, and an A standing from the Association of American Universities (AAU). To put this accomplishment into context, the AAU only accredited 16 percent of southern white public colleges and 14 percent of southern white private colleges. Jones also completed and secured the $1 million campaign begun by McKenzie, and the Board of Trustees expanded the number of Fisk alumni on the board from three to five.

The Fisk student riot did not result in the school's first African American president, but Jones did hire the first high-level African American administrators, including Juliette Derricotte (1929) as the school's first dean of women and Alrutheus Taylor as chief academic dean (1929). He also brought highly qualified, younger black faculty on board including Z. Alexander Looby (a Howard University graduate), St. Elmo Brady (a Fisk University undergraduate and the first African American to receive a Ph.D. from the University of Illinois), and Charles S. Johnson. By 1930 these new administrators and faculty began a new chapter for Fisk and its students.

Johnson earned his Ph.D. in sociology from the University of Chicago and was a director in the National Urban League in New York City in 1920. Known as an "entrepreneur of the Harlem Renaissance," he would bring his progressive and cultural background to Fisk, where he became the new head of the Department of Sociology in 1926. He would become Fisk University's first black president in 1946. Johnson sought not only to study race relations in the South but to effect positive and meaningful change. Z. Alexander Looby later emerged as an instrumental leader in Nashville's civil rights movement. Moreover, he was one of the attorneys who prevailed in the court case that desegregated Nashville's public schools.

In terms of student culture, the events of 1924–25 and the subsequent appointment of Jones brought about significant changes affecting daily student life. The lights-out curfew was lifted for men (women were still bound by the 10:00 p.m. curfew), and men and women were permitted to walk together during the day. In fact, men and women were given social time in the parlors of Jubilee Hall two nights a week; students were allowed downtown on special occasions; and dress regulations were relaxed. A new student government was organized, and smoking (for male students) was discouraged but not prohibited. For the first time ever on campus, "well-chaperoned and carefully managed dances" were allowed."[134]

Just as Fisk began to allow school dances, so did Tennessee A&I. Chaperonage still existed, but it was less focused on individual courtships and more focused on supervising larger events. Leon Foster, class of 1926, described such a dance in 1925: "On entering the gymnasium of A. and I. State College, the sound of many voices fall upon the ear.... The music floats out mingling with laughter and sweet perfume. Couples are dancing, swaying to and fro in rhythmical movement. The matron may be seen patrolling the borders of the gymnasium, peering into obscure corners and little retreats that may form suitable coves for mischievous lovers."[135] Such published accounts are a rarity from any of Nashville's black colleges, as these schools worked diligently to portray their students as orderly, pious, and hardworking. However, there remains an undeniable shift in school-sanctioned events and socially acceptable behaviors between men and women on HBCU campuses.

Tennessee A&I did not experience the same type of student unrest as Fisk, although its president, William J. Hale, would be pressured to resign under similar circumstances in 1943. Hale required faculty members and students to adhere to strict rules, including a dress code, curfew, and class attendance. There were similarities in the authoritarian approach of Fisk's McKenzie and Tennessee A&I's Hale in the early twentieth century, but student life seemed less rigid and regimented at Tennessee A&I. In 1926 one student noted a simultaneous sense of style and solemnity as he described campus life at the state's only black public college:

> In the student body of Tennessee State College, there is a peculiar blending of the characteristics of the Negro, the South, and the youth of the present day. Light-hearted, care-free, emotional, pleasure-loving, they have the real spirit of the age. ... Dancing seems their specialty.... With music or without, they practice, even in their walks, every late step with all its variations, for though in general the rhythm is the same, everyone makes his own interpretation and aids his motion by his musical swing.... Behind the smiles in those sparkling eyes, back of the laughter and jest, there is a deeper and nobler meaning. They are flowers of the race. From them must come the leaders of tomorrow.[136]

Greek life at HBCU campuses in Nashville came much later than at local white colleges. Largely this was due to differences in the purpose and mission of black schools in comparison to institutions of higher education for whites. At Fisk the first fraternal societies were established after the student riot of 1925. The board allowed President Jones and the faculty to decide, and by June 1928, Greek life had been approved at Fisk. By the start of the 1928–29 school term, there were four fraternities and two sororities. At Tennessee A&I, there were many clubs but no fraternities until 1930 with the establishment of Omega Psi Phi (Rho Psi chapter). The first sorority was Sigma Gamma Rho, chartered in 1932. By 1939 the school maintained six fraternities and three sororities.[137] Many of the Meharry, Fisk, and Tennessee A&I fraternity and sorority chapters were part of national organizations. For example, Meharry's Kappa Alpha Kappa chapter was established in 1919, while Tennessee A&I's Kappa chapter began in 1931.

In many cases, students at Fisk and Tennessee A&I were allowed to join Greek societies at Meharry, which had welcomed fraternities a decade earlier. Prior to 1928, 60 percent of Fisk men belonged to fraternities at Meharry, which took them away from campus. Many of the women were members of local civic and social clubs and organizations. In his history of Fisk, Joe Richardson concluded that Jones believed "this interfered with the 'family spirit' on campus that he was trying to build. Since the students insisted on joining such societies, Jones thought it better to have them on campus."[138]

These Greek organizations would reflect the desire of black students to socialize with their peers beyond the watchful eye of the university and brought about a new sense of student loyalty and pride for those who joined. According to the authors of *African American Fraternities and Sororities,* such organizations also served as a symbol of "assimilation into an elite white academic tradition that further distanced them from the ordinary black masses."[139] Like white fraternities and sororities, black Greek life provided bonds of brotherhood and sisterhood.[140] Unlike for whites, however, Greek life for African Americans was less focused on drinking and parties and emphasized racial uplift and service. But most important, fraternities and sororities at Fisk, Tennessee A&I, and Meharry brought social intimacy, mutual support, and status to African American students. According to authors Michael Washington and Cheryl Nuñez, "The black Greek-letter tradition was the product of the African-American struggle for recognition and respect."[141]

Conclusion

As early as 1912 the *Hustler* ran advertisements on its front page that read, "Take your girl to the game in a Main 200," accompanied by a picture of a fraternity member driving his car decorated with Vanderbilt colors and signs with his arm around his date.[142] Nashville was the "Athens of the South" for its many educational offerings, yet the city was also a modern cultural center. Commercialized leisure and recreation were important byproducts of industrialization during the New South period. This was fueled, in part, by young adults, born after the Civil War, who attended local institutions of higher education between 1880 and 1930. Particularly after 1900, this new youth culture defined the pursuit(s) of happiness for college students—driven by complex cultural forces that ultimately produced a more modern, New South identity.

With new forms of entertainment and ideas about how to spend their time outside of class, young men and women more daringly danced, drank, and socialized without the watchful eye of parents, faculty, or administrators. Literary societies and debate teams gave way to more raucous fraternities and party-minded sororities and social clubs on white campuses. College students interacted more often and with greater freedom and less formality. The shift of cultural values and eagerness of college students to embrace new forms of fun would set in motion trends that produced today's modern college experience.

Nashville's white colleges, which stretched southwest, were transformed from centers of classical learning for privileged young men to sites of amusement and play accompanied by periods of study and learning. Administrators, faculty, and trustees grappled with the "conflicting worlds of scholarship and the extracurriculum."[143] The nature of social interaction between men and women changed for several reasons, all of which were interconnected. First, more women attended college, some attending single-gender schools like Ward-Belmont and others attending traditionally male universities such as Vanderbilt. Second, off campus leisure would drastically change the social landscape and provide unchaperoned opportunities for men and women. Third, on-campus culture shifted from university-sponsored events to student-led organization and societies.

These factors combined to create a ripple effect, as a new youth culture emerged in the 1890s. This generation of young adults shaped the world of leisure and social interaction by a continual process of societal challenge, reaction, and modification. Students also rebelled against nineteenth-century constraints, which led to the formation of a more assertive, modern approach to curricular and extracurricular interaction. Some rebels, such as the Agrarians, even voiced and articulated new philosophies aimed at the entire region.

More generally, the college experience was transformed for young adults attending Vanderbilt, Ward-Belmont, and to an extent Peabody and David Lipscomb. The relationships formed on campus extended into the city, where young men and women from different schools mixed at school-sanctioned events as well as at public concerts, performances, entertainment venues, city parks, shopping districts, dances, and parties. College life grew more distracting but also more exciting.

New opportunities and venues for recreation and entertainment affected African American collegians differently from how they affected white men or even white women. It may have been cultural taboo and social suicide for a respectable young white woman to go downtown alone or be seen in Jack's Alley or the Arcade at night. However it was entirely different for young black students who risked physical safety or encounters with police if they ventured into downtown "white" establishments. Thus, African American students in Nashville stayed largely within the black cultural and commercial corridor located along Jefferson Street, which ran northwest from downtown.

For white universities, college culture by 1930 was nearly unrecognizable from the early days of the postbellum era. The sixty-five-year period following the Civil War witnessed the transformation of colleges nationwide. These changes were also prevalent on the campuses of Nashville's institutions of higher education. Expanded course offerings shifted the curricular structure from classical studies to a wider array of elective coursework. This, in turn, led to a demographic change in the makeup of the study body at most local colleges. In particular, middle-class men and women altered the on-campus dynamic. In 1910 Vanderbilt chancellor James Kirkland recognized these new developments: "There have been great changes in college life. . . . [Before] the students were all preparing to enter some profession. They rose early in the morning and closed the day with religious serves. Instead of a home, the college is now a state. College life is now a bigger thing . . . than ever before."[144]

Such changes led to greater diversity on campus, both in terms of students and courses. However, the democratization and modernization of higher education also led to an internal backlash of moneyed men who created new barriers to protect their status on campus. Greek life provided an alternative collegiate space whereby money and social status still mattered. The popularity of fraternities and sororities created new problems for universities like Vanderbilt, as the student body was divided into a hierarchy of Greeks and non-Greeks. Off-campus fraternity and sorority houses would further isolate different student groups from one another. Administrators sought to control and regulate alcohol, parties, and hazing but with only nominal success. The concurrent rise of competitive athletics would change college life as well.

5
Students of Sport
Athletics and Higher Education

The solution to problems in our colleges and universities lies not in less athletics, but in more athletics.

—Charles Young, the *Hustler* (March 14, 1907)

You are going against Yankees, some of whose grandfathers killed your grandfathers in the Civil War.

—Coach Dan McGugin to the Vanderbilt football team prior to the 1922 Michigan game

In 1885 the U.S. Bureau of Education stated, "Neither the general nor college public in the South manifests much interest in athletics or gymnastics."[1] Over the next fifty years, the public's interest in intercollegiate competition not only increased—college sports would become a major part of the modern southern identity. Even political primaries are dubbed the "SEC primary" after the NCAA's Southeastern Conference. Prior to mid-1880s universities had celebrated classic scholarship, and the public respected, albeit somewhat distantly, the academic training

FIG. 5.1. Vanderbilt vs. Ole Miss advertisement in the *Tennessean*, Sept. 28, 1929. Metropolitan Government of Nashville and Davidson County Archives.

colleges provided. As intercollegiate competition grew in the 1890s and early 1900s, it was reformed and ultimately ritualized to become a centerpiece of the modern university.[2] Nashville's symbiotic relationship with its colleges and universities came to its fullest fruition through intercollegiate sports. Because of college sports, Nashville remains a prime representative of southern-style progressivism.

Between 1865 and 1900 young men and women desired expanded options in the classroom. They also sought to throw off Victorian and antebellum restraints, instead seeking out leisure venues and activities that afforded greater autonomy. After 1900 postbellum-born men and women would complete the transformation of higher education. The modern college experience included a general education curriculum, social events, greater freedom off campus, coed student bodies, and less emphasis on religion. But campus culture was perhaps most affected by the swift and sweeping rise of competitive intercollegiate athletics, which in turn connected the university to the community.

Physical activities on college campuses evolved into opportunities for commercialized leisure and spectator sport, which helped redefine expressions of southern exceptionalism from 1885 to 1930. This exceptionalism was largely played out on the gridiron. The legitimacy gained by athletics and the ensuing, sometimes volatile relationship between higher education and the student and local community reveal the important ways in which athletic rituals and sporting spectacles resonated for those seeking to create a New South.[3]

A cultural and moral campaign in the 1890s attempted to stem the rising tide of college sports. Reformers and evangelists viewed competitive athletic contests as spaces that enabled, if not encouraged, gambling, drinking, on-field violence, and bad student behavior off campus. Such behavior, critics believed, threatened the virtuous nature of learning. Sports also met resistance from the hierarchical structure of colleges previously focused on classic study and specialized departments. After 1910 resistance to competitive sports decreased as college games were modified and regulated. Perhaps even more significant, the popularity of sports with both students and the general public outweighed academic and religious concerns—the proverbial train had left the station.

The roots of this cultural shift began in the late 1880s as southerners, in some part, replaced their allegiance to the Confederacy with an new devotion to southern colleges, and in particular, collegiate sports. Sports provided a new battleground whereby participants and audiences could represent "their" school. By 1930 many loyal fans were connected to the university as students, faculty, or alumni. However, many were simply community supporters who pledged their allegiance to a university team without ever setting foot in one of its classrooms. Vanderbilt University would be a major force in this process, not just in the South but throughout the nation. The dominant southern team in football for the first quarter of the twentieth century, Vanderbilt was a leader in the formation of college athletic rules, regulations, and conference play.

Students, alumni, and members of the community were certainly willing to pay the price of admission for sporting events, especially as rivalries intensified. Ticket sales, concession sales, merchandise, and promotion all served to create a new avenue of consumerism directly sponsored by institutions of higher education. Even student newspapers reflected the commodification of leisure through an array of advertisements for stores such as Gray and Dudley Hardware, selling "bicycles, sweaters, and athletic goods."[4] Organized athletics became closely connected to the "ideals and practices of American capitalism" as college sports developed into one of the central rituals of American life in the twentieth century.[5] As sports settled into the southern landscape, stadiums also became part of modern southern society. Stadiums, courts, tracks, and fields were distinctive man-made spaces for debating fundamental questions, among them the roles of men and women, the meanings of racial difference, and the contours of accepted social conduct.

Male sports reinforced the subordinate role of women who supported their school and cheered for "their men." While Vanderbilt, Fisk, David Lipscomb, and Ward-Belmont (and predecessor schools) all featured women's athletic teams, women's sports would develop carefully under the umbrella of education rather than "belong" to the overall community. Still, progressive views on women's health, education, clothing, and gender roles allowed for a more visible presence of young women that included competitive sports. By the time the United States approached entry into World War I, athletic participation was viewed as commonplace and suitable for young women. However, the 1920s ended with a backlash led by the Women's Division of Amateur Athletics Federation (WDAAF), which sought to eliminate intercollegiate competition and restrict women's athletic programs.

Sports at Fisk University, and to an extent Tennessee A&I, Meharry, and Roger Williams, were seen as a way for African Americans to gain respect through athletic accomplishment. Local HBCUs also believed that physical fitness was essential to students' intellectual and moral development. As the *Fisk Herald* stated in 1894, "We do believe that not only the brain but also hands and feet ought to be cultivated, for well has it been said that only strong arms can make men and nations free."[6] College sports and athletics were prominent on black campuses but most remained intramural or local-level competitions. Only Fisk competed in intercollegiate conference play before 1929.

The long-term benefits of college sport also extended to those who did not participate as athletes—both students and alumni. As Helen Horowitz argued, "Alumni with fond memories of college days emerged to endow their alma mater. Football games cultivated undergraduate loyalty, especially when the school had winning teams."[7] Ultimately the university's reputation and the very honor of its male students, in particular, became tied vicariously but inextricably to the school's athletic program. Young scholars were perhaps the brightest but no longer the best, at least not according to the general public. Instead, college athletes either defended or reaffirmed a school's prestige through victory or risked losing that honor if defeated.

The Ivory Tower, Field House, and "School Spirit"

The catalog of the University of the South in Sewanee, Tennessee, established in 1858, stated that a student should "engage in the sports which make him a true southern man, hunting, shooting, [and] riding." After the Civil War, however, southern elites began to project southern manhood on "other sports."[8] Vanderbilt, chartered in 1873, would play the University of the South in the first intercollegiate athletic competition—baseball—in Nashville in 1877. The game was unauthorized and drew condemnation from Vanderbilt's faculty and administration, who, in Paul Conkin's words, "allowed it to take place but strictly forbade any subsequent foolishness of the sort."[9] The 1877 baseball game would mark the beginning of a tenuous and precarious relationship between the ivory tower of academics and the athletic fields of collegiate sport. It would also mark a shift in meanings of masculinity and honor that complicated modern meanings of southern exceptionalism. Sports were the perfect metaphor and messenger for southern manhood in the twentieth century. Nashville would become a site for this phenomenon to, quite literally, play out.

College athletics were born out of a post–Civil War tradition that emphasized physical activity as a key to a healthy body and mind. The *Hustler* articulated this sentiment in 1899: "When a student reaches college it is certainly time that he should have some faint conception of what a great part the care of his health and physical development must play in his life. . . . First of all a man should have a strong body before he hopes to have a great mind. . . . Physical work that one so much enjoys that he takes exercise unconsciously does him good. . . . It would be folly to leave this side of your life uncared for while in college."[10] This reflected the concept of "muscular Christianity," which was a prominent theme in higher education but also larger society. Organizations such as the YMCA and the Salvation Army emphasized the body as a temple of good moral living, and healthy living would lead to the attainment of economic, spiritual, and intellectual stability.[11]

In 1881 Vanderbilt students regularly used the school's new gymnasium, modestly equipped with weights, bars, and other light equipment for exercise and workouts. In 1883 the first intramural football scrimmages were held on campus, and the baseball team regularly played local teams and traveled out of town for "away" games. An athletic association was formed in 1886, and football games between academic departments began in the late 1880s. Aside from organized team sports, Vanderbilt sponsored "class games" as early as 1880 in which respective classes competed in a variety of activities.[12] By the early 1890s basketball had gained popularity with students. Athletic events were not just about watching the game but instead became a variety show of sorts. At an 1897 Vanderbilt basketball game, the program included the following: "1. Overture by Orchestra, 2. Leaping, high dive, and Spring board Somersaults, 3. Triple acrobatic acting by two teams from Nashville Athletic Club, 4. First half of Basketball game, 5. Indian Club swinging [an exercise originating in India that involved swinging lightweight clubs to exercise the shoulder, wrist, and elbow, popular in the United States until the 1920s], 6. Last Half of Basketball game."[13]

The first public basketball game at Vanderbilt occurred in December 1901, with the sophomores beating a preselected team of five, 13–4. Although the newspaper account reported that attendance was poor, the halftime show consisted of a boxing match and fencing exhibition, and it was "on the whole a good game."[14] Many of the men's teams competed against a basketball team formed by the Nashville Athletic Club, a semiprofessional league that emerged in 1895.[15] In addition to competitive team sports, annual tennis tournaments were held at Vanderbilt, and a golf club was established in 1900.

Teams were formed in response to the popularity of sports for both participants as well as spectators. In 1896 Vanderbilt hosted a track meet, referred to as "Field Day," and competed against fifteen other colleges that belonged to the newly formed Southern Intercollegiate Athletic Association (SIAA). With nearly twenty schools competing by 1900, there were so many participants that the track had to be widened at the old Dudley Field, built in 1892. The attraction of basketball also increased quickly, and citing the "growing interest," the city formed a basketball league in 1903. The city league, which consisted of the YMCA Ramblers, Nashville Athletic Club, Tennessee Medical and Dental Departments, and Vanderbilt, would later be replaced by SIAA conference play.[16] City league basketball games were often played in a local skating rink called the Hippodrome, located across the street from Centennial Park near Vanderbilt.[17]

College games and meets were far from sophisticated. For example, when Vanderbilt's basketball team traveled to Mobile, Alabama, to play, the court was lined with chicken wire to distinguish out of bounds. In 1913 a basketball game scheduled between Vanderbilt and the YMCA Ramblers was canceled when it was discovered that two of Vanderbilt's players, Henry "Monk" Sharp and another student identified as Robinson, intended to play for the more successful Ramblers. The *Tennessean* reported: "Without these two the Vanderbilt five would have been badly crippled, since it would have been necessary to supply their places with substitutes, and therefore, they have decided to call the game off."[18] It was also not uncommon for college teams to play several games on an extended road trip. Students were excused for classes missed, which signaled the growing legitimacy of student-athletes in the eyes of the college or university administration.

The University of Nashville/Peabody had club teams and formed an athletic association that hired part-time coaches. Between 1890 and 1900, Peabody constructed a baseball field, football field, and track, but never built a gymnasium for basketball. In 1900 the college assumed financial and organizational control of athletics and adopted the colors of garnet and blue. While Peabody maintained

FIG. 5.2. Peabody College still fielded athletic teams, including football through the 1920s. A man identified as "Claude" played for Peabody from 1921–1923. Metropolitan Government of Nashville and Davidson County Archives.

its athletic program through the 1920s, it discontinued football contests with Vanderbilt. As a whole, according to Paul Conkin, "intercollegiate athletics were never as prominent at Peabody as most colleges."[19] Competitive sport also played a secondary role at David Lipscomb College. Lipscomb focused on baseball, basketball, and tennis. The school built courts and a field on its new campus in 1903, but its athletes did not compete in conference play or competitive intercollegiate seasons until after 1930.

Collegiate "football" began in 1869 with Rutgers defeating Princeton 6–4, using rules that most closely resembled those of soccer.[20] In early games a touchdown was four points, as were field goals, and the conversion "extra point" kick was two points. Two decades later, Vanderbilt's first football season was played in 1890–91, with games against Sewanee and Washington University of St. Louis twice each at the Nashville Athletic Club field downtown. Approximately two hundred fans were on hand. The team was coached by student Elliott H. Jones (class of 1891) with the following record: at Sewanee (W 22–0), Washington–St. Louis (L 24–6), Sewanee (W 26–4), and at Washington–St. Louis (W 4–0).

The first game had been played the previous year in 1890 against the University of Nashville/Peabody College, but it was the only game of the year and considered more of an exhibition. The University of Nashville's charter had been amended several times since 1874 when its literary department became part of the new normal college. Confusion grew over the names in the 1880s and 1890s, although the University of Nashville and Peabody Normal School each maintained separate boards of trust. Sources use the names interchangeably throughout the 1890s, but most of what was once the University of Nashville, including its campus, became Peabody College. That said, the first football game originated with a challenge issued by the University of Nashville/Peabody to Vanderbilt's Athletic Association. This led to a quickly called mass student meeting. A motion was made to accept the challenge because "Vanderbilt had never taken anything off of Peabody and should not do so now."[21]

The motion passed unanimously, and college football was born in Nashville. Jones, named captain, called for Vanderbilt students who had any experience with the game, which gave him an initial team of six players. Other students were recruited, and the game was held two weeks later on Thanksgiving Day at Sulphur Dell Athletic Park, with Vanderbilt defeating the "Normalites," as they were nicknamed, 40–0. Sulphur Dell was the site of Nashville's main baseball park and athletic fields, located a half mile north of the state capitol, and served as the home of the Nashville Americans (baseball) in 1895 and later the Nashville Volunteers, or Vols, from 1901 to 1963.[22] The Vanderbilt Commodores would also play and win each contest with the University of Nashville between 1892 and 1904, which largely consisted of student-athletes from its medical school, college prep departments, and some "Normalites."[23]

Historian Andrew Doyle has argued that sports, and football specifically, represented a higher sense of purpose as southern athletes fought to defend not only their colleges and universities but also their regional culture, way of life, and cavalier legacy: "Like the New South movement itself, early southern college football was an amalgamation of innovation and tradition."[24] In Middle Tennessee, Vanderbilt University, Sewanee (University of the South), and the University of Nashville/Peabody (until 1909) best exemplified these attitudes. Explicitly, football games were cast as "honor contests" between southern schools as well as with colleges outside the region. Such sentiments are best expressed in Vanderbilt's weekly six-page student newspaper, the *Hustler,* which was sponsored by the Athletic Association from 1898 to 1917. The newspaper's athletic coverage was

FIG. 5.3. Vanderbilt vs. Sewanee (University of the South), 1930. Metropolitan Government of Nashville and Davidson County Archives.

extensive, providing a play-by-play commentary on football, baseball, track, and basketball games. The *Hustler* also featured in-depth reporting of college and city-wide tennis matches, field days, and intramural or club contests as well as editorials about the athletic programs of other schools and governing bodies such as the SIAA. Beyond the student-run paper at Vanderbilt, Nashville newspapers such as the *Banner, Nashville American,* and the *Tennessean* (after 1907) also provided regular and generous coverage. Games were highly anticipated and celebrated, if won, with downtown parades and Greek society parties into the night.

At first, southern culture had rejected what they viewed as a northern invention that represented modernity and order rather than agrarianism. But by 1900, according to Doyle, "sports proponents muted this opposition by imbuing the sport with the trappings of sectional pride and the faithful sang 'Dixie' and bellowed with 'Rebel Yells.'"[25] Though no southern team defeated a major northern opponent in the first decades of college football, universities in the South described such games as "northern invasions" and congratulated returning teams for defending regional honor even after a loss. A sportswriter for the *Nashville American* even declared the 1905 Vanderbilt football loss to Michigan (0–18) as Vanderbilt's "greatest triumph since the team was organized."[26]

The *Hustler* regularly placed the high stakes of southern pride on the line, as in this promotion of an upcoming game: "If Vanderbilt beats Sewanee we will close the season with flying colors and will again be accorded the championship of all 'Dixie' in the world of college baseball."[27] In February 1898 the newspaper introduced a new baseball season with the following call: "In the North as well as in the South the teams have begun practice, and speculations are rife as to what the relative strength of the teams will be."[28] Vanderbilt planned to play Harvard, Cornell, Columbia, Brown, and Pennsylvania, but "no game has yet been scheduled with Princeton." The schedule also included an "extensive" southern tour to play smaller schools as well as the Universities of Georgia and North Carolina. The *Hustler* also noted, "Auburn and University of Alabama have organized teams, which have gone into training."[29] After 1893, Conkin noted, football and basketball "tended to diminish student support of tennis, baseball, and track, although Vanderbilt consistently came in first or second in the Southern Association track meets."[30] Events and games related to the basketball, tennis, and track and field teams were regularly and prominently published, but football proved to be more popular.

After the death of the University of Georgia's Von Gammon from injuries sustained in an 1897 football game with the University of Virginia, a reformist movement swept the South to ban the sport. Particularly, church-affiliated schools condemned what they saw as sanctioned violence and heavily criticized the side effects of bad behavior and the carnival-like atmosphere of game days. Emory, Trinity (later Duke), Furman, and Wake Forest Universities, all affiliated with the Baptist or Methodist churches, either temporarily denied the establishment of football or dissolved existing programs. Vanderbilt University, first established by the Methodists in conjunction with a $1 million endowment from Cornelius Vanderbilt, resisted this trend. Led by James Kirkland, who became chancellor in 1893, Vanderbilt continued its football program to the disappointment of many southern Methodists. Historian Andrew Doyle noted, "Football became an emotional flash point in the twenty-year struggle between Methodist conservatives and the Kirkland administration for control of Vanderbilt . . . [and] their failure to eliminate the Vanderbilt football program revealed the declining power of conservative evangelicals to define and shape southern culture."[31]

Nationwide, college sports were in dire need of regulation and uniform enforcement of standard rules, but football remained the most controversial. In 1897 the state of North Dakota introduced into its state legislature a bill to make playing football a misdemeanor.[32] Others believed that football promoted promiscuous

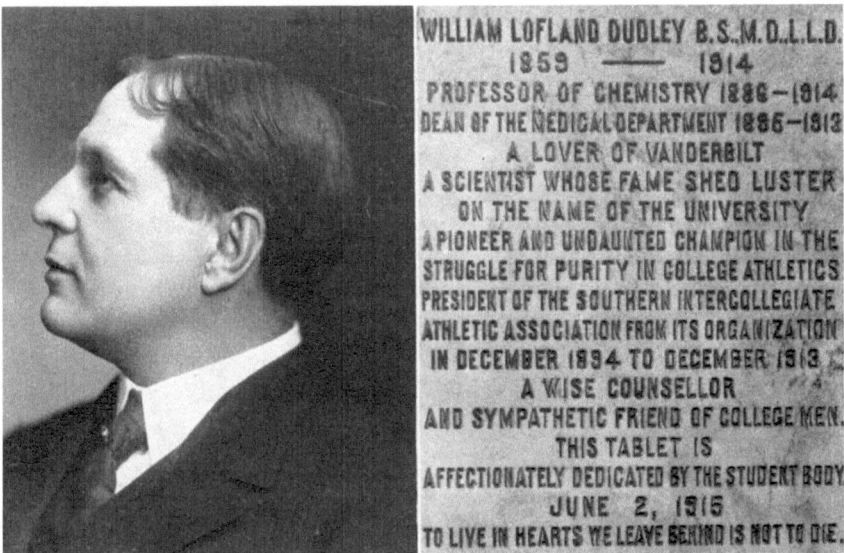

FIG. 5.4. William Dudley, Vanderbilt professor, athletic director, and founder of the SIAA which later developed into what is today the SEC. Courtesy of Ridley Wills II.

behavior, drinking, and gambling. Many argued that sports venues were not acceptable for women. Eligibility violations, cheating, and rough misconduct on field were also problematic for college football programs across the nation. Vanderbilt also fell victim to such practices. Even the *Hustler* "admitted that one player was not a student" and "older Dental and Medical students, who faced no admission requirements at all, often dominated early Vanderbilt teams, [with] players staying on the team for five or six years."[33]

In 1894 William Dudley led the effort to found the Southern Intercollegiate Athletic Association (SIAA) in Atlanta, Georgia, along with Alabama, Auburn, Georgia, Sewanee, Georgia Tech, and North Carolina. A year later, seven more colleges joined the SIAA: Cumberland University (in Lebanon, Tennessee), Louisiana State, Mississippi, Mississippi State, Tennessee, Texas, and Tulane. The SIAA was the first organized conference for college athletics in the South and governed football, baseball, basketball, and track and field for schools within its association. Known by many as the "father of southern football," Dudley came to Vanderbilt as a chemistry professor in 1886, and he later served as the dean of the Medical School from 1895 until his death in 1914. He also served as the director of affairs for the Centennial Exposition of 1897.

Led by Dudley, the SIAA drafted a constitution and bylaws to govern college sports. This included several important regulations: players must be "bona fide" students at their respective colleges, capped an athlete's eligibility at five years, banned faculty and coaches from play, defined officiating duties, denied the payment or compensation of athletes, and mandated that athletes be amateur only. The SIAA would meet annually and the organization's stated purpose (1895) was "the development and purification of college athletics throughout the South."[34] While there was no clear playoff or championship tournament structure, Vanderbilt claimed seven football titles and seven football co-championships, the most of any member school from 1894 to 1921. In 1922 Vanderbilt and other larger universities dropped out of the SIAA to join the newly formed Southern Conference, established a year earlier, in what would later become the basis for the current Southeastern Conference (SEC). The move came as the SIAA swelled to over thirty schools of all sizes, with a geographical area stretching from Texas to Virginia to Florida.[35] The SIAA was dissolved in 1942, and most of its charter schools became part of the current SEC.[36]

These reforms propelled southern football into the modern sporting age, but additional reforms would be needed after 1895. In 1902 the *Hustler* called for renewed reform: "In the South, there is need of a readjustment in the Inter-Collegiate Athletic Association, which will save us from criticism that now falls on account of a confusion of ideas as to the interpretation of certain rulings."[37] The author continued, "While it is good to have a winning combination, it is far better to have a pure combination free from ringers, semi-professionals, and those who have received pay for play."[38] Corruption and cheating was but one issue for college sports. Another involved drunken or rowdy spectators and large crowds.

In Nashville a handful of postgame events resulted in bad behavior that many blamed on football and college students. The night after the 1892 football contest between the University of Nashville/Peabody and Vanderbilt, the two schools participated in a debate. After the debate concluded and while the judges were deliberating, some Vanderbilt players "blackened the game ball" with the score 40–4 in large letters and placed it on the lectern. The presiding officer of the debate team quickly removed it but not before the audience saw it.[39] Vanderbilt students cheered, but the faculty and administration were horrified at the lack of courtesy as well as the interruption of a serious academic event.

After one game between Vanderbilt and the University of Nashville, students poured into downtown to enjoy postgame festivities when student fights erupted. In 1909 Vanderbilt defeated Auburn, and the student portion of the crowd, which included mostly young men and some young women, went from taunting to truly rowdy behavior. "Like Sherman's March through Georgia, the surging crowd started a campaign through the streets of Nashville," the *Hustler* reported.[40] Although such incidents were rare in Nashville, it did give legitimacy to the concerns of the college and community regarding competitive, school-sponsored athletics that seemed to inspire chaotic and impulsive behavior.

In 1897, while still under Methodist control, the board came close to voting on a motion that would have abolished all college athletics at Vanderbilt. This was in reaction to a violent brawl that occurred between its students and University of Nashville students in 1896. The game "degenerated into very rough play, with several kneeings of downed players . . . and after several incidents, the contending fans rushed the field and joined in pitched battle."[41] The chaos and violence made national news and "[the chancellor] was infuriated." But even so, the faculty and administration recognized the benefits of football for the university, despite reservations about the game itself. Football had increased student loyalty and enrollment, inspired an impassioned sense of school spirit, and "attracted the first broad and sustained interest on the part of Nashvillians."[42] Of course, those benefits were in addition to the potential revenue and recruitment that sports brought to Vanderbilt.

Ultimately, Vanderbilt administrators and the Board of Trust chose to focus on the pros rather than the cons of college sports. College spirit had reached a new height that demanded loyalty and support. Historian Brian Ingrassia argued that college sport was a popular activity that created a middlebrow culture, "making the world of highbrow intellectualism legible, or palatable, to the public.[43]

Modern College Sports and Urban Spaces

The development of athletic programs and spectator crowds also aided the New South's economic metamorphosis. According to Andrew Miller,

> The structure of sport began to conform to models of commercial and industrial enterprise associated with the urban North, the rituals of competition acquired added significance. . . . The rules of the games, codified and published nationwide, likewise stressed increasingly "rational" processes . . . with an emerging hierarchy of authority headed by expert, professional coaches and training.[44]

Vanderbilt began hiring part-time coaches who were recent graduates from Pennsylvania, Princeton, and Harvard, with salaries ranging from $400 to $800 for a season.[45] In 1904 Vanderbilt recruited a coach who would be instrumental

Napoleon and His Marshal Ney

DAN E. McGUGIN
Head coach of football and director of athletics.

This portly generalissimo with the good natured countenance has been directing Commodore campaigns for the past eighteen years, and is still the foxiest of them all. Besides holding down a seat in the Senate, manipulating a big law practice, dealing in oil, and countless other minor things, Old Dan is always on hand every fall to develop another grid machine out on Dudley field to uphold Vanderbilt's name in Southern football. It has been McGugin who has raised the name of Vanderbilt to such a high place in the football world.

His unfailing strategy and cunning were never displayed to better advantage than in the Texas and Georgia games of the past season, when against what were apparently overwhelming odds, he guided his fighting cohorts to victories that ultimately gave the Commodores an equal claim on the Southern title.

It has often been said that the secret of Senator Dan's success as a gridiron coach was not so much due to his cunning and strategy nor to his inside knowledge of the game, but to his strong, influential personality that causes his men to fight hard and play their best to please "Coach." Col. Dan is just in his prime as a gridiron mentor, and good for many seasons yet. May he never desert his first love.

WALLACE WADE
Full-time coach, football, basketball and baseball.

FIG. 5.5. Vanderbilt University head coach Dan McGugin and assistant coach Wallace Wade. Courtesy of Ridley Wills II.

in forming the school's early football reputation and success. Dan McGugin was hired after having played and served as an assistant coach for the University of Michigan, Vanderbilt's main northern rival during this period. McGugin was not a southerner but channeled the region's distinctive sense of honor and loyalty. In perhaps the ultimate irony, this "Yankee" cultivated immense southern pride in Nashville by building the region's preeminent program at Vanderbilt in the first quarter of the twentieth century.

Under McGugin's direction, expertise, and discipline, Vanderbilt won all nine of its games in 1904, outscoring opponents 452–4.[46] In an iconic moment, McGugin was hired full-time and joined the university's teaching faculty—the first full-time faculty member at a major southern university employed specifically to coach football. He was the head coach of Vanderbilt's football program from 1904 to 1917, and after World War I he resumed the helm, coaching from 1919 until his retirement in 1934. His total record after nearly thirty years at Vanderbilt was 197 wins, 55 losses, and 19 ties. During the first half of his tenure, "so dominant was Vanderbilt in the South that other struggling teams, such as those at Georgia, Alabama [which lost 0–78 in 1906], and Tennessee, hesitated to play the Commodores or sour-graped their one-sided losses by charging that Vanderbilt used professional athletes."[47]

Athletics emerged as a public-relations ambassador for college and universities for the better, with victories and accolades or, for the worse, with cases of on-field misbehavior or postgame fights. However, as a whole, sport was not only an instantly popular addition to campus culture, but the attendant school spirit also spilled over into the community. This represented a major shift from the formerly passive relationship between the larger college and the city. As a result, schools indulged their students, alumni, and local communities with an era of building campaigns in the 1920s, not of classrooms and libraries but of stadiums, field houses, and basketball arenas. Intercollegiate athletics were no longer simply about developing school loyalty or southern masculinity. College sport had also assumed its role as a powerful recruitment tool for future students, as well as a bridge that established a strong connection with the broader local community. Historian Frederick Rudolph wrote candidly in his seminal work *The American College and University:* "At last the American college and university had discovered something that all sorts of people cared about passionately. . . . No one had ever had to number the players in Greek class, but then no one very much cared what was going on there."[48]

Stephen Hardy, in *How Boston Played,* has described a "structural triad" that served to shape relationships within growing urban areas along with notions of leisure, recreation, and sport. Hardy argued that this triad describes humanity in its rawest forms: body (physical), mind (social), and soul (state of mind).[49] At the turn of the century, this triad of human and urban forces, constantly in motion and reacting to one another, would create a ripple effect. Emergent forms of leisure and notions of urban space produced new meanings and communities, particularly for young people and urban boosters.[50] This occurred in Nashville most predominantly on college campuses through leisure activities and sport that took place in city parks, theaters, and athletic fields.

FIG. 5.6. 1921 Vanderbilt University football team in action. The Commodores outscored its opponents 161–21 for a record of 7–0–1 (4–0–1 in conference games) and a share of the SIAA championship. Courtesy of Ridley Wills II.

Vanderbilt's student culture was ripe for college athletics, and sporting events merged with leisure and social organizations to consume the body, mind, and soul of its students. Since the 1880s Vanderbilt had featured the largest number of Greek chapters of any Nashville college, and the numbers of sponsored dances and other outings increased dramatically. While dances occurred in the late nineteenth century, the nature of dances and social interaction evolved decidedly after 1900. For example, in 1906 dances began mixing with college sports. After the Vanderbilt-Michigan baseball game, both teams met a host of other young men and women at the school's University Club, where the "local boys had a chance to take a back seat, and Michigan men were decidedly the rage."[51] Even prior to the 1922 Vanderbilt game against Michigan to dedicate the new Dudley Stadium, local newspapers were filled with ads encouraging attendees to buy the "latest fashions, hats, suits, and furs to wear to the game."[52] Joseph Frank and Son offered a pre–game day special with an extra pair of pants included with every purchase of a Fulwirth suit that "practically doubled the life of your suit for only $27.50."[53] This represented important links between and among those connected to the business community, local colleges, and the commercialization of sports.

Athletic victories helped facilitate an orderly transition to modernity on southern terms. With the advent and ascension of college sport in the United States, college loyalty cultivated pride within the larger community as well. The Vanderbilt newspaper argued that athletics promoted unity on-campus by allowing visitors to "see the beautiful athletic field, the building, and breathe the University spirit."[54] Perhaps football, more than any other sport, superseded demographic differences. Students who paid tuition to attend represented the sons and daughters of mostly the upper middle class, but community members of all socioeconomic backgrounds (including men and women) came out to watch and cheer for local college teams. Many Vanderbilt men like Daniel May, James W. Warner Jr., and Guilford Dudley Jr. were either from Nashville or planted roots in Nashville following graduation. As they moved into positions of power in local industry and commerce, they gave back to the university most noticeably through their continued support as athletic boosters or advertising sponsors.

The construction of the first Dudley Field was approved in 1892 after the administration realized that playing on a field located on campus could bring huge revenue to the school. Vanderbilt followed the leads of Yale, Harvard, and Princeton, whose games averaged over fourteen thousand in attendance, with each school netting approximately $12,000 per game.[55] By the mid-1890s, over five thousand spectators attended football games at the original Dudley Field and Stadium. Nashvillians flocked to Vanderbilt games at the old Dudley Field until 1922, but they sat on small wooden stands or milled about beyond the end zones or dugouts. This would change with the modern sports stadium.

While Nashville's football program gained considerable prestige from 1900 to 1920, visiting teams and local spectators were unimpressed with the school's athletic fields and venues. Southern college sports were seen as inferior, in part, because their facilities lagged behind those of northern schools. The campaign to build the new Dudley Stadium was part of a larger movement to raise the bar at southern colleges and universities in the 1920s. Other stadiums completed during the decade included Tennessee's Shields-Watkins Field (1921), LSU's Tiger Stadium (1924), North Carolina's Kenan Field (1927), Duke Stadium (1929), and Georgia's Sanford Stadium (1929). These "massive, reinforced-concrete stadiums" created a "visible and permanent presence for big-time football on post–World War I campuses," concluded Brian Ingrassia.[56] Dudley Stadium, the first in the South to be used exclusively for football, was single-decked with a horseshoe grandstand and concrete bleachers, originally planned to seat forty thousand but scaled back to hold more realistic crowds of twenty thousand.

The new Dudley Stadium was located near Twenty-fifth Avenue, which was serviced by one of two streetcar lines that ran on either side of campus. Students, alumni, and community members could ride public streetcars to multiple stops near the stadium, as they had with the original Dudley Stadium. In addition to streetcars, West End Avenue and Twenty-first Avenue/Hillsboro Avenue crowded with people walking to the game. Even out-of-towners riding into Union Station on the NC&St.L or L&N railroads could walk or take a short streetcar ride to Dudley Stadium.

In the 1930s the transition from public transportation to private motorcars was accompanied by the expansion of suburbia. Suburbs were also made practical by larger highways that connected the hinterland to the urban core. This made the new Dudley Stadium's location on the edge of campus even more important so that Vanderbilt might provide ample parking. Ultimately most Commodore fans, except students living on campus, traveled to games by automobile. Cars in parking lots would lead to opportunities for "tailgating"—a phenomenon that emerged as fans and alumni sought to enjoy pregame festivities.

FIG. 5.7. Completed Dudley Stadium, 1922. Metropolitan Government of Nashville and Davidson County Archives.

FIG. 5.8. The relationship between the city's business community and Vanderbilt University was not only strong, the efforts of Nashville's leading business men garnered the university's yearbook dedication in 1922. Courtesy of Ridley Wills II.

Fundraising and construction efforts for a new Dudley Stadium also directly connected the university to the city and its leaders. A local firm was awarded the building contract and several Vanderbilt alumni, who were engineers and architects in Nashville, supervised the stadium's construction.[57] The athletic association, governed by Vanderbilt faculty, alumni, students, and local community members, secured initial loans from the Vanderbilt Board of Trust for $75,000. In turn, Board Chair Whitefoord Cole led a downtown fund drive, and "both the Chamber of Commerce and civic clubs joined the effort," which raised another $80,000 in pledges.[58] Members of the Chamber of Commerce such as William Manier Sr. (class of 1881), William Manier Jr. (class of 1905), and H. G. Hill, president of the Chamber of Commerce, assisted Cole in the stadium's fundraising drive.[59] Nashville business leaders realized that the active support of football served to promote the city. Spectators who came to Nashville for games also spent money in the local economy. Urban boosters and Vanderbilt officials alike wanted visitors to have a favorable opinion of Nashville, and local community members also wanted to show off the city. As Ingrassia argued, "Athletics . . . filled the cultural gap by making universities meaningful to the public."[60]

The opening of the new Dudley Stadium allowed Vanderbilt to stage mass-marketed events that also brought positive attention to the city. Dudley Stadium, with a seating capacity of just over twenty thousand, was a tangible and visible way to "showcase the progressive urban society of the twentieth-century South."[61] Vanderbilt celebrated the opening of the "New Dudley Field" with a large parade, which began downtown and marched up Broadway and West End Avenue with student bands, floats, and flags. Tennessee Governor Alfred Taylor and even Cornelius Vanderbilt (great-great-grandson of the school's founder) attended.[62] It was a citywide affair that served as a pivotal moment connecting Vanderbilt to the larger Nashville community.

Following the parade, Coach McGugin stressed "southern honor" in his pre-game speech to the team prior to their first game in the new stadium: "You are going against Yankees, some of whose grandfathers killed your grandfathers in the Civil War."[63] Ironically, McGugin's father had been an officer in the Union army. As the Vanderbilt captain, Jess Neely, led the Commodores onto the field, the two teams met at the fifty-yard line to pose for a picture, and the game ball was dropped from an airplane and caught, after one bounce, by Coach McGugin. The band played "Vanderbilt Forever" until the final play.[64] While game ended in a scoreless tie, Vanderbilt did not lose to the "Mighty Wolverines," and the game was hailed as a victory by students, fans, and local newspapers.

The year 1922 was a banner year for Vanderbilt athletics. Its football program shared the "title" of co-champion in the newly formed Southern Conference. Throughout the 1920s the university touted its reputation as the strongest team in the conference, coming in first or second for all but two years. However, the end of the decade marked a turning point for Vanderbilt's athletic program. After thirty years of dominance in southern sports and an established competitive reputation against northern foes such as Michigan and Yale, Vanderbilt would win its last conference football title in 1923.

As flagships of the public university system improved athletics and increased enrollment, Vanderbilt was surpassed by schools such as Georgia, Tennessee, Auburn, and Alabama. "No other team did as well," Conkin noted, "but the great era was finally at an end."[65] From the 1930s on, Vanderbilt settled into the middle of the pack but would remain in the powerful SEC. Perhaps this was analogous to Nashville's standing as a New South city, as its growth spurt came to a halt with the beginning of the Great Depression.

FIG. 5.9. 1921 Vanderbilt University baseball team members. Courtesy of Ridley Wills II.

Even though Vanderbilt football may have lost some of its bragging rights after 1923, athletic victories for any southern school doubled as a moral victory for the region. No clearer evidence exists than the reaction of local newspapers in Nashville, Atlanta, Birmingham, and other southern cities after the University of Alabama defeated the University of Washington in the 1926 Rose Bowl (considered the national championship game). Headlines reflected a deep sense of southern pride and common interest. While schools in the South maintained intense rivalries, when playing teams from outside the region they rooted for one another. Further, Vanderbilt football heroes such as Jess Neely and Lynn Bomar became "big men on campus," winning victories on the field and honors from the university, including the prized Bachelor of Ugliness.

As football thrived, basketball and baseball budgets finished in the red and continued to rely on the football program's receipts. However, that did not stop Vanderbilt from adding intercollegiate sports: golf (1925), tennis (1926), and swimming (1926). These sports did not generate a financial profit, but they were immensely valuable to student culture as well as recruitment and retention. In addition to the collective school spirit that athletics inspired, team loyalty and a sense of inclusiveness for individual students who participated was also important. Many of these athletic teams achieved success; specifically, Vanderbilt's baseball program remains strong.

Perhaps more than at any other southern university, the evolution of Vanderbilt athletics exemplified tensions between the ivory tower and the athletic field and between the city and its colleges. While a major factor in the intercollegiate athletics boom from 1890 to 1930, Vanderbilt did not abandon the "collegiate" part of their mission. But by 1930 the transformation was complete. The ivory tower still bestowed the light of higher learning, but it also became a vessel that existed, in part, to illuminate the fields of play—at times even overshadowed by the stadium, court, and diamond.

African Americans and Sport

College football was the chosen sport of the white South, which, according to Hasan Kwame Jeffries, "idolized the stars of the college gridiron in much the same way as they worshipped the heroes of the Confederacy."[66] Andrew Doyle added that college sports, particularly football, in the early twentieth century South was a "stabilizing force of tradition and a resolute faith in progress.... The racial caste system ... and the all-white teams fielded by segregated southern universities embodied this social ideal well."[67] In contrast, an editorial from Howard

University's newspaper addressed the transcendent nature of sports for African Americans, proclaiming, "Athletics is the universal language."[68]

Fisk University, along with other black colleges and universities in Nashville, used athletics as a means to instill additional pride and loyalty in the school and community. Sports spurred a belief by many African Americans that athletics could be used to build relationships with whites and provide powerful lessons in "interracial education."[69] In reality, racial exclusion was the defining element in American sports from the 1890s through the 1950s, affecting HBCU campuses and the collegiate world in general.[70] On the one hand, Vanderbilt and Nashville's white leaders used modern sports to perpetuate antebellum southern values of patriarchy and white rule. On the other hand, sports provided a public sphere for African Americans and women to challenge the status quo.

From 1895 to 1920 black colleges served as the primary medium for black athletic expression.[71] Jeffries has argued that Atlanta served as the epicenter of black college sport, with Atlanta University and Morehouse College forming football teams in the 1890s. Nearby Clark College and Morris Brown College had established baseball programs by 1896, and Morehouse College formed a track team in 1907. On December 30, 1913, on the campus of Morehouse, administrators representing HBCUs throughout the South met to create the Southern Intercollegiate Athletic Conference (SIAC). Because other local African American colleges such as Roger Williams University and Meharry Medical College maintained limited athletic programs, Fisk was forced to go on the road for competition. Undeterred, Fisk traveled regularly to other southern states to play football and baseball and to participate in track meets. Along with Alabama State University, Atlanta University, Clark College, Jackson College, Morehouse College, Morris Brown College, Talladega College, and Tuskegee Institute, Fisk was a charter member of the SIAC.

Basketball began at Fisk in 1903 though the school's teams did not compete in an organized collegiate conference until 1925. The original gymnasium at Fisk was the nation's first gymnasium and mechanical laboratory on any HBCU campus. The impetus for the project was none other than W. E. B. Du Bois, who with three of his classmates formed a committee to raise the funds necessary to build the gym, which was completed in 1888.[72] Basketball, tennis, track, and baseball were largely pursued through intramural contests between classes and clubs from 1915 to 1929. In 1929 the basketball team did participate in intercollegiate competition, winning games against regional HBCU rivals such as Tuskegee, Wilberforce, and Louisville Municipal College.[73]

Fisk's first football team was organized in 1893–94 and earned the nickname "Sons of Milo" after President Erastus Milo Cravath. Soon after, they changed the team's mascot to the Fisk Bulldogs. The team was coached by Charles Snyder, who also served as the team captain and star player. Until 1907 students or former players coached Fisk's team, which was a common trend at both white and black colleges across the nation. (At Vanderbilt, Elliott H. Jones, a student-athlete elected to coach and captain the first football game, was both a player and coach from 1890 to 1892.) The success of Fisk football in contests against other HBCUs was even more pronounced than that of Vanderbilt against white schools: Fisk lost only one game between 1899 and 1904. Fisk claimed football championships in 1910, 1912, 1913, 1915, 1919, 1928, and 1929.

In 1907 football combined with music at Fisk. The football team's coach, John W. Work, doubled as the conductor of the Jubilee Singers. In a show-like spectacle, the team and the singers toured together, playing four games and singing twelve concerts.[74] Howard University traveled to Nashville in 1916 for a game against Fisk University, and the team's visit, observed sports historian Raymond Schmidt, "was the centerpiece for a number of high-class events." He added, "The entertainment provided by the city's black society was said to have portrayed Nashville as the 'Athens of the South.'"[75]

FIG. 5.10. Howard University versus Fisk University football game crowd and cheerleaders, 1919. Metropolitan Government of Nashville and Davidson County Archives.

Fisk competed on Bennett Field, described as a "plot of land between Cravath Hall and the chapel" and used as a playing field.⁷⁶ With large crowds, many times in excess of one thousand people, Bennett Field was adequate but not a true stadium. White society in Nashville may have acknowledged the athletic success of Fisk and other HBCUs, but there was little comparison to the intense local interest in and reaction to Vanderbilt's victories and losses. It was an unfortunate effect of segregation and reflective of the parallel, yet alternate realities experienced by black and white college students and institutions.

Meharry intermittently fielded a football team but rarely played any school outside of Nashville. Roger Williams also fielded a team and traveled as far as Chicago to play Wilberforce University in 1921. The *Chicago Defender* published headlines that read "Roger Williams U. Takes Wilberforce into Camp" and "Wilberforce Downs Roger Williams," with pregame tickets sold in businesses and drug stores in Ohio.⁷⁷ Existing game records show Roger Williams played Arkansas Baptist, West Kentucky Industrial, Knoxville College, and Fisk in addition to Wilberforce over a twenty-eight year period.⁷⁸ Meharry, Roger Williams, Fisk, and Tennessee A&I all maintained athletic associations, and girls engaged in sports but without a competitive intercollegiate schedule. Roger Williams's athletic program would end with its move to Memphis in the late 1920s. Meharry would phase out its athletics program as the school shifted more seriously to graduate-level and specialized coursework after the completion of its new campus and hospital in 1931.

Aside from football, Meharry Medical College, Walden University, and Tennessee A&I competed in regular tennis tournaments, starting in 1917, on courts built by Tennessee A&I students. Although there were city tennis courts, African Americans were not allowed to use whites-only public recreational facilities. Basketball was also played in a similar fashion, with most games played outdoors until 1923, when a gym was completed at Tennessee A&I on the top floor of the Men's Trades Building.⁷⁹ Local HBCUs played intramural basketball with club teams or class competitions but often played one another as well. During the 1930s Tennessee A&I used funding from the federal Works Progress Administration to build regulation tennis courts, additional stadium space, and a cinder track.⁸⁰ Tennessee A&I completed its first football field with bleacher seating in 1931.

Tennessee A&I's first baseball game was played in 1912 at Greenwood Park, a field that could be marked off as a diamond. There were no official stands for spectators. Curiously the teams were divided by marital status—married men against single men. The 1915 *Bulletin* of Tennessee A&I pictured the school's first intercollegiate baseball team, which participated in the Nashville City League through 1930. The Nashville City League included Tennessee A&I, Roger Williams University, Walden University, and Fisk University. Bobby Lovett wrote that "A&I

graduates went on to teach and coach baseball at schools across Tennessee, the South, and the nation."[81] The black community, including women, "dressed up and flocked to local baseball games, and thus men spectators dressed up too."[82] Tennessee A&I would go on to athletic greatness, particularly in track and field, in the 1960s and 1970s, but the school's sports program did not join a black intercollegiate competitive conference until 1930.

Celebrating its twenty-fifth anniversary in 1938, the Southern Intercollegiate Athletic Conference (SIAC) specifically noted the importance of Fisk University: "The rise of athletics at Fisk University has been one of the most colorful adventures in the history of Negro athletics. Fisk University was one of the first Negro colleges in the South to make athletics a part of its general college program."[83] Indeed, Fisk expanded its extracurricular sports program and engaged in intercollegiate competition in 1906, seven years before the formation of the SIAC. Despite the establishment of the SIAC in 1913, black colleges were plagued by the same irregularities that afflicted many white institutions. Fisk was listed as one of the schools in need of reform, especially after the football career of "Jumping" Joe Wiggins, who played one year at Virginia State, two years at Atlanta University, and then three years for the Fisk Bulldogs in the 1920s.

In 1918 the *Fisk University News,* following the lead of university president Fayette McKenzie, announced that "athletics needs reforming . . . in a way that would gratify the natural impulses of young men, and awaken and sustain their interest." Reflecting McKenzie's reputation as a strict disciplinarian, his report contended, "Only reform could displace the vast anomaly of organized intercollegiate athletics with its handful of highly trained players, its show games, its elaborate and costly agencies and paraphernalia, its gate-receipts, it serious interference with the work of students, its betting and gambling, and its conspicuous misrepresentation of the proper function and service of the universities."[84]

Conservative black leaders and white leaders like McKenzie were skeptical of the benefits of competitive athletics on HBCU campuses and in the local community. The Fisk team was disbanded but resumed again in the fall of 1919. That year the university was the "undisputed champion of the South" with its 39–0 win over Morehouse, but two years later McKenzie slowed the football craze by enforcing strict rules that football players receive no special treatment in the classroom and were denied even the consideration of athletic scholarships. His decision was based on several trends he found disturbing. He had received reports that the visiting Wilberforce team had acted inappropriately with vulgar language and suspected drinking on the train to Nashville. In addition, the president of Shaw University had accused Howard University's football players of "pay for play." Finally, there were reports of gambling on the outcomes of HBCU games.

These problems also existed at white colleges and universities, but many HBCU presidents (most of whom were white) felt extra pressure to distance themselves from sports that seemed to undermine the work of black universities. Many administrators were already fighting incredible odds to prove that their institutions served to educate honest and productive members of society. After McKenzie's resignation in 1925, President Jones hired Fisk alumnus Henderson Johnson (class of 1924) as the school's first athletic director. Best known as "Tubby," Johnson brought a new level of prestige to Fisk football, and the program garnered national attention in black newspapers, particularly the *Chicago Defender*. Some questioned the effect that football would have on the integrity of the school, but sports did increase school spirit and student enrollment as the black community simultaneously responded to new challenges brought about by racial segregation. The early twentieth century witnessed the increasing popularity of professional and college sport, and African American athletes seized the opportunity to showcase their talent. On a smaller scale, black schools operated like white collegiate programs with visitors and alumni attending games, hosting dances, and organizing pregame bonfires. Likewise, black college football "operated in a similar yet separate gridiron world—black All-America teams, mythical national champions, controversies," with media coverage "clearly symboliz[ing] the desire to emulate and belong to the mainstream intercollegiate football world—whether admitted or not."[85]

In 1906 the prominent African American educator Samuel Archer relayed his belief that sports would develop "qualities of self-reliance and self-control."[86] In other words, he saw college athletics as another mode of racial uplift, one that had the potential to literally even the playing field for a new generation of African Americans. Many believed that if white Americans could recognize the sporting accomplishments of blacks, then ultimately white society would accept the assimilation of educated blacks into the professional and political world. While such recognition or acceptance would not occur in Nashville before 1930, sports would indeed be a major part in the public process toward an integrated American society. This process began with Jackie Robinson, a black athlete from Georgia. Robinson would break the color barrier in Major League Baseball in 1949, five years before *Brown v. Board of Education* and fifteen years before Lyndon B. Johnson would sign major civil rights legislation. But change would come slowly and painfully to the South. Even by 1955, few were surprised when, as Hasan Kwame Jeffries noted, the governor of Georgia forbade "Georgia Tech's football team from competing in the Sugar Bowl because the school's opponent, the University of Pittsburgh, had an African American player."[87]

Most SEC schools continued to exclude African Americans from varsity sports through the 1960s. Nashville's own Perry Wallace would break the varsity sport color barrier of the Southeastern Conference in 1967 at Vanderbilt University. Wallace was the first African American varsity athlete to play under an athletic scholarship in the Southeastern Conference, and he remains a basketball legend at Vanderbilt. Football would not be desegregated in the Deep South until after 1970. The decision was not based on principle but rather on pride after Sam Cunningham, a black fullback for the University of Southern California "ran roughshod over the vaunted all-white defense" of Coach Paul "Bear" Bryant's University of Alabama squad.[88]

Black sports did not remove racial barriers in Nashville or in the South in general during the Jim Crow Era. However, it is evident that intercollegiate sport allowed African Americans, individually and collectively, to reflect the modern college experience exhibited on white campuses. By the 1930s, black college sports were supplanted by black professional leagues as the most desirable spectator sport. These leagues would dominate until white professional sports began to integrate in the 1950s, but for the first two decades of the century, black colleges served as the primary mediums for black athletic expression.[89] Like the white community, sport brought together the colleges and the broader society, but athletic victories also brought black athletes a sense of racial pride throught the universal language of athletics. Indeed college sport would ultimately help to break down color barriers on white southern campuses.

Women and Sport

Women made remarkable athletic strides from 1865 to 1930, and they used education as a platform to propel themselves into otherwise unacceptable public spheres. In doing so, these new generations of educated women helped to redefine acceptable behavior, occupation, sport, and leisure for females and between men and women in public urban spaces by the end of the Roaring Twenties.

Men's sports had previously been forbidden to women "by the dictates of decency," but the growing popularity of competitive collegiate sports and commercialized entertainment in many ways emancipated young white women, especially those of the middle and upper classes, to participate indirectly as spectators.[90] Women as "watchers" or supporters created a particularly southern environment for outdoor team sports such as baseball and football. Historian Patrick Miller noted that college baseball and football games in the South were often viewed as extended social occasions suitable for courtship in the 1880s and 1890s as "belles and beaux mingled freely along the sidelines of the field, a custom explained by the absence of grandstands during the early years."[91]

Instead of limiting the role of women at such games (as many continued to protest the inclusion of women at universities like Vanderbilt), southern men appreciated and encouraged female attendance at collegiate sporting events. Students, alumni, and administrators believed that the presence of women lent "dignity and, at the same time, a more festive air to the proceedings."[92] Girls flocked to the arenas and stadiums "where the gladiators fought," and female students from Vanderbilt were recruited as "rooters" for the games to cheer for their male counterparts. Outside of Vanderbilt's student body, young women from Ward Seminary, Belmont College, Ward-Belmont (after 1913), and Peabody College attended Vanderbilt athletic events. The biggest events were football games, of course, but female students from neighboring schools also supported men's baseball and basketball games as well as track meets. Ward-Belmont's *Milestones* recalled such collegial camaraderie in 1920: "To end the evening we had a novel experience, for Vanderbilt came to call. We met them on the North Front veranda, and for the remainder of the evening there were yells, rooting, and songs in honor of the victory over Sewanee, not to mention a number of more personal and less boisterous tête-à-têtes between sweethearts!"[93]

Significant numbers of women also participated directly in the collegiate sports movement, creating their own niche as athletes themselves. This evolved after the Civil War and followed Victorian Era trends that had already begun to emphasize the development of good health. Under the umbrella of education, women advanced their engagement in physical activity. Certain attitudes persisted about women and sports, but from the 1880s through the 1920s, young women made significant progress toward a new image that included physical education and sport.[94] Athletics and physical education reflected the "strategies New Women in the New South adopted and some of the tensions and anxieties they faced as they negotiated the contested ground of gender redefinition at the turn of the century," according to Pamela Dean.[95] Although traditional principles of femininity were in one sense a barrier for women during this time, this ideology turned on itself by allowing women to participate in more physical activities. Higher education was a powerful, although acceptable, wedge between appropriate female behavior and evolving notions of gender in the New South. Women's athletics drove the wedge further.

As the concept of the New Woman developed, social acceptance of strenuous exercise for women paralleled changes in clothing. Less restrictive clothing was also precipitated by the new trend of bicycling, which became immensely popular in the 1890s. With long skirts and several layers of underclothing, women's dress became particularly burdensome while bicycling. As early as 1897, Vanderbilt called for the creation of a Bicycle Club that seemed to suggest men and women riding together: "[The Bicycle Club] would add much to the pleasure and profit of cyclists in this university to have certain times appointed for spins to different points of interest [in the city]."[96] Whether bicycling or exercising, in 1902 the Ward Seminary student body announced, "Regardless of criticism, [we] adopt the divided skirt."[97]

The invention of elastic in the 1880s also allowed women to wear fewer layers of underclothing, while promoting the popularity of bloomers, an antebellum style of pants that became the preferred and, indeed, more modern alternative for active women in the postbellum period. By the turn of the century, the style of acceptable athletic clothing for women transformed into a new look consisting of a middy blouse, bloomers, and long, dark, woolen stockings.[98] In addition, skirts became shorter, underclothing was minimized, and many women eliminated corsets. In 1901 an article entitled "The American Girl of Today" stated, "it is interesting to note that while forty-seven percent of the girls enter schools wearing corsets, these are given up, in consequence of advice and teachings of the instructors in physical training."[99] The women's basketball teams at Ward Seminary and Vanderbilt

FIG. 5.11. Original Ward Seminary basketball team in 1897. Harpeth Hall School Archives.

wore black "dress" uniforms, long stockings, and boots from their first game in 1897 until 1910. After 1910 they traded in long, black-sleeved tops and belts for white sailor-style shirts, bloomers, and an early version of sneakers. Thus, the organization of athletics and physical activity coincided with greater numbers of women in higher education, which led to changes in health awareness, clothing reform, and notions of social independence.[100]

Basketball was the leading competitive sport for women and one that pushed the boundaries of femininity since it required the most practice, physicality, and natural ability. The first women's game in the South was held in 1893 at Newcomb College, today part of Tulane University. Newcomb faculty member Clara Gregory Baer was the first to write rules for a modified version of Naismith's game. Baer published her rules formally in 1914 and explained the evolution of the game in a way that reveals the southern complexities of sports and gender: "After a short trial of the game at Newcomb [in 1893], it was abandoned. Later, in January 1894, a modified form of basketball was substituted. The chief feature of the modified game was the introduction of dividing lines on the court to prevent the general rush after the ball. The use of the lines . . . marked the first modification, and publication, of the rules for women."[101] The lines, division of the courts, and number of players on the court limited the women's game to confined areas by designating them for offense or defense on one end of the court. This was to alleviate concerns that running up and down the court was too strenuous for girls.

Southern women's sports, like men's sports, also lagged behind the North and West. However, by 1898 Vanderbilt began to recognize the accomplishments of female athletes, even if it presented such women as atypical:

> Miss Rowena Reed of California is the pride of all college girls. She is the girl who broke the woman's record for the broad jump at Vassar by clearing 13 feet 3 inches, and has won the 120-yard hurdle race and the running high jump doing 3 feet 8 inches. Miss Reed, who is a sophomore, is 19 years old, weighs 160 pounds, and is 5 feet 8½ inches tall. She can ride, swim, fence, row, wheel, run, jump, handle Indian clubs, play football and basketball with the best.[102]

Curiously, she is described as the "pride of all college girls" even though the account of her athletic feats makes her sound quite masculine, especially considering the average height and weight of most women at that time.[103]

Over the next decade the idea of women playing sports slowly gained acceptability. Ward Seminary's athletic clubs in the late 1890s were categorized under the heading "Physical Culture" and mixed sport with exhibition. One performance included "hoop drill, German Bell exercise, Swedish gymnastics, fancy march, and combination bell and wand drill" (the last similar to present-day baton twirling).[104]

Although a minority in the student body, Vanderbilt women actively participated in student culture, ranging "from a woman editor on the *Observer* to a reporter on the *Hustler,* from a basketball team that never lost a game for several years to a girls' club."[105] Such participation mirrored national trends reflecting greater interest in women's clubs and sports. As the "Here and There" section of the *Hustler* reported in 1895, "The colleges for women are beginning to take a very active interest in athletics. Fencing is greatly in vogue at Smith College. At Vassar there was much excitement over the Fall Field Day, while since then basket-ball has become the popular pastime."[106] In 1897 the Vanderbilt women's basketball team, still a club sport, began receiving coverage in the student newspaper. One report stated, "School girls are almost as enthusiastic over the [basketball] game as the men."[107]

The first public competitive basketball game in Tennessee was between Vanderbilt and Ward Seminary in 1897. A male reporter apparently gained covert access to the game:

> In spite of the precautions and vigilance of don't-let-a-man-come-in girls . . . I gained admission to the gymnasium and hid myself in a corner. Soon the crowd began to gather, consisting of the girls' schools and old and young ladies. On the faces of the sweet schoolgirls were not seen the usual "bewitching" smiles. Something was lacking. What was it? It could not have been girlfriends, for all kinds of femininity were there. It must have been the absence of the college boys, whom, alas, the teachers had excluded from the rare sight of seeing girls play basketball.[108]

Before the game between Ward Seminary and Vanderbilt began, the doors were locked and the windows covered. The male student anticipated what was to come: "Now, . . . we will see some scratching and hair-pulling and hear a half dozen screams . . . [and] I was not deceived; they showed that they were still girls."[109] Yet, he was also surprised to see a new side of his female counterparts: "The agility of some of them was really surprising, as they got around after the ball in a manner that would put some of our gym graduates to shame."[110] The game ended in a loss for Ward Seminary, 0–5.[111] Even by the 1909–10 season, local women's basketball games were still played behind guarded doors. Team captain Ada Raines proudly admitted that the women's team maintained "winning ways," but the season's wins and losses were not officially recorded. In stark contrast, the mettle of the men seemed solely determined by wins and losses. The 1909–10 Vanderbilt yearbook boasted of the 10–3 season record of its men's basketball team with individual games scores listed.[112]

David Lipscomb College fielded a women's basketball team and tennis team by 1910, although they rarely competed against outside schools. The witty basketball program motto was "Aim at the Goal," and the players were divided into two intramural teams, with five each on "Haughty Hits" and "Dandy Doers" and six girls listed as "Scrubs" to substitute for either team. The tennis club also found a pun to spice up its image, as the team yell was "First come, first served!"[113] Lipscomb also maintained about twelve to twenty members annually from 1910 to 1917.

In the early 1900s several schools held an annual girls' tennis tournament that included students from Peabody, Ward Seminary, Belmont, and Vanderbilt. They played before a "large and enthusiastic crowd" on the grounds of the Nashville Tennis Club in Centennial Park. However, athletic contests in which females competed publicly were rare.[114] By 1910 all of Nashville's institutions of higher education featured girl's basketball and tennis teams, some were competitive while others remained at the intramural club level.[115]

As men's competition grew more intense, women's competition was presented almost as an afterthought. While men played before large crowds, women played behind closed doors. This allowed women to play sports in a way that preserved their modesty, out of public sight. Historian Pamela Dean argued that literally playing behind closed doors allowed the community to "deny the emerging reality that southern college women were in fact learning to be strong, self-reliant, and competitive, as well as graceful, loyal, and cooperative."[116] Institutional support of female athletics was nominal in coeducational schools with strong men's programs such as Vanderbilt. And yet, most administrators did not oppose physical strength and fitness for the mind and moral compass.

However, on the Vanderbilt campus, attitudes toward women and physical fitness also carried subtle hints of hostility. As the 1896–97 school term began, the first gym class was organized for female students just a year after the school issued a policy granting women more equitable access to the campus. One male student commented, "The class meets Wednesday at 8:45 a.m. to take Gym work. . . . The Co-eds should be careful not to break our springboard and vaulting bar. Positively no admittance [is permitted on this equipment]. The public need not to be alarmed to hear feminine screams issuing from our Gym; [it is] the Co-eds."[117]

Male students also complained when their access was limited, as it infringed on their previously unrestricted on-campus freedoms.[118] On a Friday in March 1897, a note appeared on the bulletin board informing men to avoid the gym that afternoon. An ironic statement appeared in the *Hustler* the following week: "Never was the importance of physical exercise so forcibly realized as when the object of this notice was discovered."[119]

Interestingly enough, it was not that Vanderbilt men resisted gym time for women but rather that they wanted to exercise alongside them. In an early call for coeducation gym classes one student commented, "We kindly submitted this time but hope this will not be repeated.... We are perfectly willing to share with the co-eds... but our only objection is to the exclusion of either sex at any time. Let us have co-gymnastics or let us have our gym."[120] Most male students did not seem to opposed women's physical education, exercise, or sport; however, they did mind when their time and space were infringed upon. Nonetheless, physical education classes would not be held with male and female students together until the 1940s, and many schools would not offer coed gym classes until the 1950s and 1960s.

After 1900, however, the acceptance of women becoming more active increased. For example, Ward Seminary announced in 1911: "Physical culture is made a special feature of Seminary life. The gymnasium and bowling alleys afford abundant indoor exercise. Lessons in swimming are offered throughout the session. In addition... the extensive campus at Ward Place furnishes abundant facilities for tennis, basketball, croquet, field hockey, and other outdoor sports."[121] After its merger Ward-Belmont continued to emphasize sports. Local schools, reflective of national patterns, struggled between preserving "womanly qualities" and encouraging physical exercise and fitness. Beyond physical education, the main argument focused on whether the playing of sports could occur without a serious challenge to a young woman's femininity.[122]

Female athletes answered this question in Nashville by revealing that they were not girls obsessed with the assumed masculinity of sports. Many of the girls participated in other extracurricular activities and maintained an active status in academic subjects such as art and literature. That is not to say that sporting success made women popular; in fact, truly gifted athletic women at coeducational institutions were shamed for not being feminine. Even worse, female athletes could be treated as freaks or outsiders and sometimes called "Amazons" by their peers.

At all-female schools the connection between sports and school spirit was more about camaraderie than competition or defending one's honor. Ward-Belmont used sports to inspire school spirit, loyalty, and unity. Ward-Belmont's Rosalyn Kirsch penned a poem popular among the girls in 1920:

> There's a school in Tennessee,
> Where we all just love to be.
> Everyone should want to see,
> The sports at W-B.
> We've tennis in the spring and fall,
> In winter we play basketball.

We stand together one and all,
And loyalty is our call.[123]

In contrast, coed school students portrayed women's sports as a reflection of the rivalry between schools and the desire to defeat local opponents. In a 1904 article, the male author lamented a two-point loss by the Vanderbilt women's basketball team against Ward Seminary:

> The game was played in the Vanderbilt gymnasium, which was decorated with gold and black streamers and pennants in honor of the occasion.... The girls in gold [Vanderbilt supporters] did all in their power to cheer the Commodores on to a long-fought victory over their hated down-town rivals.... It was none of your Out-of-my-way-please affairs, but straight, hard basketball all the way through. Not once was time taken out to fix hair, and only once was *poudre rouge* brought on the floor... but alack and alas, it was all in vain.[124]

Despite sporting success and the growth of varsity women's athletics on high school and college campuses in the Progressive Era, many educators and parents continued to view competitive sports as unladylike. This would lead to a backlash in the 1920s. As a result, many schools reduced some or all intercollegiate competition. As early as 1915 the National Education Association outlined standards in sports for girls and stated the purpose of play: "If all girls and women engaged in active sports could say, 'I play because I enjoy playing,' one of the most valuable results of play would be realized."[125]

A decade later, the movement away from competitive varsity sports was further fueled by the formation of the Women's Division of the National Amateur Athletic Federation (WDNAAF). In 1925 the WDNAAF passed a resolution barring extramural competition and publicly played games that required purchased admission. The argument against women's sports was based on fears that certain sports, namely basketball, were unhealthy and inappropriate and would lead to problems related to men's sports (gambling, violence, and cheating). Ward-Belmont and Vanderbilt followed this national trend, and while Tennessee did not ban female athletics, as the state of Colorado did in 1929, the emphasis shifted from competitive athletics to a "sports for sports' sake" mindset.[126]

Historian Pamela Grundy lamented the cultural backlash against women's sports by 1930, as "narrowing standards of conduct and appearance" called for women to be "cooperative, supportive, and sexually attractive.... Such efforts stood in dramatic contrast to those of competitive basketball, which had allowed a substantial number of young women to transcend a range of limited expectations during a crucial period in their lives."[127] Intercollegiate sports for women would not become truly mainstream until after the passage of Title IX as part of the Educational Amendments of 1972.

Female athletes during this time may not have gained the public's approbation, but their efforts and competitive spirit certainly laid the groundwork that would ultimately lead to a women's movement within sport.[128] They pursued their interest on the court and on the field with determination, keen to be involved in something new and fun, but likely not conscious of the wider feminist ramifications. Upon graduation these young women entered Nashville society and public life as educated women who also appreciated competitive sport. In these ways sport for females did connect the college to the city as an extension of the more visible role of women in society.

Conclusion

From the 1870s through the early 1900s, colleges justified sport as the physical exercise component needed to help increase the overall well-being of its students. This was the traditional view of school athletics throughout the Progressive Era. Ideas of "muscular Christianity," reinforced programs such as the YMCA, YWCA, club sports, and varsity athletics. However, athletics would shift the focus of competitive sports from moral and physical training for the body as a "temple" to a test of vicarious manhood.[129] As early as 1893 Vanderbilt's student newspaper, the *Hustler,* stated, "Athletics have become a very important and useful element in developing character and manhood in the University."[130] A decade later the newspaper defined school spirit in terms of college sport: "True college spirit is a deep permanent enthusiasm and the interest which a man feels toward his Alma Mater. . . . The student who wins his college initial upon the gridiron at Vanderbilt is a 'knight worthy of his spurs.'"[131]

Once alumni, administrators, and urban boosters joined students in their support of college sport in the early 1900s, the landscape for higher education shifted once again. Curriculum changes, coeducation, and social societies had previously changed the composition and chemistry that produced the modern college experience, but nothing would change colleges and universities more than intercollegiate competitive sport. As Frederick Rudolf observed, "once *sport* had been accepted, the *games* had to be won."[132]

Football would emerge as the backbone of a metaphorical anatomy that would support other popular sports such as baseball, basketball, track, and tennis. While controversial in the 1890s, football players by 1910 represented the collective and literal big men on campus. After reform and reluctant support from administrators, faculty, and trustees, football grew dynamically and rapidly. Instead of fighting football, university officials sought to control and co-opt the enthusiasm that the game brought to Vanderbilt and other major college campuses. This shift reflected the powerful role that youth culture played in shaping leisure in Nashville, the region, and the nation.

College sports certainly altered the fabric of American life, including life in southern urban centers. However, it remains important to recognize that the white patriarchy controlled the process and used sports, in part, to reinforce southern social order. Black college sports were popular with students and with many members of the black community. However, HBCUs did not have the facilities, funding, or booster support that white universities like Vanderbilt enjoyed. As a group and as a whole, African American students from the 1870s through the 1920s had less time and money to invest in college athletics. Meanwhile, white women were allowed to participate in athletics but were limited by administrators, funding, schedules, and public acceptance. Victorian attitudes turned to athletic victories for some women who took advantage of breaking barriers as student-athletes. But the majority of college women participated as spectators of men's sports.

Overall sports embraced visions of industrialism and structured efficiency, but more important, in the South athletics also functioned as a safety valve for white men attending institutions of higher education. College sports provided a way to prove one's worth, ability, and strength. Vanderbilt was the dominant southern team, but other southern schools had matched or surpassed the university's early athletic prowess by the mid-1920s. As college athletics necessitated bigger and better facilities, the movement from field to stadium affected Vanderbilt's relationship to the city. Dudley Stadium and Memorial Gymnasium were but part of a movement to create and invest in physical space for athletic play and spectatorship. In turn and in part, by 1930 college sports provided fertile ground for the reconceptualization of what it meant to be southern.

6

Athens of the New, New South

A Conclusion

> Nashville's value as a regional urban center is measured by its industry and innovation, yes—but the soul of the city is found in Nashville's love of music and the arts, sense of community, and commitment to higher education. Local colleges and universities have provided the foundation for the city's distinctive and successful growth for over 150 years.
>
> —Martha Rivers Ingram, interview with author, 2016

An 1885 *Memphis Ledger* editorial acknowledged the positive and progressive role that Nashville played as one of Tennessee's leading cities: "We are all proud of Nashville, not only on account of its historic associations, its commanding position, and political relations with the rest of the State, but for the intelligence, culture, and hospitality of the people."[1] Fast forward 125 years, and as Martha Rivers Ingram's opening quote suggests, Nashville still takes great pride in its reputation as a dynamic place to live, work, and learn. Present-day Nashville is in many ways a manifestation of the vision of local leaders in the New South and Progressive Eras. Its formula for success reflects Nashville's distinguished role as

FIG. 6.1. Old meets new with the Ryman Auditorium (1891) in the forefront and the AT&T building (1994), pictured in the background in 2000. This image symbolizes Nashville's unique relationship with tradition and progress in its urban core. Library of Congress.

a southern city that carefully balances notions of progress and tradition, change and continuity. Further, Nashville relishes and recognizes its reputation for higher education as a key component of what makes the city an attractive destination.

The introduction to this book began with a 2013 *New York Times* announcement that Nashville was America's new "it" city. Over the last twenty years, the city has grown, expanded, and developed new industry. The metropolitan statistical area of Nashville (Davidson County) now officially includes Murfreesboro (Rutherford County) and Franklin (Williamson County), as well as Cheatham, Robertson, Sumner, and Wilson counties according to the U.S. Office of Management and Budget. In 2000 metro Nashville's population was approximately 1.3 million.[2] In 2015, the metro area crossed the 1.8 million threshold, with predictions that it would top 2 million residents by the end of the decade.[3] By 2016, an average of 1,500 people per month moved to Nashville, totaling nearly 20,000 residents per year in addition to natural growth. Also in 2016, Nashville surpassed Memphis as the largest city in Tennessee.[4] As Mayor Karl Dean (2007–15) described the past twenty years, "Before the late 1990s, Nashville was a nice city, but now it is an exciting place; it is wide awake."[5]

The how and why of Nashville's recent success is rooted in its past. And so the story of Nashville is linked to the city's mutually beneficial relationship with local colleges and universities. This final chapter reexamines college life and the modern southern city by threading the historical narrative needle from previous chapters through to the present. These closing pages explore the relationship between Nashville and its colleges and universities after 1930 and into the twentieth-first century. As higher education and urban living continue to evolve, Nashville has perhaps earned a new title—Athens of the New, New South.

Ridley Wills II's story is one of those narrative threads. Wills is a Vanderbilt alumnus, the son of Fugitive poet Jesse Ely Wills, retired senior vice president of National Life and Accident Insurance, a third-generation member of the Vanderbilt University Board of Trust, and patriarch of one of Nashville's most historic families. Also a historian and author, Wills articulated what set Nashville apart: "The cities most closely associated with the Old South, including Charleston, New Orleans, Savannah, and Mobile, were overall uninterested in establishing commercial ties with the 'Yankees.' In contrast, Nashville and Atlanta had the sense to engage with the North after the Civil War."[6] Wills's words reinforce one of this book's major themes: the progressive attitude adopted by Nashville positively affected the city culturally and commercially, which in turn provided fertile ground for higher education. The combination of commerce, culture, and education are the reasons why Nashville maintains its enviable position as a dynamic, prosperous southern city.

Economist Richard Florida, in *Cities and the Creative Class,* argued that for positive growth a city must possess the "three Ts": Talent, Tolerance, and Technology.[7] Mayor Karl Dean said he believes that Florida provides a blueprint for cities like Nashville that hope to attract a "Creative Class" that values diversity, individuality, and quality of life. As Dean contended, "Nashville, and Tennessee in general, has always been a place of moderation that honors tradition but seeks progress."[8] He continued:

At times we do not give enough credit to what colleges and universities have meant and continue to mean to the city of Nashville. Historically higher education in Nashville remains one of our greatest strengths. These institutions are our rock in times of transition or financial downturn. Generally we have a three-prong formula for success. Higher education (intellectual), when combined with the dynamic diversity of business (commercial) and music/arts (cultural), elevates the level of discourse and strengthens our sense of community and pride. Students, faculty, and alumni are our neighbors, co-workers, and family members.[9]

The efficiency and cohesiveness of a metropolitan government structure (formed in 1963) that covers all 503 square miles of Davidson County and a forward-thinking political policy are also factors that separate Nashville from other U.S. cities. The concepts of progressive politics, urban boosterism, and an active commercial-civic elite are still very much alive in Nashville. The city of Nashville, and in particular local leaders, continues to recognize and emphasize the importance of strong institutions of higher education. Thriving colleges and universities boost the local economy, form valuable public-private partnerships, positively affect the city's spatial arrangement and urban neighborhoods, and complement the city's identity as a center of entertainment, music, publishing, healthcare, technology, and education.

In addition, many of the city's prominent families connected to industry and commerce remain heavily invested and involved in local colleges and universities. They continue a legacy of urban boosterism and business progressivism that began during the New South era. The Curb, Massey, Davis, Carell, Boyd, McKissack, and Ayers families have all been generous stewards and donors of Fisk, Meharry, Belmont, Lipscomb, and Vanderbilt. Moreover, most of these families have focused their philanthropic efforts not on one local institution but have made transformative gifts to multiple colleges and universities located in Nashville's urban core.

The city's leading philanthropic family is the Ingram family. The corporate descendent of Ingram Oil and Refining, Ingram Industries first invested in Nashville in the early 1900s. Under magnate E. Bronson Ingram II, the company expanded and divided in the 1960s and again in the 1990s after Ingram's death in 1995. From 1963 to 1995 the company ventured into publishing, technology, insurance, and other market sectors, increasing its value by over $900 million in less than thirty years. Ingram Industries and other family-related companies employ over twenty-five thousand people with its business home base in Nashville.[10]

Referred to as the "Modern Medicis," the Ingrams are committed to "the idea that somebody in society has to take responsibility for the process of cultural development," according to Mac Pirkle, former director of the Tennessee Repertory Theatre. Martha Rivers Ingram is the matriarch of the family but also, arguably, the matriarch of Nashville. Pirkle continued, "She is so confident and so visionary."[11] Ingram has devoted time and invested heavily in the city's identity and her priorities are clear. From her leading roles as an advocate, organizer, and donor for the Tennessee Performing Arts Center (1980) and the state's bicentennial celebration (1996) to the opening of the Schermerhorn Symphony Center (2006) and countless other causes, her position in Nashville's cultural and educational community is unmatched.

Notably, the Ingram family has financially contributed to Nashville's local colleges and universities to support academic programs, building projects, and general fundraising campaigns. As chairman of the Vanderbilt Board of Trust (1991–95), Bronson Ingram led a successful $500 million capital campaign, beginning with a personal gift of $25 million. Following in Bronson's footsteps, Martha and her children, John, Orrin, Robin, and David, have served or currently sit on boards of trust for educational institutions and maintain a special relationship with Vanderbilt. In 1998 the Ingram family donated Ingram Micro stock worth over $300 million. At the time, the gift was the largest-ever private donation to a college or university.[12] In 2006 Vanderbilt embarked on a venture to create a university-house system akin to those of Oxford and Cambridge. Underclassmen and women live and learn together in ten "houses," each guided by a faculty head of house. These living-and-learning communities were named the Martha Rivers Ingram Commons, in honor of her commitment to the university and belief in the community at Vanderbilt and, more broadly, in Nashville.

As the city grows (Nashville's employment numbers increased 21 percent from 2009 to 2016), so do its institutions of higher learning.[13] In addition to students, local colleges and universities employ over one hundred thousand Nashville-area residents and also provide healthcare and medical services to many who call Nashville home. Specifically, Vanderbilt University has eighty-five hundred faculty and staff, and Vanderbilt Medical Center employs nearly twenty thousand people (part-time and full-time). The larger Vanderbilt Medical Center structure serves more than sixty-three thousand pediatric and adult hospital patients per year and over 2.2 million patients when all university-related clinics are included.[14] Edith Carell Johnson, chair of the Medical Center's Board of Directors, has emphasized the undeniable local and regional significance of Vanderbilt University, Vanderbilt Medical Center, and Vanderbilt's Monroe Carell Jr. Children's Hospital:

> A 2015 economic impact report found the University and Medical Center contribute more than $8.9 billion each year in direct and indirect economic activity to Nashville and Tennessee. . . . However, Vanderbilt's true impact is felt far beyond any financial calculation. More importantly, its trainees—students from across the continuum of undergraduate and professional curricula—are positively

impacting the world each day through the education they receive. Many of our patients receive highly specialized services that are not available anywhere else in the region. Vanderbilt will continue its rich history of making important contributions to Nashville, Tennessee and the world.[15]

As Mayor Karl Dean concluded, "It is hard to think of a great city without a great research university and hospital."[16] In Nashville, Vanderbilt represents both.

In addition to the role that local universities play as employers, Davidson County boasts a total of nearly one hundred thousand college students.[17] The number of students adds to the city's ever-present youth culture, produces loyal alumni, and generates ardent support and partnerships between schools and the greater community. The availability of such varied higher education choices creates an extremely well-educated base of residents with 51.5 percent of adults twenty-five years or older having one or more years of college education and 30 percent with at least a bachelor's degree.[18] Moreover, approximately 60 percent of all graduates from two- or four-year colleges stay in the local area. Nashville remains an educational magnet, and in turn, the city benefits from talented graduates and attracts new sectors of business and growth from technology start-up companies (Nashville is sometimes referred to as the "Silicon Valley of the South") to one of the region's top healthcare and hospital networks. As the Chamber of Commerce argues, Nashville's institutions of higher education are "an integral part of the economic and cultural identity of the area," creating a "talent pipeline" that supports the local and regional workforce.[19]

Elected in 2015, Mayor Megan Barry highlights the interconnectedness between living and earning a living in Nashville: "We're very fortunate to have so many strong institutions contributing to our city's workforce and to its intellectual, cultural, and political life."[20] Nashville is better poised than many southern cities to harness rapid growth, in large part because of the "talent pipeline" that flows from local colleges and universities. One example of this phenomenon is Claire Dugan, a student in the Belmont University Honors Program. A member of the class of 2018, Dugan was drawn to Nashville from rural Iowa because of the city's promise and Belmont's reputation for music-business instruction:

> I knew that I wanted to attend a school that offered an exceptional music business program. . . . All the tools I need to capitalize on my future plans lie within a mile of each other between Belmont and Music Row. . . . Absolutely the schools benefit from the city, and in turn, I feel extremely connected to Nashville. I definitely plan on living in Nashville and working in the music industry after graduation.[21]

Anecdotes such as Dugan's are common in the business world but also carry over to local government. Mayor Megan Barry, Nashville's first female mayor stated, "Higher education was certainly the hook that lured me to Nashville. Like the previous two mayors, Karl Dean and Bill Purcell, I came here to go to graduate school at Vanderbilt, and my life was never the same after I made that decision."[22] Such examples reinforce the historical importance of local colleges and universities founded between 1865 and 1930. Schools founded during this period are not only a relevant and noteworthy part of the city's storied past; its colleges and universities are also a relevant and noteworthy part of the city's future narrative. Institutions of higher education consistently produce graduates who are ready to enter the marketplace as skilled, educated professionals—further boosting Nashville's economy and the city's progressive urban vibe. In other words, the cycle continues.

Trends in Higher Education, Post-1930

Historian Michael Dennis noted that "[higher] education has occupied a marginal place in the annals of southern progressivism, not to mention southern history. Yet it was progressive educators who championed the values of the industrializing New South."[23] In the sixty-five years between the end of the Civil War and the start of the Great Depression, Nashville earned and honed its reputation as a New South city and the "Athens of the South." By 1930 the mix of urbanization and higher education in Nashville resulted in contemporary notions of college and college life set against the backdrop of a modern southern city. From 1930 to the present, Nashville's colleges and universities continued to fill important roles as Nashville's urban culture developed. However, the niche-specific schools that served African Americans, women, and would-be teachers prior to 1930 evolved and modified as a new higher education model focused on four-year, coeducational, integrated institutions.

With few exceptions, the collegiate institutions explored in previous chapters still serve as the higher educational hubs of the city, located generally in West Nashville. Today's Nashville also includes Trevecca Nazarene University, a private college operated by the Church of the Nazarene. The school began as the Pentecostal Literary and Bible Training School in 1901. It moved to downtown Nashville permanently in 1936, a year after the school began offering collegiate classes as Trevecca Nazarene College. Its new home on the southeastern edge of downtown is located on the former campus of Walden University. Aquinas College is also worthy of mention. A Catholic college born out of the St. Cecilia Normal School in 1928, Aquinas opened its doors to the public as a junior college in 1961. In 1994 it expanded to a four-year, coed, liberal arts model and added nursing, business, and education schools. However, in 2017 the small, private, Dominican college announced it would reduce its college offerings and degree program to education only.

Higher education for women, particularly in the South, changed dramatically after 1930. Private all-female schools experienced their cultural halcyon days from 1900 to 1950; however, accreditation, changing workforce demands, and economic depression led to the decline of single-gender institutions following World War II. Ward-Belmont was no exception. The school's enrollment declined incrementally through the 1930s and 1940s. With the school in debt and the campus as its greatest asset, Dr. Robert Provine entered talks with the Tennessee Southern Baptist Convention in early 1951. The events that began in 1951 would result in the creation of a coeducational college offering full bachelor's degree programs and end Ward-Belmont's College Preparatory School and Junior College.

Under the governance of the Tennessee Baptist Convention, Belmont College reopened in the fall of 1951 as a four-year coeducational liberal arts college. While the once-prominent Ward-Belmont Music Conservatory itself closed, Belmont University continued its legacy through its signature programs in music and music business. Faced with the closure of Ward-Belmont as a single-gender institution, the local community rallied in 1951 to have an all-girls school designed to educate young women for college. Because the majority of day students in the College Preparatory Division were daughters of local families, a new high school named the Harpeth Hall School was established on a suburban estate on the edge of Belle Meade, four miles west of Ward-Belmont's campus.[24]

By 1955 the number of women's colleges in the United States had fallen to 248 and would steadily decline throughout the 1960s and 1970s. As some women's colleges closed, others adapted and survived to become accredited four-year liberal arts colleges such as Agnes Scott College in Decatur, Georgia. While other all-female schools, like Sophie Newcomb College in New Orleans, joined forces with all-male schools or began admitting men in an effort to redefine their mission as coeducational. Others ultimately embraced their role as college preparatory schools, which many had been all along, despite claims to offering at least some college-level work and the awarding of diplomas. Likewise in Nashville, the closing of Ward-Belmont opened the door for a more sustainable model of single-gender education in the form of the Harpeth Hall School. Considered Harpeth Hall's brother school, Montgomery Bell Academy is the surviving remnant of what once was the University of Nashville's college preparatory school. Montgomery Bell Academy continues to serve grades 7–12 on its west Nashville campus.

African American students and the HBCU system, also endured through a period of great change and transition after 1930. After Roger Williams's move and closure, the three remaining schools all received accreditation between 1930 and

1946. Meharry was recognized by SACS but earned different types of accreditation because of the nature of its graduate-level medical and health-related programs. In the 1950s and 1960s, Fisk, Meharry, and Tennessee State University (formerly Tennessee A&I) emerged as centers of the civil rights movement seeking to reconcile greater political enfranchisement with the racial realities of segregation in the South. Bobby Lovett noted the participation of local students who played monumental roles in the sit-in movement as well as the Freedom Ride campaigns. These included Fisk students such as Diane Nash, Vanderbilt University's James Lawson (who was expelled for his participation in the sit-in movement), John Lewis (American Baptist Theological Seminary, est. 1924), and Ernest "Rip" Patton Jr., Sandra Mitchell, and Allen Cason Jr. from Tennessee A&I. Two white students rounded out the integrated Freedom Rider group: Salynn McCollum, a student from Peabody College, and Jim Zwerg, a young white man from Wisconsin who was an exchange student at Fisk.[25]

Diane Nash, originally from Chicago, famously led twenty-five hundred marchers from Fisk to City Hall where she confronted Mayor Ben West with a question, "Do you feel it is wrong to discriminate against a person solely on the basis of their race or color?" West responded, "Yes," and the headline in the *Tennessean* the next day read, "Mayor Says Integrate Counters."[26] Within three weeks Nashville's downtown businesses and restaurants voluntarily began to dismantle Jim Crow policies that had been in place since the late 1800s.

Hundreds of students from local HBCUs and a handful of students from local white colleges participated in the civil rights movement in Nashville and helped coordinate strategy and protests across the region.[27] The success of the civil rights movement and subsequent local, state, and federal legislation would ultimately negatively impact HBCU admissions. As white colleges across the nation integrated, many making racial diversity a priority by the late 1980s, student enrollment at black colleges declined. In Nashville the school most affected by integration was Fisk University. Meharry's graduate programs were still desperately needed to train black doctors, dentists, and pharmacists, but even Meharry had to reassess academic programs and phased out its School of Nursing to cut costs.

John Thelin, in *A History of American Higher Education,* noted: "Even after the nominal integration of higher education in the South and elsewhere, the HBCUs continued to be available, effective, and attractive sources of undergraduate education." After 1978, however, and the implementation of affirmative-action policies, well-endowed historically white colleges actively began to recruit minority students, and "the HBCUs stood to lose in bidding wars."[28] All three schools struggled financially with strained budgets and sagging student enrollment from the 1970s through the 1990s.

Tennessee A&I, which became Tennessee State University in 1968, dealt with integration differently from Fisk and Meharry. As a result of a prolonged court case that began the same year, *Geier v. Tennessee,* TSU merged with the University of Tennessee–Nashville. TSU faculty member Rita Geier alleged that the creation of a local branch of the state's flagship public university, which planned to open a fully accredited four-year campus, created a dual system of higher education in Tennessee that was unfairly and inequitably based on race. Others heavily involved in the case included Raymond Richardson and Coleman McGinnis. Although the case would not be formally closed until 2001, in 1979 an agreement was reached that formally merged the predominantly white UTN with predominantly black TSU. The *Geier* case, while long and messy, would set TSU on a different trajectory from that of Fisk and Meharry and also provide the school with a second campus located downtown, where UTN had previously existed.

Given the nation's changing demographic for high school graduates and new trends in higher education, Fisk and Meharry have broadened their base to attract a variety of minority groups, while TSU has shifted to integrate along more traditional lines while still touting its HBCU status. In sum, local black colleges and universities continue to shape the city of Nashville as a center of higher education for young people of all socioeconomic and racial/ethnic backgrounds.

Reavis Mitchell, a longtime Fisk professor and local historian, said he believes that a recent effort to attract underrepresented minorities, including undocumented and other racial/ethnic minority students, is a natural extension of Fisk's mission and a way to ensure the school's long-term durability. He argued: "You have to continue to prepare people for the future. You can't lean on the past.... As long as there's a population in this country and people coming into this country who need opportunity and a welcoming place to grow, . . . then there's a role for Fisk University."[29]

Nashville's Colleges and Universities

Nearly all the colleges and universities included in this study opened their doors in the months and years immediately following the Civil War and firmly established their Nashville roots prior to 1900. From 1900 to 1930 local colleges grew and developed in different but largely positive ways—combining their institutional voices to create a rich, collective chorus. As these schools now celebrate, or prepare to celebrate, their sesquicentennial anniversaries, their survival over the past 150 years is a testament to their continued place in local history and culture and the value of higher education to Nashville's brand as a southern urban center.

Vanderbilt University and Peabody College

Vanderbilt University remains Nashville's most prestigious and largest university and plays an ever-present role in Nashville. With ten schools, nearly 4,000 degrees conferred in 2015, over 12,000 full- and part-time students in 2016, and one of the best research hospitals in the nation—Vanderbilt is the largest private employer in Middle Tennessee and the second-largest private employer in the state.[30] Originally envisioned as an alternative to Ivy League schools in the North, Vanderbilt's roots as a "Southern Ivy" are still strong—nearly 40 percent of students hail from southern states. Moreover, Vanderbilt's School of Law and School of Medicine consistently rank in the nation's top twenty. Colleges and schools for arts and sciences, business, and engineering are also ranked as top-tier programs in their respective areas.[31] Vanderbilt remains at the forefront in producing yet another generation of leaders, men and women, who will shape the "New, New South."

Longtime Chancellor James Kirkland's fearful questions about the "feminization" of the university have also been answered. In 2015 women made up 53 percent of the student body. Vanderbilt has also increased diversity in other ways, with ethnic minorities, largely Asian, African American, and Hispanic, making up over 35 percent of the undergraduate population.[32] Still, diversity remains an issue. In 2013 a grassroots group named Hidden Dores (short for Commodores) formed to "induce structural change" at Vanderbilt, while Chancellor Nicolas Zeppos declared in 2015 that diversity and inclusion were of paramount concern.[33]

Membership in fraternities and sororities has decreased from its all-time high of 85 percent in the 1960s, but 43 percent of all undergraduates still participate in traditional rush, initiation, and Greek membership in one of twenty such chapters on campus. Thus, Greek life still permeates much of Vanderbilt's student culture. The university has worked hard to reverse the negative stereotypes associated with college fraternities and sororities. Still, binge drinking and sexual assault remain a constant reminder of the powerful and dark undertow of Greek life and its propensities for parties and exclusivity.

As for college athletics, Vanderbilt is the smallest institutional member of the powerful Southeastern Conference (SEC) and the only private school in the conference. Higher tuition costs, more stringent admission standards, and curricular rigor are partly to blame for the university's lackluster athletic performance in recent decades. Vanderbilt's dominance in football waned after 1930, but in recent years its football, baseball, men's and women's basketball, and men's and women's tennis teams consistently compete at the highest levels. The schools that Vanderbilt once beat by double digits, from the 1890s through the 1920s, now dominate the SEC, and the nation. These football powerhouses include the University of Alabama, Auburn University, and the University of Tennessee, all of which have won one or more NCAA national championships in the last twenty years. Vanderbilt is also the only SEC school located in a major metropolitan area.

Despite recent historic trends, the school's athletic programs have experienced a resurgence over the last decade. Vanderbilt's recent national championships include bowling (2007), baseball (2014), and women's tennis (2015). David Williams II (J.D.), who has served as vice chancellor for athletics and university affairs, athletic director, and professor of law since 2003, is a big reason for the Commodores' athletic comeback. Williams has worked diligently to more fully integrate the school's athletic programs into student life and to connect Vanderbilt sports to the larger community. Williams also believes that the university and the city share a strong bond:

> Our fans base includes not only our alumni, students, staff, and faculty but also the Nashville public at large. We refer to this as Vanderbilt's sidewalk alumni. I believe all of the colleges in Nashville benefit from this great city, its wonderfully diverse population and its love and knowledge of sports. From the famed Tiger Belles of Tennessee State University to the recent NCAA National Championships won by Vanderbilt in three different sports, the college athletics landscape in Nashville is one that adds to the enjoyment of life in the urban location. It contributes to the honor of being the "It City."[34]

The Commodore Club, which acts as an athletic booster club and alumni network, testifies to Williams's efforts with a new advertising campaign—"Star Power: The Degree. The City. The SEC"—which clearly seeks to connect the city to the Commodores. The organization also helps defray the costs of tuition and living expenses. With an average total cost of nearly $70,000 for all school-related expenses per year, Vanderbilt's ability to provide athletic and academic scholarships as well as financial aid is paramount. Perhaps Vanderbilt's greatest weakness is the question of affordability and whether or not student demand will continue to exceed the high cost of a Vanderbilt education. As a twenty-first-century generation comes of age, overwhelmed with student debt rather than job offers, Vanderbilt's "Ivory Tower" model will no doubt be tested again.

Across the street from Vanderbilt, Peabody College continued to exist as the southern think tank of educational pedagogy and progressivism but struggled mightily after World War II. Like colleges established for other specific groups, namely women and African Americans, teacher training schools were rapidly declining as four-year colleges added departments of education that offered undergraduate and graduate programs. In 1964 Peabody added the Blair Academy of Music as a precollegiate division of its Music Department, but the strength of Peabody's music program was not enough to stabilize the larger institutional structure in the long run.[35] Peabody had managed to retain its accreditation, but by 1975 the school faced dire financial and academic straits.

In 1977 Peabody entered into merger talks with Vanderbilt and then Tennessee State University. For a time it appeared that Peabody would join forces with TSU, providing the former with public funding and long-term stability and the latter with a desired doctoral program. This alarmed Vanderbilt, which had maintained a historic relationship with Peabody since the early twentieth century.

In the 1950s Peabody and Vanderbilt formed a cooperative agreement that allowed Peabody students to participate in the Vanderbilt marching band and Vanderbilt students to take education courses at Peabody. Additionally, both schools operated under a "common calendar" and shared a library. Moreover, athletes recruited to play for Vanderbilt's varsity athletic teams could be admitted as Peabody students but play on Vanderbilt teams. This was particularly important for the Vanderbilt men's football and basketball programs, and athletic boosters previously quiet about the fate of Peabody quickly rallied to support the merger. They feared that Vanderbilt sports, already struggling to compete in the SEC, would slide even further if all student-athletes had to be accepted via Vanderbilt's more selective and stringent admission process.

Following weeks of negotiations between Peabody and TSU (and the Tennessee Board of Regents and state legislature), Peabody reentered talks with Vanderbilt, which proposed a new offer that was passed by both Boards of Trust on July 1, 1979. In 1981 Blair Academy also merged with Vanderbilt to become the Blair School of Music. Today's Peabody College continues its legacy of training educators, and while it is not an independent university, it maintains a distinct governance within Vanderbilt's larger framework. It also remains a progressive educational center with more than just a national reputation. Since 2005, the Peabody College of Education and Human Development has been ranked among the top graduate schools of education in the nation more than five times.

Belmont University and Lipscomb University

Belmont and Lipscomb Universities were both founded on religious principles. Ida Hood and Susan Heron, Belmont's cofounders, were not Baptists nor was the school affiliated with any Protestant denomination. But like many schools in the late nineteenth century, Belmont was spiritually centered with required chapel and modest-dress requirements. Lipscomb was founded with an intentional parochial purpose as a Church of Christ–governed institution. As many colleges and universities moved to more secular models of higher education, Belmont moved in the opposite direction. When Ward-Belmont closed, it was purchased by the Tennessee Southern Baptist Convention and remained a Baptist institution from 1951 until 2004. Since 2004, the school has been nondenominational but proudly proclaims its "student-centered Christian community." Lipscomb has perhaps changed the least from its original mission and structure of any other local college.

These two universities have also contributed to the spatial arrangement of the city. Both campuses line Belmont Boulevard and back up to the 12th South neighborhood, making these areas prime locations for retail shops, restaurants, and residents in west Nashville. Former Mayor Karl Dean, a Vanderbilt alumnus and Belmont faculty member, suggests that the most consequential decision for Belmont and Lipscomb leaders was to continue investing and building during the Great Recession. As a result, both schools have emerged as "national universities" attracting many out-of-state students.[36]

These two schools are also the most popular private-university options for high school graduates from the metro Nashville area. In part, that is because they have much higher acceptance rates than Vanderbilt, lower costs (approximately $45,000 total in 2015), and are centrally located close to downtown Nashville. They have also capitalized on Nashville's reputation for music and music-related industry, as well as other industrial sectors including healthcare, finance, and technology.

Belmont specifically promotes and specializes in majors that align with two of Nashville's most successful industries: music (performance, entertainment, and business) and healthcare. With over 7,000 students, more than 5,800 of whom are undergraduates, 61 percent of its student body is female as of 2016. Belmont is organized into eleven colleges and schools and in the last five years it has established a law school (J.D.) and pharmacy school (Pharm.D.), casting a wider net to attract local residents for postgraduate studies, and perhaps more important, potential out-of-state students.[37] For on-campus students, Belmont offers nine social fraternities and sororities, but they do not have the same influence on student culture as at Vanderbilt. Ward-Belmont's Club Village is no more, but Greek and club life at Belmont remains more inclusive than fraternities and sororities at larger public and more elite universities.

Lipscomb University, with 3,000 undergraduate and 1,650 graduate students in 2016, has perhaps made the biggest splash on the local college scene. A school with meager beginnings and a strict religious curriculum and school culture seemed an unlikely candidate for major mainstream growth. Gaining status as a junior college in the 1940s, Lipscomb was accredited by SACS as a four-year institution in 1954. For the next fifty years, Lipscomb remained a small college, with a fairly stable enrollment of several hundred students. However, its location in west Nashville and administrative decisions to expand the school's broad-base appeal changed the trajectory of the school, beginning in 1988 with its first master's program in education. In 2007 Lipscomb introduced its first doctoral degree programs (doctor of education and doctor of ministry) and expanded its master's and specialist degree programs.

Since the 1990s Lipscomb's recruitment and public relations efforts have increased while campus rules based on Church of Christ doctrine have relaxed. For example, rules relating to dorm living and curfew are less restrictive, with most changes implemented in the last ten years. The school now employs faculty who are non-Church of Christ, and in fact, Lipscomb has become the college choice for many Muslim students. Nashville's large immigrant populations, many of whom are Kurdish, are attracted to Lipscomb because of its emphasis on modesty and morality. Lipscomb may encourage students to "Go Greek," but the school's fraternities and sororities exist to create "God-honoring relationships, develop student leaders, and promote on-campus student involvement."[38] Lipscomb still requires twice-weekly chapel attendance and all undergraduate students take three Bible classes: the Story of Jesus, the Story of the Church, and the Story of Israel.

Unlike Belmont, Lipscomb's official denominational ties remain. However, Belmont continues to emphasize its Christian-school status. In certain ways, balancing religious and academic interests in higher education can be precarious, limiting a university's recruitment to a specific niche. Since 2000 Belmont and Lipscomb seem to have found that balance, and the next two decades are full of promise and possibility for two universities that have grown at a faster rate than the city of Nashville. However, Belmont and Lipscomb should not lose sight of the liberal arts curriculum that attracts top-tier students and should avoid the "customer" phenomenon that favors the business model of higher education.

Core members of Nashville's "Athens of the New, New South" image, Lipscomb and Belmont have benefited tremendously from their prime locations near downtown as the urban core has gentrified and revitalized. Both schools continue to tout their location as a recruitment tool. Lipscomb president Dr. L. Randolph Lowry views the city of Nashville as "the university's campus and the world as its classroom."[39] Lowry made certain that Lipscomb University was part of the Equal Chance for Education (ECE) program along with Trevecca, Cumberland, Fisk, Belmont, and Watkins. The ECE provides scholarships and funding for undocumented student who are academically prepared and professionally driven but do not qualify for student loans or financial aid.[40]

In addition to participating in the ECE program, Belmont's president Bob Fisher helped lead an initiative called "Bridges to Belmont." Launched in 2013, "Bridges to Belmont" provides full-tuition scholarships and a summer transition program for twenty-five local graduating seniors from Metropolitan Nashville Public Schools (MNPS).[41] In 2014, then–Nashville Mayor Karl Dean also praised the enduring ties between Belmont and the Nashville community and referred to the university as "Nashville's own stimulus program," while also noting that its graduates represented the "ideal citizen of the city of Nashville."[42]

Belmont and Lipscomb have also developed a sports rivalry. While neither school fields a football team, they are both members of NCAA's Division I and compete in soccer, softball, cross-country, baseball, and tennis. Basketball matchups between the Belmont Bruins and the Lipscomb Bisons have grown in intensity, represented by increased attendance, media coverage, and local bragging rights. Called the "Battle of the Boulevard" because of the schools' close proximity along Belmont Boulevard, this game is highly anticipated and reaffirms the power of sports to build school spirit and rally community support. Specifically, the Belmont men's and women's basketball teams have also gained national notoriety with recent appearances in the NCAA national tournament.

Tennessee State University

Tennessee State University advertises as a public university, HBCU, and as a "comprehensive, urban, coeducational, land-grant institution" located in the heart of Nashville. Although the school desegregated in the early 1970s, the student body remains majority black (75 percent black, 22 percent white) as of 2016. Carefully balancing its HBCU tradition with present educational trends, the school's growth continues to impress. With eight colleges and schools, forty-five undergraduate majors, and thirty-one graduate programs (including seven doctoral degrees), TSU enrolls more Nashvillians than any other four-year university in Davidson County.[43] It is also the most affordable option with tuition of less than $8,000 per year. Many first-generation college students pass through the halls of TSU.

TSU's school culture in 2016 is a mix of on-campus undergraduates, commuter undergraduate students, off-campus students enrolled in "TSU @ a Distance" online courses, and commuter graduate students. Students are thus part of the TSU community on multiple levels and to varying degrees—with a sense of camaraderie but with less cohesiveness than other local colleges and universities. However, there are approximately ten local chapters of national Greek social clubs and over one hundred student organizations. Perhaps Tennessee State's greatest source of school pride is its storied athletic program, with seventeen Olympic gold medalists from 1955 to 1985, including Wilma Rudolph, Wyomia Tyus, and Chandra Cheeseborough. Coach Ed Temple, the legendary TSU track-and-field coach of the Tigers and famed Tiger Belles, also coached two Olympic teams. Today's TSU athletic teams compete in NCAA Division I with consistently successful football and basketball programs.

Celebrating its centennial celebration in 2012, TSU's Dr. Bobby L. Lovett, a member of the history faculty from 1973 to 2011, published *A Touch of Greatness*. Lovett's institutional history highlights the school's commitment to educational and life achievement as well as the continued challenges of higher education for African Americans living or attending college in the South. With nearly nine thousand students on two campuses, TSU is the second-largest university in Nashville behind Vanderbilt. In order to sustain continued growth in the twenty-first century, the university must harness growth in ways that strengthen, rather than strain, institutional infrastructure and academic rigor.

Fisk University and Meharry Medical College

Both Fisk University and Meharry Medical College have endured difficult circumstances in recent years. TSU's model for growth and success, following its merger with the short-lived University of Tennessee–Nashville (1968–79), has certainly played a role in Fisk University's struggle to attract and retain students. With a number of program offerings, higher rates of admission, and lower costs, many African Americans from Nashville and across the state have chosen to attend TSU over Fisk. In 2011 Fisk's student body dwindled to less than 550 students. The last several years have witnessed a full SACS reaccreditation, increased contributors, the school's sesquicentennial anniversary, and the appointment of Dr. Kevin D. Rome as the sixteenth university president. For the 2017–2018 academic year, Fisk boasted an enrollment of over 850 students, a 56 percent increase over the last six years.

In 2014 then-president H. James Williams declared, "The Fisk Renaissance is truly underway" and announced plans for a new residence hall, the first new construction on campus in nearly forty years.[44] Fisk is divided into two major college divisions that offer undergraduate and graduate programs: the School of Humanities and Social Sciences and the School of Natural Sciences, Mathematics, and Business. Fisk University also sponsors four men's and six women's sports that compete in the National Association of Intercollegiate Athletics, a league associated with smaller schools. Fisk is also home to nine national sororities and fraternities, continuing its tradition of Greek life.

Although Fisk remains a small liberal arts college, it has maintained academic excellence, a testament to the school's commitment to a liberal arts education born from a post–Civil War model that resisted industrial training. Fisk is one of four HBCUs to earn a tier-one ranking on the list of Best National Liberal Arts Colleges by *U.S. News and World Report.* In 2016 the university was awarded a $5 million grant from the Center of Research Excellence in Science and Technology, a division of the National Science Foundation, to establish a Center for Biological Signatures and Sensing. The school's already strong science program produces more African American graduates who go on to earn doctoral degrees in the natural sciences than any other HBCU school in the nation; many of whom continue on at Meharry Medical College, reaffirming the bond between the two colleges.

In the twenty-first century Meharry Medical College features a Medical School, Dental School, and Graduate School; it is also home to the Robert Wood Johnson Center for Health Policy. Meharry does not offer undergraduate degrees, in line with its historic foundation as a postgraduate institution of higher education and medical training. Like Lipscomb University and the Church of Christ, Meharry still maintains denominational ties to the United Methodist Church, as did Central Tennessee College (from which Meharry originated). Meharry struggled in the late 1980s and 1990s, losing its accreditation for pediatrics, surgery, and ob-gyn residency training programs, but it has recently experienced a renaissance of its own. Bringing its endowment up to $139 million, embarking on a $70 million fundraising campaign, and installing its twelfth president, James E. K. Hildreth, in 2015, Meharry has shifted its message from "surviving to thriving."[45] In fact, among Nashville colleges and universities, Meharry's endowment is second only to Vanderbilt.

Meharry's student population of approximately 830 students might seem small, but the college seeks to increase the quality of instruction, not necessarily the size of its student body. Still predominantly African American, the college also includes white, Asian, Hispanic, and Native American students. Meharry's enrollment is at desired capacity, and competitiveness is at an all-time high with over two thousand applicants competing for fewer than two hundred slots annually. Meharry is one of the top five producers of African American Ph.D. degrees in the country, and approximately 20 percent of all black dentists in the United States are Meharry alumni.

If one still questions the relevance of Fisk and Meharry today, one need look no further than national politics and culture. Then-presidential candidate Hillary

Clinton visited Nashville on February 28, 2016, to deliver a speech. Her stop was not at Vanderbilt or Belmont (which held a presidential debate in 2008), but at Meharry. She argued that higher education should "allow students to refinance loans and create special funds that would be dedicated to helping those attending black colleges and universities."[46] Likewise, the Fisk Jubilee Singers continue to bring prestige and recognition to the university, an intangible source of pride and a historic connection that connects the school to the broader community. With sold-out shows and tours across the Southeast and the United States, the Jubilee Singers won the National Medal of Arts in 2008 and were nominated for a Grammy in 2009 in the category of "best gospel performance." Meharry and Fisk are both heavily involved in local partnerships and collaborations, particularly in social work and healthcare, which stem from strong histories of community service. President Hildreth also hopes to increase federal funding with a strategy that builds in part on existing partnerships with Vanderbilt and Tennessee State Universities, while also forging new institutional relationships with other Middle Tennessee colleges and universities.[47] Meharry University proudly boasts: "Our bond with Nashville is intricate, strong, and mutually respectful. All Meharrians are Nashvillians, whether for a season or a lifetime."[48]

Conclusion

The Metropolitan Transit Authority, Nashville's current bus system, is one key to the city's future growth. With proposals to enhance and improve public transportation, Mayor Megan Barry has made public transportation a priority. Just as electric streetcars once connected the downtown core to local schools, there is a special MTA bus route worthy of note. It was not designed to be symbolic, but it is nevertheless. Route 21, named the University Connector, runs a loop with stops at Vanderbilt, Belmont, Lipscomb, Meharry, Fisk, and TSU.[49] It symbolizes the literal and metaphorical connection between Nashville and its institutions of higher education. The University Connector is a testament to the interactive and cyclical relationship between the city and its colleges—each informing the other, shaping campuses and curricula as well as the larger urban landscape. Nashville, as Athens of the South, represents a distinctive identity that embraces higher education, college life, and urbanization—inextricably linked and historically bonded. May it always be so.

Appendix
Nashville Maps

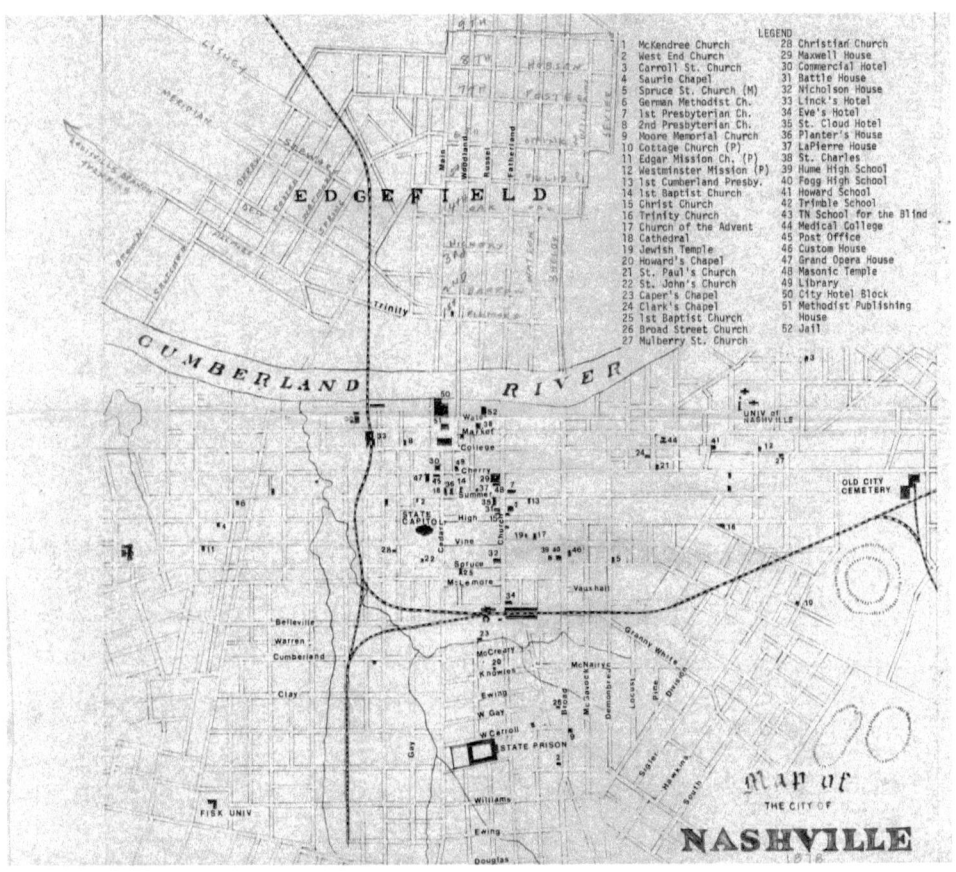

1878 map. Courtesy of Ridley Wills II.

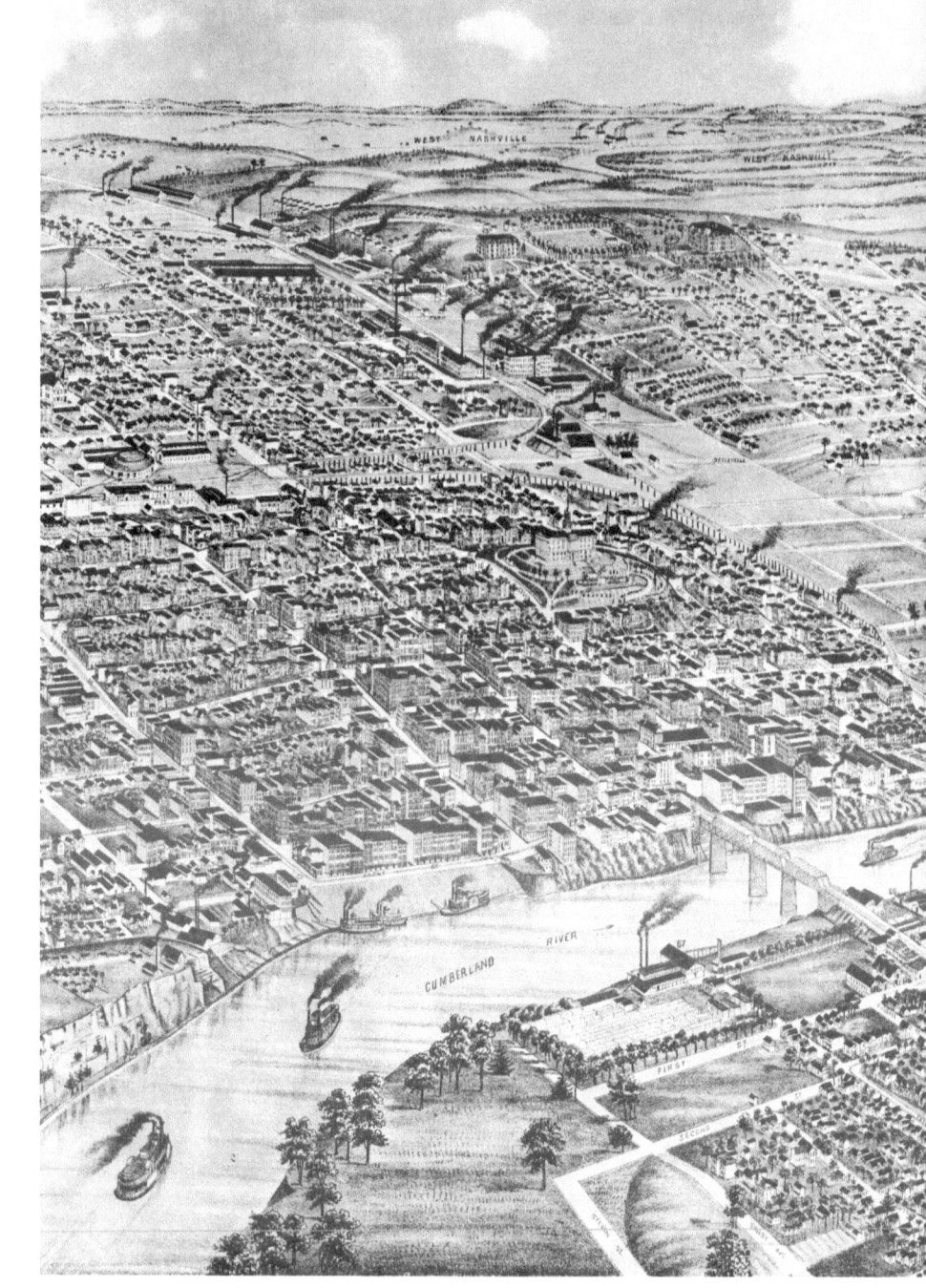

1880s map looking West.
Courtesy of Ridley Wills II.

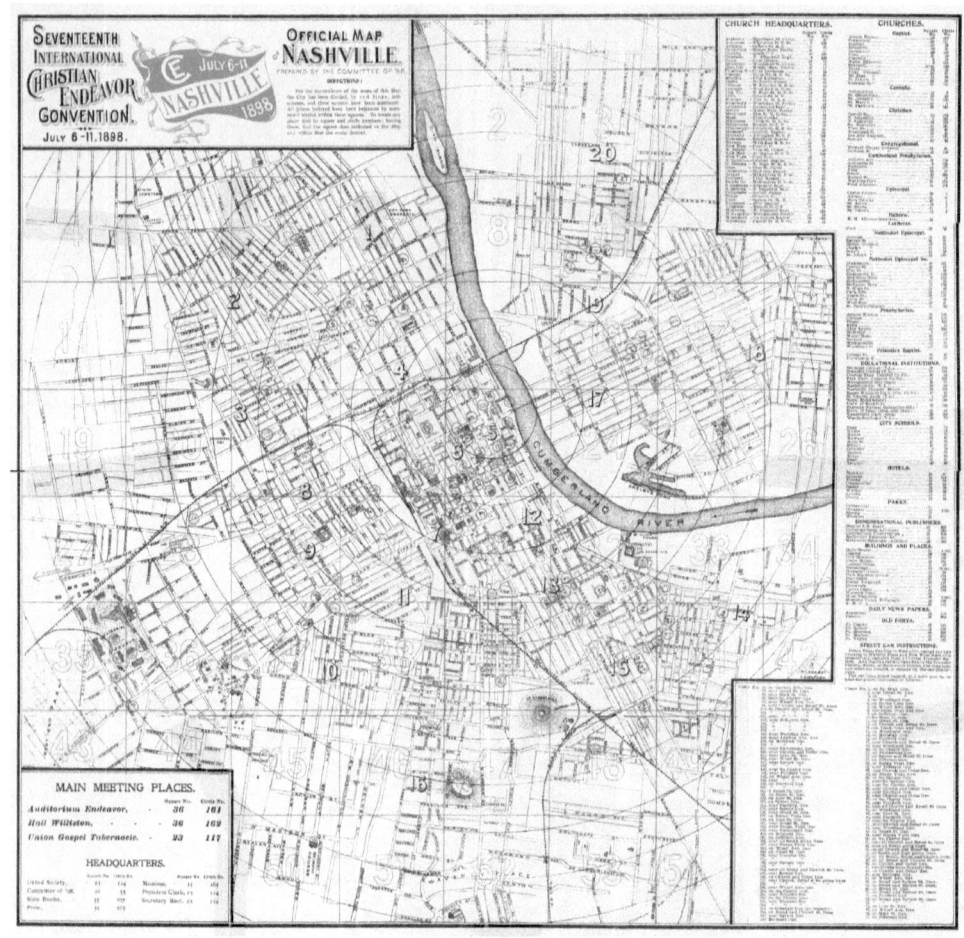

1898 map. Courtesy of Ridley Wills II.

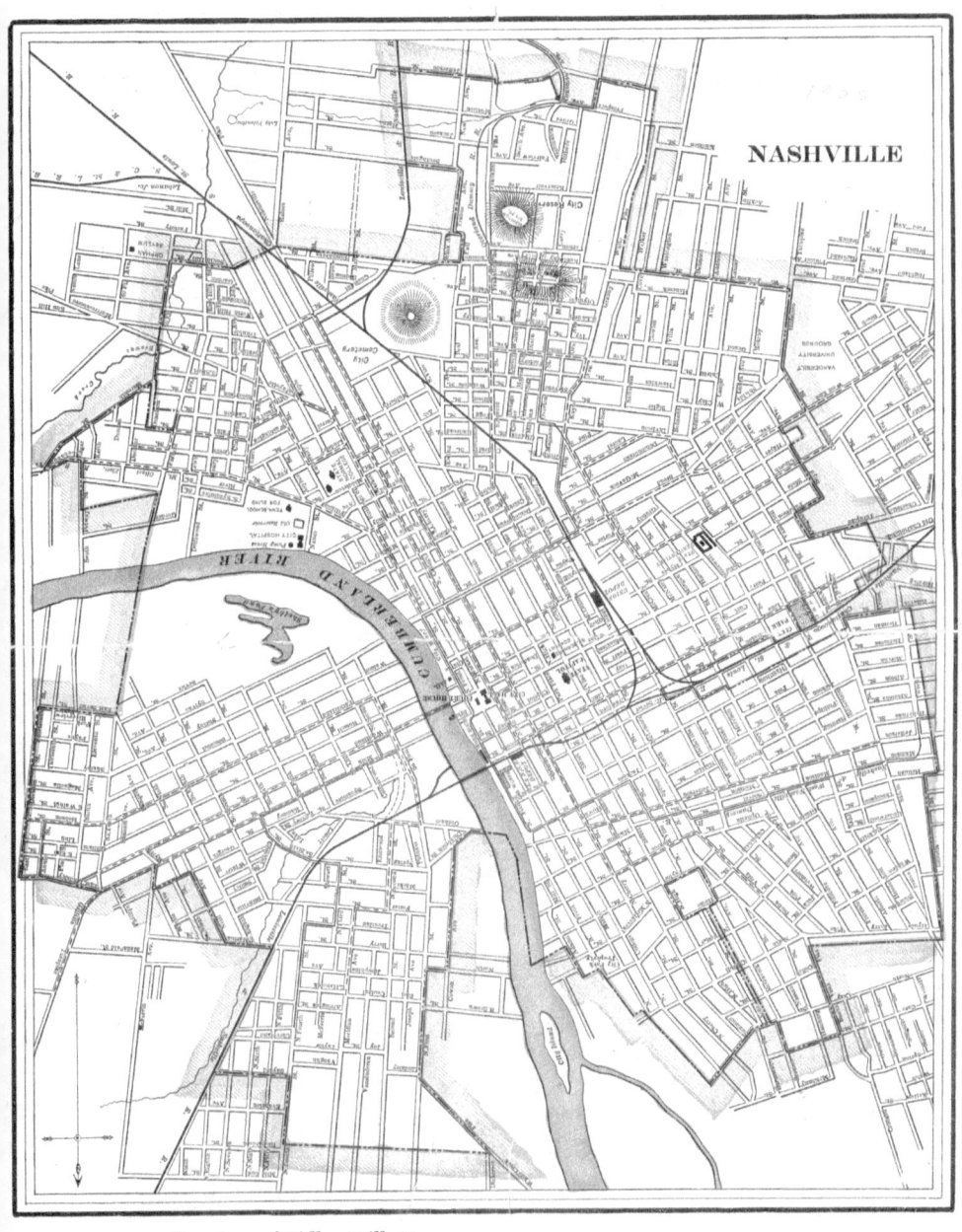

1900 map. Courtesy of Ridley Wills II.

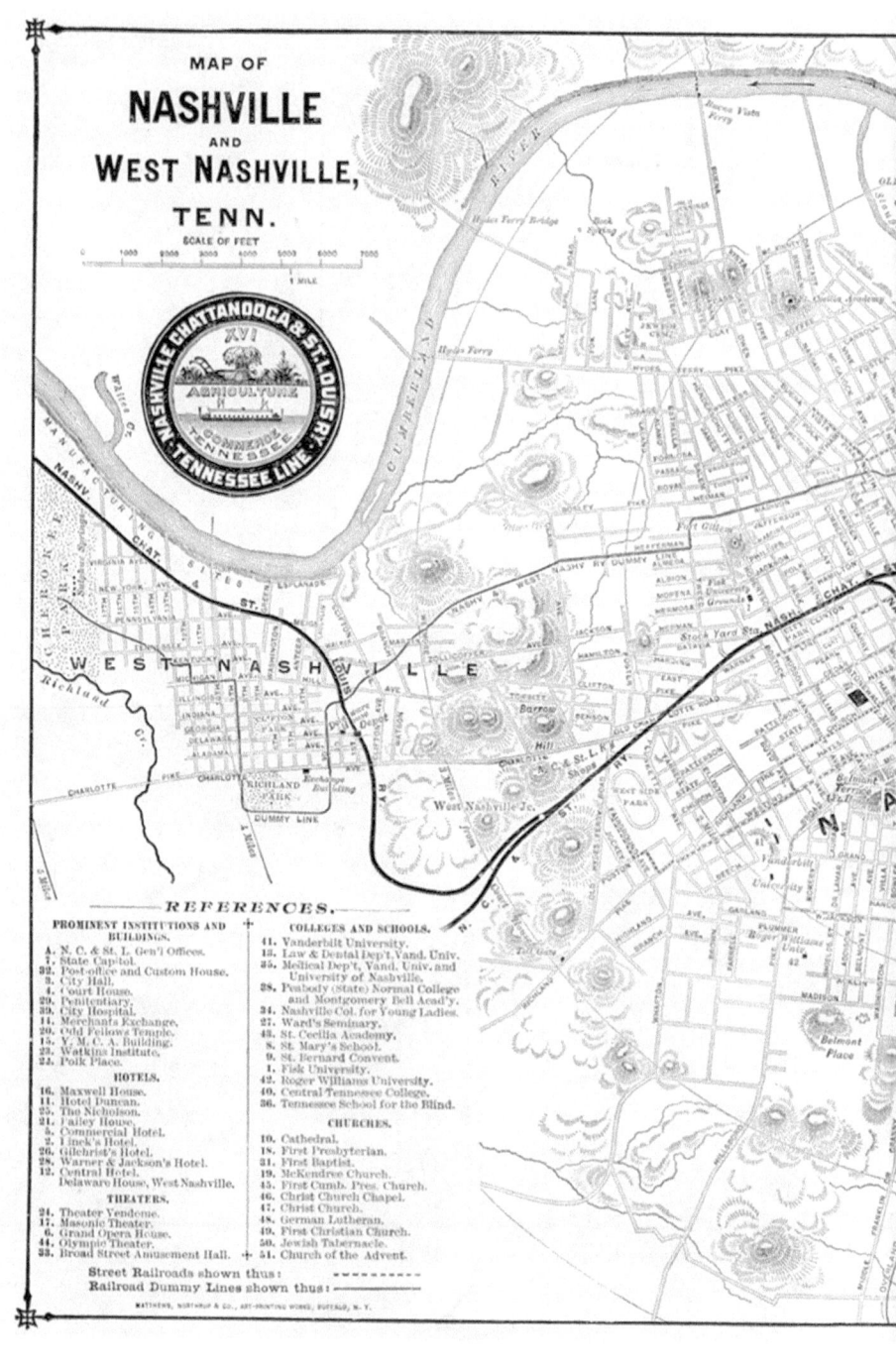

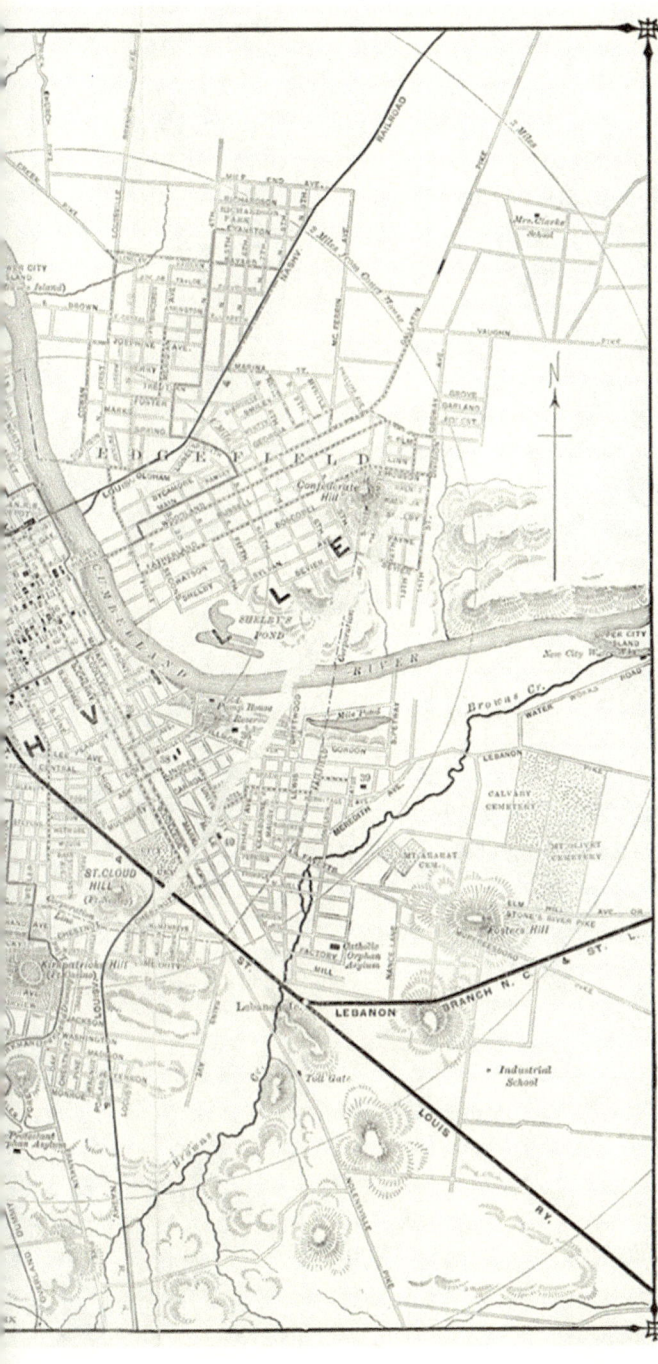

1907 map. Courtesy of Ridley Wills II.

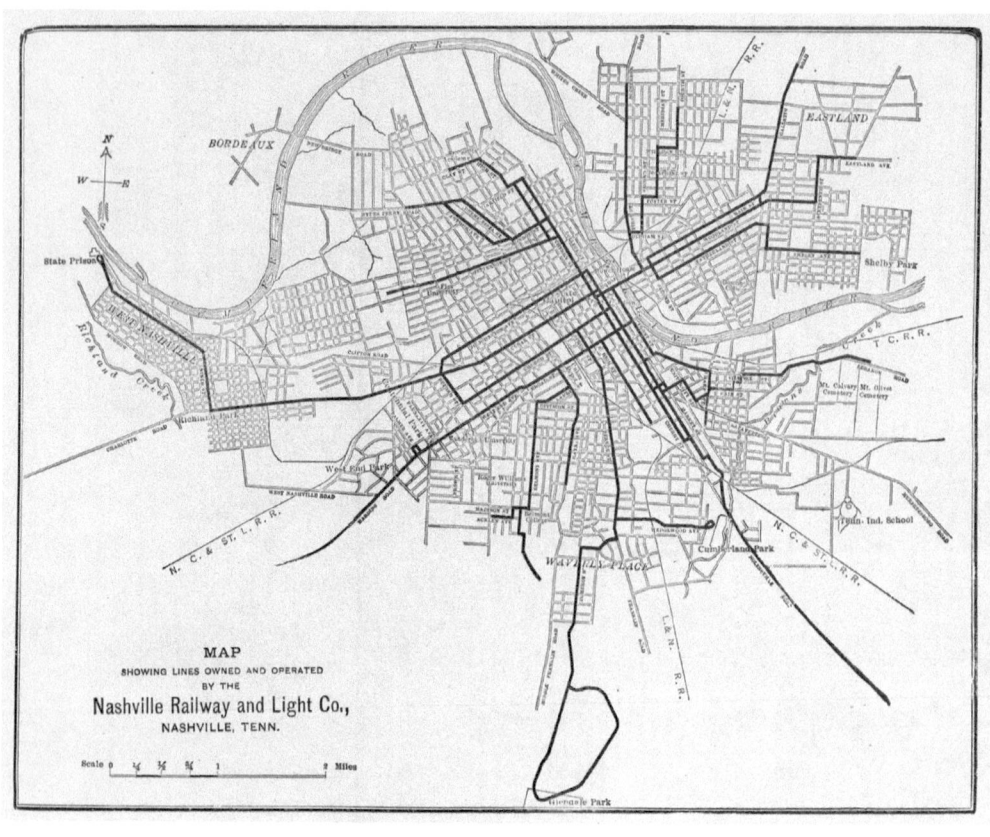

1913 Nashville Electric Railway map. Courtesy of Ridley Wills II.

Notes

Introduction

1. Kim Severson, "Nashville's Latest Big Hit Could Be the City Itself," *New York Times*, January 8, 2013, http://www.nytimes.com/2013/01/09/us/nashville-takes-its-turn-in-the-spotlight.html (accessed August 13, 2016).

2. Henry McRaven, *Nashville, "Athens of the South"* (Chapel Hill, NC: Scheer and Jervis, 1949), vii. Middle Tennessee and Nashville were first called "Athens of the South" as early as the 1850s with already established schools such as Cumberland College (1842), the University of Nashville (1826), and the University of the South (1857) in nearby Sewanee.

3. See also: Robert Wiebe, *The Search for Order, 1877–1920* (New York: Hill and Wang, 1967). Wiebe argues that during the Gilded Age/Progressive Era, urban areas grew and increasingly connected to smaller "island" communities. In Nashville, as the downtown grew, suburban communities such as Belle Meade emerged, further extending the size and scope of the city. Likewise, outlying areas such as Murfreesboro and Lebanon were more accessible to Nashville as the city grew, connected by railroads prior to the Civil War.

4. Mike Ramirez, "The Lost Cause in a New South City: Nashville, 1890–1910," in "Nashville as Historical Laboratory, 1977–1978," a collection of student papers archived at the Vanderbilt University Library.

5. U.S. Census Reports, 1880–1940.

6. Ramirez, "The Lost Cause in a New South City," 3.

7. For more see Don Doyle, *New Men, New Cities, New South: Atlanta, Nashville, Charleston, Mobile, 1860–1910* (Chapel Hill: University of North Carolina Press, 1990). See also Lawrence Larson, *The Urban South: A History* (Lexington: University Press of Kentucky, 1990); Arthur M. Schlesinger, *A History of American Life*, vol. 12, *The Rise of the City, 1878–1898* (New York: Macmillan, 1931); Edwin Mims, *The Advancing South: Stories of Progress and Reaction* (Garden City, NY: Doubleday, Page, 1926); and Raymond Mohl, *The New City: Urban America in the Industrial Age, 1860–1920* (Arlington Heights, IL: Harlan Davidson, 1985).

8. *Memphis Ledger,* 1885, taken from *W. E. Ward's Seminary Annual Announcement,* 1885–1886, 19. The rest of the quotation states, "We are all proud of Nashville, not only on account of its historic associations, its commanding position, and political relations with the rest of the State, but for the intelligence, culture, and hospitality of the people."

9. Quoted in Edward L. Ayers, *The Promise of the New South: Life after Reconstruction* (New York: Oxford University Press, 1992), 63.

10. Several of these schools have multiple iterations of their official institutional titles due to mergers, accreditation, or simply symbolic name changes to reflect the changing nature of the school. I have chosen to use the school names listed above both for consistency but also simplicity. For clarity, however, the following schools underwent name changes. Today's Lipscomb University began as the Nashville Bible School, renamed David Lipscomb College (1918) after the passing of one of its founders and administrators but was called "Lipscomb" for short. In 1988 the school was renamed Lipscomb University after expanding its offerings to include doctoral work. When established in 1912, the full-name of today's Tennessee State University was the Tennessee Agricultural and Industrial State Normal School, which was later shortened to Tennessee A&I in 1927. The Southern Association of Colleges and Schools granted accreditation in 1946, and five years later, the State Board of Education approved the school's university status. It official name was changed to Tennessee State University in 1968. The Ward-Belmont School began as two separate women's schools: Ward Seminary (1865) and Belmont College for Young Women (1890). After their merger in 1913, Ward-Belmont offered three different divisions: college preparatory, music conservatory, and junior college (after 1925). The school was sold to the Tennessee Baptists in 1951 and reopened in the fall of 1951 as a four-year coeducational liberal arts college. The college preparatory division moved farther west and opened as the Harpeth Hall School on a new campus. The college dropped the name Ward and reassumed the name Belmont College, as its name was based on the location of the campus on a former antebellum estate of the same name. In 1991 the school changed its name to Belmont University and also began a long process that would result in its eventual legal separation from the Tennessee Baptist Convention.

11. See Don H. Doyle, *Nashville in the New South, 1890-1930* (Knoxville: University of Tennessee Press, 1985). His work provided much of the background and information underlying this book's exploration of urbanization and education. While Doyle argued that Nashville did not truly become an "Athens of the South" until after 1920, this book will argue that many modern notions of education, urbanization, and leisure were set in motion by Nashville's younger progressive generation in the late 1800s.

12. See Mabel Newcomer, *A Century of Higher Education for American Women* (New York: Harper and Brothers, 1959); and Nancy F. Cott, *The Grounding of Modern Feminism* (New Haven, CT: Yale University Press, 1987).

13. See also Shirley Ardener, *Women and Space: Ground Rules and Social Maps* (New York: St. Martin's, 1981).

14. For analysis of the shift from Victorian to progressive values, specifically in relation to gender, see Carroll Smith-Rosenberg, *Disorderly Conduct: Visions of Gender in Victorian*

America (New York: Knopf, 1985). For more on the leisure revolution, see Dale Somers, "The Leisure Revolution: Recreation in the American City, 1820–1920," *Journal of Popular Culture* 5 (Summer 1971): 125–47.

15. Michael Dennis, *Lessons in Progress: State Universities and Progressivism in the New South, 1880–1920* (Urbana: University of Illinois Press, 2001), 3, 251.

16. Laurence R. Veysey, *The Emergence of the American University* (Chicago: University of Chicago, 1965), 5.

17. Ibid., 265.

18. For more, see Michael McGerr, *A Fierce Discontent: The Rise and Fall of the Progressive Movement in America, 1870–1920* (New York: Free Press, 2003).

19. Arthur Cohen, *The Shaping of American Higher Education: Emergence and Growth of the Contemporary System* (San Francisco: Jossey-Bass, 1998), 97, 101, 114.

20. James W. Fraser, *Preparing America's Teachers: A History* (New York: Teachers College Press, 2007), 51–53.

21. John Dewey was a leading force behind what became the junior college movement. This movement resulted in today's community college system, which offers a two-year, associate degree.

22. The NTA is today the National Education Association (NEA). The NTA initially formed in 1857 with meetings in New York.

23. The democratization of education was not a new concept, but the emphasis on democratic education increased with the growth of government, immigration, women's education, African American education, and the Morrill Land Acts of 1862 and 1890. For more on reform and pedagogical developments, John Dewey's works must be consulted. See his *Democracy and Education* (New York: Macmillan, 1944); *Experience and Education* (New York: Collier, 1938); and *Moral Principles in Education* (Boston: Houghton Mifflin, 1909).

24. Christopher Lucas, *American Higher Education: A History* (New York: Macmillan, 2006), 152. See also Ronald K. Goodenow and Arthur O. White, eds., *Education and the Rise of the New South* (Boston: Hall, 1981); and Warren H. Button and Eugene F. Provenzo, eds., *History of Education and Culture in America,* 2nd ed. (Englewood Cliffs, NJ: Prentice Hall, 1989).

25. For more see Andrew David Holt's seminal work: *Struggle for a State System of Public Schools in Tennessee, 1903-1936*, Contributions to Education 753, Teachers College, Columbia University (New York: Teachers College, Columbia Univ., 1938).

26. Charles Lee Lewis, *Philander Priestly Claxton: Crusader for Public Education* (Knoxville: University of Tennessee Press, 1948), 164–65.

27. Ibid., 3.

28. Ibid., 84.

29. Ibid., 172.

30. Lewis quotes a *Tennessean* editorial published in 1943 following Claxton's retirement from his last position as president of Austin Peay State University: "Tennessee is proud to have furnished Claxton to the nation for a long and distinguished career as Commission of Education, but the work that he did within the state's own borders holds in fondest memory

and likes to recall him as the young evangel of educational advance carrying the campaign for a better public school system into the hills and hamlets of the commonwealth" (ibid., 299).

31. For a more thorough treatment of Charles Dabney and public universities in the South, see Dennis, *Lessons in Progress*.

32. Doyle, *Nashville in the New South*, 201. For a report on Tennessee's colleges and universities just after World War I, see George F. Zook, *A Survey of Higher Education in Tennessee, 1924: By the United States Bureau of Education* (Nashville: Tennessee College Association, 1926).

33. McGerr, *Fierce Discontent*, 110.

34. Ibid.

35. Glenda Elizabeth Gilmore, *Gender and Jim Crow: Women and the Politics of White Supremacy in North Carolina, 1896–1920* (Chapel Hill: University of North Carolina Press, 1996), 148. For a broad treatment of progressivism, see Allen Davis, *Spearheads for Reform: The Social Settlements and the Progressive Movement, 1890–1914* (New Brunswick, NJ: Rutgers University Press, 1984).

36. John R. Thelin, *A History of American Higher Education*, 2nd ed. (Baltimore: Johns Hopkins University Press, 2011), 127–34.

37. In addition to the colleges and universities briefly introduced below, there were other notable educational institutions in Nashville, but these do not fit this book's parameters as their role was limited to smaller preparatory schools or theological seminaries during this period. They include Wallace University School (1886–1944), Battleground Academy (1889–present), Montgomery Bell Academy (1867–present), University School of Nashville (1915–present), St. Cecelia Academy (1860–present), the Harpeth Hall School (1865–present), American Baptist Theological Seminary (1924-present), and Trevecca Nazarene (1901–present).

38. Paul Conkin, *Gone with the Ivy: A Biography of Vanderbilt University* (Knoxville: University of Tennessee Press, 1985), 23.

39. J. H. Kirkland, "Private Gifts to Education," *Independent* 54 (April–June, 1902): 983.

40. T. J. Stiles, "The Commodore's Civil War," *Vanderbilt Magazine,* April 11, 2011, http://news.vanderbilt.edu/vanderbiltmagazine/the-commodores-civil-war/ (accessed April 19, 2016). Cornelius Vanderbilt died on January 4, 1877.

41. Conkin, *Gone with the Ivy*, 88–90, 102, 259–88.

42. Ibid., 7–34.

43. Helen Lefkowitz Horowitz, *Campus Life: Undergraduate Cultures from the End of the Eighteenth Century to the Present* (New York: Knopf, 1987), 108.

44. "History of Vanderbilt University," Vanderbilt University website, http://www.vanderbilt.edu/about/history/ (accessed March 12, 2015). Vanderbilt's student enrollment by 1950 exceeded 3,500 students.

45. Conkin, *Gone with the Ivy*, 133.

46. Vanderbilt University has been accredited by the Commission on Colleges of the Southern Association of Colleges and Schools since 1895. It also holds specialized accredi-

tation from thirteen institutions, including the American Bar Association (1925), the American Psychological Association (1959), and the Association of Theological Schools (1938).

47. Meharry also separated as an independent institution from Walden University in 1915 and completed its new hospital facility in the late 1920s, signaling the growth of healthcare and medical services for both the white and black local community.

48. John A. M'Ewen, *An Address Delivered at the Laying of the Corner Stone of the University of Nashville* (Nashville: John T. S. Fall, 1853).

49. Paul Conkin, *Peabody College: From a Frontier Academy to the Frontiers of Teaching and Learning* (Nashville: Vanderbilt University Press, 2002), 73. The Western Military Institute closed its doors in 1862 during the Civil War. See also: J. L. M. Curry, *A Brief Sketch of the Peabody Education Fund Through Thirty Years* (New York: John Wilson and Son, 1898).

50. "A Great Aid to Southern Education," *Public Opinion* 38 (June 1905): 203.

51. Peabody was known as one of the earliest American industrial philanthropists, contributing to a number of causes including the Peabody Trust in Britain and the Peabody Institute and George Peabody Library in Baltimore. His philanthropy emphasized education and the arts; he was motived by his own lack of education and exposure to the cultural arts as a child and young adult.

52. *Proceedings of the Trustees of the Peabody Education Fund, from Their Original Organization, on the 8th of February, 1867* (Cambridge, MA: John Wilson and Son, 1875), 1–7.

53. Conkin, *Peabody College*, 111–16.

54. Ibid., 133. Payne also heavily emphasized exercise and gymnastics and required students to spend at least three hours in the gender-segregated gymnasium under instructor supervision.

55. Ibid., 169–80.

56. Mary A. Evins, ed., *Tennessee Women in the Progressive Era: Toward the Public Sphere in the New South* (Knoxville: University of Tennessee Press, 2013), 193.

57. S. P. Pittman, *Lipscomb's Golden Heritage, 1891–1941* (Nashville: Associated Ladies for Lipscomb, 1983), 6. Although the school was Nashville Bible College for half of the period examined, I will use identify the school as Lipscomb or David Lipscomb College for consistency.

58. James D. Anderson, *The Education of Blacks in the South, 1860–1935* (Chapel Hill: University of North Carolina Press, 1988), 7.

59. Courses in expression contained instruction in public speaking, recitation, and etiquette.

60. Anderson, *The Education of Blacks in the South,* 10–23; *Annual Announcement of the Nashville Bible School, 1914–1915* (Nashville: McQuiddy Printing, 1914), 18–33.

61. Anthony LaBue, "Teacher Certification in the United States: A Brief History," *Journal of Teacher Education* 11, no. 2 (1960): 147–72.

62. Pittman, *Lipscomb's Golden Heritage,* 23.

63. Ibid., 24.

64. Trevecca Nazarene was another religious school; it was founded in 1901 by Presbyterian minister J. O. McClurkan. It opened as the Pentecostal Literary and Bible Training School. The school claimed to offer bachelor's degrees as early as 1910 and changed its name to Trevecca College for Christian Workers. In 1917 it became the official college for the Church of the Nazarene. The school experienced several moves and financial problems, and Trevecca Nazarene College would not become accredited until 1969. For the purposes of this book, Trevecca will not be considered, as it was not a part of Nashville's emerging, mainstream college culture from 1865 to 1930.

65. "Ward Seminary Founded During Post-War Chaos," *Ward-Belmont Hyphen*, November 3, 1934, 1. The *Ward-Belmont Hyphen* was the weekly student periodical from 1913 to 1951. Ward Seminary first opened under the name W. E. Ward's Seminary.

66. William Thomas Hale and Dixon Lanier Merritt, *History of Tennessee and Tennesseans* (Chicago: Lewis, 1913), 1,494.

67. *Nashville Banner,* April 13, 1925.

68. See also Ivar Lou Myhr Duncan, *A History of Belmont College* (Nashville: Belmont College, 1966); and Louise Douglas Morrison, *A Voyage of Faith: The Story of Harpeth Hall* (Nashville: Harpeth Hall, 1980).

69. *AMA [American Missionary Association] Proceedings,* 1865, n.p.

70. Reavis Mitchell, "Fisk University," *Tennessee State University Library Digital Collection,* http://ww2.tnstate.edu/library/digital/FISKU.HTM (accessed August 13, 2016).

71. Gustavus D. Pike, *The Jubilee Singers and Their Campaign for Twenty Thousand Dollars* (Boston: Lee and Shepard, 1873). World tours by the Jubilee Singers continued to subsidize the university's financial costs well into the twentieth century.

72. Accreditation page, Fisk University website, https://www.fisk.edu/about/accreditation (accessed March 10, 2015).

73. Anderson, *Education of Blacks in the South,* 250.

74. Fisk would not become officially accredited by SACS until 1930 but remains the first African American college in the nation to receive an A standing. In 1933 the Association of American Universities also gave Fisk an "A" standing. In both cases, accreditation most likely was delayed because Fisk was a predominantly African American college.

75. *Baptist Home Mission Monthly* 11, no. 1 (January 1889): 148–50.

76. "Roger Williams University," *America's Lost Colleges,* http://www.lostcolleges.com/#!roger-williams/c6ri (accessed July 31, 2016).

77. *Catalog of the Officers and Students of Roger Williams University,* 1884–1885, 23.

78. Steve Hoskins, "American Baptist Theological Seminary," *Tennessee Encyclopedia of History and Culture* http://tennesseeencyclopedia.net/entry.php?rec=1567 (accessed August 16, 2016). The American Baptist Theological Seminary opened its own campus in south Nashville 1924, but in 1934 it purchased the former campus of Roger Williams University and returned to its original Nashville location. While remaining a small school, it would play a major role in Nashville's civil rights movement. It was renamed American Baptist College in 1971.

79. Frances Meharry, *History of the Meharry Family in America* (Lafayette, IN: Lafayette Printing, 1925), 369.

80. Walden University was first established in 1865 but was renamed Central Tennessee College after the school received its state charter in 1867.

81. James Summerville, *Educating Black Doctors: A History of Meharry Medical College* (University of Alabama Press, 1983), 10–18.

82. Although Morehouse College in Atlanta maintained a rigorous curriculum and emerged as a major competitor with Fisk and Meharry in the 1920s and 1930s, the Morehouse School of Medicine was not established until 1975.

83. Bobby L. Lovett, *A Touch of Greatness: A History of Tennessee State University* (Macon, GA: Mercer University Press, 2013), 9-20. The Land Grant College Act of 1862 and the Hatch Act of 1887 were pivotal to the development of a public system of higher education.

84. *Tennessee State University 75th Anniversary: Some Traditions Are Forever* (Nashville: Tennessee State University, 1987), 4. This remains the current motto for Tennessee State University.

85. Ibid., 5–6. Tennessee Agricultural and Industrial State Normal School changed to Tennessee Agricultural and Industrial State Normal College in 1925. The school was not accredited as a college until 1933.

86. To clarify the author's intent and use of the term, it is important to define "gender." Gender is often confused with sex, but sex generally refers to biology and anatomy. By contrast, gender refers to a set of qualities and behaviors that society expects from a female or male. New opportunities as a result of "college life" involved men and women, both white and black.

Chapter 1

1. *Nashville Banner,* June 29, 1914, 5.

2. *Souvenir of Nashville Tennessee* (Columbus, Ohio: Ward Bros., 1884), n.p.

3. *Official Guide to Tennessee Centennial and City of Nashville,* (Nashville: Marshall Bruce Co., 1897), 84.

4. *Birmingham Ledger,* reprinted in *Nashville Banner,* June 29, 1914, 5.

5. Ibid.

6. Ibid.

7. Henry Grady, *The "New South" Speech*, December 22, 1886, http://historymatters.gmu.edu/d/5745/ (accessed August 6, 2016).

8. Arthur Colyar, "Nashville," *New England Magazine* 1 (Sept. 1889), 138.

9. Sarah McCanless Howell, "The Editorials of Arthur S. Colyar: Nashville Prophet of the New South," *Tennessee Historical Quarterly* 27, No. 3 (Fall 1968), 276.

10. Jackson Lears, *The Making of Modern America, 1877–1920* (New York: Harper Perennial, 2009), 149.

11. Walter Durham, *Reluctant Partners: Nashville and the Union, 1863–1865* (Knoxville: University of Tennessee Press, 1987), xxii-xxiii.

12. Modernity is defined as a temporal period that is discontinuous with the past because of social and cultural changes. It does not dismiss tradition, but modernity does imply change, typically in the form of certain understandings of progress or improvement. Life is fundamentally different when measured by premodern and modern standards. For more see Wiebe, *Search for Order.*

13. Dan R. Frost, *Thinking Confederates: Academia and the Idea of Progress in the New South* (Knoxville: University of Tennessee Press, 2000), xiii.

14. Ethos is used here to represent a distinguishing characteristic, sentiment, moral nature, or guiding beliefs of a person, group, or institution. In this case, it describes the cityscape of Nashville.

15. Dewey W. Grantham, *Southern Progressivism: The Reconciliation of Progress and Tradition* (Knoxville: University of Tennessee Press, 1983), 271.

16. Bruce G. Harvey, *World's Fairs in a Southern Accent: Atlanta, Nashville, and Charleston, 1895–1902* (Knoxville: University of Tennessee Press, 2014), xxi. Planning for the exposition began in 1894, and the cornerstone of the Parthenon was laid in October 1895.

17. Doyle, *Nashville in the New South,* 7.

18. Herman Justi, ed., *Official History of the Tennessee Centennial Exposition 1897* (Nashville: Brandon, 1898), 20.

19. J. B. Killebrew, "J. B. Killebrew's Recollections of My Life," Southern Historical Collection, Wilson Library, University of North Carolina at Chapel Hill, available online at http://www2.lib.unc.edu/mss/inv/k/Killebrew,J.B.html (accessed March 1, 2016). J. B. Killebrew attended the University of North Carolina in the 1850s and was a farmer and lawyer who later served as editor of the *Southern Planter,* Tennessee's superintendent of public education, and state's commissioner of agriculture. Killebrew lost most of his wealth in after the stock market crash of 1929.

20. *Catalogue and Announcement of the Ward-Belmont School, 1919–1920,* 6.

21. Ayers, *Promise of the New South,* 64.

22. Dewey A. Grantham, "The Contours of Southern Progressivism," *American Historical Review* 86, no. 5 (1981): 1045. See also Grantham, *Southern Progressivism.*

23. Frost, *Thinking Confederates,* xiii.

24. For more see Leslie Brown, *Upbuilding Black Durham: Gender, Class, and Black Community Development in the Jim Crow South* (Chapel Hill: University of North Carolina Press, 2008); and Rand Dotson, *Roanoke, Virginia, 1882–1912: Magic City of the New South* (Knoxville: University of Tennessee Press, 2007).

25. James T. Bell, *Reports of Departments of the City of Nashville* (Nashville: Brandon, 1889), 7–8.

26. *Nashville City Directory* (Nashville: Brandon, 1890), iv.

27. U.S. Census Reports, 1890; U.S. Census Reports, 1920.

28. Mark B. Riley, "Edgefield: A Study of Nashville's First Suburb," *Tennessee Historical Quarterly* 37, no. 2 (1978): 139. This development was also made possible by the incorporation of the Nashville and Edgefield Street Railroad Company in 1866 that provided transportation to South Tenth Street in downtown Nashville.

29. Ibid., 154.

30. Acklen died on May 4, 1887, while on a shopping trip to New York City. She is buried in Nashville's Mt. Olivet Cemetery in a family mausoleum with her first two husbands and nine of her ten children. Mark Brown, "Adelicia Acklen," *Tennessee Encyclopedia of History and Culture,* online edition, https://tennesseeencyclopedia.net/entry.php?rec=1 (accessed November 1, 2015).

31. Kathy L. London, "The Belmont Neighborhood, 1900–1920: Prevailing Southernism," 9, in "Nashville as a Historical Laboratory" collection.

32. Cindy Young, "The Growth and Development of the Richland–West End Neighborhood," 3, in "Nashville as a Historical Laboratory" collection.

33. Julia Beach, "Belle Meade Country Club and Urbanization, 1900–1920," 11, in "Nashville as a Historical Laboratory" collection.

34. Lawrence W. Levine, *Highbrow/Lowbrow: The Emergence of Cultural Hierarchy in America* (Cambridge, MA: Harvard University Press, 1988).

35. Blaine A. Brownell and David R. Goldfield, eds. *The City in Southern History* (Port Washington, NY: Kennikat Press, 1977), 134–36. According to the *Nashville City Directory* for 1880, Nashville maintained thirteen wards. Downtown was still a major residential area with the white professional class living in Ward 1, surrounded by African American neighborhoods in Wards 2 and 4. Also close to the downtown center, Wards 3, 5, and 6 maintained a racial and socioeconomic mix. Wards 7–9, 11, and 12 were home to the middle- and upper-class. By 1920 the city had expanded to over twenty-five city wards. See also Doyle, *Nashville in the New South,* 78–86.

36. E. W. Crozier, *Nashville Blue Book: Selected Names of Nashville and Suburbs* (Nashville: Brandon, 1896); *Dau's Society Blue Book of Selected Names of Nashville and Suburbs* (New York: Dau, 1907); *The Wayne Handbook of Nashville,* 1897.

37. Baltzell, *Philadelphia Gentlemen,* 386.

38. Ibid., 292–334.

39. For more on the shift from "walking city" to public transportation and suburbs see Sam Bass Warner, *Streetcar Suburbs: The Process of Growth in Boston, 1870–1900,* 2nd ed. (Cambridge, MA: Harvard University Press, 2009).

40. William Waller, ed., *Nashville in the 1890s* (Nashville: Vanderbilt University Press, 1970), 4.

41. "Interview with Mary Hamilton Thompson Orr (1879–1968)" courtesy of Ophelia Thompson Paine, c.1965; *Vanderbilt University Annual Announcement,* 1893-94, 126.

42. West End Avenue and Twenty-First Avenue merged to form Broadway, which was the main downtown thoroughfare, ending at the Cumberland River.

43. Statistics taken from the "Model T Ford Club of America," September 1, 2015, http://www.mtfca.com/ (accessed August 7, 2016).

44. Powell, "Politicians and Public Policy," 35–36.

45. Thomas C. Hanchett, *Sorting Out the New South City: Race, Class, and Urban Development in Charlotte, 1875–1975* (Chapel Hill: University of North Carolina Press, 1998), 10, 32.

46. Amy Price, "Urbanization of Nashville from 1908–1917: The Role of Commercial and Civic Clubs," 1–12, in "Nashville as a Historical Laboratory" collection.

47. E. Digby Baltzell, *Philadelphia Gentlemen: The Making of a National Upper Class* (New York: Free Press, 1958), 386.

48. *Nashville American,* December 11, 1896, as quoted in Waller, *Nashville in the 1890s,* 7.

49. Judith Sealander, *Grand Plans: Business Progressivism and Social Change in Ohio's Miami Valley, 1890–1929* (Lexington: University Press of Kentucky, 1988), 10–11.

50. For more on the Thompson family, see Ophelia Thompson Paine, *Glen Leven: A Family Story* (Sewanee, TN: Tree of Life Memoirs, 2016).

51. Conkin, *Peabody College,* 120.

52. Bill Carey, "A Place for a Damned Fool or an Eskimo," *Nashville Post,* March 22, 2000, http://www.nashvillepost.com/home/article/20446258/a-place-for-a-damned-fool-or-an-eskimo (accessed April 7, 2016).

53. "Martha's Mettle," *Vanderbilt Magazine,* September 2, 2011, http://news.vanderbilt.edu/vanderbiltmagazine/marthas-mettle/ (accessed April 7, 2016). There have been many contributions by the Ingram family over the years; however, two gifts are worthy of note here. Hortense Bigelow Ingram is credited with gifts totaling nearly $1 million dollars at the time of her death in 1979.

54. Daniel May Papers, 1890–1982, Tennessee State Library and Archives.

55. Ibid.

56. William Waller, *Nashville, 1900 to 1910* (Nashville: Vanderbilt University Press, 1972), 110.

57. Craig Havighurst, *Air Castle of the South: WSM and the Making of Music City* (Urbana: University of Illinois Press, 2007), 7–8.

58. Cheek-Neal Coffee Company was sold to Postum Company, better known today as General Foods, in 1928 for $42 million dollars. Carroll Van West, "Cheekwood Botanical Garden and Museum of Art," *Tennessee Encyclopedia of History and Culture,* online edition, https://tennesseeencyclopedia.net/entry.php?rec=237 (accessed March 22, 2016).

59. *Peabody Reflector* 40, no. 1 (1967): 19.

60. *Vanderbilt University Quarterly* 13, no. 1 (1913): 8; *Vanderbilt University Quarterly* 7, no. 1 (1907): 127.

61. James William "Billy" Warner III, Obituary, *Tennessean,* August 10, 2015.

62. Black Bottom, which stretched from First to Fifth Avenue South, was home to many of the city's African Americans, as well as Irish and Jewish immigrants. It was also near the city's shipping wharfs, and river workers frequented saloons and other less than reputable establishments.

63. Doyle, *Nashville in the New South,* 80. For more see chapter 7, "Progressive Nashville and the Rise of Boss Howse," 143–82.

64. Ibid., 168.

65. Precisely because of his attention to minorities in poor neighborhoods, Howse mobilized an African American bloc vote for his reelection. Solomon Parker Harris ran and won as part of Howse's city council, the first African American since the 1880s. Howse's failure to enforce the state's prohibition law resulted in his removal from office in 1915.

66. Don Doyle, "Hilary Howse," *Tennessee Encyclopedia of History and Culture,* online edition, http://tennesseeencyclopedia.net/entry.php?rec=665 (accessed April 4, 2015).

67. Ibid.

68. *Yearbook of the Nashville Board of Trade* (Nashville: Marshall and Bruce, 1907–8), 4. Nashville's business sector created the Board of Trade as early as 1855. The Board of Trade consolidated with the Commercial Club and renamed it the Chamber of Commerce in 1894. In 1908 the original name, the Board of Trade, reemerged after a merger between the Chamber of Commerce and the Retail Merchants' Association.

69. Anne Firor Scott, "Women, Religion, and Social Change in the South, 1830–1930," in Samuel S. Hill Jr. et al., *Religion and the Solid South* (Nashville: Abingdon Press, 1972), 92–95. Also see Dewey W. Grantham, *The Democratic South* (Athens: University of Georgia Press, 1963).

70. *Nashville Banner,* June 29, 1914.

71. See chapter 2, "Modern Belle," for more discussion on how some women gained autonomy based on individual accomplishments while many others achieved prosperity and effected reforms because of the position of their families (either fathers, husbands, or other prominent male family members).

72. Carole Bucy, *Women Helping Women: The YWCA of Nashville, 1898–1998* (Nashville: J. S. Sanders, 1998), 8.

73. Ibid., 55–59.

74. John A. Simpson, *Edith D. Pope and Her Nashville Friends: Guardians of the Lost Cause in the* Confederate Veteran (Knoxville: University of Tennessee Press, 2003), 128.

75. Price, "Urbanization of Nashville," 5.

76. Charlotte A. Williams, *The Centennial Club of Nashville: A History from 1905–1977* (Nashville: Centennial Club, 1978), 13.

77. Simpson, *Edith D. Pope and Her Nashville Friends,* 128.

78. Alison Isenberg, *Downtown America: A History of the Place and the People Who Made It* (Chicago: University of Chicago Press, 2005), 15.

79. Maureen Flanagan, *Seeing with Their Hearts: Chicago Women and the Vision of the Good City* (Princeton, NJ: Princeton University Press, 2002), 10.

80. *Vanderbilt University Quarterly* 10, no. 1 (1910): 146. Samuel Keith died in 1909.

81. Mary Ellen Pethel, *Home Sweet Home: A History of the West End Home Foundation,* archival exhibit text, Nashville Metropolitan Library (October 2014–March 2015). In addition to the Board of Directors, the Young Peoples Auxiliary, later renamed the Young Women's Auxiliary, was organized to help with daily operations and fundraising. In 1909 construction began on a new home located on West End Avenue, which served the organization for over seventy years.

82. "Former L&C Head Dies," *Nashville Post,* June 14, 2002, https://www.nashville-post.com/news/2002/6/13/former_lc_head_dudley_dies (accessed December 4, 2015); Ann Marie Deer Owens, "BOT Member, Community, and Business Leader Dudley Dies," *Vanderbilt Register,* June 24, 2002, http://news.vanderbilt.edu/archived-news/register/articles/index-id=6292.html (accessed December 3, 2014),.

83. Margaret Ripley Wolfe, *Daughters of Canaan: A Saga of Southern Women* (Lexington: University Press of Kentucky, 1995), 141.

84. Ibid.

85. Carole Stanford Bucy, "Anne Dallas Dudley," *Tennessee Encyclopedia of History and Culture,* online edition, http://tennesseeencyclopedia.net/entry.php?rec=406 (accessed December 4, 2015). The Maternal Welfare Organization brought birth control pioneer Margaret Sanger to Nashville in 1938 for a lecture and lesson on the purpose and use of birth control.

86. Railroads running in and out of the city, such as the L&N and the NC&St.L, were segregated as early as 1895. The Separate Car Law was a local ordinance affecting public transportation, including city streetcars and trolleys.

87. Lester Lamon, *Black Tennesseans, 1900–1930* (Knoxville: University of Tennessee Press, 1977), 24. Boyd also headed the National Doll Company, which issued the first African American baby doll for sale by any company.

88. *Nashville Banner,* July 1905; June 1907.

89. For more see Neill Griffin, "The Jim Crow Streetcar Boycott in Nashville," 1–15, in "Nashville as a Historical Laboratory" collection.

90. Lamon, *Black Tennesseans.* Lester Lamon noted that black per capital income, job and educational opportunities, and political influence still paled in comparison to those of white Southerners.

91. James C. Napier was born outside the city limits, but called Nashville home for his entire life. He was educated at Wilberforce and Oberlin Colleges before earning his law degree at Howard University. He served on the city council in Nashville in 1870 and 1878–84. In 1898 he ran for Congress but was unsuccessful. Beginning in 1903, Napier played a leadership role in the Black Business League and became register of the Treasury of the United States Bank. In addition to his role in founding the Globe Publishing Company, he also helped start the One Cent Savings Bank, a bank predominantly for African Americans. R. F. Boyd was president of the Baptist Publishing Board, a division of the National Publishing Board. For more see August Meier, *Negro Thought in America* (Ann Arbor: University of Michigan Press, 1963), 124.

92. Lamon, *Black Tennesseans,* 156. See also Henry Lewis Suggs, ed., *The Black Press in the South, 1865–1979* (Westport, CT: Greenwood, 1983).

93. *Globe,* March 21, 1913, 4. For more see Lamon, *Black Tennesseans.*

94. Brownell and Goldfield, *The City in Southern History,* 119. Yet, in 1917 there remained problems of racial violence. In response to several lynchings in Tennessee, the Law and Order League was formed in 1918. For more see chapter 4, "Continuity and Change: Southern Urban Development, 1860–1900," in *The City in Southern History,* where

Howard N. Rabinowitz focuses largely on race and municipal policies. See also Doyle, *Nashville in the New South,* 87–142; and Eleanor W. Bryan, "The Negro in Nashville from 1900 to 1920," in the "Nashville as a Historical Laboratory" collection.

95. Reavis L. Mitchell Jr., "George Edmund Haynes," *Tennessee Encyclopedia of History and Culture,* online edition, https://tennesseeencyclopedia.net/entry.php?rec=614 (accessed August 6, 2016). Portions of this section reprinted with permission by University of Georgia Press taken from: Mary Ellen Pethel, "Lift Every Female Voice: Education and Activism in Nashville's African American Community, 1870–1940," in *Tennessee Women,* vol. 2, ed. Beverly Bond and Sarah W. Freeman, 239–69 (Athens: University of Georgia Press, 2015).

96. Cynthia Neverdon-Morton, *Afro-American Women of the South and the Advancement of the Race, 1895–1925* (Knoxville: University of Tennessee Press, 1989), 166.

97. *Yearbook of the Nashville Board of Trade,* 10.

98. U.S. Census Report, 1900.

99. For more see James F. Blumenstein and Benjamin Walter, eds., *Growing Metropolis: Aspects of Development in Nashville* (Nashville: Vanderbilt University Press, 1975).

100. Lears, *Making of Modern America,* 134.

Chapter 2

1. *The Iris* (Ward Seminary annual), 1903, 70.

2. Ibid.

3. Ibid., 70–71. The topic of gender is not limited to women nor is discussion of race limited to African Americans. However, when discussing gender and race, this chapter is predominantly focused on traditional shifts regarding white and African-American women rather than more modern constructions of manhood and masculinity that were important to white and black male college students. In addition, "whiteness" was taken for granted at all of Nashville's college and universities, unless the institutions were specifically established for African Americans.

4. Helen Lefkowitz Horowitz, *Alma Mater: Design and Experience in the Women's Colleges from Their Nineteenth-Century Beginnings to the 1930s,* 2nd ed. (Amherst: University of Massachusetts Press, 1993), xxiv.

5. This new image is similar to the national trend and image of the Gibson Girl that emerged in the 1890s. The Gibson Girl was seen as All-American, a female who could play sports and place an emphasis on education while still remaining rational and aristocratic. See also Carl J. Schneider and Dorothy Schneider, *American Women in the Progressive Era, 1900–1920* (New York: Anchor Books, 1993).

6. Evins, *Tennessee Women in the Progressive Era,* xii.

7. David Gold and Catherine L. Hobbs, *Educating the New Southern Woman: Speech, Writing, and Race at the Public Women's Colleges, 1884–1945* (Carbondale: Southern Illinois University Press, 2014), 3.

8. Barbara Solomon, *In the Company of Educated Women: A History of Women and Higher Education in America* (New Haven, CT: Yale University Press, 1985), 83.

9. Sarah Stage and Virginia B. Vincenti, eds., *Rethinking Home Economics: Women and the History of a Profession* (Ithaca, NY: Cornell University Press, 1997), 32.

10. Ibid.

11. Amy Thompson McCandless, *The Past in the Present: Women's Higher Education in the Twentieth-Century American South* (Tuscaloosa: University of Alabama Press, 1999), 18–19.

12. *Hustler,* January 13, 1898, 3.

13. Irene Harwarth, *Women's Colleges in the United States: History, Issues, and Challenges* (Washington D.C.: U.S. Department of Education, 1997), 8.

14. Elizabeth Avery Colton, "Standards of Southern Colleges for Women," *School Review* 20 (September 1912): 458–75.

15. See chapter 1 for discussion of the creation of the U.S. Department of Education as well as accreditation agencies such as the NTA, SACS, ACA, and SACW. These organizations and departments were formed between 1857 and 1900.

16. McCandless, *The Past in the Present*, 17. McCandless defined "twoness" as being southern and being female.

17. Amy McCandless, "Maintaining the Spirit and Tone of Robust Manliness: The Battle against Coeducation at Southern Colleges and Universities, 1890–1940," *NWSA Journal* 2, no. 2 (1990): 199.

18. Conkin, *Peabody College,* 119.

19. *Vanderbilt University Annual Announcement,* 1908–1909.

20. As course offerings and academic majors expanded, nursing, education, domestic science, languages, and literature were largely encouraged as acceptable majors for females. See Conkin, *Gone with the Ivy,* 276–77, 290–303.

21. *Hustler,* May 16, 1907, 2. Godbey would graduate with a B.S. and begin her teaching career at Howard-Payne College as a math professor.

22. *Hustler,* October 10, 1895, 4.

23. The Founder's Medal received by Celia Rich is not the same as the Founder's Medal given by the Society for the History of Natural History or as part of the Gold Medal prize awarded by the Royal Geographical Society. Rather, it was an award given by Vanderbilt University; similar awards were bestowed by many colleges and universities as the highest honor within an institution for academic excellence.

24. *Commencement Courier,* June 15, 1898, 3.

25. Ibid.

26. *Catalog of the Vanderbilt Chapter of Phi Beta Kappa,* 1914.

27. *Commencement Courier,* June 19, 1900, 3.

28. Ibid., 11.

29. *Annual Announcements of the Nashville Bible School, Inc.* (Nashville: McQuiddy Printing Company, 1903), n.p.

30. *Ward Seminary Bulletin,* 1909–1910, 2.

31. Ibid.

32. Joan Marie Johnson, *Southern Women at the Seven Sister Colleges: Feminist Values and Social Activism, 1875–1915* (Athens: University of Georgia Press, 2008), 23.

33. Mary Ellen Pethel, *All-Girls Education from Ward Seminary to Harpeth Hall, 1865–2015* (Charleston, SC: History Press), 15.

34. *Ward-Belmont Bulletin* 6 (September 1918): 75.

35. *Annual Announcement and Catalog of the Ward-Belmont School*, 1924–1940.

36. Ibid.

37. *The Iris*, vol. 4, 1902, n.p.

38. *Ward Seminary Bulletin* 45 (1909–1910): 79.

39. *Belmont College for Young Women Prospectus*, n.d.

40. *Nashville Daily American*, September 5, 1890, 5.

41. *The Aitrop* (Belmont College annual), 1904; *Milady in Brown*, 1905–1913.

42. *Milady in Brown*, 1905. Muskogee became part of the Creek Indian Territory after the Indian Removal Act of 1830. The city was also the site of the region's U.S. Indian Agency, which is today a museum in Muskogee, Oklahoma.

43. Ibid., 17–20. The girls formed "State Clubs" based on states with a significant and fairly consistent number of students in the student body. For example, the 1905 *Milady in Brown* shows the number of students as follows: Kentucky, 17; Missouri, 12; Louisiana, 4; Tennessee, 43; Texas, 21; Mississippi, 12; Illinois, 9; Alabama, 10; and Arkansas, 9.

44. Colton, "Standards of Southern Colleges for Women," 460, 463.

45. *Annual Catalog and Announcement for the Ward-Belmont School*, 1917–1925.

46. Evins, *Tennessee Women in the Progressive Era*, 210.

47. Conkin, *Peabody College*, 151, 220.

48. Ibid., 212. Not until 1929 did the school determine that high school records must show three completed units of English.

49. Ibid.

50. William Payne served earlier as president of Peabody College, 1888–1901. He expected women to pursue the L.I. (Licentiate of Instruction) certificate that only allowed them teacher certification for primary or secondary education. Sherman Dorn, *A Brief History of Peabody College* (Nashville: Vanderbilt University Press, 1996), 11.

51. Conkin, *Peabody College*, 12. For more on the legacy of Bruce Payne, see "President Bruce Ryburn Payne: In Memoriam," *Peabody Reflector* 10, no. 6 (1937): 213–14.

52. *Hustler*, March 17, 1899, 2.

53. Ibid.

54. The Seven Sisters, a consortium of prestigious East Coast liberal arts colleges for women, originally included Mount Holyoke, Vassar, Smith, Wellesley, Bryn Mawr, Barnard, and Radcliffe. The association was formed in 1915 when four of the schools met to discuss fundraising. Today five of the Seven Sisters remain women's colleges. Vassar became coeducational in 1969 and Radcliffe merged with Harvard in 1977. The name "Seven Sisters" has its origins in Greek mythology. It refers to the seven daughters of Atlas who were changed into stars by Zeus. For more on the history of these schools, see Horowitz, *Alma Mater*.

For more on southern women who attended schools in the north, see Johnson, *Southern Women at the Seven Sister Colleges.*

55. Christie Farnham, *The Education of the Southern Belle: Higher Education and Student Socialization in the Antebellum South* (New York: New York University Press, 1994). For more general commentary on women's changing roles in southern society, see the following anthologies: Janet L. Coryell, Martha H. Swain, Sandra Gioia Treadway, and Elizabeth Hayes Turner, eds., *Beyond Image and Convention: Explorations in Southern Women's History* (Columbia: University of Missouri Press, 1998); Janet L. Coryell, Thomas H. Appleton Jr., Anastatia Sims, and Sandra Gioia Treadway, eds., *Negotiating Boundaries of Southern Womanhood* (Columbia: University of Missouri Press, 2000); and Michele Gillespie and Catherine Clinton, eds., *Taking off the White Gloves: Southern Women and Southern Historians* (Columbia: University of Missouri Press, 1998).

56. Jill K. Conway, "Perspectives on the History of Women's Education in the United States," *History of Education Quarterly* 14 (Spring 1974): 1–12. Conway's study begins with the first school to accept female students, Oberlin College, in the 1830s. Conway found that 60–70 percent of women who graduated from institutions of higher education (most notably in the Northeast) rejected conventional marriage and remained single. See also: Carole Lasser, ed., *Educating Men and Women Together* (Urbana: University of Illinois Press, 1987) and also Charlotte W. Conable, *Women at Cornell: The Myth of Equal Education* (Ithaca, NY: Cornell University Press, 1977).

57. Lynn Gordon, *Gender and Higher Education in the Progressive Era, 1890–1920* (New Haven, CT: Yale University Press, 1990). Also, for a period analysis of women's education, see Anna C. Brackett, *Woman and the Higher Education* (New York: Harper and Brothers, 1893).

58. Conkin, *Peabody College,* 141. "Even discounting blacks, who were not eligible," Conkin continues, "the poorest white families were almost never in a position to provide even an eighth-grade education for their children, who at a young age had to go to work on a farm or in a cotton mill"(141).

59. For more on the role of state colleges and universities in southern educational reform and progressivism see Dennis, *Lessons in Progress.* Also see Gold and Hobbs, *Educating the New Southern Woman.*

60. *Observer,* March 3, 1904, 3.

61. *Annual Announcement for Ward's Seminary for Young Ladies,* 1885–1886. 1.

62. *Milestones,* 1929, 217.

63. Ilana DeBare, *Where Girls Come First: The Rise, Fall, and Surprising Revival of Girls' Schools* (New York: Penguin, 2004), 92. Such festivals occurred nationally at most all-female schools until the 1960s.

64. Johnson, *Southern Women at the Seven Sister Colleges,* 15.

65. Ibid., 111. Northern colleges did not fare much better. Sixty percent of female graduates of northern colleges married upon graduation or soon after and did not seek employment.

66. *Hustler,* October 1906, 2.

67. *Hustler,* March 15, 1906, 3. "Mrs. Grundy" was a symbolic turn-of-the-century stock character meant to represent rigid respectability, priggishness, and strict propriety.

68. *Hustler,* May 16, 1907, 2. For more see Johnson, *Southern Women at the Seven Sister Colleges.*

69. Robert Winthrop, "Tribute to Eben Sperry Stearns, D.D., L.L.D., chancellor of the University, and president of the Normal college at Nashville, Tennessee," *Annual Meeting of the Trustees of the Peabody Education Fund in New York* (Cambridge, MA: John Wilson and Son, 1887), 3–6.

70. Conkin, *Peabody College,* 118. John Berrien Lindsley is less well known but perhaps more influential to the development of Tennessee during and after the Civil War. He was the son of Philip Lindsley who founded the University of Nashville and also had strong ties to Vanderbilt University and Peabody College. At the University of Nashville, Berrien Lindsley began a Medical Department in 1850 and remained a professor of chemistry until 1873. He succeeded his father as chancellor of the university in 1855 and helped restore the University of Nashville to its prewar status in terms of budget, course offerings, and campus buildings. He also revitalized the Literary Department. In addition he played a significant role in secondary education with the founding of Montgomery Bell Academy (1867), was selected as superintendent of Nashville Public Schools (1866), led efforts to form the Tennessee College of Pharmacy (1870), and served on the Tennessee Board of Education (1877–1897).

71. Ibid., 119.

72. *Milestones* (Ward-Belmont annual), 1916, 97.

73. Republican motherhood emerged from the Enlightenment and the American Revolution and emphasized that citizens must be educated to be virtuous. Therefore, women must be educated to teach their children. The cult of domesticity, or cult of true womanhood, was prevalent in some form from the mid-1800s through the 1950s. This belief held that the world of work and leisure was for men and full of violence, immorality, and cutthroat competition. Instead, women and the home were seen as moral havens that should be protected and revered. In this private sphere, women were deemed "queen," thus retaining more power and autonomy in the home in exchange for their absence in the public sphere.

74. Megan Elias, *Stir It Up: Home Economics in American Culture* (Philadelphia: University of Pennsylvania Press, 2010), 1. The home economics movement evolved as a "science" and academic subject out of the Morrill Land-Grant universities and later with the Smith-Hughes Act of 1917.

75. Mary Hoffschwelle, "Science of Domesticity: Home Economics at George Peabody College for Teachers, 1914–1939," *Journal of Southern History* 57, no. 4 (1991): 680.

76. *Milady in Brown* (Belmont College annual), 1910, 229.

77. *Milady in Brown,* 1911, 3.

78. *Milestones,* 1916, 9.

79. Elias, *Stir It Up,* 16.

80. *Milady in Brown,* 1910, 128.

81. Hoffschwelle, "Science of Domesticity," 659.

82. *Annual Catalog and Announcement for the Ward-Belmont School,* 1924–1925, 22. Emphasis on *Progressive* in original.

83. Charlotte Angstman, "College Women and the New Science," *Popular Science Monthly* 53 (May 1898): 679. See also Stage and Vincenti, *Rethinking Home Economics,* 32–33.

84. Conkin, *Gone with the Ivy,* 285–88.

85. Hoffschwelle, "Science of Domesticity," 677–80.

86. *Ward-Belmont Conservatory of Music Catalog,* 1929–1930, 11. Excerpts of this passage are reprinted from *All-Girls Education from Ward Seminary to Harpeth Hall, 1865-2015* with permission by the History Press.

87. Conkin, *Gone with the Ivy,* 79–82.

88. Conkin, *Gone with the Ivy,* 302.

89. Ibid. The first official dean of women was not Stella Vaughn, but rather Dr. Ada Bell Stapleton from the University of London. Kirkland likely hired her because she shared his philosophy, implementing a strict double standard and limiting the opportunities of Vanderbilt women to participate fully in college culture. As Conkin stated, "She was no feminist."

90. Pittman, *Lipcomb's Golden Heritage,* 7. The school was incorporated in 1901, naming David Lipscomb, W. H. Dodd, J. R. Ward, C. A. Moore, J. C. McQuiddy, and W. R. Chambers as incorporators. These men were all prominent members of the Nashville community. David Lipscomb was a teacher and administrator who dedicated his career to the school. J. C. McQuiddy owned one of the main publishing houses in Nashville. Yet, Harding was opposed to the idea of incorporation and subsequently resigned.

91. Joe M. Richardson, *A History of Fisk University: 1864–1946* (Tuscaloosa: University of Alabama Press, 1980), 60. See also Nancie Caraway, *Segregated Sisterhood: Racism and the Politics of American Feminism* (Knoxville: University of Tennessee Press, 1991).

92. For more on each of these schools see: "A Little Old School for Women's History Month," Nashville Public Library, https://library.nashville.org/blog/2016/03/little-old-school-womens-history-month (access July 31, 2016); Robert Boyte Crawford Howell (1878-1955) Papers, 1838–1963, Tennessee Department of State, State Library and Archives, Microfilm Accession No. 1270 (1972); "Elizabeth Burges Buford, President of Buford College, c. 1912" *Nashille Public Library Online Collection,* http://nashville.contentdm.oclc.org/cdm/ref/collection/nr/id/2304 (accessed July 31, 2016).

93. *Hustler,* December 19, 1895, 3.

94. *Annual Announcement for Ward's Seminary for Young Ladies,* 1885–1886.

95. Conkin, *Peabody College,* 119. In 1872 Sears achieved a milestone as the first female president of a public college, the Mankato Normal School, today part of the Minnesota State University system. After making controversial statements about the role of women, Sears was dismissed after only one year. Shortly after, she moved to Nashville to accept a mathematics position at the newly formed State Normal School. Sears was also an ardent suffragist, retired from Peabody in 1907, and received the first Carnegie retirement award in Tennessee. She died in 1929.

96. Ibid. Some male teachers were more qualified in terms of their academic résumés.

97. *Annual Announcement of the Nashville Bible College*, 1903–1904, 1909–1910, 1914–1915.

98. Thomas Woody, *A History of Women's Education in the United States* (New York: Science Press, 1929), 329.

99. Ibid.

100. Excerpt from *Tennessean*, 1912, taken from *Concerning Miss Edith Margaret Smaill*, brochure, Belmont University Special Collections.

101. "Harvard Men Try Out for Wellesley Parts," *Harvard Crimson*, February 8, 1932. Portions of this analysis and primary source quotes are reprinted with the permission of the Tennessee Historical Society.

102. "Story of Belmont," *Blue and Bronze*, Belmont College literary magazine, 1913, 19–20.

103. *Vanderbilt University Board of Trust*, June 1913.

104. James Kirkland, *Commencement Address of the Fiftieth Anniversary of Vanderbilt University*, 1925. Miss Vaughn also wrote a personal history of Vanderbilt, although no complete draft remains, this was one of the earliest historical accounts written about the university.

105. *Tennessean*, October 24, 1960, 21.

106. "2015 Vanderbilt HOF Class Announced, " Vanderbilt University Commodores website, November 10, 2015, http://www.vucommodores.com/genrel/111015aac.html (accessed March 31, 2016).

107. W. E. Ward, "The Coming Woman," *Annual Commencement of W. E. Ward's Seminary for Ladies*, 1885–1886, 25.

108. Lori Bland Bateman, "Separation, Coordination, and Coeducation: Southern Baptist Approaches to Women's Higher Education, 1880–1920," *Baptist History and Heritage* 38, no. 3 (2003): 92.

109. Conkin, *Gone with the Ivy*, 213–14.

110. Ibid.

111. Elizabeth was born in 1898 and later married Greek scholar Benjamin Meritt. Kirkland's wife was Mary Henderson, a Knoxville, Tennessee, native. They married in 1895 after he arrived in Nashville in 1893 to assume the Vanderbilt chancellorship.

112. Conkin, *Peabody College*, 136.

113. *Peabody Reflector* 2, no. 3 (1893): 83–87.

114. Ibid.

115. Ibid.

116. Conkin, *Peabody College*, 137. Julia Sears taught at Peabody for thirty years, retiring in 1907. Her portrait, which hangs in the chapel among those of prominent male presidents and leaders, is the only one of a woman.

117. Ibid. Male students who were part of the SATC were allowed to take some regular classes in addition to military training.

118. *Milestones*, 1918, 77.

119. Ibid., 189–90.

120. Ward, "The Coming Woman," 25.

121. Marjorie Spruill Wheeler, ed., *Votes for Women! The Woman Suffrage Movement in Tennessee, the South, and the Nation* (Knoxville: University of Tennessee Press, 1995), 162–63.

122. *Hustler,* September 30, 1896, 1.

123. *Hustler,* May 16, 1907, 2.

124. Rosalyn Terborg-Penn, *African American Women in the Struggle for the Vote* (Bloomington: Indiana University Press, 1998), 9. See also: Anita Goodstein, "A Rare Alliance: African American and White Women in the Elections of 1919 and 1920," *Journal of Southern History* 64, no. 2 (April 1998), 219-246.

125. *Mass Meeting Tonight,* 1920, Tennessee State Library and Archives Broadside Collection.

126. *The Truth about the Negro,* 1920, Tennessee State Library and Archives Broadside Collection.

127. *Fisk Herald,* March 1889, 9.

128. Evins, *Tennessee Women in the Progressive Era,* 193.

129. Amy Thompson McCandless, "Progressivism and the Higher Education of Southern Women," *North Carolina Historical Review* 70, no. 3 (1993): 320–23. Also see Harwarth, *Women's Colleges in the United States,* 8–10.

Chapter 3

1. W. E. B. Du Bois, *The Souls of Black Folk* (Chicago: A. C. McClurg, 1903). For a complete biography and excellent analysis of Du Bois's life, see David Levering Lewis, *W. E. B. Du Bois, 1868–1919: The Biography of a Race* and *W. E. B. Du Bois, 1919–1963: The Fight for Equality and the American Century* (New York: Henry Holt, 1994, 2001). The opening quote is taken from Pike, *Jubilee Singers,* 26, 28.

2. Clarence L. Mohr, "Minds of the New South: Higher Education in Black and White, 1880–1915," *Southern Quarterly* 46, no. 4 (2009): 14.

3. Dennis, *Lessons in Progress,* 259.

4. W. E. B. Du Bois, "The Talented Tenth," in *The Negro Problem: A Series of Articles by Representative Negroes of To-day* (New York: James Pott, 1903), 75.

5. "Special Correspondence of The New York Evening Post," reprinted in Louis R. Harlan and Raymond W. Smock, eds., *Booker T. Washington Papers,* vol. 10, 1909–1911 (Urbana: University of Illinois, 1981), 211.

6. Booker T. Washington, "From an Address by Booker T. Washington at The Negro Baptist Convention, September 19, 1913," Booker T. Washington Society website, http://www.btwsociety.org (accessed January 19, 2015).

7. In Harlan and Smock, *Booker T. Washington Papers,* 212.

8. Crystal deGregory, "Raising a Nonviolent Army: Four Nashville Black Colleges and the Century-Long Struggle for Civil Rights" (Ph.D. diss., Vanderbilt University, 2011), 230.

9. Bobby L. Lovett, *The African American History of Nashville, Tennessee, 1780–1930* (Fayetteville: University of Arkansas Press, 1999), 130.

10. In Harlan and Smock, *Booker T. Washington Papers*, 211.

11. Mohr, "Minds of the New South," 15.

12. Ibid.

13. Ridgely Torrence, *The Story of John Hope* (New York: Macmillan, 1948), 114–15.

14. Bobby L. Lovett, *The Civil Rights Movement in Tennessee* (Knoxville: University of Tennessee Press, 2005), 45–60.

15. Du Bois, "The Talented Tenth," 33.

16. deGregory, "Raising a Nonviolent Army," 3, 29.

17. *Official Catalogue of the Tennessee Centennial Exposition* (Nashville, 1897), 57.

18. Nathan Cardon, "The South's 'New Negroes' and African American Visions of Progress at the Atlanta and Nashville International Expositions," *Journal of Southern History* 80, no. 2 (2014): 303.

19. Justi, *Official History of the Tennessee Centennial Exposition*, 195–96.

20. Justi, *Official History of the Tennessee Centennial Exposition*, 197, as quoted in Richard Couto, "Race Relations and Tennessee Centennials," *Tennessee Historical Quarterly* 55, no. 2 (1996): 151.

21. Ibid.

22. Couto, "Race Relations and Tennessee Centennials," 145–46.

23. Cardon, "South's 'New Negroes' and African American Visions of Progress," 319–20. Worthy of note, the National Association of Colored Women drafted and passed their first constitution as they met in Nashville in conjunction with the Centennial Exposition. Their efforts to demand racial equality on streetcars was largely unsuccessful in the city.

24. Ibid.

25. Fran Paden, "Moffat, Mary Adelene, 1862–1956," *The Pathfinder* (Grundy County Historical Society), 9, no. 1 (2004), 30. Living in Boston as an adult, she served on the Executive Board of the NAACP for several years and was named "best friend of race" by the Boston Literary and Historical Association in 1912.

26. According to Adelene Moffat's great-great niece Fran Paden, Moffat retrospectively wished she had given her address a different name. She felt that it was misleading to describe herself as a southern woman because she did not live in the South during her adult life. She could easily be compared to the Grimke sisters, helping lead the abolition and women's rights movements. In fact, Moffat was also an advocate for women's suffrage as well as for the kindergarten movement.

27. Adelene Moffat, *Views of a Southern Woman: An Address before the Third Annual Conference of the National Association for the Advancement of Colored People* (New York: Allied Printing, 1911), n.p.

28. *Fisk Herald*, January 1889, 9.

29. *Catalog of Fisk University*, 1904–1905, 21. For more see Marcus S. Cox, *Segregated Soldiers: Military Training at Historically Black Colleges in the Jim Crow South* (Baton Rouge: Louisiana State University Press, 2013).

30. Grace Elizabeth Hale, *Making Whiteness: The Culture of Segregation in the South, 1890–1940* (New York: Vintage Books, 1998), 199–227. See also Jacqueline Royster, ed.,

Southern Horrors and Other Writings: The Anti-Lynching Campaign of Ida B. Wells, 1892–1900 (New York: Bedford/St. Martin's, 1996), a collection of Ida B. Wells's antilynching writings.

31. *Crisis,* March 1911.

32. Kathy Bennett, "Lynching," *Tennessee Encyclopedia of Culture and History,* online edition, https://tennesseeencyclopedia.net/entry.php?rec=816 (accessed January 20, 2016); Couto, "Race Relations and Tennessee Centennials," 145. Numbers of lynchings swelled in the 1890s. Historian Richard A. Couto reported that in Tennessee about ten African American men were lynched annually during the decade.

33. Bennett, "Lynching."

34. Minnie Lou Crosthwaite to Thomas E. Jones, January 22, 1934, as quoted in deGregory, "Raising a Nonviolent Army," 220.

35. Bennett, "Lynching."

36. Kate Herndon Trawick, "The Exposure of Womanhood through Lynching," *Fisk University News,* October 1917, 27–28. Trawick was the general secretary of the YWCA. She also gives the statistic that "the number of rapes by Negroes was 1.8 per 100,000 of the population. Rape by whites was 0.6 per 100,000" (29). It is unknown where Trawick drew her information.

37. Ibid., 28.

38. *Race Problems of the South: Report of the Proceedings of the First Annual Conference Held under the Auspices of The Southern Society for the Promotion of the Study of Race Conditions and Problems in the South at Montgomery, Alabama* (Richmond, VA: B. F. Johnson, 1900), 37. The printed transcript of this conference contains more than a dozen speeches made by local officials who served across the South in larger towns and industrializing cities. Their opinions range across a wide spectrum of feelings about race and class in the South. This quotation is not representative of all views presented.

39. Bobby L. Lovett, "Tennessee State University: A Synopsis of 'A Touch of Greatness,' 1912–2012," *Engaged: The Journal of Tennessee State University* 1, no. 11 (2012): 3. In the 1870s African Americans made up approximately 30 percent of Nashville's population, with their numbers peaking at 39 percent in 1890 and returning to 29 percent by 1925 during the Great Migration.

40. Department of the Interior, Bureau of Education, *Negro Education.* Other census population totals can be found at http://www.census.gov/population/cencounts/tn190090.txt (accessed July 31, 2016).

41. Department of the Interior, Bureau of Education, *Negro Education: A Study of the Private and Higher Schools for Colored People in the United States,* Bulletin 1916, no. 38, vol. 2 (Washington, DC: Government Printing Office, 1917), 527.

42. Ibid. The Bureau of Education was a federal agency that operated from 1867 to 1972 to guide educational policy and measure educational standards from state to state. The bureau's "organizational descendant" is the National Center for Education Statistics (NCES), part of the Institute of Education Sciences in the U.S. Department of Education.

43. Department of the Interior, Bureau of Education, *Negro Education,* 22.

44. Thomas Jesse Jones, *Educational Adaptations: Report of Ten Years Work of the Phelps-Stokes Fund, 1910–1920* (New York: Phelps-Stokes Fund, c. 1920), 27. Jones identified four main groups whose cooperation and coordination was necessary in order to advance African American education: "1—all Negroes; 2—all the white South; 3—all philanthropists who are supporting Negro schools or all boards and agencies acting for these donors; and 4—all denominational bodies which are conducting colored schools," (27).

45. Department of the Interior, Bureau of Education, *Negro Education*, 62. Of Tennessee's 473,088 African Americans in 1910, nearly 40 percent officially maintained membership in Protestant congregations, led by Baptists and Methodists.

46. Mohr, "Minds of the New South," 16–17. See also Atticus Greene Haygood, *Our Brothers in Black* (New York: Phillips and Hunt, 1881).

47. *Hearings Before the Committee on Agriculture,* 62nd Congress, 2nd Session, in James Carroll Napier Papers, Fisk University, as quoted in Lester Lamon, "The Tennessee Agricultural and Industrial Normal School: Public Education for Black Tennesseans," *Tennessee Historical Quarterly* 32, no. 1 (1973): 42–43. Napier was seeking equal funding on behalf of Nashville's efforts to open and operate the new Tennessee A&I Normal School.

48. Anderson, *Education of Blacks in the South*, 238–39.

49. Isabel Smith Gates, *The Life of George Augustus Gates* (Boston: Pilgrim Press, 1915).

50. Bobby L. Lovett, *A Touch of Greatness: A History of Tennessee State University* (Macon, GA: Mercer University Press, 2013), 1–12.

51. Ibid.

52. Lovett, "Tennessee State University: A Synopsis," 8.

53. Ibid., 7.

54. Ibid., 8. Regardless of regional reluctance on the part of white taxpayers, the opening of schools such as Tennessee A&I increased the number of southern public colleges for African Americans to sixteen by 1915.

55. Ibid., 26.

56. *Bulletin, Tennessee A. and I. State Teachers College* 18, no. 3 (1929): 1.

57. F. Erik Brooks and Glenn L. Starks, *Historically Black Colleges and Universities: An Encyclopedia* (Santa Barbara, CA: Greenwood, 2011), 18, 75.

58. Jones, *Educational Adaptations*, 21. The report also noted that "greater public cooperation with classes on race questions in white colleges were held by the YMCA and Southern Sociological Congress and Southern University Race Commission" (21).

59. Ibid., 27.

60. In the Bureau of Education's 1916 report, *Negro Education*, Howard University was listed as the most reputable black college. For more on accreditation standards, see Anderson, *Education of Blacks in the South*, 238–78.

61. Department of the Interior, Bureau of Education, *Negro Education*, 59.

62. Ibid., 64.

63. Ibid., 51. Also see Introduction, Kenneth W. Goings and Raymond A. Mohl, eds., *The New African American Urban History* (Thousand Oaks, CA: Sage, 1996).

64. Lovett, "Tennessee State University: A Synopsis," 18–20. According to Lovett, SACS created a two-tiered system whereby black colleges and universities received either an "A" or "B" level designation rather than equal membership with white institutions.

65. *The Radio*, 1926, 28.

66. Ibid., 30–39.

67. Commencement Day Program, Tennessee A&I Normal School, 1928.

68. The Phelps Stokes Fund remains one of the most influential programs for minority-education funding. Caroline Phelps Stokes was one of the first female philanthropists and used her wealth to provide resources and support for the underprivileged. Stokes was born in New York into a wealthy philanthropic and reform-minded family. Her father founded the American Bible Society and New York Peace Society, while her mother was an abolitionist and director of the New York Colored Orphan Asylum. Caroline Phelps Stokes traveled across the country as well as the world, giving of her time and money. She also spent a great deal of time in the South and donated generously to Hampton Institute as well as Tuskegee. Although the endowment was not formed until 1911 (she died in 1909), the fund bearing her name has sponsored educational surveys and research for over one hundred years. Booker T. Washington and Thomas Jesse Jones were instrumental in the direction and allocation of the Phelps Stokes Fund. Jones distributed funds needed to provide job training for many African Americans throughout the South, particularly in Georgia, Alabama, and Tennessee.

69. C. G. Woodson, "Thomas Jesse Jones," *Journal of Negro History* 35 (January 1950): 107–9. See also Donald Johnson, "W. E. B. Du Bois, Thomas Jesse Jones and the Struggle for Social Education," *Journal of Negro History* 85 (Summer 2000): 78–81.

70. *Fisk Herald*, February 1889, 1.

71. Industrial or vocational education could be divided into nine categories according to the U.S. Census Report of 1916. The following list shows the categories as well as the percentage of Americans employed in each classification: (1) manufacturing/mechanical, 30.8 percent; (2) agricultural/forestry/animal husbandry, 26.3 percent; (3) trade/commerce, 10.2 percent; (4) domestic/personal service, 8.2 percent; (5) clerical, 7.5 percent; (6) transportation, 7.4 percent; (7) professional service, 6.25 percent; (8) extraction of minerals, 2.6 percent; and (9) public service, 1.75 percent. See Arthur F. Payne, *Administration of Vocational Education: With Special Emphasis on the Administration of Vocational Industrial Education under the Federal Vocational Education Law* (New York: McGraw-Hill, 1924), 3–17.

72. *Catalogue of the Officers and Students of Fisk University, 1885–1886* (Nashville: Wheeler, Osborn and Duckworth, 1886), 37.

73. Ibid.

74. Tennessee Agricultural and Industrial State Normal School became Tennessee State University in 1968.

75. Lovett, *Touch of Greatness*, 16–24.

76. Ibid.

77. Ibid., 12–14. Chattanooga bid $71,000 while Nashville's local government committed $80,000.

78. Bobby L. Lovett, "William Jasper Hale," *Tennessee Encyclopedia of History and Culture,* online edition, https://tennesseeencyclopedia.net/entry.php?rec=584 (accessed January 19, 2016).

79. The Harmon Award, as it was commonly called, was given in eight categories from 1926 to 1930 and included other notable winners such as Langston Hughes, John Hope, James Weldon Johnson, and Julius Rosenwald.

80. *Ayeni,* yearbook of Tennessee A&I, 24–59.

81. "William Jasper Hale, 1874–1944," Tennessee State University website, http://ww2.tnstate.edu/library/digital/hale.htm (accessed January 19, 2016).

82. Anderson, *Education of Blacks in the South,* 248.

83. Morehouse College is a private black men's liberal arts college in Atlanta, Georgia. Morehouse was first founded in 1867 as a seminary but renamed in 1913 after Henry Morehouse, who served as an administrator. The college offered programs in the fields of business, education, humanities, and the sciences. It is part of an educational consortium of six institutions, including Spelman College (for women). The school's most notable alumnus is Martin Luther King Jr.

84. Du Bois, "The Talented Tenth," 47.

85. As early as 1889, Fisk self-proclaimed, "Fisk University is, without a doubt, the most widely known school for colored people in the world," (*Fisk Herald,* October 1889, 1). For more on Fisk graduates, see Reavis Mitchell Jr., *Thy Loyal Children Make Their Way: Fisk University Since 1866* (Nashville: Fisk University Press, 1995).

86. Department of the Interior, Bureau of Education, *Negro Education,* 64.

87. Jones, *Educational Adaptations,* 50.

88. According to several catalogs from the late 1890s and early 1900s, the curriculum remained virtually the same. A sample curriculum included: freshman year—Latin, Greek, mathematics, English, and history; sophomore year—Greek, science (physiology and botany), history, rhetoric, and mathematics; junior year—Latin, science (physics and astronomy), German, Greek, and English literature; senior year—psychology, English literature, science (chemistry), political economy, ethics, sociology, logic, and geology. Except for the senior year, six weeks a year were dedicated to study of the Bible.

89. The master's degree offered at Fisk during this time does not compare with the requirements of a modern master's degree. Further, there were no specific academic fields in which students received their degree. Still, this was not atypical of most colleges in the United States, especially in the South. Degree requirements became more standardized after World War I, when accreditation agencies, along with the Bureau of Education, formulated a more specific outline of requirements. The full description of master's degree requirements at Fisk in the 1904–1905 catalog is as follows: "Conferred on BA of Fisk or other colleges on the presentation of evidence that they have made satisfactory progress in liberal studies after graduation. In general, the requirements will be the equivalent of a year of systematic study, not professional. Each professor is authorized to arrange with any graduate of the Classical Department a course of advanced work in any of the lines of study included in his professorship. After conferring with the student, he will determine the authors to be studied,

fix the limit of time of preparation, and arrange for the examinations. Each professor will submit his conclusions to the Faculty for approval, and when the aggregate of approved work by any students shall be considered equivalent to a year of regular study, he will be recommended for the Degree of Master of Arts" (*Catalog of Fisk University,* 1904–1905), 20.

90. Andrew Ward, *Dark Midnight When I Rise: The Story of the Fisk Jubilee Singers* (New York: HarperCollins, 2000), 82-94.

91. Richardson, *History of Fisk University,* 27.

92. Bureau of Education, *Negro Education,* 536. Although the American Missionary Association (AMA) is usually credited with the school's initial establishment, the report notes additional support given by the Western Freedmen's Aid Commission.

93. W. E. B. Du Bois began his public speaking while at Fisk and served as editor of the *Herald,* the school newspaper, for one year.

94. Fayette Avery McKenzie, *Ideals of Fisk: Inaugural Address of Doctor Fayette Avery McKenzie, on the Occasion of His Inauguration as the Fourth President of Fisk University, Nashville, Tennessee, November 9, 1915* (Nashville [1915]), 10.

95. Francille Rusan Wilson, *The Segregated Scholars: Black Social Scientists and the Creation of Black Labor Studies, 1890–1950* (Charlottesville: University of Virginia Press, 2006), 123. Woodson was the author of *A Century of Negro Migration* (1918).

96. Wilson, *Segregated Scholars,* 110.

97. Richardson, *History of Fisk University,* 64.

98. Link, *Paradox of Southern Progressivism,* 230. Charles Johnson's degree from the University of Chicago in Sociology was a Ph.B. (Bachelor of Philosophy), which was awarded prior to the establishment of the Ph.D. or B.A. in sociology. His work in Mississippi, supported by the Rosenwald Fund not the U.S. Public Health Service study, produced two books: *Shadow of the Plantation* and *Growing Up in the Black Belt.*

99. Many graduates continued their education elsewhere. A consistent number of Fisk graduates went on to Meharry Medical College and later practiced medicine, dentistry, pharmacy, or nursing. Others went to schools in the Northeast.

100. According to Joe Richardson, of those still living in 1900, 8 were college professors, 46 were school principals, 165 were teachers in either normal/high schools or grammar schools, 20 were ministers, 9 were lawyers, 16 were in professional schools, 13 were in business, 9 worked for the federal government, 2 were editors of newspapers, 1 served as a college president, and 45 were housewives.

101. Richardson, *History of Fisk University,* 53.

102. Ibid., 537. Further, as a whole, from 1910 to 1917 the school's budget, including income and expenditures, hovered around $50,000, while the property of the school was valued at over $525,000. Eighty-five of the students hailed from Nashville, but an estimated 150 traveled to Fisk from other parts of Tennessee and an astounding 266 came from out of state or abroad.

103. *Reports of the Freedmen's Aid Society,* Third Annual Report, 8. For more on African American teacher training and education in Nashville see: Sonya Yvette Ramsey,

Reading, Writing, and Segregation: A Century of Black Women Teachers in Nashville (University of Illinois Press, 2008).

104. James Summerville, *Educating Black Doctors: A History of Meharry Medical College* (Tuscaloosa: University of Alabama Press, 1983), ix.

105. Walden College began first as Central Tennessee College and was renamed after a prominent bishop of the Methodist Episcopal Church North in 1900. The Freedmen's Aid Society also funded the school. In 1915 the school changed its name from Walden University to Walden College.

106. deGregory, "Raising a Nonviolent Army," 66.

107. Ibid.

108. Throughout the first decades of the twentieth century, tuberculosis was one of the top three causes of mortality among African Americans in urban areas. For more see Samuel Kelton Roberts, *Infectious Fear: Politics, Disease, and the Health Effects of Segregation* (Chapel Hill: University of North Carolina Press, 2009).

109. Summerville, *Educating Black Doctors*. According to the Historically Black Colleges and Universities Network, today Meharry Medical College is the largest private, historically black institution exclusively dedicated to educating health care professionals and biomedical scientists in the United States ("The History of Historically Black Colleges and Universities," http://www.hbcunetwork.com/The_History_Of_HBCUs_Timeline.cfm).

110. Department of the Interior, Bureau of Education, *Negro Education*, 532–35. Walden offered subjects that served as preparation for collegiate work, including Latin for four years, foreign language for two years, mathematics and English for three years, and science for two and a half years. In addition, the school offered sociology, psychology, Greek, and philosophy.

111. Ibid.

112. The Nursing School closed in 1962. According to the *Tennessean* (February 11, 2015), "Lyttle served as vice president and later president of the National Association of Colored Graduate Nurses. In 1948 she became administrator of school health programs at the University of California, and later she became the superintendent of the National Baptist Bath House Hospital in Hot Springs, Arkansas, where she met S. M. Frazier, whom she married in 1954. In 1946, Meharry Medical College dedicated a residence hall in her name. Lyttle-Frazier died on Aug. 7, 1983."

113. Darlene Clark Hine, *Black Women in White: Racial Conflict and Cooperation in the Nursing Profession, 1890–1950* (Bloomington: Indiana University Press, 1989).

114. Millie E. Hale, ed., *Hale Hospital Review and Social Service Quarterly* 1, no. 4 (1922): 3.

115. Axel C. Hansen, "George W. Hubbard Hospital, 1910–1961," *Journal of the National Medical Association* 54, no. 1 (1962): 8.

116. Ibid.

117. Hansen, "George W. Hubbard Hospital, 1910–1961,": 2–3.

118. Ibid., 10.

119. Bobby L. Lovett, *The African-American History of Nashville, Tennessee, 1780–1930: Elites and Dilemmas* (Fayetteville: University of Arkansas Press, 1999), 129. See also Arnold Taylor, *Travail and Triumph: Black Life and Culture in the South since the Civil War* (Westport, CT: Greenwood, 1976).

120. Ibid.

121. *The Journal of the American Dental Association* 32, vol. 11 (June 1945), 667; *Journal of the American Medical Association,* 43 (August 14, 1943), 14

122. Reavis Mitchell Jr., "Meharry Medical College," *Tennessee Encyclopedia of Culture and History,* online edition, http://tennesseeencyclopedia.net/entry.php?rec=885 (accessed January 13, 2016).

123. Summerville, *Educating Black Doctors.*

124. President Herbert Hoover to Dr. John J. Mullowney, telegram, November 27, 1931, Meharry University Special Collections.

125. *Crisis,* November 1911, 62.

126. Elizabeth Gilmore also notes the exponential growth of white female teachers and credits this growth with the expansion of African American primary and secondary education.

127. Sonya Yvette Ramsey, *Reading, Writing, and Segregation: A Century of Black Women Teachers in Nashville* (Champaign, IL: University of Illinois Press, 2008), 2.

128. Richardson, *History of Fisk University,* 54.

129. Ibid., 53.

130. Ibid., 160.

131. Ibid., 161.

132. *Some Traditions are Forever: 75th Anniversary of Tennessee State University* (Nashville: Tennessee State University, 1987), 6. The school still maintained a High School Division often referred to as "The Academy." Many academy students continued their education in the Tennessee A&I Collegiate Department, but it was not considered a traditional college-preparatory school. The academy was ultimately closed.

133. *The Radio,* 1925, 11.

134. *The Radio,* 1926, 13–21.

135. According to historian Mary Hoffschwelle, a state law passed in 1901 prohibited teachers from instructing students of a different race. Though it was not always enforced, especially in higher education, it was technically illegal for whites to teach in black schools.

136. *The Radio,* 1926, 1–29.

137. Ibid., 22.

138. *The Radio,* 1925–1927.

139. *The Radio,* 1925, 62. Tennessee A&I produced many black teachers who did not graduate with diplomas but rather with certificates of licensure, which at that time required, on average, one year of training beyond secondary school coursework.

140. The Nashville Normal and Theological Institute received a charter and incorporated as Roger Williams University in 1883. Most funding for the school came from the Ameri-

can Baptist Home Mission Society. In 1866, the school was originally named the Nashville Normal and Theological Institute. Roger Williams University merged with LeMoyne-Owen College in Memphis, which traces its roots back to 1862, when classes were first taught by men and women of the American Missionary Association (AMA). According to the College Board Annual Survey of Colleges the first five historically African American schools are: (1) 1837, Cheyney University of Pennsylvania; (2) 1854, Lincoln University of Pennsylvania; (3) 1856, Wilberforce University (Ohio); (4) 1857, Harris-Stowe State College (Missouri); and (5) 1862, LeMoyne-Owen College (Tennessee).

141. Department of the Interior, Bureau of Education, *Negro Education,* 540.

142. Ibid.

143. Ibid., 539.

144. Lovett, *Touch of Greatness,* 46.

145. *Catalog of Fisk University,* 1895–1896, 38.

146. *Commencement Address,* Meharry Medical College, 1897.

147. Schwager, "Educating Women in America," 336–37.

148. Linda Perkins, "The National Association of College Women: Vanguard of Black Women's Leadership and Education, 1923–1954," *Journal of Education* 172 (1990): 65–75. See also Stephanie Shaw, *What a Woman Ought to Be and to Do: Black Professional Women Workers in the Jim Crow Era* (Chicago: University of Chicago Press, 1996).

149. Ibid.

150. *Fisk Herald,* June 1890, 6–7, 10–11. Also like Ward-Belmont and David Lipscomb College, female Fiskites were required to wear uniforms designed and approved by the faculty in 1904–5. The following is a description: "Daily uniform was white shirt-waist suit, skirt and waist without trimming except tucks. This suit can be made at home. Hats furnished and no other hats allowed. No silk or satin dress skirts or waists, no silk or ribbon sashes. Elaborate and expensive trimmings are forbidden" (*Catalog of Fisk University,* 1904–1905, 22).

151. *Catalog of Fisk University,* 1895–1896, 67.

152. Ibid., 37. The industrial kitchen was furnished and funded by the John F. Slater Fund, which like the Phelps Stokes Fund gave money toward developing industrial education.

153. *Catalog of Fisk University,* 1904–1905, 10–11.

154. Ibid., 63.

155. Emily Scarbrough, "'Fine Dignity, Picturesque Beauty, and Serious Purpose': The Reorientation of Suffrage Media in the Twentieth Century" (master's thesis, Eastern Illinois University, 2015), p. 24, available online at The Keep, Eastern Illinois University, Masters Theses, Paper 2033, http://thekeep.eiu.edu/theses/2033 (accessed March 23, 2016).

156. Gilmore, *Gender and Jim Crow,* 147.

157. Jacqueline Rouse, *Lugenia Burns Hope: Black Southern Reformer* (Athens: University of Georgia Press, 2004). The couple left Nashville in 1898 after John accepted a position at Atlanta Baptist College; he would be appointed president of Morehouse College in 1906 and Atlanta University in 1929.

158. Lovett and Wynn, *Profiles of African Americans in Tennessee*, 131–32. Moreover, Nettie Langston Napier, wife of prominent black businessman James C. Napier, was also active in the community. She was a pioneer for impoverished black children, forming Nashville's Day Home Club in 1907 (Lovett and Wynn, 95, 137).

159. Ward, *Dark Midnight When I Rise*, 402–3; Lovett and Wynn, *Profiles of African Americans in Tennessee*, 12–13, 81–82, 121–32. It is important to note that Mary Church Terrell and Ida B. Wells were also native Tennesseans (from Memphis). Both publicly advocated women's rights and education for African Americans while denouncing segregation and lynching.

160. Jessie Carney Smith, *Notable Black American Women*, Book II (Detroit: Gale, 1996), 156. Excerpts from this page are reprinted from *Tennessee Women Volume II* (2015) with permission from University of Georgia Press. In 1878 local black businessman James C. Napier was elected to the Nashville City Council, and his resolution requesting that the city's Board of Education hire black teachers was adopted, though with conditions that delayed implementation.

161. Howard N. Rabinowitz, *Race, Ethnicity, and Urbanization: Selected Essays* (Columbia: University of Missouri Press, 1994), 103, 116. Surprisingly, pay for black teachers in Nashville was equal to that of whites during the 1880s when the Board of Education passed a new salary schedule in 1889. Also of note, in 1887 nearly half of all African American applicants passed the city's teacher examination with the one of the top ten scores citywide earned by a young Fisk student named William Edward Burghardt Du Bois (109).

162. Summerville, *Educating Black Doctors*, 32.

163. Gilmore, *Gender and Jim Crow*, 149. For discussions of white women and gender hierarchies in the Confederacy see Drew Gilpin Faust, *Mothers of Invention: Women of the Slaveholding South in the American Civil War* (Chapel Hill: University of North Carolina Press, 2004). For discussions of gender and race in the early antebellum era, see Catherine Clinton in *The Plantation Mistress* (New York: Pantheon, 1983).

164. Jones, *Jeanes Teacher in the United States*, 7.

165. *Fisk University News*, October 1917, 1–3.

166. *Some Reports of a Trip Made by Booker T. Washington of Tuskegee Institute through the State of Tennessee, November 18–28, 1909*, reprinted from the *New York Evening Post* (N.p., n.d.), 13.

167. Richardson, *History of Fisk University*, 49.

168. Du Bois, *Souls of Black Folk*, chapter 6.

169. McKenzie, "Ideals of Fisk," 4.

170. Paul Finkelman, ed., *Encyclopedia of African American History, 1896 to Present* (New York: Oxford University Press, 2009), 399.

171. Adam Fairclough, *A Class of Their Own: Black Teachers in the Segregated South* (Cambridge, MA: Belknap Press of Harvard University Press, 2007), 5–9.

172. Lovett, "Tennessee State University: A Synopsis," 8.

173. In Harlan and Smock, *Booker T. Washington Papers*, 211.

174. Ibid., 211–12.

Chapter 4

1. *The Iris,* 1902 (annual of Ward Seminary), vol. 4, 57–58.

2. For more on working-class women and leisure, see Kathy Peiss, *Cheap Amusements: Working Women and Leisure in Turn-of-the-Century New York* (Philadelphia: Temple University Press, 1986). Peiss argues that working class women gained access to public space but not necessarily for reasons of individual or collective empowerment.

3. Woodrow Wilson, "What Is a College For?" in *The Papers of Woodrow Wilson,* vol. 19, ed. Arthur Link (Princeton, NJ: Princeton University Press, 1975), 344–46, as quoted in Horowitz, *Campus Life,* 102.

4. *Hustler,* February 3, 1910, 3.

5. Horowitz, *Campus Life,* 97.

6. The two most influential works that define heterosocial and homosocial relationships are Peiss, *Cheap Amusements,* and Gordon, *Gender and Higher Education in the Progressive Era.* Other important works include John C. Spurlock and Cynthia A. Magistro, *The Transformation of American Women's Emotional Culture* (New York: New York University Press, 1998); and Kevin White, *The First Sexual Revolution: The Emergence of Male Heterosexuality in Modern America* (New York: New York University Press, 1993).

7. Paula S. Fass, *The Damned and the Beautiful: American Youth in the 1920s* (New York: Oxford University Press, 1977), 7.

8. For more on the working class, gender, and leisure see Georgina Hickey, *Hope and Danger in the New South City: Working-Class Women and Urban Development in Atlanta, 1890–1940* (Athens: University of Georgia Press, 2003).

9. Justi, *Official History of the Tennessee Centennial Exposition.*

10. See also Richard Butsch, ed., *For Fun and Profit: The Transformation of Leisure into Consumption* (Philadelphia: Temple University Press, 1990). For more on the influence of women as independent consumers, see Liette Gidlow, *The Big Vote: Gender, Consumer Culture, and the Politics of Exclusion, 1890s–1920s* (Baltimore: Johns Hopkins University Press, 2004).

11. Lawrence Levine, *Highbrow/Lowbrow: The Emergence of Cultural Hierarchy in America* (Cambridge, MA: Harvard University Press, 1988).

12. Thus, changes in the late nineteenth century and early twentieth century reflect a broader social pattern of segmentation and commodification of the broader American society.

13. For more on other entertainments for mass audiences, see John Kasson, *Amusing the Millions: Coney Island at the Turn of the Century* (New York: Hill and Wang, 1978). Amusement parks were another major outlet of heterosocial leisure provided by entrepreneurs seeking profits by offering an exciting escape from the working world. According to Kasson, amusement parks emerged as laboratories of the new mass culture. Kasson concluded that they represented an "artificial distraction for an artificial life," whereby the age of scarcity transformed into a fake world of abundance (10).

14. *Hustler,* March 3, 1910, 4–5.

15. Ridley Wills, *Belle Meade Country Club: The First One Hundred Years* (Nashville: Hillsboro Press, 2001), 5-6. The Nashville Golf Club included opportunities for hunting, tennis, and riding, as well as other outdoor activities.

16. The first public golf course did not open until 1924 when Nashville added a course to Shelby Park. For more on Nashville's golf courses, see Wills, *Belle Meade Country Club*; and Julia Beach, "Belle Meade Country Club and Urbanization, 1900–1920," 1–3, in "Nashville as a Historical Laboratory" collection.

17. Various reports found in the *Hustler, Nashville Banner,* and Ward-Belmont social programs show that many events were held at the Belle Meade Country Club, the University Club, and the Hermitage Club. It is also important to note that the Hermitage and Centennial Clubs were located downtown, and clubwomen often sponsored social events such as an annual ball and regular dinners.

18. *W. E. Ward's Seminary Annual Announcement,* 1896–1897, 42.

19. Ridley Wills II, *Lest We Forget* (Franklin, Tenn.: Plumbline Media, 2013), 98.

20. *Hustler,* March 5, 1908, 3.

21. *Hustler,* March 22, 1906, 6.

22. Waller, *Nashville in the 1890s,* 118–39.

23. "Tennessee State Fair Grounds," Historic Nashville website, April 1, 2009, https://historicnashville.wordpress.com/tag/tennessee-state-fair-grounds/ (accessed March 22, 2016). The track was temporarily closed to harness racing in 1906 when the state passed laws that made betting on horseracing illegal.

24. Lewis Smith Maiden, *Highlights of the Nashville Theater, 1876–1890* (New York: Vantage Press, 1979), 120–28. This book gives a factual and chronological account of performers, shows, and theater attendance during the fourteen-year period.

25. *W. E. Ward's Seminary Annual Announcement,* 1896–1897, 42; *Nashville Banner* advertisements, 1917.

26. Maiden, *Highlights of the Nashville Theater,* ii.

27. Martha Ingram, *Apollo's Struggle: A Performing Arts Odyssey in the Athens of the South, Nashville, Tennessee* (Nashville: Hillsboro Press, 2004), 47–166.

28. *Nashville American,* January 9, 1894, as quoted in Waller, *Nashville in the 1890s,* 122–23. For more on the development of theater, see Levine, *Highbrow/Lowbrow.*

29. Ingram, *Apollo's Struggle,* 47-50.

30. William U. Eiland, *Nashville's Mother Church: The History of the Ryman Auditorium* (Nashville: Opryland USA, 1992), 35.

31. Ibid., 13.

32. Ibid., 1-25.

33. Ibid., 25–46.

34. Rosalyn Kirsch scrapbook, 1916–1918, Belmont Special Collections. See also Jim Cullen, *The Art of Democracy: A Concise History of Popular Culture in the United States* (New York: Monthly Review Press, 2002).

35. Eiland, Nashville's Mether Church, 48. For post–World War I developments, see Pamela Grundy, "'We Always Tried to Be Good People': Respectability, Crazy Water Crystals, and Hillbilly Music on the Air, 1933–1935," *Journal of American History* 81 (March 1995): 1591–1620.

36. Mary Daly McWilliams scrapbook, 1916–1918, Belmont Special Collections.

37. *Nashville Banner,* July 4, 1914, 1.

38. Rosalyn Kirsch scrapbook. See also: Lauren Rabinovitz, *For the Love of Pleasure: Women, Movies, and Culture in Turn-of-the-Century Chicago* (New Brunswick, NJ: Rutgers University Press, 1998).

39. *Chat,* May 11, 1895, as quoted in Waller, *Nashville in the 1890s,* 128.

40. Randy McBee, *Dance Hall Days: Intimacy and Leisure among Working-Class Immigrants in the United States* (New York: New York University Press, 2000). The largest group that frequented downtown dance halls in urban areas was the working class.

41. Various accounts of school and social club dances can be found in the *Hustler,* 1905–17. See also newspaper clippings, Margueritte Griffith Witherspoon scrapbook, 1916–1918, Belmont Special Collections; and Doyle, *Nashville in the New South.*

42. *Hustler,* April 5, 1911.

43. Witherspoon scrapbook. Although many dances had themes, certain functions maintained an odd and peculiar twist. Sponsored as a "kid party," all attendees dressed in children's-style clothes, nibbled on candy and peppermint, and danced to the Vito orchestra in the school's gymnasium.

44. Lears, *No Place of Grace,* 3–47, 103–30. For a poignant primary source, see Joseph Lee, *Play and Playgrounds,* American Civic Association, Department of Public Recreation, Leaflet no. 11, January 1908.

45. The National Recreation Bureau was formed in 1906, while the National Park System began in the same year through the establishment of Yellowstone Park. New York City opened legendary Central Park in 1851, becoming the first city to establish a municipal park and ensuring no further development on the property. This desire to return to an idealized nature in an age of urbanization is documented in Peter Schmidt, *Back to Nature: The Arcadian Myth in Urban America* (Baltimore: Johns Hopkins University Press, 1990). See also David Schuyler, *The New Urban Landscape: The Redefinition of Urban Form in Nineteenth-Century America* (Baltimore: Johns Hopkins University Press, 1986).

46. Leland R. Johnson, *The Parks of Nashville* (Nashville: Metropolitan Nashville and Davidson County Board of Parks and Recreation, 1986), 21–43. The members of the Park Board all served on the committee that organized the Centennial Exposition. They were Major F. P. McWhirter, R. M. Dudley, Ben Lindauer, Colonel S. A. Champion, and Major E. C. Lewis. Some of the land designated for parks was gained through court action, some deeded from the railroad, and other property purchased from individuals.

47. Ingram, *Apollo's Struggle,* 100.

48. *Globe,* July 12, 1912, 1. For more on parks in lower-income areas, see Johnson, *Parks of Nashville,* 73–78.

49. *Hustler,* March 9, 1900, 4.

50. Ibid.
51. *Hustler,* February 8, 1900, 1. See also Peiss, *Cheap Amusements.*
52. *Hustler,* October 10, 1907, 4.
53. Horowitz, *Alma Mater,* 150–51.
54. Ibid., 150–57.
55. Henry Seidel Canby, *College Sons and College Fathers* (Freeport, NY: Books for Libraries Press, 1915), 145–47.
56. *Hustler,* February 3, 1910, 1.
57. Horowitz, *Campus Life,* 89.
58. Fass, *Damned and the Beautiful,* 157–58.
59. Nicholas L. Syrett, *The Company He Keeps: A History of White College Fraternities* (Chapel Hill: University of North Carolina Press, 2009), 57, 122.
60. Conkin, *Gone with the Ivy,* 76.
61. Ridley Wills II, interviewed May 14, 2016, by Mary Ellen Pethel, Nashville, TN.
62. Syrett, *Company He Keeps,* 129–30.
63. Horowitz, *Campus Life,* 62.
64. *Hustler,* October 11, 1900, 3. The sorority began with nine members, who initiated four more women into the sorority that year. Although both began solely as local sororities, Phi Kappa Upsilon merged with the nationally recognized Kappa Alpha Theta in 1904, and in 1909 Theta Delta Theta became a part of the Delta Delta Delta national organization. The *Hustler* also announced the initial beginnings of Theta Delta Theta: "The colors are magenta and cerise, and the flowers are red and pink carnations. The pin is kite-shaped with the letters Theta Delta Theta in black on a red scroll across the top. In the lower point is a sun."
65. *Hustler,* October 1, 1909, 5.
66. *Hustler,* October 26, 1905, 4.
67. *The Comet,* 1909.
68. Conkin, *Gone with the Ivy,* 218.
69. Syrett, *Company He Keeps,* 151–53.
70. Ibid., 163.
71. Ibid., 165.
72. Ibid., 191.
73. *Vanderbilt University Quarterly,* January-March 1911, 19–20.
74. Conkin, *Gone with the Ivy,* 219.
75. *The Commodore,* 1911, 196.
76. "Kings Among Men: Part One," *Hustler,* October 3, 2013, http://www.vanderbilthustler.com/life/college_culture/article_42b0b48e-2c45-11e3-b08c-001a4bcf6878.html (accessed February 14, 2016).
77. Ibid; *The Commodore,* 1893.
78. "Kings Among Men."
79. Ibid.
80. Conkin, *Gone with the Ivy,* 209.
81. Ibid., 220–21.

82. Ibid., 307.

83. Ibid., 60.

84. *Caduceus of Kappa Sigma* 20, No. 1 (October 1905): 230.

85. Alexander Heard, *Speaking of the University: Two Decades at Vanderbilt University* (Nashville: Vanderbilt University Press, 1995), 56. There was one year during the B.U.'s existence where there was no winner. In 1909, the result listed as "no election." The winner, Noel Thomas Dowling, learned that the ballot box had been stuffed, with many of his supporters voting twice. He declared the election unfair and would not accept the honor. Dowling became a well-known constitutional law professor at Columbia University.

86. Witherspoon Scrapbook. After graduation, Griffith married Harry Witherspoon at the age of eighteen.

87. *The Iris,* 1905–1917; *The Ark,* 1910; *The Zenith,* 1914, 1916. For more on changing social interaction in the Gilded Age/Progressive Era, see Smith-Rosenberg, *Disorderly Conduct;* Peiss, *Cheap Amusements;* and McBee, *Dance Hall Days.*

88. John Crowe Ransom Papers, Vanderbilt University Special Collections, Jean and Alexander Heard Library, Nashville, TN.

89. "The Fugitives and Agrarians," Jean and Alexander Heard Library, Vanderbilt University website, http://www.library.vanderbilt.edu/speccol/vuhistory/fugitives_agrarians .php (accessed Feb. 12, 2016). Elliott was one of Davidson's classmates, a Vanderbilt graduate (B.A., 1917; M.A., 1920), a member of the Vanderbilt faculty for a year, a Rhodes Scholar, and an Oxford University Ph.D. He later became a renowned political scientist for nearly forty years at Harvard.

90. Conkin, *Gone with the Ivy,* 313.

91. Ibid., 322.

92. Harry Ransom Center, University of Texas at Austin, http://www.hrc.utexas.edu/ (accessed February 12, 2016).

93. *I'll Take My Stand* (New York: Harper and Brothers, 1930), 359.

94. Ibid., 20. For more see: Paul Conkin, *The Southern Agrarians* (Knoxville: University of Tennessee Press, 1988); and Don Doyle, *Nashville Since the 1920s* (Knoxville: University of Tennessee Press, 1985).

95. Horowitz, *Alma Mater,* 4.

96. Solomon, *In the Company of Educated Women,* 95. See chapter 7 for a general treatment of the dimensions of the collegiate experience for women.

97. Davis, "A Quiet, Even Growth," 6.

98. Ibid., 7.

99. Ibid.

100. Ibid.

101. *Annual Announcement of Ward Seminary,* 1894–1895, 38.

102. Ibid.

103. Horowitz, *Alma Mater,* 149–50.

104. *Announcement and Prospectus of Belmont College,* 1891, 24–25.

105. *Announcement and Prospectus of Belmont College,* 1895, 24.

106. Ibid. Day students often carried letters and correspondence to Vanderbilt or other local young men for boarding students.

107. *The Aitrop,* 1904, 63–70.

108. *Musical Herald,* 1908 (London: J. Curwen & Sons), 4.

109. *The Aitrop,* 1904, 63–70.

110. Ibid.

111. *Announcement and Prospectus of Belmont College,* 1906, 8.

112. Willye O. Smith, "Halloween Night," *Blue and Bronze,* 1904, 21–22.

113. Gilbertine Moore, *Gilly Goes to Ward-Belmont* (Nashville: Benson Printing, 1973), 26.

114. *The Aitrop,* 1904, n.p.

115. Moore, *Gilly Goes to Ward-Belmont,* 22-23.

116. Ibid., 28.

117. Sarah Bryan Benedict, Sarah Colley Cannon, and Mary Elizabeth Cayce, "The Bells of Ward-Belmont: A Reminiscence," *Tennessee Historical Quarterly* 30 (Winter 1971): 381.

118. The debate team only had four members, so most Fisk men opted to pursue other clubs and societies.

119. Rodney T. Cohen, *Fisk University* (Charleston, SC: Arcadia Publishing, 2001), 30.

120. M. Deborah Bialeschki, "'You Have to Have Some Fun to Go Along with Your Work': The Interplay of Race, Class, Gender and Leisure in the Industrial New South,'" *Journal of Leisure Research* 30, no. 1 (1998): 95–101.

121. Cohen, *Fisk University,* 44. The Decagynian Club defected from the Lyceum Club, the only other women's club at that time. As Rodney T. Cohen recounted, "When approached by the members about a name, Professor Chase replied humorously with 'Call yourselves the Decagynians—the ten married women'" (44).

122. Richardson, *History of Fisk University,* 90.

123. Ibid., 75.

124. Lovett, *African American History of Nashville, Tennessee,* 164.

125. President's Report, *Fisk University News* 14, no. 1 (1924), as quoted in Christopher Nicholson, "To Advance a Race: A Historical Analysis of the Intersection of Personal Belief, Industrial Philanthropy and Black Liberal Arts Higher Education in Fayette McKenzie's Presidency at Fisk University, 1915–1925" (Ph.D. diss., Loyola University Chicago, 2011), Loyola eCommons, http://ecommons.luc.edu/luc_diss/153), 222 (accessed January 30, 2016).

126. Richardson, *History of Fisk University,* 91–92.

127. Ibid.

128. Ibid., 96.

129. Lovett, *African American History of Nashville,* 166.

130. Ibid.

131. McKenzie to P. D. Cravath, Nashville, April 16, 1925, McKenzie Papers, as quoted in Lovett, *African American History of Nashville,* 166.

132. Lovett, *African American History of Nashville,* 166.

133. Ibid., 167.

134. Richardson, *History of Fisk University,* 106.
135. *The Radio,* 1926, 90.
136. Ibid., 90–91.
137. Lovett, *Touch of Greatness,* 66–67.
138. Richardson, *History of Fisk University,* 107–8.
139. Tamara L. Brown, Gregory S. Parks, and Clarenda M. Phillips, *African American Fraternities and Sororities: The Legacy and Vision* (Lexington: University Press of Kentucky), 171.
140. Ibid., 42.
141. Ibid, 171.
142. *Hustler,* September 1912, 1.
143. Horowitz, *Campus Life,* 91.
144. *Hustler,* February 3, 1910, 1–2.

Chapter 5

1. The *Bulletin* of the Bureau of Education, as quoted in Patrick M. Miller, "The Manly, the Moral, and the Proficient: College Sport in the New South," *Journal of Sport History* 24, no. 3 (1997): 286.
2. Brian Ingrassia, *The Rise of Gridiron University: Higher Education's Uneasy Alliance with Big-Time Football* (Lawrence: University Press of Kansas, 2012), 4.
3. Miller, "The Manly, the Moral, and the Proficient," 286.
4. *Hustler,* May 7, 1896, 2.
5. Pamela Grundy, "From Amazons to Glamazons: The Rise and Fall of North Carolina Women's Basketball, 1920–1960," *Journal of American History* 87 (June 2000): 114.
6. *Fisk Herald,* November 1894.
7. Horowitz, *Campus Life,* 108.
8. Miller, "The Manly, the Moral, and the Proficient," 286.
9. Conkin, *Gone with the Ivy,* 58.
10. *Hustler,* October 12, 1899, 3–4.
11. Edward Ward Carmack, *Character: Or, The Making of the Man* (Nashville: McQuiddy Printing Company, 1909). This text was used widely in Nashville to teach the tenets of "Muscular Christianity." Dudley A. Sargent also contributed to this doctrine.
12. *Hustler,* March 9, 1900, 4.
13. *Hustler,* February 4, 1897, 1. For more on "Muscular Christianity," see Harvey Green, *Fit for America: Health, Fitness, Sport, and American Society* (New York: Pantheon, 1986). For general works about the rise of sport in American, see Foster Rhea Dulles, *America Learns to Play: A History of Popular Recreation, 1607–1940* (Gloucester, MA: Peter Smith, 1963); Steven A. Riess, *City Games: The Evolution of American Urban Society and the Rise of Sports* (Urbana: University of Illinois Press, 1991); and Benjamin Rader, *American Sports: From the Age of Folk Games to the Age of Spectators* (Englewood Cliffs, NJ: Prentice Hall, 1983).

14. *Hustler,* December 12, 1901, 1

15. In an 1899 program, gymnastics were performed before the basketball exhibit, and the program reported that "the entertainments given were noted for their high class and cleanliness in every respect" (Nashville Public Library, unprocessed).

16. *Hustler,* November 19, 1903, 3.

17. The Hippodrome was razed in 1968.

18. Quoted in Traughber, *Nashville Sports History,* 79.

19. Conkin, *Peabody College,* 141–43. Peabody did play the Universities of Tennessee, Texas, Virginia, and Kentucky in football through the 1910s. Also see "Athletics," *University of Nashville Bulletin of Information, Peabody College,* 1902, 9–13.

20. Six years later Harvard would defeat Yale in a rugby-like contest that would develop into American-style football. In 1876 Harvard, Columbia, Princeton, and Yale established the first conference, the Intercollegiate Football Association. Under the association's rules each team was allowed fifteen players on the field, playing two forty-minute halves; the game involved a combination of kicking and carrying the ball.

21. Traughber, *Nashville Sports History,* 31-36.

22. For more on Sulphur Dell, see Kent Whitworth, "Historic Stadiums," *Tennessee Encyclopedia of History and Culture,* online edition, http://tennesseeencyclopedia.net/entry.php?rec=1252 (accessed April 10, 2016).

23. Ridley Wills II interview.

24. Andrew Doyle, "Turning the Tide: College Football and Southern Progressivism," *Southern Cultures* 3, no. 3 (1997): 29.

25. Ibid.

26. Ibid.

27. *Hustler,* May 15, 1902, 2.

28. *Hustler,* February 3, 1898, 1.

29. Ibid.

30. Conkin, *Gone with the Ivy,* 141.

31. Andrew Doyle, "Foolish and Useless Sport: The Southern Evangelical Crusade Against Intercollegiate Football," *Journal of Sport History* 24, no. 3 (1997): 333–34.

32. *Hustler,* February 4, 1897, 4.

33. Conkin, *Gone with the Ivy,* 138.

34. *Southern Intercollegiate Athletic Association Handbook,* 1895, Vanderbilt University website, http://www.library.vanderbilt.edu/speccol/exhibits/Athletics/SIAA_handbook1895.pdf (accessed April 20, 2015).

35. Roger Saylor, *Southern Intercollegiate Athletic Association,* College Football Historical Society, http://library.la84.org/SportsLibrary/CFHSN/CFHSNv06/CFHSNv06n2g.pdf (accessed March 1, 2015).

36. Some of the original schools joined other conferences such as the Atlantic Coast Conference (ACC) and the Big 12.

37. *Hustler,* January 1902, 1.

38. Ibid.

39. Traughber, *Nashville Sports History*, 35.

40. *Hustler,* November, 4, 1909, 1. It is likely that women involved in this event were not Vanderbilt students but rather the dates of male students.

41. Conkin, *Gone with the Ivy,* 139

42. Ibid.

43. Ingrassia, *Rise of the Gridiron University,* 4.

44. Miller, "The Manly, the Moral, and the Proficient," 290.

45. Ibid., 296.

46. Conkin, *Gone with the Ivy,* 214–15. It should be noted that while he was hired as a full-time coach, McGugin returned to Michigan to practice law until 1908. Even after he permanently relocated to Nashville, he opened a corporate law office downtown and continued to practice law through his coaching tenure. In addition McGugin regularly taught courses in Vanderbilt's law school.

47. Ibid.

48. Frederick Rudolph, *The American College and University* (New York: Knopf, 1962), 378–87.

49. Steven Hardy, *How Boston Played: Sport, Recreation, and Community, 1865–1915* (Knoxville: University of Tennessee Press, 2003). More specifically, the first category, "body," involves the city's physical structure (e.g., the Irish ghetto in Boston's North End created by immigration, roads, parks, and municipal districts). The second, "mind," deals with social structures and the physiology and interaction between individuals and groups (e.g., transportation patterns, public transportation, and shopping districts). The third category Hardy describes as "state of mind," or identity/loyalty (e.g., Yankees, Red Sox, Bostonian). For more on urban space and gender, see Sarah Deutsch, *Women and the City: Gender, Space, and Power in Boston, 1870–1940* (New York: Oxford University Press, 2000).

50. The community remained an active agent in shaping its own notion of modern leisure. Driving this commodification was the influence of a youth culture, produced in large part by the expanse of higher education and shifts in acceptable behavior for women.

51. *Hustler,* March 26, 1906, 3. There were chaperones at the dance.

52. Bill Traughber, "Vandy Ties Michigan in 1922," *Commodore History Corner,* 2006, http://www.vucommodores.com/ot/history-corner-083006.html (accessed April 10, 2015).

53. *Hustler,* October 1, 1922, 2–4.

54. *Hustler,* November 19, 1903, 3.

55. *Hustler,* March 3, 1898, 4. Eight years later, as Vanderbilt began to charge more consistently for tickets they set a range of prices. College game tickets were no less than four cents and no more than $1.12.

56. Ingrassia, *Rise of the Gridiron University,* 168–69.

57. Traughber, "Vandy Ties Michigan in 1922."

58. Conkin, *Gone with the Ivy,* 309.

59. *American City* 27, nos. 4–6 (1922, 517, *The Scroll of Phi Delta Theta Fraternity,* 1903.

60. Ingrassia, *Rise of the Gridiron University,* 3.

61. Doyle, "Turning the Tide," 46.
62. Conkin, *Gone with the Ivy,* 309.
63. Traughber, "Vandy Ties Michigan in 1922."
64. Ibid.
65. Conkin, *Gone with the Ivy,* 311.
66. Hasan Kwame Jeffries, "Fields of Play: The Mediums through Which Black Athletes Engaged in Sports in Jim Crow Georgia," *Journal of Negro History* 86, no. 3 (2001): 271.
67. Doyle, "Turning the Tide," 48.
68. *Hilltop* (Howard University newspaper), April 1924, from Patrick B. Miller, "To 'Bring the Race along Rapidly': Sport, Student Culture, and Educational Mission at Historically Black Colleges during the Interwar Years," *History of Education Quarterly* 35, no. 2 (1995): 111.
69. Miller, "To 'Bring the Race along Rapidly,'" 111–12.
70. Jeffries, "Fields of Play," 264–75.
71. Ibid., 264–65. See also S. H. Archer, "Football in Our Colleges," *Voice of the Negro* 3 (March 1906): 199–205.
72. Richardson, *History of Fisk University,* 157–59; Cohen, *Fisk University,* 97–115. In 1949 the gymnasium became the Van Vechten Gallery, and in 1950 the Henderson A. Johnson Gymnasium was completed.
73. Cohen, *Fisk University,* 111–16.
74. Richardson, *History of Fisk University,* 157.
75. Raymond Schmidt, *Shaping College Football: The Transformation of an American Sport, 1919–1930* (Syracuse, NY: Syracuse University Press, 2007), 134.
76. Richardson, *History of Fisk University,* 99.
77. *Chicago Defender,* November 7, 12, 1921. Wilberforce was a Methodist school, and Roger Williams was a Baptist school.
78. College Football Data Warehouse website, http://www.cfbdatawarehouse.com (accessed April 18, 2016).
79. Lovett, *Touch of Greatness,* 285.
80. Ibid., 287.
81. Lovett, *A Touch of Greatness,* 288.
82. Ibid.
83. "Silver Jubilee, SIAC," as quoted in Cohen, *Fisk University,* 97.
84. *Fisk University News,* September 1918, 6.
85. Ibid.
86. Ibid.
87. Jeffries, "Fields of Play," 271.
88. Ibid.
89. Ibid.
90. Rudolph, *American College and University,* 378–87.
91. Miller, "The Manly, the Moral, and the Proficient," 301.
92. Ibid.

93. *Milestones,* November 1920, 197.

94. Ellen W. Gerber, *Innovators and Institutions in Physical Education* (Philadelphia: Lea and Febiger, 1971); Margaret A. Lowe, *Looking Good: College Women and Body Image, 1875–1930* (Baltimore: Johns Hopkins University Press, 2003).

95. Pamela Dean, "'Dear Sister' and 'Hated Rivals': Athletics and Gender at Two New South Women's Colleges, 1893–1920," *Journal of Sport History* 24 (Fall 1997): 341.

96. *Hustler,* April 14, 1897, 1.

97. *The Iris,* vol. 4, 1902, n.p.

98. A "middy" blouse was a loose-fitting top with a large, navy-style collar, and "bloomers" were knee-length, baggy pants similar to "knickerbockers" worn by young men.

99. Geo. J. Engelmann, "The American Girl of Today," *American Physical Education Review,* March 1901, 35–66. See also Anne O'Hagag, "The Athletic Girl," *Munsey's Magazine* 25 (August 1901): 730–37.

100. Elizabeth Halsey, *Women in Physical Education* (New York: G. D. Putnam's Sons, 1961), 5–100. For more on the connections between physical activity and physical appearance for women, see Lowe, *Looking Good.* For a more specific treatment of women's physical education and sport in a college setting, see Adam R. Hornbuckle, "Women's Sports and Physical Education at the University of Tennessee, 1899–1939" (master's thesis, University of Tennessee, Knoxville, 1983). As with the professionalization of academic disciplines and professional and academic associations, women also gained from this movement with the founding of the Association for the Advancement of Physical Education (1885) and the *American Physical Education Review,* as well as the publication of Gertrude Dudley and Frances A. Kellor's *Athletic Games in the Education of Women* (1909).

101. Clara Gregory Baer, *Newcomb College Basket Ball Guide for Women, Collegiate Rules* (New Orleans: H. Sophie Newcomb Memorial College for Women, The Tulane University of Louisiana, 1914), 3.

102. *Hustler,* March 3, 1898, 4.

103. The average height of white women in the United States in 1895 was approximately five feet three inches, while the average weight was 125 pounds.

104. *The Iris,* vol. 4, 1902, 83.

105. *Observer,* 1909, 213. The *Observer* was a published periodical of Vanderbilt; the *Hustler* was the school's weekly newspaper. Also, the girls' basketball team first formed during the 1896–97 school year.

106. *Hustler,* December 12, 1895, 3.

107. *Hustler,* February 3, 1898, 1.

108. *Hustler,* March 17, 1897, 1.

109. Ibid.

110. Ibid.

111. Ibid.

112. Bill Traughber, "Vandy's Men's and Women's 1909–1910 Seasons," *Commodore History Corner,* February 6, 2007, 3–4.

113. *The Ark* (Nashville Bible College), vol. 1, 1910, 11–68.

114. *Hustler,* May 17, 1906. Many other reports reveal the rise of tennis and golf through club teams; however, most seem to be either limited to men or do not specifically mention women as participants.

115. Carl E. Klafs, *The Female Athlete* (St. Louis: C. V. Mosby, 1973).

116. Dean, "'Dear Sisters' and 'Hated Rivals,'" 353.

117. *Hustler,* September 30, 1896, 3. Two years later, the *Hustler* (March 3, 1898) carried the admiring description of female athlete Rowena Reed of Vassar quoted earlier in this chapter.

118. McCandless, "Maintaining the Spirit and Tone of Robust Manliness," 199.

119. *Hustler,* March 17, 1897, 1.

120. Ibid.

121. *Ward Seminary Bulletin,* 1911, 63.

122. Shelia Scraton, *Shaping Up to Womanhood: Gender and Girls' Physical Education* (Buckingham, UK: Open University Press, 1992), 29. See also Martha Verbugge, *Able-Bodied Womanhood: Personal Health and Social Change in Nineteenth-Century Boston* (New York: Oxford University Press, 1988).

123. Kirsch Scrapbook.

124. *Hustler,* 1, February 1904.

125. *Standards in Sports for Girls and Women* (Washington, DC: AAHPER, 1915), 16.

126. Jimmy Bryant, "From the UCA Archives: A Brief History of Women's Basketball," *Log Cabin Democrat* (Conway, AR), November 13, 2011, http://thecabin.net/sports/college (accessed April 25, 2015).

127. Grundy, "From Amazons to Glamazons," 141.

128. Mary Ellen Pethel, "Sport and the Outward Life: Young Women Athletes as Progressive Players," in *Tennessee Women in the Progressive Era: Toward the Public Sphere in the New South,* ed. Mary A. Evins (Knoxville: University of Tennessee Press, 2013), 235–39.

129. See also: Robin Bachin, *Building the Southside: Urban Space and Civic Culture in Chicago, 1890–1919* (Chicago: University of Chicago Press, 2004).

130. *Hustler,* November 23, 1893, 1.

131. *Hustler,* March 19, 1903, 2.

132. Rudolph, *American College and University,* 378–87.

Chapter 6

1. *Memphis Ledger,* 1885, from *W. E. Ward's Seminary Annual Announcement,* 1885–1886, 19.

2. U.S. Census, 2000.

3. Metropolitan Statistical Areas, 2015, http://www.census.gov/popest/data/metro/totals/2015/files/CBSA-EST2015-alldata.csv (accessed April 26, 2016). Davidson County has a population of over 700,000 residents.

4. "Nashville vs. Memphis? We win!" *Tennessean,* May 31, 2016, 1.

5. Karl Dean, mayor of Nashville (2007–15), Belmont professor of history and political science, interviewed May 17, 2016, by Mary Ellen Pethel, Nashville, TN.

6. Ridley Wills II, interviewed May 14, 2016, by Mary Ellen Pethel, Nashville, TN.

7. For more see Florida, *Cities and the Creative Class* (New York: Routledge, 2004).

8. Dean interview.

9. Ibid.

10. David R. Logsdon, "Erskine Bronson Ingram," *Tennessee Encyclopedia of History and Culture,* online edition, http://tennesseeencyclopedia.net/entry.php?rec=685 (accessed May 14, 2016).

11. E. Thomas Wood, "The Empire Strikes Back: Protecting the Ingram Family Fortunes," *Nashville Scene,* June 6, 1996, http://www.nashvillescene.com/nashville/the-empire-strikes-back/Content?oid=1180527 (accessed May 14, 2016).

12. William H. Honan, "Vanderbilt U. Receives a Gift of $300 Million," *New York Times,* December 1, 1998, http://www.nytimes.com/1998/12/01/us/vanderbilt-u-receives-a-gift-of-300-million.html (accessed May 1, 2016).

13. Getahn Ward, "Can Nashville's Growth Continue?" *Tennessean,* August 15, 2015, http://www.tennessean.com/story/money/real-estate/2015/08/14/population-gains-key-nashville-job-growth/31509555/ (accessed May 3, 2016).

14. "Working at VU," Vanderbilt University website, http//www.vanderbilt.edu/work-at-vanderbilt-working-at-vu.php (accessed May 8, 2016). Figures related to patients served taken from an interview with Edith Carell Johnson, chair of Vanderbilt University Medical Center's Board of Directors, by Mary Ellen Pethel, Nashville, TN, May 17, 2016.

15. Johnson interview.

16. Dean interview.

17. The statistic of over 100,000 students in metro Nashville includes students attending one of five community colleges or twenty-six vocational and technical schools. While some of these are for-profit institutions, like the University of Phoenix, most are traditional nonprofit schools operating on private or public funding.

18. Ibid.

19. "Talent Pipeline," Nashville Chamber of Commerce and Economic Development website, http://www.nashvilleareainfo.com/homepage/human-capital/higher-education (accessed May 9, 2016). In sum, there are sixteen four-year and postgraduate institutions in Davidson County and twenty-one in the Metropolitan Nashville area.

20. Megan Barry, mayor of Nashville (2015–present), interviewed May 19, 2016, by Mary Ellen Pethel, Nashville, TN.

21. Claire Dugan, Belmont University Honors Program student, interviewed May 13, 2016, by Mary Ellen Pethel, Nashville, TN. Dugan is pursuing a B.B.A. (Bachelor of Business Administration).

22. Barry interview.

23. Michael Dennis, "The Illusion of Relevance: Southern Progressives and American Higher Education," *Journal of the Historical Society* 8, no. 2 (2008): 229.

24. The school continues many of the traditions first begun at Ward's Seminary and Belmont College for Young Women. Today, Harpeth Hall is open to grades five through twelve. There is no official relationship between Belmont University and the Harpeth Hall School.

25. Lovett, *Touch of Greatness*, 144. For more on the state's civil rights movement, see Lovett, *Civil Rights Movement in Tennessee*.

26. "Mayor Says Integrate Counters," *Tennesseean*, 1, April 20, 1960.

27. Several student leaders of the civil rights movement in Nashville were students at the American Baptist College, a small college with less than two hundred enrolled students, which opened in 1924. Its most notable graduate is John Lewis. In 2013 the school was designated as an HBCU.

28. Thelin, *History of American Higher Education*, 348.

29. Adam Tamburin, "At 150 Fisk University Celebrates Rich History, New Era," *Tennessean,* January 9, 2016, http://www.tennessean.com/story/news/education/2016/01/08/150-fisk-university-celebrates-rich-history-new-era/78256502/ (accessed May 8, 2016).

30. The ten schools within the Vanderbilt University framework are the College of Arts and Sciences, Blair School of Music, Divinity School, School of Engineering, Graduate Schools, Law School, School of Medicine, School of Nursing, Owen Graduate School of Management, Peabody College, and Division of Unclassified Studies.

31. Jim Patterson, "Vanderbilt's Peabody No. 1 Education School for Fifth Consecutive Year," *Vanderbilt News,* March 12, 2013, http://news.vanderbilt.edu/2013/03/usnews-graduate-2013/ (accessed May 8, 2016).

32. "Race and Ethnic Distribution: Undergraduate." Vanderbilt Institutional Research Group, https://virg.vanderbilt.edu/virgweb/ (accessed April 28, 2016).

33. Guy Russo and Erin Logan, "Vanderbilt Universities Wants Our Bodies But Not Our Baggage," *Huffington Post,* November 16, 2015, www.huffingtonpost.com/erin-logan/vanderbilt-university-wants-our-bodies-b_8572830.html (accessed April 30, 2016).

34. David Williams II, Vanderbilt University vice chancellor for athletics and university affairs, athletic director, and professor of law, interviewed May 11, 2016, by Mary Ellen Pethel, Nashville, TN.

35. Ingram, *Apollo's Struggle*, 197–206. Ingram's book gives a fascinating and complete history of the Blair Academy of Music, from its inception in 1964 to the present, as one of the premier music schools in the South.

36. Karl Dean interview.

37. The eleven colleges include Gordon E. Inman College of Health Sciences and Nursing, Mike Curb College of Entertainment and Music Business, Jack C. Massey College of Business, College of Liberal Arts and Social Sciences, College of Law, College of Pharmacy, College of Visual and Performing Arts, College of Sciences and Mathematics, University College of Adult Degree Programs, College of Theology and Christian Ministry, and Interdisciplinary Studies and Global Education. Belmont University had an 82 percent acceptance rate in 2015.

38. "Go Greek," Lipscomb University website, http://www.lipscomb.edu/gogreek (accessed May 7, 2016).

39. "L. Randolph Lowry III," Lipscomb University website, https://secure.lipscomb.edu/president/biography (accessed May 6, 2016).

40. For more see: Equal Chance for Education, www.equalchanceforeducation.com (accessed August 29, 2016).

41. "University Announces Full Scholarship Program for Nashville Students," *Belmont Vision*, March 26, 2013, http://belmontvision.com/2013/03/university-announces-new-scholarship-program-for-local-students/ (accessed May 9, 2016).

42. "Belmont Breaks Ground on Wedgewood Academic Center," *Belmont Vision,* May 24, 2012, http://belmontvision.com/2012/05/belmont-breaks-ground-on-wedgewood-center/ (accessed May 7, 2016).

43. The eight schools and colleges include Agriculture, Human, and Natural Sciences; Business; Education; Engineering; Graduate Studies and Research; Health Sciences; Liberal Arts; Life and Physical Sciences; and Public Service. TSU has also ventured into the world of online degree programs.

44. William Williams, "Fisk President Discusses Historic University's Current State, Future," *Nashville Post,* September 29, 2014, https://www.fisk.edu/articles/president-nashvillepost (accessed May 2, 2016).

45. Adam Tamburin, "New Meharry President: Go 'from Surviving to Thriving,'" *Tennessean,* July 5, 2015, www.tennessean.com/story/news/eduction/2015/07/05/new-meharry-sees-path-forward-past-lessons/29739189/ (accessed May 2, 2016).

46. Joel Ebert, "Clinton Makes Closing Arguments in Tennessee," *Tennessean,* February 29, 2016, http://www.tennessean.com/story/news/politics/2016/02/28/hillary-clinton-speak-nashvilles-maherry-medical-college-today/80925186/ (accessed May 1, 2016).

47. "James Hildreth Named Meharry's Next President," *Tennessean,* July 5, 2015, 1.

48. "Life in Nashville," Meharry Medical College website, http://www.mmc.edu/prospectivestudents/nashville.html (accessed May 8, 2016).

49. This route was designed and created under the Dean administration after the completion of the 28th Avenue Connector which provided a more accessible and convenient route between Charlotte Avenue and West End Avenue.

Bibliography

Archival Collections

Belmont University Special Collections
    "Background and History of Belmont College." N.p., 1964
    Concerning Miss Edith Margaret Smaill. Brochure, 1912
    Kirsch, Rosalyn. Scrapbook, 1918–1919
    McWilliams, Mary Daly. Scrapbook, 1916–1918
    Witherspoon, Margueritte Griffith. Scrapbook, 1916–1918
Meharry University Special Collections
    Mullowney, John J. Papers
Tennessee State Library and Archives
    Broadside Collection
    Howse, Hilary E. Papers
    May, Daniel. Papers. May Hosiery Mill, Box 9
    McKenzie, Fayette Avery. Collection, III-B-5, 6
Vanderbilt University Archives, Jean and Alexander Heard Library
    Kirkland, James. Papers. High Schools and Universities, Box 13, File 76, 16–18, 1905
    Merriam, Lucius. Vanderbilt University: Higher Education in Tennessee, Box 23, File 88, 1–8
Vanderbilt University Special Collections, Jean and Alexander Heard Library
    College General Curriculum, Box 23, Files 4–15
    Education General, Box 23, File 9, 1–2
    "Nashville as a Historical Laboratory, 1977–1978." Manuscripts of twenty-five research papers written by students enrolled in the History 295 (Nashville and the Urban South) class, taught by Professor Don H. Doyle

at Vanderbilt University in spring semester 1977 and fall semester 1978. For a complete list of the papers, see https://www.library.vanderbilt.edu/speccol/findingaids/nashvilleashistoricallaboratory.pdf.

Ransom, John Crow. Papers.

Vanderbilt Institutional Research Group. https://virg.vanderbilt.edu/virgweb.

Periodicals

The Aitrop, Belmont College annual
Announcement and Prospectus of Belmont College
Announcement of the Meharry Medical Department of Central Tennessee College with Catalogue of Students and Graduates
Annual Announcement for Ward's Seminary for Young Ladies (also *W. E. Ward's Seminary Annual Announcement*)
Annual Announcement of the Nashville Bible School (Inc.)
Annual Catalog and Announcement of the Ward-Belmont School for Young Women
The Ark, Nashville Bible College annual
Belmont Vision, student newspaper of Belmont College
Blue and Bronze
Bulletin, Tennessee A. and I. State Teachers College
Bulletin of the Tennessee Agricultural and Industrial State Normal School
Catalog of the Officers and Students of Fisk University, Nashville, Tenn. (also *Catalog of Fisk University*)
Catalog of the Officers and Students of Roger Williams University
Catalogue of the Officers and Students of the University of Nashville, including the State Normal, Montgomery Bell, and Medical Department
Chicago Defender
Collier's
Commencement Courier, Vanderbilt University
The Commodore, Vanderbilt University annual
Confederate Veteran
Crisis: A Record of the Darker Races, newspaper of NAACP
Fisk Herald
Fisk University News
Globe
Havalind Acts, David Lipscomb College student newspaper
Hilltop, Howard University student newspaper
Hustler, Vanderbilt University student newspaper
Industrial Arts Magazine
The Iris, Ward Seminary annual
Meharry News
Memphis Ledger

Milady in Brown, Belmont College annual
Milestones, Ward-Belmont School annual
Nashville American
Nashville Banner
Nashville City Directory
New York Times
Observer, Vanderbilt University
Peabody Reflector
The Radio, annual of Tennessee Agricultural and Industrial State College
The Talisman, Nashville College for Young Ladies annual
Tennessean
Tennessee College Magazine
University of Nashville Bulletin of Information, Peabody College
Vanderbilt Magazine
Vanderbilt University Annual Announcement
Vanderbilt University News
Vanderbilt University Quarterly
Ward Seminary Bulletin
Ward-Belmont Bulletin
Ward-Belmont Conservatory of Music Catalog
Ward-Belmont Hyphen
The Zenith, Nashville Bible College annual

Interviews

Megan Barry
Anne Davis
Karl Dean
Claire Dugan
Martha Rivers Ingram
Edith Carell Johnson
David Williams II
Ridley Wills II

Published Primary Sources

Alumni Directory of Peabody College, 1877–1909. Nashville: Alumni Association of Peabody College, 1909.
AMA [American Missionary Association] *Proceedings,* 1865.
American City 27, nos. 4–6 (1922).
Angstman, Charlotte. "College Women and the New Science." *Popular Science Monthly* 53 (May 1898): 674–90.

Annual Commencement of W. E. Ward's Seminary for Ladies, 1885–1886.
Annual Reports of the City of Nashville, 1874, 1877, 1880–1915. Nashville: Albert B. Tavel, 1887.
Archer, S. H. "Football in Our Colleges." *Voice of the Negro* 3 (March 1906): 199–205.
Baer, Clara Gregory. *Newcomb College Basket Ball Guide for Women, Collegiate Rules.* New Orleans: H. Sophie Newcomb Memorial College for Women, Tulane University of Louisiana, 1914.
Baptist Home Mission Monthly 11, no. 1 (1889).
Barney, Elizabeth C. "The American Sportswoman." *Fortnightly Review* 56 (1894): 263–77.
Baxter, Sylvester. "The Economic and Social Influences of the Bicycle." *Arena* 6 (October 1892): 578–83.
Bell, James T. *Reports of Departments of the City of Nashville.* Nashville: Brandon, 1889.
Belmont College for Young Women Prospectus. N.d.
Brackett, Anna C. *Woman and the Higher Education.* New York: Harper and Brothers, 1893.
Caduceus of Kappa Sigma 20 (October 1905).
Canby, Henry Seidel. *College Sons and College Fathers.* Freeport, NY: Books for Libraries Press, 1915.
Carmack, Edward Ward. *Character: Or, The Making of the Man.* Nashville: McQuiddy, 1909.
Catalog of the Vanderbilt Chapter of Phi Beta Kappa. Phi Beta Kappa, 1914.
Colton, Elizabeth Avery. "Standards of Southern Colleges for Women." *School Review* 20 (September 1912): 458–75.
Commencement Address. Meharry Medical College, 1897.
Commencement Address of the Fiftieth Anniversary of Vanderbilt University. Vanderbilt University, 1925.
Commencement Day Program. Tennessee A&I Normal School, 1928.
Crozier, E. W. *Nashville Blue Book: Selected Names of Nashville and Suburbs.* Nashville: Brandon Printing Co., 1896.
Curry, J. L. M. *A Brief Sketch of the Peabody Education Fund Through Thirty Years.* New York: John Wilson and Son, 1898.
Dau's Society Blue Book of Selected Names of Nashville and Suburbs. New York: Dau, 1907.
Department of the Interior, Bureau of Education. *Negro Education: A Study of the Private and Higher Schools for Colored People in the United States.* Bulletin 1916, no. 38, vol. 2. Washington, DC: Government Printing Office, 1917.
Dewey, John. *Democracy and Education.* New York: Macmillan Publishing, 1944.
———. *Experience and Education.* New York: Collier Books, 1938.
———. *Moral Principles in Education.* Boston: Houghton Mifflin, 1909.
Du Bois, W. E. B. *The Souls of Black Folk.* Chicago: A. C. McClurg, 1903.
———. "The Talented Tenth." In *The Negro Problem: A Series of Articles by Representative Negroes of To-day,* 31–75. New York: James Pott, 1903.

Engelmann, Geo. J. "The American Girl of Today." *American Physical Education Review* 3 (1901): 35–66.
Gannett, Kate Well. "The Transitional American Woman." *Atlantic Monthly* 46 (December 1880): 817–23.
Garrigues, Henry. "Woman and the Bicycle." *Forum* 20 (January 1896): 578–87.
Gates, Isabel Smith. *The Life of George Augustus Gates.* Boston: Pilgrim Press, 1915.
Gordon, M. K. "Reform of School Athletics." *Century,* n.s. 57 (Jan. 1910): 469–71.
"A Great Aid to Southern Education." *Public Opinion* 38 (June 1905): 529.
Hale, Millie E., ed. *Hale Hospital Review and Social Service Quarterly* 1, no. 4 (1922).
Hale, William Thomas, and Dixon Lanier Merritt. *History of Tennessee and Tennesseans.* Chicago: Lewis, 1913.
Harlan, Louis R., and Raymond W. Smock, eds. *Booker T. Washington Papers.* Vol. 10, *1909–1911.* Urbana: University of Illinois, 1981.
"Harvard Men Try Out for Wellesley Parts: Innovation Calls for Men to Carry Male Roles in 'The Man of Destiny' Under Auspices of Dramatic Club." *Harvard Crimson,* February 8, 1932.
Haygood, Atticus Greene. *Our Brothers in Black.* New York: Phillips and Hunt, 1881.
Heard, Alexander. *Speaking of the University: Two Decades at Vanderbilt University.* Nashville: Vanderbilt University Press, 1995.
Hill, David Spence. *Introduction to Vocational Education.* New York: Macmillan, 1920.
Holden, Alyce K. "Secular Music in Nashville, 1800–1900." Thesis, Fisk University, 1940.
Huggins, Mollie. *Tennessee Model Household Guide: Practical Help in the Household.* Nashville: Publishing House Methodist Episcopal Church South, 1897.
Jones, Thomas Jesse. *Educational Adaptations: Report of Ten Years' Work of the Phelps-Stokes Fund, 1910–1920.* New York: Phelps-Stokes Fund [c. 1920].
Josephsson, Axel. "Bicycles and Tricycles." *Twelfth Census of the United States, 1900.* Vol. 10, 325–39. Washington D.C., 1902.
Justi, Herman, ed. *Official History of the Tennessee Centennial Exposition 1897.* Nashville: Brandon Printing Co., 1898.
Killebrew, J. B. "J. B. Killebrew's Recollections of My Life." Southern Historical Collection, Wilson Library, University of North Carolina at Chapel Hill. Available online at http://www2.lib.unc.edu/mss/inv/k/Killebrew,J.B.html (accessed March 1, 2016).
Kirkland, James H. "Private Gifts to Education." *Independent* 54 (April–June 1902): .
Lee, Joseph. *Play and Playgrounds.* American Civic Association, Department of Public Recreation. Leaflet no. 11. January 1908.
Lockwood, Francis Cummins. *The Freshman and His College: A College Manual.* Boston: D. C. Heath, 1913.
Lyttle, Hulda M. "A School for Negro Nurses: At the George W. Hubbard Hospital and Meharry Medical College, Nashville, Tennessee." *American Journal of Nursing* 39, no. 2 (1939): 133–38.

McKenzie, Fayette Avery. *Ideals of Fisk: Inaugural Address of Doctor Fayette Avery McKenzie, on the Occasion of His Inauguration as the Fourth President of Fisk University, Nashville, Tennessee, November 9, 1915.* Nashville [1915].

Meharry, Frances. *History of the Meharry Family in America.* Lafayette, IN: Lafayette Printing, 1925.

Metropolitan Statistical Areas, Office of Management and Budget, 2015. http://www.census.gov/popest/data/metro/totals/2015/files/CBSA-EST2015-alldata.csv. Accessed April 26, 2016.

M'Ewen, John A. *An Address Delivered at the Laying of the Corner Stone of the University of Nashville.* Nashville: John T. S. Fall, 1853.

Moffat, Adelene. *Views of a Southern Woman: An Address before the Third Annual Conference of the National Association for the Advancement of Colored People.* New York: Allied Printing, 1911.

Nashville Board of Trade. *Yearbook of the Nashville Board of Trade.* Nashville: Marshall and Bruce, 1907–1908.

Nashville Departmental Annual Reports, 1894–1898. Nashville: Brandon Printing, 1898.

Official Catalogue of the Tennessee Centennial Exposition. Nashville, 1897.

O'Hagag, Anne. "The Athletic Girl." *Munsey's Magazine* 25 (August 1901): 730–37.

Paxson, Frederic L. "The Rise of Sport." *Mississippi Valley Historical Review* 4 (September 1917): 143–68.

Pike, Gustavus D. *The Jubilee Singers and Their Campaign for Twenty Thousand Dollars.* Boston: Lee and Shepard, 1873.

Proceedings of the Trustees of the Peabody Education Fund, from Their Original Organization, on the 8th of February. Cambridge, MA: John Wilson and Sons, 1875.

Race Problems of the South: Report of the Proceedings of the First Annual Conference Held under the Auspices of the Southern Society for the Promotion of the Study of Race Conditions and Problems in the South at Montgomery, Alabama. Richmond, VA: B. F. Johnson, 1900.

"Report of the President to the Board of Trustees of George Peabody College for Teachers." *Reports of the President: George Peabody College for Teachers.* Vol. 2, June 1920.

Reports of the Freedmen's Aid Society. Third Annual Report. 1868.

Sargent, Dudley A. *Health, Strength and Power.* Boston: H. M. Caldwell, 1904.

———. "The Place for Physical Training in the School and College Curriculum." *American Physical Education Review* 5 (March 1900): .

The Scroll of Phi Delta Theta Fraternity, 1903.

Smith, Charles Foster. "Southern Colleges and Schools." *Atlantic Monthly* 54 (1884): 548–56.

Some Reports of a Trip made by Booker T. Washington of Tuskegee Institute through the State of Tennessee, November 18–28, 1909. Reprinted from the *New York Evening Post.* N.p., n.d.

Southern Intercollegiate Athletic Association Handbook (1895), Vanderbilt University website, http://www.library.vanderbilt.edu/speccol/exhibits/Athletics/SIAA _handbook1895.pdf. Accessed April 20, 2015.

Standards in Sports for Girls and Women. Washington, DC: AAHPER, 1915.

Stanton, Elizabeth. "Women in Athletics." *North American Review* 3 (1882): 513–17.

Tennessee Baptist Convention Minutes, 1897.

Third Annual Conference of the National Association for the Advancement of Colored People. New York: Allied Printing, 1911.

United States Census Reports, 1880–1920; 1930; 2000.

Vanderbilt University Board of Trust, 1910–1913.

Washington, Booker T. "From an Address by Booker T. Washington at The Negro Baptist Convention, September 19, 1913." Booker T. Washington Society *website,* http://www.btwsociety.org. Accessed January 19, 2015.

The Wayne Handbook of Nashville, 1907.

Wells, Kate G. "The Transitional American Women." *Athletic Monthly* 11, no. 2 (1880): 821–23.

Winthrop, Robert. "Tribute to Eben Sperry Stearns, D. D., L. L. D., chancellor of the University, and president of the Normal college at Nashville, Tennessee." *Annual Meeting of the Trustees of the Peabody Education Fund in New York* (Cambridge, MA: John Wilson and Son), 1887.

Woodruff, Clinton Rogers. *Proceedings of the Atlantic City Conference for Good City Government and the Twelfth Annual Meeting of the National Municipal League.* National Municipal League, 1906.

Woody, Thomas. *A History of Women's Education in the United States.* New York: Science Press, 1929.

Yearbook of the Nashville Board of Trade. Nashville: Marshall and Bruce, 1907–1908.

Zook, George F., ed. *A Survey of Higher Education in Tennessee, 1924: By the United States Bureau of Education.* Nashville: Tennessee College Association, 1926.

Secondary Sources

Allison, Clinton B. "Philander Priestly Claxton." *Tennessee Encyclopedia of Culture and History.* Online edition, http:tennesseeencyclopedia.net (accessed October 20, 2015).

Anderson, Benedict. *Imagined Communities.* 3rd ed. London: Verso, 2006.

Anderson, James D. *The Education of Blacks in the South, 1860–1935.* Chapel Hill: University of North Carolina Press, 1988.

Ardener, Shirley. *Women and Space: Ground Rules and Social Maps.* New York: St. Martin's Press, 1981.

Ayers, Edward L. *The Promise of the New South: Life after Reconstruction.* New York: Oxford University Press, 1992.

Bachin, Robin. *Building the South Side: Urban Space and Civic Culture in Chicago, 1890–1919.* Chicago: University of Chicago Press, 2004.

Baker, Paula. "The Domestication of Politics: Women and American Political Society, 1780–1920" *American Historical Review* 89 (June 1984): 620–47.

Baltzell, E. Digby. *Philadelphia Gentlemen: The Making of a National Upper Class*. New York: Free Press, 1958.

Barth, Gunther. *City People: The Rise of Modern City Culture in Nineteenth-Century America*. New York: Oxford University Press, 1980.

Bateman, Lori B. "Separation, Coordination, and Coeducation: Southern Baptist Approaches to Women's Higher Education, 1880–1920." *Baptist History and Heritage* 38, no. 3 (2003): 88–99.

Bell, Daniel. *The Reforming of General Education: The Columbia College Experience in its National Setting*. New York: Columbia University Press, 1966.

Benedict, Sarah Bryan, Sarah Colley Cannon, and Mary Elizabeth Cayce. "The Bells of Ward- Belmont: A Reminiscence." *Tennessee Historical Quarterly* 30 (Winter 1971): 345–68.

Bennett, Bruce, ed. *The History of Physical Education and Sport*. Chicago: Athletic Institute, 1972.

Bennett, Kathy. "Lynching." *Tennessee Encyclopedia of Culture and History*. Online edition, https://tennesseeencyclopedia.net/entry.php?rec=816. Accessed January 20, 2016.

Bernhard, Virginia, Betty Brandon, Elizabeth Fox-Genovese, Theda Perdue, and Elizabeth H. Turner, eds. *Southern Women: Hidden Histories of Women in the New South*. Columbia: University of Missouri Press, 1994.

Bialeschki, M. Deborah. "'You Have to Have Some Fun to Go Along with Your Work': The Interplay of Race, Class, Gender and Leisure in the Industrial New South." *Journal of Leisure Research* 30 (1998): 79–101.

Blair, Karen J. *The Clubwoman as Feminist: True Womanhood Redefined, 1868–1914*. New York: Holmes and Meier, 1980.

Blumstein, James F., and Benjamin Walter, eds. *Growing Metropolis: Aspects of Development in Nashville*. Nashville: Vanderbilt University Press, 1975.

"Brief History of Lipscomb University." Lipscomb University website, http://www.lipscomb.edu/page.asp?SID=4&Page=2393. Accessed September 10, 2015.

Brooks, F. Erik, and Glenn L. Starks. *Historically Black Colleges and Universities: An Encyclopedia*. Santa Barbara, CA: Greenwood, 2011.

Brown, Leslie. *Upbuilding Black Durham: Gender, Class, and Black Community Development in the Jim Crow South*. Chapel Hill: University of North Carolina Press, 2008.

Brown, Mark. "Adelicia Acklen." *Tennessee Encyclopedia of History and Culture*. Online edition, https://tennesseeencyclopedia.net/entry.php?rec=1. Accessed November 1, 2015.

Brown, Tamara L., Gregory S. Parks, and Clarenda M. Phillips. *African American Fraternities and Sororities: The Legacy and the Vision*. Lexington: University Press of Kentucky, 2005.

Brownell, Blaine A., and David R. Goldfield, eds. *The City in Southern History: The Growth of Urban Civilization in the South.* Port Washington, NY: Kennikat Press, 1997.

Bryant, Jimmy. "From the UCA Archives: A Brief History of Women's Basketball." *Log Cabin Democrat* (Conway, AR), November 13, 2011, http://thecabin.net/sports/college. Accessed April 25, 2015.

Bucy, Carole Stanford. "Anne Dallas Dudley." *Tennessee Encyclopedia of History and Culture.* Online edition, http://tennesseeencyclopedia.net/entry.php?rec=406. Accessed December 4, 2015.

———. *Women Helping Women: The YWCA of Nashville, 1898–1998.* Nashville: J. S. Sanders, 1998.

Bulger, Margery A. "American Sportswomen in the 19th Century." *Journal of Popular Culture* 16, no. 2 (1982): 1–16.

Bullock, Henry Morton. *A History of Emory University.* Nashville: Parthenon Press, 1936.

Burt, Jesse C. *Nashville: Its Life and Times.* Nashville: Tennessee Book Company, 1959.

Butsch, Richard, ed. *For Fun and Profit: The Transformation of Leisure into Consumption.* Philadelphia: Temple University Press, 1990.

Button, H. Warren, and Eugene F. Provenzo, eds. *History of Education and Culture in America.* 2nd ed. Englewood Cliffs, NJ: Prentice Hall, 1989.

Calhoun, Charles, ed. *The Gilded Age: Perspectives on the Origins of Modern America.* 2nd ed. New York: Rowman and Littlefield, 2007.

Campbell, Barbara Kuhn. *The "Liberated" Woman of 1914: Prominent Women in the Progressive Era.* Ann Arbor: University of Michigan Press, 1979.

Caraway, Nancie. *Segregated Sisterhood: Racism and the Politics of American Feminism.* Knoxville: University of Tennessee Press, 1991.

Cardon, Nathan. "The South's 'New Negroes' and African American Visions of Progress at the Atlanta and Nashville International Expositions." *Journal of Southern History* 80, no. 2 (2014): 287–326.

Carey, Bill. *Fortunes, Fiddles and Fried Chicken: A Nashville Business History.* Franklin, TN: Hillsboro Press, 2000.

———. "A Place for a Damned Fool or an Eskimo." *Nashville Post,* March 22, 2000, http://www.nashvillepost.com/home/article/20446258/a-place-for-a-damned-fool-or-an-eskimo. Accessed April 7, 2016.

———. "Stargazing, Vanderbilt Football and 'Bachelor of Ugliness' Reigned 100 Years Ago." *Vanderbilt Register,* December 20, 2013.

"Centennial Park." Nashville Metro Parks *website,* https://www.nashville.gov/Parks-and-Recreation/Parks/Centennial-Park.aspx. Accessed April 15, 2015.

"Charles Dana Gibson and the Gibson Girls." Lively Roots website, http://www.livelyroots.com/things/gibsongirl.htm. Accessed on April 10, 2008.

Clinton, Catherine. *The Other Civil War: American Women in the Nineteenth Century.* New York: Farrar, Straus and Giroux, 1984.

———. *The Plantation Mistress.* New York: Pantheon, 1983.

Cohen, Arthur. *The Shaping of American Higher Education: Emergence and Growth of the Contemporary System.* San Francisco: Jossey-Bass, 1998.

Cohen, Michael David. *Reconstructing the Campus: Higher Education and the American Civil War.* Charlottesville: University of Virginia Press, 2012.

Cohen, Rodney T. *Fisk University.* Charleston, SC: Arcadia Publishing, 2001.

Coleman, David. "The History of Historically Black Colleges and Universities." HBCU Connect website, http://hbcuconnect.com/history.shtml. Accessed September 13, 2015.

College Football Data Warehouse website, http://www.cfbdatawarehouse.com. Accessed April 18, 2016.

Collins, L. M. *One Hundred Years of Fisk University Presidents, 1875–1975.* Nashville: Hemphill's Creative Printing, 2002.

Conable, Charlotte Williams. *Women at Cornell: The Myth of Equal Education.* Ithaca, NY: Cornell University Press, 1977.

Conkin, Paul E. *Gone with the Ivy: A Biography of Vanderbilt University.* Knoxville: University of Tennessee Press, 1985.

———. *Peabody College: From a Frontier Academy to the Frontiers of Teaching and Learning.* Nashville: Vanderbilt University Press, 2002.

Conway, Jill K. "Perspectives on the History of Women's Education in the United States." *History of Education Quarterly* 14 (Spring 1974): 1–12.

Coryell, Janet L., Martha H. Swain, Sandra Gioia Treadway, and Elizabeth Hayes Turner, eds. *Beyond Image and Convention: Explorations in Southern Women's History.* Columbia: University of Missouri Press, 1998.

Coryell, Janet L., Thomas H. Appleton Jr., Anastatia Sims, and Sandra Gioia Treadway, eds. *Negotiating Boundaries of Southern Womanhood: Dealing with the Powers That Be.* Columbia: University of Missouri Press, 2000.

Cott, Nancy F. *The Grounding of Modern Feminism.* New Haven, CT: Yale University Press, 1987.

Couto, Richard. "Race Relations and Tennessee Centennials." *Tennessee Historical Quarterly* 55, no. 2 (1996): 144–59.

Cox, Marcus S. *Segregated Soldiers: Military Training at Historically Black Colleges in the Jim Crow South.* Baton Rouge: Louisiana State University Press, 2013.

Cullen, Jim. *The Art of Democracy: A Concise History of Popular Culture in the United States.* New York: Monthly Review Press, 2002.

Davis, Allen. *Spearheads for Reform: The Social Settlements and the Progressive Movement, 1890–1914.* New Brunswick, NJ: Rutgers University Press, 1984.

Davis, Janet. *The Circus Age: Culture and Society under the American Big Top.* Chapel Hill: University of North Carolina Press, 2002.

Dean, Pamela. "'Dear Sister' and 'Hated Rivals': Athletics and Gender at Two New South Women's Colleges, 1893–1920." *Journal of Sport History* 24 (1997): 341–57.

DeBare, Ilana. *Where Girls Come First: The Rise, Fall, and Surprising Revival of Girls' Schools.* New York: Penguin, 2004.

deGregory, Crystal. "Raising a Nonviolent Army: Four Nashville Black Colleges and the Century-Long Struggle for Civil Rights." Ph.D. diss., Vanderbilt University, 2011.

Dennis, Michael. "The Illusion of Relevance: Southern Progressives and American Higher Education." *Journal of the Historical Society* 8, no. 2 (2008): 229–71.

———. *Lessons in Progress: State Universities and Progressivism in the New South, 1880–1920*. Urbana: University of Illinois Press, 2001.

Deutsch, Sarah. *Women and the City: Gender, Space, and Power in Boston, 1870–1940*. New York: Oxford University Press, 2000.

Dickenson, W. Calvin. "Temperance." *Tennessee Encyclopedia of Culture and History*. Online edition, https://tennesseeencyclopedia.net/entry.php?rec=1302. Accessed September 13, 2015.

Dorn, Sherman. *A Brief History of Peabody College*. Nashville: Vanderbilt University Press, 1996.

Dotson, Rand. *Roanoke, Virginia, 1882–1912: Magic City of the New South*. Knoxville: University of Tennessee Press, 2007.

Doyle, Andrew. "Causes Won, Not Lost: College Football and the Modernization of the American South." *International Journal of the History of Sport* 11, no. 2 (1994): 231–51.

———. "Foolish and Useless Sport: The Southern Evangelical Crusade Against Intercollegiate Football." *Journal of Sport History* 24, no. 3 (1997): 317–40.

———. "Turning the Tide: College Football and Southern Progressivism." *Southern Cultures* 3, no. 3 (1997): 28–51.

Doyle, Don H. "Hilary Howse." *Tennessee Encyclopedia of History and Culture*. Online edition, http://tennesseeencyclopedia.net/entry.php?rec=665. Accessed April 4, 2015.

———. *Nashville in the New South, 1880–1930*. Knoxville: University of Tennessee Press, 1985.

———. *Nashville since the 1920s*. Knoxville: University of Tennessee Press, 1985.

———. *New Men, New Cities, New South: Atlanta, Nashville, Charleston, Mobile, 1860–1910*. Chapel Hill: University of North Carolina Press, 1990.

Dulles, Foster Rhea. *America Learns to Play: A History of Popular Recreation, 1607–1940*. Gloucester, MA: Peter Smith, 1963.

Duncan, Ivar Lou Myhr. *A History of Belmont College*. Nashville: Belmont College, 1966.

Durham, Walter. *Reluctant Partners: Nashville and the Union, 1863–1865*. 1985. Reprint, Knoxville: University of Tennessee Press, 2008.

Ebert, Joel. "Clinton Makes Closing Arguments in Tennessee." *Tennessean*, February 29, 2016, http://www.tennessean.com/story/news/politics/2016/02/28/hillary-clinton-speak-nashvilles-maherry-medical-college-today/80925186/. Accessed May 1, 2016.

Edwards, Rebecca. *New Spirits: Americans in the Gilded Age, 1865–1905*. New York: Oxford University Press, 2006.

———. *Angels in the Machinery: Gender in American Party Politics from the Civil War to the Progressive Era*. New York: Oxford University Press, 1997.

Eiland, William U. *Nashville's Mother Church: The History of the Ryman Auditorium.* Nashville: Opryland USA, 1992.

Elias, Megan. *Stir It Up: Home Economics in American Culture.* Philadelphia: University of Pennsylvania Press, 2010.

Evins, Mary A., ed. *Tennessee Women in the Progressive Era: Toward the Public Sphere in the New South.* Knoxville: University of Tennessee Press, 2013.

Ezzell, Tim. *Chattanooga, 1865–1900: A City Set Down in Dixie.* Knoxville: University of Tennessee Press, 2013.

Fairclough, Adam. *A Class of Their Own: Black Teachers in the Segregated South.* Cambridge, MA: Belknap Press of Harvard University Press, 2007.

Farnham, Christie Anne. *The Education of the Southern Belle: Higher Education and Student Socialization in the Antebellum South.* New York: New York University Press, 1994.

Fass, Paula. *The Damned and the Beautiful: American Youth in the 1920s.* New York: Oxford University Press, 1977.

Faust, Drew Gilpin. *Mothers of Invention: Women of the Slaveholding South in the American Civil War.* Chapel Hill: University of North Carolina Press, 2004.

Finkelman, Paul, ed. *Encyclopedia of African American History, 1896 to Present.* New York: Oxford University Press, 2009.

"Fisk University." *The American Experience Series,* 2000. PBS website, http://www.pbs.org/wgbh/amex/singers/peopleevents/pande06.html. Accessed January 20, 2016.

Flanagan, Maureen. *Seeing with Their Hearts: Chicago Women and the Vision of the Good City, 1871–1933.* Princeton, NJ: Princeton University Press, 2002.

Florida, Richard. *Cities and the Creative Class.* New York: Routledge, 2004.

"Former L&C Head Dies." *Nashville Post,* June 14, 2002, https://www.nashvillepost.com/news/2002/6/13/former_lc_head_dudley_dies. Accessed December 4, 2015.

Fraser, James W. *Preparing America's Teachers: A History.* New York: Teachers College Press, 2006.

Frost, Dan R. *Thinking Confederates: Academia and the Idea of Progress in the New South.* Knoxville: University of Tennessee Press, 2005.

"The Fugitives and Agrarians." Jean and Alexander Heard Library, Vanderbilt University website, http://www.library.vanderbilt.edu/speccol/vuhistory/fugitives_agrarians.php. Accessed Feb. 12, 2016.

Gasman, Marybeth, and Roger L. Geiger, eds. *Higher Education for African Americans Before the Civil Rights Era, 1900–1964.* New Brunswick, NJ: Rutgers University Press, 2012.

Gerber, Ellen W. *Innovators and Institutions in Physical Education.* Philadelphia: Lea and Febiger, 1971.

Gidlow, Liette. *The Big Vote: Gender, Consumer Culture, and the Politics of Exclusion, 1890s–1920s.* Baltimore: Johns Hopkins University Press, 2004.

Gillespie, Michele, and Catherine Clinton, eds. *Taking Off the White Gloves: Southern Women and Southern Historians.* Columbia: University of Missouri Press, 1998.

Gilmore, Glenda Elizabeth. *Gender and Jim Crow: Women and the Politics of White*

Supremacy in North Carolina, 1896–1920. Chapel Hill: University of North Carolina Press, 1996.
"Go Greek." Lipscomb University website, http://www.lipscomb.edu/gogreek. Accessed May 7, 2016.
Goings, Kenneth W., and Raymond A. Mohl, eds. *The New African America Urban History*. Thousand Oaks, CA: Sage, 1996.
Gold, David, and Catherine L. Hobbs. *Educating the New Southern Woman: Speech, Writing, and Race at the Public Women's Colleges, 1884–1945*. Carbondale: Southern Illinois University Press, 2014.
Goldin, Claudia. "The Female Labor Force and American Economic Growth, 1890–1980." In *Long-Term Factors in American Economic Growth,* ed. Stanley L. Engerman and Robert E. Gallman, 557–604. University of Chicago Press, 1986. Available online at http://www.nber.org/chapters/c9688.pdf. Accessed October 30, 2015.
"Good to Be Greek." *Vanderbilt Magazine,* April 7, 2010, http://news.vanderbilt.edu/vanderbiltmagazine/good-to-be-greek/. Accessed May 5, 2016.
Goodenow, Ronald K., and Arthur O. White, eds. *Education and the Rise of the New South*. Boston: Hall, 1981.
Gordon, Lynn. *Gender and Higher Education in the Progressive Era, 1890–1920*. New Haven, CT: Yale University Press, 1990.
———. "The Gibson Girl Goes to College: Popular Culture and Women's Higher Education in the Progressive Era, 1890–1920." *American Quarterly* 39 (Summer 1987): 211–30.
Grantham, Dewey W. "The Contours of Southern Progressivism." *American Historical Review* 86, no. 5 (1981): 1035–59.
———. *The Democratic South*. Athens: University of Georgia Press, 1963.
———. *Southern Progressivism: The Reconciliation of Progress and Tradition*. Knoxville: University of Tennessee Press, 1983.
"Greek Life." Belmont University website, http://belmont.edu/organizations/greek/index.html. Accessed May 7, 2016.
Green, Harvey. *Fit for America: Health, Fitness, Sport, and American Society*. New York: Pantheon, 1986.
Grundy, Pamela. "From Amazons to Glamazons: The Rise and Fall of North Carolina Women's Basketball, 1920–1960." *Journal of American History* 87 (June 2000): 112–46.
———. "'We Always Tried to Be Good People': Respectability, Crazy Water Crystals, and Hillbilly Music on the Air, 1933–1935." *Journal of American History* 81 (March 1995): 1591–1620.
Guy-Sheftall, Beverly. "Black Women and Higher Education: Spelman and Bennett Colleges Revisited." *Journal of Negro Education* 51 (1982): 278–86.
Hackney, Sheldon. "Origins of the New South in Retrospect." *Journal of Southern History* 38 (May 1972): 191–216.
Hale, Grace Elizabeth. *Making Whiteness: The Culture of Segregation in the South, 1890– 1940*. New York: Vintage Books, 1998.

Halsey, Elizabeth. *Women in Physical Education*. New York: G. D. Putnam's Sons, 1961.
Hanchett, Thomas. *Sorting Out the New South City: Race, Class, and Urban Development in Charlotte, 1875–1975*. Chapel Hill: University of North Carolina Press, 1998.
Hansen, Axel C. "George W. Hubbard Hospital, 1910–1961." *Journal of the National Medical Association* 54, no. 1 (1962): 1–16.
Hardy, Stephen. *How Boston Played: Sport, Recreation, and Community, 1865–1915*. Knoxville: University of Tennessee Press, 2003.
Harvey, Bruce G. *World's Fairs in a Southern Accent: Atlanta, Nashville, and Charleston, 1895–1902*. Knoxville: University of Tennessee Press, 2014.
Harwarth, Irene. *Women's Colleges in the United States: History, Issues, and Challenges*. Washington D.C.: U.S. Department of Education, 1997.
Havighurst, Craig. *Air Castle of the South: WSM and the Making of Music City*. Chicago: University of Illinois Press, 2007.
Hickey, Georgina. *Hope and Danger in the New South City: Working-Class Women and Urban Development in Atlanta, 1890–1940*. Athens: University of Georgia Press, 2003.
Higginbotham, Evelyn Brooks. *Righteous Discontent: The Women's Movement in the Black Baptist Church, 1880–1920*. Cambridge, MA: Harvard University Press, 1993.
Hine, Darlene Clark. *Black Women in White: Racial Conflict and Cooperation in the Nursing Profession, 1890–1950*. Bloomington: Indiana University Press, 1989.
"History of Vanderbilt University." Vanderbilt University website, http://www.vanderbilt.edu/about/history/. Accessed March 12, 2015.
Hoffschwelle, Mary S. "The Science of Domesticity: Home Economics at George Peabody College for Teachers, 1914–1939." *Journal of Southern History* 57, no. 4 (1991): 659–80.
Holden, Alyce K. "Secular Music in Nashville, 1800–1900." Thesis, Fisk University, 1940.
Honan, William H. "Vanderbilt U. Receives a Gift of $300 Million." *New York Times*, December 1, 1998, http://www.nytimes.com/1998/12/01/us/vanderbilt-u-receives-a-gift-of-300-million.html. Accessed May 1, 2016.
Hornbuckle, Adam R. "Women's Sports and Physical Education at the University of Tennessee: 1899–1939." Thesis, University of Tennessee, 1983.
Horowitz, Helen Lefkowitz. *Alma Mater: Design and Experience in the Women's Colleges from Their Nineteenth Century Beginnings to the 1930s*. 2nd ed. Amherst: University of Massachusetts Press, 1993.
———. *Campus Life: Undergraduate Cultures from the End of the Eighteenth Century to the Present*. New York: Knopf, 1987.
Howell, Reet, ed. *Her Story in Sport*. New York: Leisure Press, 1982.
Ingram, Martha. *Apollo's Struggle: A Performing Arts Odyssey in the Athens of the South, Nashville, Tennessee*. Franklin, TN: Hillsboro Press, 2004.
Ingrassia, Brian. *The Rise of Gridiron University: Higher Education's Uneasy Alliance with Big-Time Football*. Lawrence: University Press of Kansas, 2012.
Isaac, Paul E. *Prohibition and Politics: Turbulent Decades in Tennessee, 1886–1920*. Knoxville: University of Tennessee Press, 1965.

Isenberg, Alison. *Downtown America: A History of the Place and the People Who Made It*. Chicago: University of Chicago Press, 2005.
Israel, Charles A. *Before Scopes: Evangelicalism, Education, and Evolution in Tennessee, 1870–1925*. Athens: University of Georgia Press, 2004.
"James Hildreth Named Meharry's Next President." *Tennessean,* July 5, 2015, 1.
Jeffries, Hasan Kwame. "Fields of Play: The Mediums through Which Black Athletes Engaged in Sports in Jim Crow Georgia." *Journal of Negro History* 86 (2001): 264–75.
Johnson, Donald. "W. E. B. Du Bois, Thomas Jesse Jones and the Struggle for Social Education, 1900–1930." *Journal of Negro History* 85 (Summer 2000): 71–95.
Johnson, Joan Marie. "Job Market or Marriage Market? Life Choices for Southern Women Educated at Northern Colleges, 1875–1915." *History of Education Quarterly* 47, no. 2 (2007): 149–72.
———. *Southern Women at the Seven Sister Colleges: Feminist Values and Social Activism, 1875–1915*. Athens: University of Georgia Press, 2010.
Johnson, Leland R. *The Parks of Nashville: A History of the Board of Parks and Recreation*. Nashville: Metropolitan Nashville and Davidson County Board of Parks and Recreation, 1986.
Jones, Lance G. E. *The Jeanes Teacher in the United States, 1908–1933: An Account of Twenty-Five Years' Experience in the Supervision of Negro Rural Schools*. Chapel Hill: University of North Carolina Press, 1937.
Judson, Sarah Mercer. "Leisure Is a Foe to Any Man: The Pleasures and Dangers of Leisure in Atlanta during World War I." *Journal of Women's History* 15 (2003): 92–115.
Kasson, John F. *Amusing the Millions: Coney Island at the Turn of the Century*. New York: Hill and Wang, 1978.
Kennard, June A. "History of Physical Education." *SIGNS* 2 (4, 1977): 835–42.
Kerber, Linda. *No Constitutional Right to Be Ladies: Women and the Obligations of Citizenship*. New York: Hill and Wang, 1999.
Kirby, Jack Temple. *Darkness and the Dawning: Race and Reform in the Progressive South*. Philadelphia: J. B. Lippincott, 1972.
Klafs, Carl E. *The Female Athlete*. St. Louis: C. V. Mosby, 1973.
Klein, Maury. *History of the Louisville and Nashville Railroad*. New York: MacMillan, 1972.
Knowles, Malcolm S. *The Adult Education Movement in the United States*. New York: Holt, Rinehart and Winston, 1962.
Kolko, Gabriel. *Railroads and Regulation, 1877–1916*. New York: Norton, 1965.
Kyriakoudes, Louis M. *The Social Origins of the Urban South*. Chapel Hill: University of North Carolina Press, 2003.
"L. Randolph III." Lipscomb University website, https://secure.lipscomb.edu/president/biography (accessed May 6, 2016).
LaBue, Anthony. "Teacher Certification in the United States: A Brief History." *Journal of Teacher Education* 11 no. 2 (1960): 147–72.

Lamon, Lester. *Black Tennesseans, 1900–1930*. Knoxville: University of Tennessee Press, 1977.

——. "The Tennessee Agricultural and Industrial Normal School: Public Education for Black Tennesseans." *Tennessee Historical Quarterly* 32, no. 1 (1973): 42–58.

Larson, Lawrence. *The Urban South: A History*. Lexington: University Press of Kentucky, 1990.

Lasser, Carol, ed. *Educating Men and Women Together*. Urbana: University of Illinois Press, 1987.

Lears, Jackson. *Rebirth of a Nation: The Making of Modern America, 1877–1920*. New York: HarperCollins, 2009.

Lears, T. J. Jackson. *No Place of Grace: Antimodernism and the Transformation of American Culture, 1880–1920*. New York: Pantheon, 1981.

Lee, Mabel. *A History of Physical Education and Sports in the U.S.A.* New York: John Wiley and Sons, 1983.

Leloudis, James L. *Schooling the New South: Pedagogy, Self, and Society in North Carolina, 1880–1920*. Chapel Hill: University of Chapel Hill Press, 1996.

Levine, Lawrence W. *Highbrow/Lowbrow: The Emergence of Cultural Hierarchy in America*. Cambridge, MA: Harvard University Press, 1988.

Lewis, Charles L. *Philander Priestley Claxton: Crusader for Public Education*. Knoxville: University of Tennessee Press, 1948.

Lewis, David Levering. *W. E. B. Du Bois, 1868–1919: The Biography of a Race*. New York: Henry Holt, 1994.

——. *W. E. B. Du Bois, 1919–1963: The Fight for Equality and the American Century*. New York: Henry Holt, 2001.

"Life in Nashville." Meharry Medical College website, http://www.mmc.edu/prospectivestudents/nashville.html (Accessed May 8, 2016).

Link, Arthur S., and Richard McCormick. *Progressivism*. Arlington Heights, IL: Harlan Davidson, 1983.

Link, William A. *The Paradox of Southern Progressivism, 1880–1930*. Chapel Hill: University of North Carolina Press, 1992.

Logan, Erin, and Guy Russo. "Vanderbilt University Wants Our Bodies but Not Our Baggage." *Huffington Post*. November 16, 2015, http://www.huffingtonpost.com/erin-logan/vanderbilt-university-wants-our-bodies_b_8572830.html. Accessed April 30, 2016.

Logsdon, David R. "Erskine Bronson Ingram." *Tennessee Encyclopedia of History and Culture. Online edition,* http://tennesseeencyclopedia.net/entry.php?rec=685. Accessed May 14, 2016.

Lovett, Bobby L. *The African-American History of Nashville, Tennessee, 1780–1930: Elites and Dilemmas*. Fayetteville: University of Arkansas Press, 1999.

——. *The Civil Rights Movement in Tennessee: A Narrative History*. Knoxville: University of Tennessee Press, 2005.

———. "Roger Williams University." *Tennessee Encyclopedia of History and Culture.* Online edition, https://tennesseeencyclopedia.net/entry.php?rec=1147. Accessed September 13, 2015.

———. "Tennessee State University." *Tennessee Encyclopedia of History and Culture.* Online edition, https://tennesseeencyclopedia.net/entry.php?rec=1358.

———. "Tennessee State University: A Synopsis of 'A Touch of Greatness,' 1912–2012." *Engaged: The Journal of Tennessee State University* 1, no. 11 (2012): 1–23.

———. *A Touch of Greatness: A History of Tennessee State University.* Macon, GA: Mercer University Press, 2013.

———. "Walden University." Tennessee State University Library Digital Collection, http://ww2.tnstate.edu/library/digital/walden.htm. Accessed October 18, 2015.

———. "William Jasper Hale." *Tennessee Encyclopedia of History and Culture.* Online edition, https://tennesseeencyclopedia.net/entry.php?rec=584. Accessed January 19, 2016.

Lovett, Bobby L., and Linda T. Wynn, eds. *Profiles of African Americans in Tennessee.* Nashville: Annual Local Conference on Afro-American Culture and History, 1996.

Lowe, Margaret A. *Looking Good: College Women and Body Image, 1875–1930.* Baltimore: Johns Hopkins University Press, 2003.

Lucas, Christopher. *American Higher Education: A History.* New York: Macmillan, 2006.

Lykes, Richard Wayne. *Higher Education and the United States Office of Education, 1867–1953.* Washington D.C.: Bureau of Postsecondary Education, United States Office of Education, 1975.

Lystra, Karen. *Searching the Heart: Women, Men, and Romantic Love in Nineteenth-Century America.* New York: Oxford University Press, 1989.

Maiden, Lewis Smith. *Highlights of the Nashville Theater, 1876–1890.* New York: Vantage Press, 1979.

Matthews, Jean V. *The Rise of the New Woman: The Women's Movement in America, 1875–1930.* Chicago: Ivan R. Dee, 2003.

McBee, Randy. *Dance Hall Days: Intimacy and Leisure among Working-Class Immigrants in the United States.* New York: New York University Press, 2000.

McCandless, Amy Thompson. "Maintaining the Spirit and Tone of Robust Manliness: The Battle against Coeducation at Southern Colleges and Universities, 1890–1940." *NWSA Journal* 2, no. 2 (1990): 199–216.

———. *The Past in the Present: Women's Higher Education in the Twentieth-Century American South.* Tuscaloosa: University of Alabama Press, 1999.

———. "Progressivism and the Higher Education of Southern Women." *North Carolina Historical Review* 70, no. 3 (1993): 320–23.

McCormick, Richard L. "The Discovery That Business Corrupts Politics: A Reappraisal of the Origins of Progressivism." *American Historical Review* 86, no. 2 (1981), 247–74.

McGerr, Michael. *A Fierce Discontent: The Rise and Fall of the Progressive Movement in America, 1870–1920.* New York: Free Press, 2003.

McRaven, Henry. *Nashville, "Athens of the South."* Chapel Hill, NC: Scheer and Jervis, 1949.

Meier, August. *Negro Thought in America*. Ann Arbor: University of Michigan Press, 1963.

Miller, Patrick B. "'The Manly, the Moral and the Proficient': College Sport in the New South." *Journal of Sport History* 24, no. 3 (1997): 285–316.

———. "To 'Bring the Race along Rapidly': Sport, Student Culture, and Educational Mission at Historically Black Colleges during the Interwar Years." *History of Education Quarterly* 35, no. 2 (1995): 111–33.

Mims, Edwin. *The Advancing South: Stories of Progress and Reaction*. Garden City, NY: Doubleday, Page, 1926.

Mitchell, Reavis, Jr. "George Edmund Haynes." Tennessee Encyclopedia of History and Culture. Online edition, https://tennesseeencyclopedia.net/entry.php?rec=614.

———. "Meharry Medical College." *Tennessee Encyclopedia of Culture and History*. Online edition, http://tennesseeencyclopedia.net/entry.php?rec=885. Accessed January 13, 2016.

———. *Thy Loyal Children Make Their Way: Fisk University Since 1866*. Nashville: Fisk University Press, 1995.

Model T Ford Club of America website, http://www.mtfca.com. Accessed September 13, 2015.

Mohl, Raymond. *The New City: Urban America in the Industrial Age, 1860–1920*. Arlington Heights, IL: Harlan Davidson, 1985.

Mohr, Clarence L. "Minds of the New South: Higher Education in Black and White, 1880–1915." *Southern Quarterly* 46, no. 4 (2009): 8–34.

Montgomery, Rebecca S. *The Politics of Education in the New South: Women and Reform in Georgia, 1890–1930*. Baton Rouge: Louisiana State University Press, 2006.

Moore, Gilbertine. *Gilly Goes to Ward-Belmont*. Nashville: Benson Printing, 1973.

Morrison, Louise Douglas. *A Voyage of Faith: The Story of Harpeth Hall*. Nashville: Harpeth Hall, 1980.

Neverdon-Morton, Cynthia. *Afro-American Women of the South and the Advancement of the Race, 1895–1925*. Knoxville: University of Tennessee Press, 1989.

Newcomer, Mabel. *A Century of Higher Education for American Women*. New York: Harper and Brothers, 1959.

Nicholson, Christopher. "To Advance a Race: A Historical Analysis of the Intersection of Personal Belief, Industrial Philanthropy and Black Liberal Arts Higher Education in Fayette McKenzie's Presidency at Fisk University, 1915–1925." Ph.D. diss., Loyola University Chicago. Loyola eCommons, http://ecommons.luc.edu/luc_diss/153. Accessed January 30, 2016.

"Our Mission and History." Montgomery Bell Academy website, http://www.montgomerybell.edu/Page/About-MBA/Our-Mission—History. Accessed September 30, 2015.

Owens, Ann Marie Deer. "BOT Member, Community, and Business Leader Dudley Dies." *Vanderbilt Register,* June 24, 2002, http://news.vanderbilt.edu/archived-news/register/articles/index-id=6292.html. Accessed December 3, 2014.

Pace, Robert. *Halls of Honor: College Men in the Old South.* Baton Rouge: Louisiana State University Press, 2011.

Paden, Fran. "Moffat, Mary Adalene, 1862–1956." *Grundy County History,* 2004, Revised 2008.

Paine, Ophelia Thompson. *Glen Leven: A Family Story.* Sewanee, TN: Tree of Life Memoirs, 2016.

Patterson, Jim. "Vanderbilt's Peabody No. 1 Education School for Fifth Consecutive Year." *Vanderbilt News,* March 12, 2013, http://news.vanderbilt.edu/2013/03/usnews-graduate-2013/.

Payne, Arthur F. *Administration of Vocational Education: With Special Emphasis on the Administration of Vocational Industrial Education under the Federal Vocational Law.* New York: McGraw-Hill, 1924.

Peiss, Kathy. *Cheap Amusements: Working Women and Leisure in Turn-of-the-Century New York.* Philadelphia: Temple University Press, 1986.

Perkins, Linda. "The National Association of College Women: Vanguard of Black Women's Leadership and Education, 1923–1954." *Journal of Education* 172 (1990): 65–75.

Perry, Elisabeth Israels. "Men Are from the Gilded Age, Women Are from the Progressive Era." *Journal of the Gilded Age and Progressive Era* 1 (January 2002): 25–48.

Pethel, Mary Ellen. *All-Girls Education from Ward Seminary to Harpeth Hall, 1865–2015.* Charleston, SC: History Press, 2015.

———. *Home Sweet Home: A History of the West End Home Foundation.* Archival exhibit text. Nashville Metropolitan Library, October 2014–March 2015.

———. "Lift Every Female Voice: Education and Activism in Nashville's African American Community, 1870–1940." In *Tennessee Women,* vol. 2, ed. Beverly Bond and Sarah Wilkerson-Freeman, 239–69. Athens: University of Georgia Press, 2015.

———. "Sport and the Outward Life: Young Women Athletes as Progressive Players." *Tennessee Women in the Progressive Era: Toward the Public Sphere in the New South.* ed. Mary A. Evins . Knoxville: University of Tennessee Press, 2013.

Pfeifer, Michael J. *Rough Justice: Lynching and American Society, 1874–1947.* Urbana: University of Illinois Press, 2004.

Pittman, S. P. *Lipscomb's Golden Heritage, 1891–1941.* Nashville: Associated Ladies for Lipscomb, 1983.

Rabinovitz, Lauren. *For the Love of Pleasure: Women, Movies, and Culture in Turn-of-the-Century Chicago.* New Brunswick, NJ: Rutgers University Press, 1998.

Rabinowitz, Howard N. *Race, Ethnicity, and Urbanization: Selected Essays.* Columbia: University of Missouri Press, 1994.

Rader, Benjamin. *American Sports: From the Age of Folk Games to the Age of Spectators.* Englewood Cliffs, NJ: Prentice Hall, 1983.

Ramsey, Sonya Yvette. *Reading, Writing, and Segregation: A Century of Black Women Teachers in Nashville.* Urbana: University of Illinois Press, 2007.

Redlich, Fritz. "Leisure-Time Activities: A Historical, Sociological, and Economic Analysis." *Explorations in Entrepreneurial History* 3 (1965): 3–23.

Richardson, Joe M. *A History of Fisk University: 1865–1946*. Tuscaloosa: University of Alabama Press, 1980.

Riess, Steven A. *City Games: The Evolution of American Urban Society and the Rise of Sports*. Urbana: University of Illinois Press, 1991.

Riley, Mark B. "Edgefield: A Study of Nashville's First Suburb." *Tennessee Historical Quarterly* 37, no. 2 (1978): 125–45.

"Robert Fisher, Ph.D." Biographical sketch. Meharry Medical College website, https://www.mmc.edu/about/rwjf/docs/robert_fisher_bio.pdf. Accessed May 6, 2016.

Roberts, Samuel Kelton. *Infectious Fear: Politics, Disease, and the Health Effects of Segregation*. Chapel Hill: University of North Carolina Press, 2009.

Rosoff, Nancy G. "'Every Muscle Is Absolutely Free': Advertising and Advice about Clothing for Athletic American Women." *Journal of American Culture* 25 (2002): 25–31.

Royster, Jacqueline, ed. *Southern Horrors and Other Writings: The Anti-Lynching Campaign of Ida B. Wells, 1892–1900*. New York: Bedford/St. Martin's, 1996.

Rudolph, Frederick. *The American College and University*. New York: Knopf, 1962.

———. *Curriculum: A History of the American Undergraduate Course of Study Since 1636*. San Francisco: Jossey-Bass, 1977.

Saylor, Roger. Southern Intercollegiate Athletic Association, College Football Historical Society website, http://library.la84.org/SportsLibrary/CFHSN/CFHSNv06/CFHSN v06n2g.pdf. Accessed March 1, 2015. Master's thesis.

Scarbrough, Emily. "'Fine Dignity, Picturesque Beauty, and Serious Purpose': The Reorientation of Suffrage Media in the Twentieth Century." Master's thesis, Eastern Illinois University, 2015. Available online at The Keep, Eastern Illinois University, Thesis, Paper 2033, http://thekeep.eiu.edu/theses/2033. Accessed March 23, 2016.

Schlesinger, Arthur M. *A History of American Life*. Vol. 12, *The Rise of the City, 1878–1898*. New York: Macmillan, 1931.

Schmidt, Peter. *Back to Nature: The Arcadian Myth in Urban America*. Baltimore: Johns Hopkins University Press, 1990.

Schmidt, Raymond. *Shaping College Football: The Transformation of an American Sport, 1919–1930*. Syracuse, NY: Syracuse University Press, 2007.

Schneider, Carl J., and Dorothy Schneider. *American Women in the Progressive Era, 1900–1920*. New York: Anchor, 1993.

Schuyler, David. *The New Urban Landscape: The Redefinition of Urban Form in Nineteenth-Century America*. Baltimore: Johns Hopkins University Press, 1986.

Schwager, Sally. "Educating Women in America." *SIGNS* 12 (Winter 1987): 336–56.

Scott, Anne Firor. *The Southern Lady: From Pedestal to Politics, 1830–1930*. Chicago: University of Chicago Press, 1970.

———. "Women, Religion, and Social Change in the South, 1830–1930." In Samuel S. Hill Jr., with Edgar T. Thompson, Anne Firor Scott, Charles Hudson, and Edward S. Gaustad. *Religion and the Solid South*. Nashville: Abingdon Press, 1972.

Scraton, Shelia. *Shaping Up to Womanhood: Gender and Girls' Physical Education*. Buckingham, UK: Open University Press, 1992.

Sealander, Judith. *Grand Plans: Business Progressivism and Social Change in Ohio's Miami Valley, 1890–1929.* Lexington: University of Kentucky Press, 1988.
Seiter, Courtney. "Nashville: 'It' City." *Tennessean,* October 8, 2014, 1.
"The Seven Sisters." Mt. Holyoke College website, http://www.mtholyoke.edu/cic/about/12812.shtml. Accessed March 3, 2016.
Shaw, Stephanie. *What a Woman Ought to Be and to Do: Black Professional Women Workers in the Jim Crow Era.* Chicago: University of Chicago Press, 1996.
Simpson, John A. *Edith Pope and Her Nashville Friends: Guardians of the Lost Cause in the* Confederate Veteran. Knoxville: University of Tennessee Press, 2003.
Smith, Jessie Carney. *Notable Black American Women.* Book II. Detroit: Gale, 1996.
Smith-Rosenberg, Carroll. *Disorderly Conduct: Visions of Gender in Victorian America.* New York: Knopf, 1985.
Solomon, Barbara M. *In the Company of Educated Women: A History of Women and Higher Education in America.* New Haven, CT: Yale University Press, 1985.
Somers, Dale A. "The Leisure Revolution: Recreation in the American City, 1820–1920." *Journal of Popular Culture* 5 (Summer 1971): 125–47.
Spears, Betty. "The Emergence of Women in Sport." *Women's Athletics: Coping With Controversy.* Washington D.C.: AAHPER Publications, 1974.
Spurlock, John C., and Cynthia A. Magistro. *The Transformation of American Women's Emotional Culture.* New York: New York University Press, 1998.
Stage, Sarah, and Virginia Vincenti. *Rethinking Home Economics: Women and the History of a Profession.* Ithaca, NY: Cornell University Press, 1997.
Stiles, T. J. "The Commodore's Civil War." *Vanderbilt Magazine,* April 11, 2011, http://news.vanderbilt.edu/vanderbiltmagazine/the-commodores-civil-war/. Accessed April 19, 2016.
Suggs, Henry Lewis, ed. *The Black Press in the South, 1865–1979.* Westport, CT: Greenwood, 1983.
Summerville, James. *Educating Black Doctors: A History of Meharry Medical College.* Tuscaloosa: University of Alabama Press, 1983.
Syrett, Nicholas L. *The Company He Keeps: A History of White College Fraternities.* Chapel Hill: University of North Carolina Press, 2009.
"Talent Pipeline." Nashville Chamber of Commerce and Economic Development website, http://www.nashvilleareainfo.com/homepage/human-capital/higher-education. Accessed May 9, 2016.
Tamburin, Adam. "At 150 Fisk University Celebrates Rich History, New Era." *Tennessean,* January 9, 2016, http://www.tennessean.com/story/news/education/2016/01/08/150-fisk-university-celebrates-rich-history-new-era/78256502/. Accessed May 8, 2016.
———. "New Meharry President: Go 'from Surviving to Thriving.'" *Tennessean,* July 5, 2015, www.tennessean.com/story/news/eduction/2015/07/05/new-meharry-sees-path-forward-past-lessons/29739189/. Accessed May 2, 2016.
Tanner, Daniel, and Laurel Tanner. *History of the School Curriculum.* New York: Macmillan, 1990.

Taylor, Arnold. *Travail and Triumph: Black Life and Culture in the South since the Civil War*. Westport, CT: Greenwood, 1976.
"Tennessee State Fair Grounds." Historic Nashville website, April 1, 2009, https://historic nashville.wordpress.com/tag/tennessee-state-fair-grounds/. Accessed March 22, 2016.
Tennessee State University 75th Anniversary: Some Traditions Are Forever. Nashville: Tennessee State University, 1987.
Terborg-Penn, Rosalyn. *African American Women in the Struggle for the Vote, 1850–1920*. Bloomington: Indiana University Press, 1998.
Thelin, John R. *A History of American Higher Education*. 2nd ed. Baltimore: Johns Hopkins University Press, 2011.
Tindall, George B. *The Emergence of the New South, 1913–1945*. Baton Rouge: Louisiana State University Press, 1967.
Torrence, Ridgely. *The Story of John Hope*. New York: Macmillan, 1948.
Traughber, Bill. *Nashville Sports History: Stories from the Stands*. Charleston, SC: History Press, 2010.
———. "Stella Vaughn Pioneered Women's Sports." *Commodore History Corner*, 2007, 1–3.
———. "Vandy Ties Michigan in 1922." *Commodore History Corner*, 2006, http://www.vucommodores.com/ot/history-corner-083006.html. Accessed April 10, 2015.
———. "Vandy's Men's and Women's 1909–1910 Seasons." *Commodore History Corner*, 2007, 1–4.
Uffelman, Minoa, Ellen Kanervo, Phyllis Smith, and Eleanor Williams, eds. *The Diary of Nannie Haskins Williams: A Southern Woman's Story of Rebellion and Reconstruction*. Knoxville: University of Tennessee Press, 2014.
"University Announces Full Scholarship Program for Nashville Students." *Belmont Vision*, March 26, 2013, http://belmontvision.com/2013/03/university-announces-new-scholarship-program-for-local-students/. Accessed May 9, 2016.
Verbugge, Martha. *Able-Bodied Womanhood: Personal Health and Social Change in Nineteenth-Century Boston*. New York: Oxford University Press, 1988.
Veysey, Laurence R. *The Emergence of the American University*. Chicago: University of Chicago Press, 1970.
Waller, William, ed. *Nashville in the 1890s*. Nashville: Vanderbilt University Press, 1972.
———. *Nashville, 1900–1910*. Nashville: Vanderbilt University Press, 1970.
Ward, Andrew. *Dark Midnight When I Rise: The Story of the Fisk Jubilee Singers*. New York: HarperCollins Publishers, 2000.
Ward, Getahn. "Can Nashville's Growth Continue?" *Tennessean*, August 15, 2015, http://www.tennessean.com/story/money/real-estate/2015/08/14/population-gains-key-nashville-job-growth/31509555/. Accessed May 3, 2016.
Warner, Sam B, *Streetcar Suburbs: The Process of Growth in Boston, 1870–1900*. 2nd ed. Cambridge, MA: Harvard University Press, 2009.
West, Carroll Van. "Cheekwood Botanical Garden and Museum of Art." *Tennessee Encyclopedia of History and Culture*. Online edition. https://tennesseeencyclopedia.net/entry.php?rec=237. Accessed March 22, 2016.

Wheeler, Marjorie Spruill. *New Women of the New South: The Leaders of the Woman Suffrage Movement in the Southern States*. New York: Oxford University Press, 1993.

———. *Votes for Women! The Woman Suffrage Movement in Tennessee, the South, and the Nation*. Knoxville: University of Tennessee Press, 1995.

White, Kevin. *The First Sexual Revolution: The Emergence of Male Heterosexuality in Modern America*. New York: New York University Press, 1993.

Whitworth, Kent. "Historic Stadiums." *Tennessee Encyclopedia of History and Culture*. Online edition, http://tennesseeencyclopedia.net/entry.php?rec=1252. Accessed April 10, 2016.

Wiebe, Robert. *The Search for Order, 1877–1920*. New York: Hill and Wang, 1967.

Wiggins, Sam P. *Higher Education in the South*. Berkeley, CA: McCutchan, 1966.

"William Jasper Hale, 1874–1944." Tennessee State University website, http://ww2.tnstate.edu/library/digital/hale.htm. Accessed January 19, 2016.

Williams, Charlotte A. *The Centennial Club of Nashville: A History from 1905–1977*. Nashville: Centennial Club, 1978.

Williams, William. "Fisk President Discusses Historic University's Current State, Future." *Nashville Post,* September 29, 2014, https://www.fisk.edu/articles/president-nashvillepost. Accessed May 2, 2016.

Wills, Ridley. *Belle Meade Country Club: The First 100 Years*. Nashville: Hillsboro Press, 2001.

———. *Jessie and Ridley: They Made a Difference*. LaVergne, TN: Ridley Wills, 2008.

Wilson, Francille Rusan. *The Segregated Scholars: Black Social Scientists and the Creation of Black Labor Studies, 1890–1950*. Charlottesville: University of Virginia Press, 2006.

Wolfe, Margaret Ripley. *Daughters of Canaan: A Saga of Southern Women*. Lexington: University Press of Kentucky, 1995.

Wood, Thomas E. "The Empire Strikes Back: Protecting the Ingram Family Fortunes." *Nashville Scene,* June 6, 1996, http://www.nashvillescene.com/nashville/the-empire-strikes-back/Content?oid=1180527. Accessed May 14, 2016.

Woodson, C. G. "Thomas Jesse Jones." *Journal of Negro History* 35 (January 1950): 107–9.

Woodward, C. Vann. *Origins of the New South, 1877–1913*. Baton Rouge: Louisiana State University Press, 1960.

Youngs, Larry. "The Sporting Set Winters in Florida: Fertile Ground for the Leisure Revolution, 1870–1930." *Florida Historical Quarterly* 84 (Summer 2005): 57–78.

Index

accreditation 9, 86, 106, 118, 120, 125, 126, 190, 240, 241, 245, 284n 64
    Association of American Universities 26, 190
    Association of Colleges for Negro Youth 121
    Association of Collegiate Alumnae 9, 87
    Association of Negro Colleges and Secondary Schools 131
    National Colored Teachers' Association 9, 121, 125
    National Education Association 11, 23
    National Teachers Association 9
    Southern Association of College Women 9
    Southern Association of Colleges and Schools 9, 15, 21, 23, 26, 120, 190, 241, 247
    Southern Educational Association 9, 10
Acklen, Adelicia 23, 43, 44, 269n30
Addams, Jane 60, 145
administration. *See faculty*
admission. *See curricula, requirements*
Agnes Scott College 69, 240
Agrarians 177–80, 193
Alabama 11, 75, 96, 115, 130, 200
all–female education. *See single gender education*
alumni 1, 30, 49, 72, 101, 102, 111, 114, 115, 128–32, 136–38, 144–46, 169, 185, 188, 190, 197, 213, 221, 223, 230, 231, 235, 238, 239, 246, 250
American Association of University Women 92
American Baptist Theological Seminary 28, 112, 241, 264n37, 266n78, 304n27
American Dental Association 136
American Medical Association 135, 136
American Missionary Association 24, 25, 119
antebellum. *See Old South*
Aquinas College 239, 240
Arcade 156, 194
Arkansas 11, 75, 130
Association of University Professors 94
Athens of the South (Athens of the New South) 1, 2, 32, 34, 160, 193, 218, 235, 239, 251
athletics 6, 7, 32, 48, 70, 91, 96, 99, 166, 167, 169, 170, 175, 194, 195–231, 235, 243, 248, 250

331

athletics (cont'd)
    African American 7, 188,
        216–22, 231, 250
    facilities, fields, and stadiums
        6, 15, 65, 70, 96, 154, 175,
        191, 199, 200, 201, 207–20,
        226–27, 229, 231
    intramural 92, 198, 199, 203,
        217, 219, 227, 230
    men 7, 87, 99, 161, 195–216,
        222, 225, 228, 230–31,
        243, 248, 298n19–20
    women 7, 65, 70, 91, 184,
        222–31, 243, 249, 301n98,
        301n100, 301n103,
        301n105
Atlanta 3, 39, 40, 41, 58, 124, 216, 217, 235
Atlanta University 109, 110, 121, 147, 186, 217, 220
Auburn University 204, 205, 207, 215, 244

"Bachelor of Ugliness" 176, 216, 295n85
Baptist church 22, 108, 119, 140, 145, 204, 245, 246
Barnard College 79
Barry, Megan 238, 251
Belle Meade 43, 44, 45, 56, 157
Belle Meade Country Club 44, 157, 163
Belmont Boulevard and surrounding neighborhood 43, 44, 45, 55, 95, 246
Belmont College for Young Women 4, 10, 23, 44, 47, 49, 54, 55, 69, 73, 75–77, 81, 87, 88, 92, 94, 95, 104, 155, 167, 177, 180–84, 223, 227
Belmont Mansion (Belle Monte) 47, 181
Belmont University 104, 236, 238, 245, 245–48, 251, 298n37
Bethlehem House 60, 120
bicycles 162, 197, 223
Birmingham 3, 33, 34, 35, 40, 41, 58, 216
black elite 6
Blair Academy of Music, 245

Board of Education (Nashville) 50
Board of Trade 53, 55, 60, 188, 214, 238, 271n68
Boards of Trust 13, 18, 25, 48, 49, 50, 51, 59, 70, 114, 115, 118, 119, 128, 145, 148, 170, 174, 187, 188, 189, 190, 193, 202, 207, 214, 231, 235, 236, 245
Boscobel College 93
Boston 2, 11, 94
Boyd, Richard Henry (R.H.) 57, 58, 59, 119, 125, 135, 188, 236
Boyd, Robert Fulton 134, 135
Broadway Avenue 156, 161, 172, 214
Brown University 204
Bruce, John Edward 113
Bryn Mawr College 79
Buford College 93
Bureau of Education. *See Department of Education*

campus 25, 48, 69, 96, 99, 177–91, 227, 231
Carell family 236, 237
Carnegie, Andrew (and Carnegie Foundation) 128, 136
Centennial Club 54, 55, 68, 157
Centennial Exposition (1897) 34, 37, 39, 40, 47, 55, 57, 62, 112, 154, 164, 205
Centennial Park 44, 57, 164, 200, 227
Central Tennessee College 28, 110, 132, 146, 250
Chamber of Commerce. *See Board of Trade*
chapel 26
Charlotte 3, 40, 47
Charlotte Avenue 43, 47, 132
Chattanooga 40, 124, 146
Cheek family 51, 63, 68
Cheek–Neal Company 50, 270n58
Chicago 2, 11, 38, 39, 55, 141, 221
Church of Christ 20, 85, 92, 176, 246, 247, 250

Church Street 50
Civil Rights movement 112, 241, 242
Civil War 2, 4, 16, 18, 21, 22, 25, 31, 37, 38, 49, 55, 61, 79, 97, 103, 110, 112, 152, 154, 170, 187, 193, 194, 199, 223, 235, 239, 242, 250
Clark College (University) 217
Claxton, Philander P. 10, 11, 30, 119
clubs 6, 63, 69, 92, 96, 106, 152, 153, 157, 158, 163, 164, 166, 168, 173, 175, 176, 177, 178, 183, 186, 187, 188, 193, 203, 210, 214, 217, 225, 226, 230, 243, 246, 275n43
coeducation 6, 20, 68, 70, 71, 72, 82, 86, 97, 102, 104, 106, 142, 152, 167, 227, 228, 229, 230, 239, 240
college preparatory. *See secondary schools*
Columbia University 46, 87, 95, 122, 130, 139, 204
Colyar, Arthur 2, 34, 35, 63
commercial–civic elite. *See urban boosters*
commercialized leisure 6, 61, 152–65, 197, 209, 210, 211, 218, 220, 222, 293n43, 299n50
Cornell University 10, 95, 204
Cotton States and International Exposition (1895) 40, 122
Cravath, Erastus 25, 127, 145, 217
Crosthwaite, Minnie Lou 57, 115, 145, 146
cult of domesticity 86, 106
Cumberland College (University) 16, 205, 247
Cumberland Park 158
curricula 5–15, 18, 20, 24, 26, 28, 30, 31, 54, 73, 75, 79, 81, 86, 87, 91, 92, 101, 106, 118, 121, 123–25, 127, 128, 139, 140, 141, 143, 193, 194, 230, 240, 243, 246, 250
    courses 8, 10, 11, 14, 18–20, 26, 54, 70, 73, 75, 77, 79, 81, 86, 92, 98, 110, 123, 125, 127, 138–41, 168, 169, 194, 219, 240, 244, 248, 249
    departments/schools 4, 8, 10, 15–18, 22, 28–30, 71, 75, 77, 81, 87, 90–94, 110, 123, 130–32, 135, 139, 141, 143, 169, 175, 177, 197, 199, 241, 243, 244–250
    requirements 10, 15, 18, 30, 70, 78, 81, 86, 98, 106, 120, 128, 132, 137, 139, 173, 180, 181, 243, 246, 247, 250

Dabney, Charles 11
David Lipscomb College (Nashville Bible College) 3, 10, 20–22, 35, 41, 45, 47, 68, 69, 72, 85, 86, 92–94, 140, 155, 157, 162, 166, 176, 177, 183, 193, 201, 226, 227
Davidson, Donald 177–79
Davidson Academy 2, 16
Day Homes' Club, 144, 146
Dean, Karl 235, 238, 239, 246, 248
degrees 9, 10, 14, 15, 18, 19, 20, 21, 23, 71, 75, 78, 79, 83, 86, 91, 92, 98, 103–6, 120, 122, 123, 126, 127, 134, 135, 137, 139, 140–43, 167, 190, 238, 239, 240, 243, 246, 247, 248, 250
Department of Education (U.S.) 9, 11, 26, 81, 117, 121, 122, 127, 128, 132, 141, 195
departments/schools. *See curricula*
Dewey, John 10
domestic science. *See home economics*
Du Bois, W.E.B. 6, 107, 109, 111, 112, 115, 120–22, 126, 128–30, 147, 188, 189, 217, Ch. 3 n. 161
Dudley, Anne Dallas 54, 56, 57, 68, 102
Dudley, Guilford Jr. 56, 57, 63, 211
Dudley, Guilford Sr. 56
Dudley, William Lofland 205, 206

Dudley Field (Dudley Stadium) 15, 200, 211, 214, 231
Duke University 3, 16, 37, 46, 204, 211

East Tennessee State University 10
Edgefield 41, 42
Emory University 3, 16, 37, 46, 118, 204
Endowments 11, 12, 26, 92, 119, 128, 169, 188, 204
extracurricular 48, 69, 91, 152, 153–71, 174, 176, 185, 193, 220, 228

faculty/administration 10, 11, 13, 14, 15, 18, 20, 26, 49, 72, 73, 79, 82, 93, 95, 96, 98, 99, 118, 120, 121, 124–26, 129, 130, 135, 138, 139, 141, 148, 153, 158, 169, 173, 174, 177, 180, 187, 188, 190, 191, 193, 197, 205, 206, 207, 209, 213, 223, 227, 230, 231, 244, 247, 249
"finishing school" 24, 73, 75, 82, 87, 104, 144
Fisk Jubilee Singers 25, 26, 107, 119, 127, 128, 142, 145, 187, 218, 251
Fisk University 3, 4, 6, 24, 25, 26, 30, 35, 42, 43, 45, 47, 49, 51, 52, 54, 58, 59, 60, 68, 92, 93, 101, 103, 107, 109–21, 123, 124, 126, 127–32, 134–37, 139, 141–48, 186–92, 216–22, 236, 237, 241, 242, 247, 249–51, 295nn88–89, 286n100, 286n102, 289n150
fraternities. *See Greek life*
Frazer, Sadie Warner 57
Freedman's Bureau (Freedman's Aid Society) 24, 25, 28, 29, 119
Fugitives 177–80, 235

Garland, Landon C. 11, 170
Gates, George A. 119, 128, 187
See *Geier v. Tennesee* 242
General Education Board (and Fund) 11, 19, 26, 119, 121, 136

George Peabody College for Teachers. *See Peabody College*
Georgia 11, 115, 137, 205, 207, 221, 240
Georgia Tech 205, 221
Germantown 45, 52
Gilded Age 154, 158
Glen Leven 49
Glendale Park 164, 165
Godbey, Lois 70, 83
Goucher College 69, 74
Grady, Henry 35, 63
Grand Ole Opry 50, 161
Granny White Pike 21, 92, 157
Great Depression 4, 38, 73, 104, 112, 215, 239
Great Recession 246
Greek life 6, 66, 96, 153, 163, 167–78, 180, 182, 185, 186, 187, 192–94, 210, 243, 246–50, Ch. 4 n. 64
Greenwood Park 145, 164, 219
Grizzard, Ephraim 115

H.G. Hill Company 51, 214
Hadley Park 52, 59, 165
Hale, John Henry 134, 135, 189
Hale, Millie E. 134, 135
Hale, William J. 115, 120, 121, 123, 124, 125, 191
Hampton Institute 122
Harding, James A. 20, 92
Harpeth Hall School 240, 262n10, 264n37, 304n24
Harris, Richard 25, 187
Harvard University 10, 46, 73, 94, 139, 204, 207, 211
Hayes, Rutherford B. 61
Haygood, Atticus Greene 118
Haynes, Elizabeth Ross 130, 131
Haynes, George Edmund 130, 131
Heron, Susan L. 23, 95, 181, 245
Hill, Richard 112
Hillsboro Road 47, 140, 212

334 Index

Hippodrome Skating Rink 158, 200
historically black colleges and universities (HBCUs) 6, 26, 30, 59, 68, 107–50, 153, 155, 185–92, 217–22, 231, 240, 241, 242, 248–51
home economics 68, 78, 86, 87, 88, 89, 92, 94, 105, 139, 143
Hood, Ida E. 23, 95, 181, 245
Hooper, Ben 124
Hoover, Herbert 101, 136
Honky Tonk Row 161
Hope, John 27, 110, 145, 285n79
Hope, Lugenia 145, 189n157
hospitals 29, 30, 36, 119, 133, 134, 135, 136, 219
Howard Female College 114
Howard University 26, 120, 121, 124, 139, 147, 186, 189, 190, 216, 218, 220
Howse, Hilary 51, 60, 124
Hubbard, George W. 29, 30, 133, 135
Hume–Fogg High School 52

industrial education 17, 108, 109, 111–13, 122–26, 128, 141, 147, 148, 250, 284n71
industrialization 3, 10, 11, 35, 37, 80, 105, 122, 125, 179, 193, 234
Ingram family 49, 160, 233, 236, 237, 270n53
Iroquois Steeplechase 56
irregular students 69, 77, 93

Jack's Alley 156, 194
Jackson, Andrew 154
Jefferson Street 43, 59, 132, 194
Jim Crow laws. *See segregation*
Johnson, Charles Spurgeon 131, 190, 286n98
Johnson, Henderson 221
Jones, Thomas Elsa 190, 192, 221
Jones, Thomas Jesse 121, 122, 123, 127, 283nn44–45
Jubilee Singers. *See Fisk Jubilee Singers*
Julius Rosenwald Fund 121, 136, 141

Junior Colleges 4, 9, 23, 77, 91, 93, 104, 239, 240, 247, 262n10, 263n21

Keith, Elizabeth 54, 55, 56
Keith, Samuel J. 55
Kentucky 11, 75
Kentucky Military Academy 49
Killebrew, George W. 40, 68
Killebrew, J.B. 39, 68, 263n19
Kirkland, James H. 13, 14, 15, 48, 90, 91, 96–98, 101, 153, 169, 173, 179, 194, 204, 243
Kirkland, Marion Palmer 71
Kirsch, Rosaylyn 161, 162, 228
Knoxville 40, 117, 146, 219
Ladies' Hermitage Association 55, 68

Lea, Luke 157
leisure. *See commercialized leisure*
Lemoyne Owen College 28
Lewis, John 112, 241
Lindsley, John Berrien 16, 84, 277n70
Lindsley, Philip 2, 16, 49
Lipscomb, David 20, 278n90
Lipscomb College. *See David Lipscomb College*
Lipscomb University 236, 245, 246, 247, 250, 251
"Lost Cause" 2, 7, 37
Louisiana 11, 75, 115
Louisiana State University 205, 211
lynching 115, 116, 275n32
Lyttle–Frazier, Hulda 133, 134

Mann, Horace 10
Martin's Female College 95
Maryville College 123
mass entertainment. *See commercialized leisure*
Massachusetts 9, 17, 128
Maxwell House Hotel (Maxwell House Coffee) 50, 51, 157

May, Daniel 50, 211
May, Jacob 50
May Day 81, 82, 104
McGugin, Dan 195, 208, 209, 214, 299n46
McKenzie, Fayette A. 48, 115, 129, 130, 146, 187, 188, 189, 190, 191
Meharry Medical College 3, 4, 6, 10, 28, 29, 30, 42, 43, 45, 47, 49, 59, 89, 92, 110, 111, 119–21, 126, 127, 129, 132–37, 139, 141, 144, 146–48, 192, 217, 219, 236, 241, 242, 249–251
Memphis 3, 10, 28, 41, 58, 110, 115–17, 146, 154, 233, 235
Merrill, James 143
Methodist church 13, 119, 173, 204, 207, 250
Middle Tennessee State University 10
Millie E. Hale Hospital 89
Mississippi 11, 75, 115, 205
Moffat, Adelene 114, 281nn25–26
Montgomery Bell Academy 16, 18, 240, 264n37, 277n70
Moore, Bellina A. 141
Moore, Ella Sheppard 145
Moore, George 145
Morehouse University 110, 121, 139, 217, 220, 285n83
Morrill Land Grant 124
Morris Brown College 217
Mount Holyoke College 79
movies 162, 164, 174
Mullowney, John J. 136
"muscular Christianity" 184, 186, 199, 230
music 1, 6, 23, 32, 45, 50, 86, 90, 91, 94, 106, 138, 139, 156, 158, 160, 161, 184, 191, 214, 233, 236–38, 240, 245, 246, 251
municipal housekeeping 6, 54, 55, 144
municipal government (Nashville). *See Nashville local government*

Napier, James C. 57, 59, 60, 63, 112, 119, 125, 133, 146, 187, 188, 189, 272n91, 283n47
Napier, Nettie 57
Nash, Diane 241
Nashville Athletic Club (City League) 199, 200, 201, 219
Nashville Bible College. *See David Lipscomb College*
Nashville Centennial 113
Nashville Equal Suffrage League 57, 102
Nashville League on Conditions among Negroes 60
Nashville local government (schools) 48, 51–52, 57, 59, 141, 146, 190, 236, 248, 251
Nashville Negro Board of Trade (Negro Business League) 59, 60, 119
Nashville Relief Society 56, 68
National American Woman Suffrage Association 57, 102
National Association for the Advancement of Colored People (NAACP) 114, 116, 145, 188
National Association of Colored Women's Clubs 144, 145
National Association of Intercollegiate Athletics 250
National Collegiate Athletic Association (NCAA) 195, 244, 248, 249
National Educational Association 95, 229
National Life and Accident Insurance (WSM) 50, 161, 235
National Urban League 131, 189
neighborhoods 41–48, 55, 236, 239, 269n35, 270n62
New Orleans 36, 41, 235, 240
New South 4, 5, 7, 10, 16, 17, 31, 35, 37, 40, 41, 42, 48, 49, 50, 51, 53, 61, 68, 69, 102, 104, 114, 122, 132, 152, 172, 178, 193, 197, 202, 215, 223, 233, 239, 243
New York 2, 11, 153, 188, 234

"new woman" 5, 24, 66, 67, 106, 223, 273n5
Nineteenth Amendment 57, 68, 92, 95, 99, 100, 101, 102, 103, 105
normal schools (training) 9, 17, 78, 84, 98, 105, 106, 121, 126, 127, 138, 139, 140, 202
North Carolina 16
nursing 68, 89, 90, 105, 106, 110, 132, 133, 239, 241, 287n112

Old South 2, 37, 39, 45, 80, 114, 170, 181, 216, 235
Old Woman's Home 55, 271n81

Panic of 1893 39
Parks Commission 164, 165, 293n46
Parthenon 1, 32, 39, 47
Patterson, Malcolm R. 119, 120
Payne, Bruce 48, 78, 98, 99
Payne, William 18, 19, 78, 98, 275n50
Peabody, George (Peabody Education Fund) 17, 19
Peabody College (Peabody Normal School) 3, 4, 10, 16–21, 23, 26, 35, 41, 44, 45, 47–52, 54, 57, 60, 68–70, 78, 83, 84, 86, 88, 90, 92–94, 98, 101, 105, 120, 140, 153, 155, 166–68, 176, 177, 193, 200–202, 206, 223, 227, 241, 244, 245
Peay, Austin 124
pedagogy. *See normal schools (training)*
Phelps Stokes Fund 119, 122, 284n68
Philadelphia 23, 39, 95
physical education 10, 69, 70, 78, 86, 96, 105, 139, 223, 224, 225, 228, 301n100
Polk, James K. 154
Porter, James 18, 19, 98
Presbyterian church 16, 180
Price's College for Ladies 93, 98
Princeton University 46, 152, 201, 204, 207, 211
Printer's Alley 156

Progressive Era (progressivism) 3, 5, 8, 11, 31, 37, 38, 40, 48, 57, 62, 65, 70, 80, 88, 93, 105, 112, 114, 118, 127, 131, 139, 143, 145, 154, 162, 175, 196, 214, 227, 229, 230, 233, 235, 236, 239, 243, 245
   business progressives. *See urban boosters*
   social reform (urban reform) 6, 37, 40, 53, 59, 62, 63, 68, 86, 88, 105, 106, 131, 141, 144, 148, 175, 187
Prohibition 53
public schools. *See secondary school education*
public transportation 42, 46, 47, 49, 62, 80, 113, 157, 161, 164, 185, 212, 251, 305n49

Radcliffe College 79
railroads 2, 3, 36, 40, 48, 49, 63, 164, 171, 212, 261n3, 272n86
Randolph–Macon College 69, 74
Ransom, John Crowe 177–79
Reconstruction 9, 40, 112, 148
Republican Motherhood 86, 277n73
Rice, Ada Scott 57
Richards, Ellen 87, 89
Richland 45
Richmond 41
Robertson, Felix 49
Rockefeller, John D. (Rockefeller Foundation) 11, 90, 119, 121, 136
Roger Williams University 3, 6, 10, 26, 41, 47, 58, 68, 92, 110, 111, 119, 121, 139, 140, 141, 143, 145, 147, 148, 217, 219, 288n140
Roosevelt, Theodore 161
Rosenwald Fund. *See Julius Rosenwald Fund*
Rutgers University 201
Ryman Auditorium 103, 108, 159, 160, 161, 163, 234

Index   337

San Francisco 39
Sears, Julia 94, 99, 278n95, 279n116
secondary school education (college preparatory) 11, 17, 19, 22, 23, 28, 52, 73, 77, 78, 79, 94, 104, 105, 117, 122, 123, 124, 127, 138, 139, 140, 141, 190, 229, 240, 242, 246, 248
segregation 5, 58, 60, 109, 111, 112, 113, 126, 144, 147, 148, 165, 171, 188, 189, 190, 216, 221, 222, 241, 242
seminary 23, 65, 75, 78, 81, 104
Seven Sisters 87, 275n54
Sevier, John 84
Sevier Park 44
Sewanee: University of the South 198, 199, 201, 202, 203, 204, 205, 223
Shaw University 220
Shelby Park 164
single gender (all–female or all–male) education 23, 65, 66, 67, 68, 69, 70, 77, 78, 82, 86, 93, 97, 99, 104, 106, 152, 167, 180–85, 228, 229, 240, 240
Smaill, Edith 94, 95
Smith College 79, 226
social reform. *See Progressive Era*
Sophie Newcomb Memorial College 69, 225, 240
sororities. *See Greek life*
South Carolina 11
Southeastern Conference (SEC) 195, 206, 215, 221, 222, 243
Southern Agrarians. *See Agrarians*
"southern belle" 5, 6, 65, 79, 81, 93, 97, 106, 184, 222
Southern Intercollegiate Athletic Association (SIAA) 15, 200, 203, 204, 205, 206, 217, 220
southern pride (southern honor) 7, 23, 36, 38, 46, 181, 197–204, 207–9, 211, 214–16, 231
sports. *See athletics*
stadiums. *See athletics, facilities*

Stapleton, Ada Bell 96, 278n89
Stearns, Eben 84
streetcars. *See public transportation*
suburbs 4, 45, 46, 47, 62, 157, 212, 240
suffrage. *See Nineteenth Amendment*
Sulphur Dell 158, 202
Sylvan Park 45

Taft, William Howard 118, 161
Talented Tenth 6, 107, 111, 121, 126, 127
Tate, John Allen 177–79
Taylor, Alfred 214
Taylor, Georgia Gordon 145
Taylor, Preston 59, 119, 125, 145, 164
teacher certification (teacher training) 10, 18, 20, 26, 78, 84, 86, 121, 122, 123, 126, 127, 134, 136, 137, 139, 140, 143, 146, 148, 244, 245
Temple, Ed 249
Tennessee 2, 10, 11, 21, 30, 39, 55, 73, 75, 78, 80, 81, 90, 100, 102, 108, 115–18, 119, 123–25, 131, 140, 145, 146, 214, 226, 229, 233, 235, 236, 243
Tennessee A&I 3, 4, 6, 10, 30, 42, 43, 45, 52, 59, 68, 80, 92, 110, 111, 114, 115, 118–26, 136, 138–40, 143, 147, 148, 191, 192, 219, 220, 241, 242, 288n132, 288n139
Tennessee Equal Suffrage Association 57, 102
Tennessee Polytechnic (Tennessee Technological University) 10
Tennessee State Fair 158, 159
Tennessee State University 110, 241, 242, 244, 245, 248, 249, 251, 262n10, 305n43
Texas 11, 75, 115, 205, 206
theaters 151–63
Thomas, John W. 112
Thompson, John 49
"Tiger Belles" 244, 249
Townsend, Arthur 145

transportation. *See public transportation*
Trawick, Kate Herndon 116, 282n36
Trevecca Nazarene University 239, 247, 263n37, 264n64
Trinity University. *See Duke University*
trustees. *See Boards of Trust*
Tulane University 205, 225
Tuskegee Institute (Tuskegee Model) 30, 109, 122, 123, 126, 139, 217

Union Station 36, 125, 171, 172, 212
Union Transportation Company 58
University of Alabama 204, 205, 109, 215, 216, 222, 244
University of Chicago 10, 74, 95, 131, 135
University of Georgia 204, 205, 209, 211, 215
University of Michigan 18, 204, 208, 210, 214, 215
University of Mississippi 196
University of Nashville 2, 15, 16, 18, 20, 29, 49, 51, 52, 70, 78, 84, 200, 202, 206, 207, 240
University of North Carolina 204, 205, 211
University of Pennsylvania 204, 207
University of Tennessee 11, 20, 78, 205, 211, 215, 242, 244
University of Virginia 204
urban boosters 5, 35, 36, 39, 48, 52, 53–56, 63, 114, 119, 125, 148, 209, 211–14, 230, 231, 235, 236, 243
U.S. Bureau of Education. *See Department of Education*

Vanderbilt, Cornelius 11, 13, 214
Vanderbilt Medical Center 15, 84, 237, 238, 303n14
Vanderbilt University 3, 11, 14, 15, 16, 18–21, 23, 26, 28, 29, 35, 37, 41–47, 49–52, 54, 55, 67–71, 73, 75, 78, 80, 82–85, 88–91, 93, 95, 97, 98, 99, 101, 102, 105, 120, 140, 151, 153, 155, 157, 158, 159, 161, 162, 163, 165–81, 185, 193–97, 199, 200–217, 222–31, 235–41, 243–46, 251, 304n30
Vassar College 74, 75, 79, 95, 225, 226
Vaughn, Stella 96
Vaughn, William 96
Vendome Theater 151, 163
Virginia 69, 121, 122, 206, 220
vocational education. *See industrial education*

Wake Forest University 204
Walden College (Walden University) 28, 30, 110, 132, 134, 139, 146, 147, 239, 287n110
Ward, Eliza H. 22, 57, 180, 181
Ward, Sara Coney 57
Ward, William E. 22, 57, 68, 97, 101, 180, 181
Ward Seminary 4, 10, 22, 23, 44, 47, 52, 54, 55, 57, 65, 69, 72–75, 77, 81, 85, 87, 93, 94–96, 104, 151, 155, 157, 165–67, 177, 180–82, 184, 223–29
Ward–Belmont School 3, 4, 10, 22, 23, 35, 41, 44, 45, 49, 51, 52, 55, 57, 67, 69, 78, 81, 82, 85, 88, 90, 91, 93, 100, 101, 153, 155, 156, 159, 162, 163, 166–69, 177, 180, 183, 184, 193, 223, 228, 229, 240, 246, 292n17
Warden, Margaret Lindsley 57
Warner, James William 51, 157, 211
Warner, Percy 48, 63, 165
Warner Parks 164, 165
Warren, Robert Penn 177–79
Washington, Booker T. 6, 10, 30, 59, 108, 109, 111, 112, 119, 121, 122, 128, 145, 147, 148, 149, 161, 187
Washington, Margaret Murray 128, 145
Washington D. C. 139, 145
Washington University 201, 202

Index 339

Wellesley College 74, 75, 79, 98
Wells, Ida B. 116
West, Ben 241
West End Avenue 41–43, 44, 46, 47, 158, 212, 214
Western Military Institute 16
Wheeler, Emma R. 146
White, George L. 127
Wilberforce University 217, 219, 220
Williams, David II 244, 305n34
Wills, Jesse 50, 177–79, 235
Wills, Ridley 50, 177–79
Wills, Ridley II 50, 235
Wilson, Woodrow 85, 152, 153
Woman's Club 68, 92
Woman's Missionary Union (Council) 60, 144, 145

women's colleges (schools). *See single-sex education*
World War I 9, 47, 92, 99, 100, 101, 102, 104, 110, 136, 142, 147, 167, 175, 211
World War II 104, 112, 244

Yale University 46, 94, 169, 211, 215
Young Ladies' Auxiliary 68
Young Men's Christian Association (YMCA) 131, 175, 176, 186, 199, 200, 230
Young Women's Christian Association (YWCA) 54, 91, 131, 146, 176, 184, 230
    Blue Triangle Branch 54, 146
youth culture 5, 151–94, 196, 231, 238, 249–51

Zeppos, Nicolas 243

www.ingramcontent.com/pod-product-compliance
Lightning Source LLC
Chambersburg PA
CBHW060513080526
44586CB00012B/464